JACK HOBBS

Leo McKinstry writes regularly for the *Daily Express*, the *Daily Mail* and the *Spectator*. He has written nine books, including a life of Geoff Boycott, which was named one of the finest ever cricket books in a recent *Wisden* poll. His biography of Jack and Bobby Charlton was a top-ten best-seller and won the WHSmith Sports Book of the Year award. His biography of Alf Ramsey won the WHSmith Football Book of the Year award. His study of the Liberal Prime Minister Lord Rosebery won Channel Four Political Book of the Year. His most recent books are a trilogy about the RAF in the Second World War.

Born in Belfast in 1962, he was educated in the west of Ireland and at Cambridge University. He is married and lives in Kent and Provence.

LEO McKINSTRY

JACK HOBBS

England's Greatest Cricketer

YELLOW JERSEY PRESS
LONDON

Published by Yellow Jersey Press 2012

2 4 6 8 10 9 7 5 3 1

Copyright © Leo McKinstry 2011

Leo McKinstry has asserted his right under the Copyright, Designs
and Patents Act 1988 to be identified as the author of this work

First published in Great Britain in 2011 by
Yellow Jersey Press

Yellow Jersey Press
Random House, 20 Vauxhall Bridge Road,
London SW1V 2SA

www.vintage-books.co.uk

Addresses for companies within The Random House Group Limited can be found at:
www.randomhouse.co.uk/offices.htm

The Random House Group Limited Reg. No. 954009

A CIP catalogue record for this book
is available from the British Library

ISBN 9780224083300

The Random House Group Limited supports The Forest Stewardship Council (FSC®),
the leading international forest certification organisation. Our books carrying the
FSC label are printed on FSC® certified paper. FSC is the only forest certification scheme
endorsed by the leading environmental organisations, including Greenpeace.
Our paper procurement policy can be found at
www.randomhouse.co.uk/environment

MIX
Paper from
responsible sources
FSC® C016897

Typeset by Palimpsest Book Production Limited, Falkirk, Stirlingshire
Printed and bound in Great Britain by CPI Group (UK) Ltd, Croydon CR0 4YY

This book is dedicated to Brook Sinclair

Contents

Introduction

Monday 17 August 1925, Taunton, Somerset

The county cricket ground in the market town of Taunton had never seen anything like it: at each entrance was a vast throng of spectators, eager anticipation written on their faces. At the railway station, special steam trains from London disgorged more supporters, all of them desperate to witness the historic event. Normally almost empty, the small press box overflowed with national newspaper journalists and sketch writers. In front of the stands newsreel cameramen set up their equipment, ready to capture the moment of glory for cinema audiences. Photographers perched awkwardly on the corrugated tin roofs of the pavilion and nearby buildings, their determination to record the vital stroke triumphing over their personal safety.

Inside the visitors' dressing room on that crisp August morning, the tension mounted as the start of play approached. No one seemed more nervous than the Surrey opening batsman Jack Hobbs. Usually so serene, he was now in a state of constant agitation, fiddling with his pads or pacing across the wooden floor. His anxiety was understandable because the public's attention, both at the ground and across the country, was entirely focused on his performance. Nothing else in the match between Surrey and Somerset seemed to matter. For weeks he had been forced to endure this remorseless burden, ever since his prolific form earlier in the 1925 season had brought him close to the record of the Victorian titan W.G. Grace in scoring 126 centuries during a first-class career. When Grace had retired almost twenty years earlier, it had been widely thought that his achievement would never be equalled. But now, despite reaching the age of forty-two, Hobbs was on the verge of the milestone after hitting no fewer than twelve centuries by mid-July. Just one more hundred would put him on a par with the Grand Old Man. With Hobbs scoring so profusely in the first three months of the 1925 summer, the nation had become obsessed with the record. Every innings he played was greeted by the public as another step towards the summit; every appearance was given intensive coverage by the press. 'England is waiting for news in an expectant hush. We shall hold our breath as hopefully as any man in Surrey and crow as lustily when the great figures break at last on the telegraph board,' stated an editorial in *The Times* in late July, capturing the national mood of mounting excitement.

But for one of the few times in his career, Hobbs had buckled under the pressure. Suddenly, after the torrent of the early season, the runs dried up. His instinctive mastery over his opponents' bowling vanished. Batting became an ordeal, each setback only adding to his sense of frustration. Even when he made a reasonable score, the press declared that he had 'failed' simply because he had not reached the century mark. Once in early August, after making 54 on his home ground of the Oval against a formidable Nottinghamshire attack, he had returned to the pavilion in near silence, so deep was the feeling of gloom in the crowd at his dismissal. The wait for the record, dragging on for week after week, had turned into a form of agony for the public and Hobbs himself. 'The mental strain was beginning to tell,' he later confessed. 'It seemed the whole circus was following me round. The newspapers were working everybody into a fever state.'

Surrey's visit to Taunton, however, had brought hope that the record might finally be in his grasp. On the first day of the match, Saturday 15 August 1925, Hobbs had batted through the late afternoon after Somerset had been cheaply dismissed. It had been a scratchy innings, lacking in Hobbs's usual elegance, confidence and timing. He had been caught off a no-ball, survived a loud appeal for lbw, given a near chance to mid-on and, towards the close of play, had almost been run-out. But somehow he had survived: 91 not out. After the rest day, just nine more runs would be needed on the Monday morning. The proximity to Grace's record drove the cricket world and the public to new paroxysms of excitement, as Hobbs became only too aware as he walked from his hotel on Sunday morning to attend church. 'I was the object of such embarrassing attention that I did not venture out again,' he revealed in a subsequent interview. That Sunday evening he had eaten his meal in the hotel, whose dining-room windows overlooked the Taunton railway station. From his table, Jack could glimpse the stream of reporters and photographers pouring into town after the arrival of the last train from London.

The atmosphere the next morning, Monday 17 August, was electric. 'Will Hobbs hit The Nine?' asked the *Daily Express.* 'One word has been on the lips of all Taunton and all Somerset today – the magic word "Hobbs".' So great was the crush of people at the ground that John Daniell, the Somerset captain, had to go into the Surrey dressing room to ask for permission to delay the start in order that more spectators could be admitted before the gates were closed. Percy Fender, the Surrey captain, and Hobbs agreed, though the hiatus only worsened the batsman's nerves. 'I had just the experience that was likely to make me more fidgety than ever – namely the experience of hanging about, waiting for the critical moment. It is something like sitting in a dentist's chair,' he wrote. Eventually, more than 10,000 fans crammed into the stands and the terraces.

At twenty-five past eleven, almost half an hour after the scheduled start, the umpires emerged from the pavilion, followed by the Somerset team. Then a huge cheer went up as Hobbs, accompanied by his fellow Surrey batsman Douglas Jardine, came into the arena. All eyes immediately turned to Hobbs's slim wiry figure of medium height. His steps were neat, almost feline. His forearms were strong and sunburnt. His bronzed face, with alert brown eyes and rather beaky nose, was cast in shadow by the peak of the dark blue MCC touring cap that Hobbs usually preferred to wear rather than the chocolate colour of Surrey. The famous wide smile, so well known to cricket supporters across the world, was absent, replaced by a look of apprehensive determination. As was his superstitious habit, Hobbs touched the peak of his cap several times while walking to the middle. On reaching the pitch, he took guard from the umpire, twirled the bat several times in his hands, gave his characteristic shrug of his shoulders before settling into his slightly open-chested stance.

The first bowler of the day was Raymond Robertson-Glasgow, an amateur, Oxford blue, schoolmaster and deep admirer of Hobbs. 'He was always, to me, the greatest player of the lot,' Robertson-Glasgow later said in a BBC interview. But that day he had no intention of making it easy for his hero. He marched to the end of his run, then turned. A hush descended on the capacity crowd. At the batting crease, Hobbs waited, taut with concentration and tapping his left foot on the ground. As Robertson-Glasgow reached his delivery stride, Hobbs adopted his usual set of movements in anticipation of his stroke, swinging his bat into a high, straight backlift, moving both his hands further down the handle, then shifting his right foot back and across the crease so that he covered all three stumps. The first ball was on middle stump and kept low, an awkward one to face right at the start of play. But he negotiated it safely with a backward defensive. The next delivery was less demanding. It slid towards the leg-side and Hobbs pushed it easily for a single, a stroke that had brought him thousands of runs in the preceding twenty years of his first-class career. He now needed just eight more.

The next few overs remained a grim struggle as Robertson-Glasgow and his Somerset colleague Jim Bridges kept up their accuracy. 'Almost all the time I was on the rack,' recalled Hobbs. At one stage, Hobbs leapt on a rare half-volley from Bridges and drove it through the covers, but a tremendous diving stop by a fielder in the deep prevented the boundary. Then, with six runs still required for the century, Robertson-Glasgow made his first error, pitching short on the leg-side while over-stepping the crease. The umpire yelled, 'No-ball!' Hobbs pivoted on the back foot and, with the fluid ease that was his trademark, pulled high over square leg. For a glorious second, it looked like the ball might sail into the crowd for six, a fitting way to reach the century. But the ball fell short. Two runs were still wanted. Moments later, he dabbed an off-side delivery to point and raced through for a quick single. There was just one run needed now, yet Somerset would not relent, the bowling still as sharp as ever.

The intensity of the climax reduced the crowd to complete silence. Finally, in the middle of the sixth over, the breakthrough came as Hobbs hit an inswinger from Bridges through the close field on the leg-side. Immediately he and Jardine set off for the crucial single. Long before they had reached either end, the crowd had erupted in ecstasy. Traditional British reserve disappeared as spectators deliriously waved hats or hand-kerchiefs. Wild cheering echoed round the ground, so loud that it could even be heard on the edges of Taunton. For the first time that morning, Hobbs broke into a grin, doffing his cap to acknowledge the thunderous applause. He then took from his pocket a telegram that he had written earlier in the dressing room and beckoned the groundsman onto the field so it could be delivered. It was addressed to his wife Ada, who was currently holidaying with their four children at Margate. The message simply read: 'Got it at last, Jack'. The overwhelming relief reflected in those five simple words to this wife was also etched on his beaming face. After the groundsman had taken the telegram, the Somerset players gathered round Hobbs to shake his hand and slap him on the back. The mood was further lightened by the sudden appearance on the field of the Surrey captain Percy Fender, whose crinkly black hair, thick moustache, and round spectacles made him one of the more distinctive figures in English cricket and, in his later years, gave him a passing resemblance to the American comic Groucho Marx. With an air of a waiter rather than his county captain, Fender carried out a goblet of straw-coloured liquid for Hobbs, who took a sip and then raised the vessel to the crowd, prompting yet another prolonged outburst of cheers. At the time, most people presumed it was a glass of champagne but actually it was only ginger ale, for Hobbs at this stage of his career was a teetotaller, on health rather than moral grounds.

Predictably Hobbs was not able to sustain his concentration after reaching the historic landmark. He was out soon afterwards, caught behind off Bridges for the addition of just one run. But the adulation continued long after he was dismissed. Telegrams flooded into the Surrey dressing room at Taunton and the club's office at the Oval. One was addressed to 'The Greatest Cricketer in the World'. Another just said, 'Superman, Taunton.' In a wireless interview at the end of the 1925 season, Hobbs said that he was 'staggered at the number and heartiness of the congratulations that reached me'. The deluge only grew when, in Surrey's second innings at Taunton, Hobbs hit his second century of the match, thereby surpassing W.G. Grace's record. Liberated from the chains of public expectation, Hobbs returned to his usual commanding style. Robertson-Glasgow remembered the 127th century as very different to the one made by Hobbs on the previous day. It was, he wrote, an innings 'full of beauty, carefree and brilliant of stroke'. So relaxed was Hobbs that, according to the *Daily Sketch*, on reaching his second hundred, 'he blew a kiss airily in the direction of the pavilion'.

Across the nation, Hobbs was now acclaimed as the greatest sportsman of his age. 'Jack Hobbs has taken the sporting world by storm. In two days and the same match he has equalled and surpassed the greatest feat ever performed in the annals of cricket,' declared the *Daily Mirror*. Even King George V, a monarch notorious for his gruff reticence, sent a fulsome message of congratulations from Balmoral via his secretary Lord Stamfordham, expressing 'much pleasure' at Hobbs's 'remarkable success, whereby you have established a new and greater record in the history of our National Game'. Nor could the non-cricket world ignore the event. 'Britain welcomes a new cricket hero,' the *New York Times* told its readers, explaining that, 'England has been in something akin to ferment this summer.' A ferment of a different sort arose in Britain's Indian Empire in the wake of Hobbs's triumph. On the day that Hobbs beat Grace's record, the *Star* published a cartoon by the brilliant New Zealand-born illustrator David Low, later to be renowned for his savage depictions of the European dictators of the 1930s. This 1925 cartoon, which perfectly captured the Hobbs mania that had gripped Britain, showed the Surrey player, bat in hand, towering over a series of other historical figures, including Columbus, Lloyd George, Caesar and Charlie Chaplin. Fatefully, Low also inserted in the line-up the Prophet Muhammad, standing on a pedestal and gazing up at Hobbs. When the image appeared in the Indian papers, it caused fury in the Muslim population, not just because Islam regards any portrayal of the Prophet as sacrilegious, but also because Muhammad was placed in a position of inferiority to a mere cricketer. According to the Calcutta correspondent of the *Morning Post*, the Hobbs cartoon 'convulsed many Muslims in speechless rage. Meetings were held and resolutions were passed.' So serious was the problem that the Indian Viceroy, the Marquess of Reading, wrote to the Cabinet in London to convey the feelings of Muslim outrage.

The tumult in India was only an extreme instance of the passions that Hobbs aroused in the summer of 1925. In the history of English cricket, no individual challenge has ever engrossed the public more than Hobbs's quest to equal W.G. Grace's record of centuries. Indeed, in all British domestic sport, the only parallel is the FA Cup Final of 1953, when almost the whole nation outside Bolton was desperate for Stanley Matthews's Blackpool side to win. It is perhaps telling that Matthews was a similar character to Hobbs: uniquely talented, working-class, modest, diffident, ascetic, a supreme professional who went on playing at the top flight past his fiftieth birthday. Just as Matthews' victory in

1953 forever cemented his status as the people's champion, so the events at Taunton in 1925 turned Jack Hobbs into a national icon. He was inundated with offers to appear in films, go on the stage, broadcast to the country, endorse advertising campaigns and write books. The Liberal Party even asked him to stand for Parliament under their banner, an appeal that Hobbs courteously turned down, citing both his fear of public speaking and his desire to continue as a professional cricketer.

The climactic outpouring of enthusiasm for Hobbs showed how cricket in the 1920s, far more than today, was truly the national English sport. Unlike football, its popularity spread across all classes and all regions, from the mining communities in Derbyshire to the patrician enclave of the MCC at Lord's. Ashes Tests were major national events, while county championship matches regularly attracted capacity crowds, particularly those involving Surrey or Yorkshire. The game's following was further boosted by the arrival of the wireless and the cinema in the first half of the twentieth century, bringing a new intimacy and immediacy to coverage. When the BBC was established in 1922, 600,000 people held radio licences. By 1930 that figure had risen to 5 million. Similarly, the cinema became part of the fabric of social life, with half a million people going to the movies at least twice a week in the early 1920s. It was also the era when the popular press expanded their circulations exponentially, complete with photographs and in-depth sports reports. All four of the mass-market papers, the *Mail,* the *Express,* the *Herald* and the *Mirror,* sold more than a million copies each day. As a result of these developments, top cricketers like Hobbs became household names. Furthermore, cricket's popularity fed on a powerful sense of national pride. It was seen as more than just a game. It was a national institution, the mirror into England's soul, its ethos of fair play, decency and honour said to reflect the best of the English character. This attitude was summed up by an editorial in *The Times* in 1928 which stated that cricket was 'English as nothing else, perhaps, is English; the greatest of all games played in the best of settings and in the finest spirit'. Even some foreign observers agreed with this verdict. The German writer Rudolf Kircher felt that cricket was 'pre-eminently English', a 'product of English temperament' and 'the most typical of all English games'. In this context, Jack Hobbs, as the greatest cricketer of his age, was seen by extension as one of the greatest of all Englishmen, the classic archetype of the modest and manly hero. 'No picture of the life of our time, set down in terms of personalities who command public attention, would be complete without him . . . He is the most representative man of the most English thing we have done in the world of recreation,' wrote the political journalist Alfred Gardiner in a perceptive essay in the summer of 1926.

In the years that followed the Taunton triumph, Hobbs's fame and hold on public affection continued to grow. His soubriquet of 'The Master' was fully deserved. He kept piling up the batting records during the remaining nine seasons of his first-class career, hitting another sixty-eight centuries to take his total to an incredible 197. Still a dominant figure on the international stage, he helped England to win the Ashes at the Oval in 1926 with one of the most skilful centuries every scored against Australia. At the age of forty-six during the 1928/9 tour of Australia, he became the oldest man in history to make a Test century, another of his records that will probably never be beaten. When he finally bowed out of first-class cricket at the end of the 1934 season, he was universally hailed as the greatest cricketer of his time and a model for all sportsmen. Almost two decades later, in Queen Elizabeth's Coronation Honours of 1953, he became the first professional cricketer to be knighted. He was 'the ideal of every cricketer, a legendary figure far beyond the bounds of the game he so richly adorned', said the spin bowler Ian Peebles, who played in Hobbs's last Ashes series. The doyenne of cricket writers Neville Cardus described him as 'one of the chosen few, because he was able to do things at the game beyond the reach of the skill and character of others'. The sense of awe that he inspired has never been extinguished. On his eightieth birthday in 1962, Sir Jack revealed that he had received a flood of telegrams, cards and letters. 'They say the public has a very short memory. I have not found it so,' he said with his trademark smile.

The same pattern continued long after his death the following year. When *Wisden* chose its five cricketers of the twentieth century for the Millennial edition of the almanac in 2000, Sir Jack Hobbs was named in third place, behind Sir Donald Bradman and Sir Garfield Sobers. Given that he first appeared for England before Bradman or Sobers had even been born, this accolade was a remarkable tribute to the continuing impact of his greatness. The verdict of the *Wisden* judges, reached through a ballot of a hundred experts from across the cricket world, reflected the historic importance he had for the development of the game. As the Australian writer Gideon Haigh, a member of the panel, said, 'Hobbs challenged the key assumption that no professional could bat as well as the thoroughbred amateur.' More romantically, the Sri Lankan correspondent Gerry Vaidyasekera voted for Hobbs because he was 'a batsman with a charming smile and a kind heart'. In a further reflection of the longevity of his name, Hobbs also cropped up in the 2008 hit movie *Slumdog Millionaire*. In the plot of this multi-Oscar-winning film, the hero Jamal appears as a contestant on the Indian version of the quiz show *Who Wants To Be a Millionaire?* The penulti-mate question is: which cricketer scored the most centuries in first-class cricket? Jamal chooses the correct answer and later goes on to win the top prize.

The phenomenal appeal of Sir Jack Hobbs through successive gener-ations was largely based on his astounding feats as a batsman. With a career aggregate of 61,237 runs, he not only scored more heavily than anyone else in the history of the first-class game but he also advanced the art of batting with an assured technique that combined solid defence with stylish attack. Hobbs first played for Surrey in 1905, at the height of the Edwardian 'Golden Age' when the majesty of batsmanship was thought to reside in flowing front-foot drives through the off-side and straight. But Hobbs, while incorporating the grandeur of Edwardian forward offence, expanded his method to include attacking and defensive strokes all round the wicket off either foot. Indeed the speed of his footwork and the range of his strokeplay became two of the prime assets in his armoury, to the delight of crowds and the despair of bowlers. There was an air of the cavalier about him in the years before the First World War, especially in his daring cuts and pulls. 'He was a mighty proposition in those days. He seemed at his best to have two strokes and plenty of time for every ball bowled,' wrote his fellow England player Frank Woolley of his aggressive style. In the post-war era, Hobbs reined in some of his attacking instincts, partly because of his increasing years, partly because of the burden of public expectations, as he explained once in a BBC interview. 'In those early days, I had all the strokes. I hadn't the same fear of getting out. I had the joy of life, whatever it was. After the war, when they started talking about W.G. and I started really making a name for myself, it was the figures that counted all the time. Unless I'd got so many runs I'd failed. I was cautious.'

The loss of exuberance in his stroke-play should not be exaggerated.

Throughout the 1920s, Hobbs remained a dominant force at the wicket, superbly equipped to master almost any opposition. The umpire Frank Chester, who saw nearly all the great players of the first half of the twentieth century, told a story that graphically illustrated Hobbs's commanding ability. In one match against Australia, Hobbs had to face the intimidating Australian fast bowler Jack Gregory, who had long caused terror in the ranks of Englishmen with his speed and bounce. Gregory, a wholehearted cricketer, was bowling flat out yet Hobbs appeared completely unruffled. 'His eyesight was so keen and his reaction so swift that he could step into line and place the ball wherever he wished, and it seemed that he had all the time in the world to do it,' recalled Chester. Exasperated by Hobbs's poise, Gregory turned to Chester and asked, 'Am I bowling fast, Frank?'

'You're bowling too fast for most batsmen but this chap is different. He's such a great player that he's making you look slow.'

On other occasion, in a match against Surrey at the Oval, the Yorkshire bowler George Macaulay encountered Hobbs for the first time. 'I hope we win the toss and put 'em in. I've heard about this Master. Well, I'll show him who's the Master if we do.' Yorkshire won the toss and duly opted to bowl. Hobbs scored 76 runs in forty-eight minutes, including 56 off Macaulay. When he departed, the Yorkshireman said, 'Well, they tell me he's the Master. But I think he's God Almighty.'

For all his prolificacy, Hobbs was no brutal run machine. It is not entirely true, as is often claimed, that he was utterly uninterested in records; his nervousness in the midsummer of 1925 is proof of that. But he was never obsessed with the runs for their own sake and would often throw away his wicket in county games through reckless hitting after he reached the hundred-mark. In his own words, he liked to 'enjoy' himself and 'give the opposing bowlers a sporting chance', the sort of attitude which outraged the much more ruthless Don Bradman. 'I can find no merit in the action of any player who deliberately gets out when his side still requires runs. That is not playing for the team,' Bradman once wrote. Nor was there anything savage about Hobbs's style. On the contrary, his batting had an easy aesthetic grace, something that further enhanced his popularity. He was almost incapable of ugliness or awkwardness, as Jack Fingleton, the Australian cricketer and journalist, recalled. 'Although figures indicate the greatness of Hobbs, they don't convey the grandeur of his batting, his faultless technique and the manner in which he captivated those who could recognise and analyse style . . . He was always attractive to watch – a neat, compact figure, faultlessly attired in flannels – whether he was moving along at a fast rate or was on the defensive.' There was nothing hurried, contrived or mechanical about his movements. Everything that he did appeared to be natural and balanced. In his 1926 essay, Alfred Gardiner wrote of the 'loose free action' of Hobbs at the crease and the 'economy of motion, no idle expenditure of effort for display or restlessness, no hint of egotism or self-consciousness'. Hobbs and his bat, continued Gardiner, 'are of a piece. The bat is so controlled, so responsive, that it seems only an extension of himself. It is not an instrument but a limb, a part of the anatomy, answering his thought as hand and eye answer it.'

Apart from the artistry and sheer weight of runs, the other feature of Hobbs's batting was his ability on a difficult wicket. His remarkable judgement, cool temperament and skill at playing the ball late made him unequalled as a player in such situations, especially when there was vicious turn on a drying pitch. On this kind of sticky wicket, wrote the long-serving Middlesex professional Harry Lee, 'Hobbs was truly the Master, and the more we lesser mortals were aware of our own limitations in such circumstances, the more we admired him.' In fact, many contemporary players and writers believed that Hobbs's genius on bad pitches made him the finest batsman of them all, even surpassing Don Bradman, who had by far the highest average in Test cricket but at times struggled in damp conditions that favoured the bowler. The tough, unsentimental Warwickshire all-rounder Bob Wyatt, who captained Hobbs in his very last Test and played regularly against Bradman during the 1930s, said that 'in spite of Bradman's great records, I've always thought that Hobbs was a still better batsman. That may seem startling when you compare some of Bradman's record scores with Hobbs's highest totals, but I'm taking into account the art of batsmanship in every department.' Hobbs 'got many of his runs and many of his centuries on extremely difficult wickets. When he was in his prime it was absolutely impossible for any bowler to keep him quiet on any type of wicket,' argued Wyatt, whereas 'whenever Bradman encountered a sticky wicket he hardly bothered to try . . . He had the perfect poise as the well-built Hobbs but he lacked the something extra when a batsman's qualities are given the most searching test of all.' Some Australians were inclined to agree with this verdict, such as Bert Oldfield, the great wicketkeeper of the interwar years. Though he believed that Bradman was the greatest 'run-getter' in the history of the game, Oldfield wrote that 'under all types of conditions, on fast, rain-affected or crumbling wickets, against the swinging new ball or the turning old ball, Jack Hobbs was the cleverest batsman I have seen.' Even Bradman himself admitted that Hobbs was 'the best equipped batsmen of all, in the technical sense – English or Australian. I could detect no flaw in attack or defence.'

Yet Sir Jack Hobbs's lasting influence in cricket was built on more than just his batsmanship. The decency of his character also played a vital part in the public's adoration. In his gentleness and modesty he was a living contradiction of the theory that only self-interested men can reach the top of competitive sport. To his admirers, he embodied the high ethical standards that were believed to make cricket a uniquely civilising force. Both on and off the field, he was a true gentleman: an honourable player, a loyal husband to his wife Ada, a good father to his four children and a devout Christian in the Anglican Church. 'He was incapable of anything paltry or mean,' said the England fast bowler Harold Larwood, adding, 'I've never met a more modest man or one who is more considerate of others.' A powerful moral code infused his actions, reflecting his simple adherence to the tenets of his religious faith. 'I think I have always tried to be good, even if I have failed miserably,' he once wrote. Most of his contemporaries would have strongly disagreed with the second part of that sentence. 'He was as straight as a gun barrel, utterly trustworthy and disliked by no one,' said Errol Holmes, his last captain at Surrey. Another Surrey leader, Henry Leveson Gower, who commanded the side in the Edwardian era and later served as Chairman of the England selectors, wrote that 'no sportsman more truly deserved the hero-worship that Hobbs attained, while certainly nobody ever bore such unbounded popularity with such modesty. You could not turn his head. You could never imagine him suffering from conceit.' Within cricket circles, there were numerous stories of his kindness towards other players, even those in the opposition. One who experienced this generosity of spirit at first hand was Bill Andrews, the Somerset fast-medium bowler who made his debut in 1930. Early in his career, he played in a match against Surrey at the Oval, and towards the end of the first day he found himself at deep mid-on. Hobbs had been in his most fluent form that Saturday evening but eventually he overreached himself, trying to pull Somerset's off spinner through mid-wicket. The ball shot up in the air towards Andrews. 'It was coming straight for me. I even had time to notice that the great batsman was beginning his walk back to the pavilion. I got right under the ball and dropped it – and I wish the ground could have swallowed me up.' At the close of play, Andrews walked off the field disconsolately and wandered into the pavilion to have a bath. 'It was quite a long way from the Surrey dressing room but almost immediately I discovered Jack Hobbs standing over me. He profusely apologised for walking away from the wicket as I moved for the catch. And he assured me he had dropped similar catches in his career.' When Andrews turned up at the Oval on the following Monday morning, he went to nets where 'Jack found me out again. Once more he was very kind.'

Hobbs's compassion extended far beyond cricket. He was a keen supporter of charities, gave away most of his memorabilia, including his England caps, to well-wishers, and diligently answered all his sack-loads of fan mail with his own hand, even though his lack of education made it a laborious task. Throughout his career and in retirement, he constantly performed acts of benevolence. 'I don't think any young cricketer ever went to him for help or guidance or even an autograph without being satisfied. He was the kindest, gentlest, most generous of men,' said the writer John Arlott, an admirer who, in Hobbs's retirement, became a close friend.

On another occasion, Arlott said that Hobbs was 'the best man I ever knew in my life. I would say this even if he had never made a run. There was something almost Christ-like about him, there really was,' a remark that perhaps highlights the dangers of excessive hero worship. But Hobbs's moral strength could not overshadow the essential light-heartedness of his character. His deep religious beliefs never made him a puritan or a prig. By nature, he was warm and optimistic, not given to introspection or moralising. 'Cricket ain't fun,' the austere Yorkshire all-rounder Wilfred Rhodes once famously said, but Hobbs's approach to the game was the refutation of that. To him, cricket was more than just his profession; it was also a source of profound pleasure. On his retirement he said that 'no other walk in life could have provided me with the same happiness. It has been a wonderful life. I have enjoyed every minute of it.'

Just as in his batting, he generally maintained a sense of balance in his outlook, neither crowing in success nor becoming morose in failure.

Even in the harsh competitive arena of Test cricket, he tried to keep a cheerful disposition. In his very last Ashes series in 1930, during the Old Trafford Test, he was felled by a rearing ball from the Australian paceman Tim Wall. Having taken the blow in the middle of his body, he collapsed to the ground. The Australians gathered round him anxiously, while a doctor, who happened to be watching, ran onto the field to see if he could help. After making his way through the circle of players, the doctor peered over the injured veteran. Hobbs looked up and, with that habitual smile, said, 'Have you got a cigar on you, Doc?' The whole Australian team burst out laughing. Even when Hobbs was bowled by a full toss from Arthur Mailey in the first innings of the vital 1926 Oval Test, he walked away from the crease with a wry grin on his face. His good humour was further reflected in his boyish love of practical jokes. Among his fellow cricketers, he was notorious for his frivolous pranks and tricks, such as surreptitiously removing a stump and taking it into the pavilion at the tea interval or deceitfully telling the square leg umpire that the new batsman was a left-hander, so the official had to run over to the other side of the field, only to hear Jack vainly trying to suppress a laugh as the incomer took up a right-hander's guard. In one festival game at Folkestone in 1927, Hobbs decided to enliven proceedings by slipping a bread roll into his pocket after lunch. On the fall of the first wicket in the afternoon, he whipped out the roll and gave it to the bowler just as the new batsman Lionel Tennyson, the aristocratic, free-scoring captain of Hampshire, strode to wicket. Seconds later, Tennyson watched open-mouthed in astonishment as this piece of bread floated through the air towards him. 'Fooling others was the great hobby of Jack Hobbs,' said the Surrey bowler Bill 'Razor' Smith, who played alongside Hobbs throughout the pre-war era. 'If you sat down carelessly you would find that you had ruined a new straw hat – always your own. To accept a cigarette from Jack was to ask for trouble – there would probably be a firework thrown in. He would join in a quiet game of poker and on being called, turn up a "Royal Flush" – from another pack. Nobody could lose their temper, as Jack's laugh was so infectious, but we were all glad to see him stay in and make runs, knowing that, for the time being at least, we were safe.' His last Surrey captain Errol Holmes thought that his 'greatest charm was that he had never really grown up and he still enjoyed a leg-pull more that most men'.

Yet it would be a serious mistake to see Hobbs as a paragon of unremitting virtue and merriment. He has often been painted as the epitome of the Corinthian spirit of fair play, but the truth is that Hobbs could be a hard-nosed, at times even cynical, professional. Amid all the accolades for his artistry, one less edifying aspect of his play was his exploitation of the lbw law of his era, which stipulated that no batsman could be given out to any ball that did not pitch directly in line with the stumps. This rule meant that batsmen could constantly use their pads as a second line of defence. Indeed, Neville Cardus once wrote that any player who allowed himself to be bowled by an off-break was either a fool or a hero. With his fine judgement of line and length, Hobbs was a skilled practitioner at the dark art of pad play, but it was a practice that provoked bitter controversy, since it was seen as unfair to the bowler and an encouragement to negative batting. In 1923 *Wisden* argued that 'nothing could be more flagrantly opposed to the true spirit of cricket', though it was not until 1935, a year after Hobbs had retired, that the law was finally changed. Nor did he always live up to his high reputation for honourable conduct. On occasions, his determination to preserve his wicket exceeded his sportsmanship. As a young Middlesex fast bowler, Gubby Allen was once left deeply disillusioned when, opening the bowling for the Gentlemen against the Players in 1925, he thought he had Hobbs caught by the keeper off a blatant edge. It was, said Allen, 'the most tremendous tickle' but Hobbs refused to walk and, to the amazement of the fielding side, he was given not out. Allen continued the story. 'When Jack got up to my end, I said at the end of the over, "Jack, you know you hit that, don't you?"

'"I did no such thing, G.O.," he replied (he always called me G.O.). I was really rather shattered. I admired Jack Hobbs, he had helped me a lot and I thought he could do no wrong and certainly would never tell a lie.'

A short while later, Hobbs and Allen were up at Scarborough, this time playing on the same side. When they were in the field Allen, still annoyed at what had happened, went up to Hobbs at cover and said, 'Now look, Jack, you hit that ball in the Gents versus Players match, didn't you?'

'Of course I did, G.O. But you mustn't say that in front of the umpire. It's unfair on him and furthermore, if I had, he would almost certainly have given me out at the next opportunity.'

A similar mix of surprise and anger ran through the Australian team during the Headingley Test of 1930, when Hobbs failed to walk after he fell to a legitimate diving catch at short leg by Ted a'Beckett. Following a tense delay and a loud, unanimous appeal by the Australians, the square leg umpire gave Hobbs out. Even then, he appeared to leave the crease only with the greatest reluctance, though subsequent press photos showed that the catch had been made cleanly. Later, after the close of play, Hobbs went into the Australian dressing room to explain his hesitation at the wicket, only to be met with a barrage of abuse from the vice-captain Vic Richardson, who told him to check the scoreboard.

Hobbs's professional instinct for pursuing his own cause was also highlighted in the way he could farm the strike, sometimes to the exasperation of his batting partners. 'Jack was very good at counting balls in an over and very good at pinching the bowling,' Wilfred Rhodes once said in a BBC interview. The same sentiment was echoed by Andy Sandham, Hobbs's Surrey partner of the 1920s and 1930s. Once, during an MCC tour of India, Bob Wyatt was batting with Sandham and found him regularly stealing the strike at the end of an over. 'I jokingly complained to him, to which he retorted that he'd had to put up with a lot of that from Jack Hobbs and he didn't see why he shouldn't get his own back now,' recalled Wyatt.

Hobbs certainly had no Franciscan spirit of self-denial when it came to taking financial advantage of his fame. Haunted by financial insecurity as a result of the impoverishment of his upbringing, he lent his name to a bewildering range of advertising campaigns and sponsorship deals. 'Right from his boyhood days Jack Hobbs never went without his Quaker Oats. He knew no surer or nicer way of getting nerve-nourishing Vitamin B, vital to guard against "nerviness", poor appetite and indigestion,' ran one typical advertisement in 1924. Waterman fountain pens, Barry's tailored suits, Berkeley armchairs, and Alkia Saltrates were among the other products he endorsed in the early 1920s, as well as the more predictable line of promoting cricket gear like Summers Brown 'Force' bats and 'Ovalba' white cleaner. A whiff of hypocrisy could be found in his eagerness to endorse several cigarette brands. In his 1935 autobiography, he admitted smoking a pipe but warned, 'As for cigarettes, if you wish to remain in the pink of conditions, keep well away from them.' Yet Hobbs was quite happy to advertise Sarony silk cut Virginia, telling potential customers, 'A Sarony after an innings or a spell of fielding is a pleasure indeed.'

There was also a negative side to his gentle character, in that he loathed responsibility and shied away from confrontation. Several leading professionals, including his greatest England batting partner Herbert Sutcliffe, felt that he could have done more to push for the Test captaincy at a time when the MCC establishment held that the position must be reserved exclusively for amateurs. In truth, Hobbs hated the burden of responsibility. Even at Surrey, if the usual skipper Percy Fender was absent on business, he was reluctant to take on the job temporarily, even though his standing was so much higher than any of his colleagues. When he occasionally assumed the leadership, as in the Gents v Players matches of the 1920s, he did not universally impress as a natural captain. In fact, the bilious Arthur Carr, who led Nottinghamshire for much of the post-war era, wrote of Hobbs, 'Captaincy was never one of his strong suits. I have seen him in charge of a side several times and if I may say so, I thought he was a rotten captain.' Hobbs's dislike of confrontation was manifested during the notorious Bodyline series of 1932/3, which he covered as a journalist for the *Star*. Hobbs had a vitally important role during that tour, not only because he was one of the few English reporters in Australia but also because the lustre of his name meant that he could have exerted a decisive influence on events. Forthright criticism from Hobbs might have brought an end to England's dangerous tactic of bowling short at the Australian batsmen, or at least woken the British public up to the reality of what was happening. But instead, keen to avoid becoming embroiled in politics and fearful of offending Douglas Jardine, the implacable England leader who was also Hobbs's club captain, he sent home a series of largely anodyne cables. It was only when he arrived back in Britain that he openly condemned Bodyline. By then it was too late.

Hobbs shied away from confrontation in a literal sense when the First World War began in 1914. The majority of professional cricketers joined the armed forces in the first two years of the conflict but Hobbs was not one of them. Instead he opted to work at a munitions factory, while also finding work as a cricket coach at the elite public school of Westminster. Given the scale of the carnage that engulfed western Europe, Hobbs later admitted to some embarrassment over his initial avoidance of military service. In his defence he cited both family duties and his failure to realise the seriousness of the war. Yet this was not the most controversial feature of his war years. In May 1915 he signed as a professional in the Bradford League, a decision that sparked an

explosive row in Yorkshire at a time when the Second Battle of Ypres
was at its height in the blood-soaked trenches of Belgium and the
Lusitania had just been torpedoed by a German U-boat with the loss
of over 1,000 lives. Lord Hawke, the autocratic guiding force of Yorkshire
cricket, described the signing of Hobbs as 'scandalous' and 'a most
unfortunate state of affairs considering the present crisis', a stance that
the Bradford League ferociously rejected, claiming that the local people
needed weekend entertainment to distract them from the miseries of
war. Hobbs's close involvement in the Bradford League ended when
he was conscripted into the Royal Flying Corps in 1916, though the
hostility between him and Lord Hawke was to last right up to the 1930s,
contradicting the myth that Hobbs had no enemies in the cricket world.
'He was a silly old fool and he never had a kind word to say about
me,' Hobbs once wrote privately. More painfully for Hobbs, the bad
feeling extended to his own family, for all but one of his five brothers
joined up in 1914 and two of them were badly injured. According to
Mark Hobbs, one of his descendants, the disparity in service led to
some friction. 'I think the animosity in the family, which I picked up,
comes from the fact that others were expected to serve and Jack didn't
because of his position as a cricketer,' he says.

Hobbs's early war years, the most contentious of his career, represent
a fascinating episode yet it has never been covered before in his own
books or in any profiles. It should not be allowed, however, to detract
from his greatness. Sir Jack Hobbs was, of course, neither saintly nor
Christ-like and he would have shuddered at the thought of being considered in such terms. He was a very human figure, with light and shade,
flaws and strengths, in his character. Like all great men who spend
decades in the limelight, it was inevitable that his story should contain
incendiary rows as well as crowning successes. But his significance, not
just for cricket but for wider British society, cannot be disputed. Through
his outstanding batsmanship and the quiet dignity of his personality,
he dramatically raised the status of professional cricketers. When he
first played for Surrey, the game still operated in a semi-feudal fashion.
Pay was poor, security almost non-existent. 'I am a hired servant on
low wages,' Wilfred Rhodes once commented rue-fully. The paid players
had to lead almost separate existences from the privileged amateurs,
who usually had their own dressing rooms, lunches, railway carriages
and hotel accommodation. Built on naked snobbery against the

professionals, cricket in the Edwardian age was riddled with injustices. Farcically, many amateurs actually had higher earnings from the game than the paid cricketers because of manipulation of expenses or bogus employment as club officials. But by the time Hobbs reached his peak, the structure of cricket had been transformed. The first-class arena was now dominated by professionals, who were respected and well rewarded, much to the anguish of some traditionalist diehards who wailed at the decline of amateur influence. Professionals 'are vastly overpaid for their efforts . . . Players of today can and do afford to buy motorcars,' moaned E.H.D. Sewell, who detected a creeping political motivation behind the change. 'The whole crusade against the so-called dividing line between amateur and professional is Communistic, if not Bolshevist in tendency.'

Jack Hobbs was no Bolshevik, but his influence was crucial to the progress of professionalism. The very idea of keeping down this national hero, simply because he was paid for his brilliance, would have repelled most of the British public. Moreover, Hobbs elevated his profession in certain direct ways. In 1924/5 he told the MCC that he would refuse a place on the tour to Australia unless he could bring his wife Ada. Such a demand from a professional would have been treated with disdain in the Edwardian age, but because of Hobbs's importance to the England team, the MCC acceded. Similarly, in 1926, when the England captain Arthur Carr was taken ill during the Old Trafford Test, Hobbs temporarily took charge, becoming the first ever professional to lead England out on home turf. Again this is something that would have been unthinkable when Hobbs began. By the time he retired eight years later, the standing of professionals had risen even further. No longer artisans, their pay was on a par with doctors and bank managers and stockbrokers. 'The county cricketer has become a man of bourgeois profession,' noted Neville Cardus with a twinge of regret.

Hobbs's own journey was symbolic of the change, from the dire poverty of late-Victorian Cambridge to the affluent respectability in mid-1930s suburbia, with his villa in Wimbledon, his membership of the local golf club and his children at private schools. But, even in stratified England, Hobbs could never be defined by a single class. Perhaps more than any other celebrity of his age, he was symbolic of England and its values. In his famous wartime essay 'The Lion and the Unicorn', George Orwell wrote that 'the gentleness of English civilisation is perhaps its most marked characteristic. You notice it the instant you set foot on

English soil. It is a land where bus conductors are good-tempered and policemen carry no revolvers.' This was the spirit that Jack Hobbs so perfectly encapsulated. He managed to be both a star and Everyman, another reason he was beloved by a public that recognised one of their own. It was a quality extolled by the Labour politician Harold Laski in an eloquent tribute to Hobbs written in 1931. 'In some ways I think Mr Hobbs is the typical Englishman of legend. You would never suspect from meeting him that he was an extraordinary person. He never boasts about himself. His private convictions are not cast at the public. He gets on with the job quietly, simply, efficiently. You could sit next to him in the Tube and remark nothing save a shrewd kindliness in his face, a certain quiet distinction of bearing. You would remark nothing in what he says until he is aroused. But then you would find whatever he feels he feels deeply; all that he thinks he has deliberated over until, as conviction, it has become a real part of himself.' Hobbs had shown 'as finely as any living man,' concluded Laski, 'what is meant by playing the game'.

1
'Better Make a Cricketer of That Kid'

The idea of Cambridge in the late-Victorian age conjures up a string of romantic images: the port making its way round the table at a lavish dinner in a wood-panelled hall; undergraduates in boaters and striped blazers punting lazily along the river Cam; earnest dons scurrying along medieval cloisters, their black gowns billowing behind them; muffins toasting by the fire in a student's private set of rooms; tiaras and necklaces glittering in the soft light from the chandeliers at a College Ball.

But there was another late-Victorian Cambridge. It was an entirely different world, one of squalor and poverty, of narrow streets and cramped houses, of endless grime and ceaseless work. This was the hardened world into which John Berry Hobbs was born in 16 December 1882, the son of a roofing slater. He was named John after his father; Berry was the maiden surname of his mother, Flora Matilda, the daughter of Elijah Berry who during his working life was variously employed as a shoemaker, baker and labourer. At the time of his birth, Jack's parents were living in Elijah's small cottage at 8 Brewhouse Lane, a rundown street in a poor working-class district in the east of the town. Soon afterwards, they moved nearby to their own home at 4 Rivar Place, a two-storey house in a red-brick terrace where they were to reside throughout Jack's upbringing.

He was the eldest of twelve children, six brothers and six sisters, with a nineteen-year gap between him and the youngest child, Gwen. Even by Victorian standards it was a large family, though Jack's mother was stoical about the burden, not least because the children were raised with a robust moral regime that encouraged respect and diligence. 'They learnt obedience and never caused me any anxiety. My husband and I were always strict with the children but he was always kind to them and me. The atmosphere was one of kindness and affection and we all considered one another. Besides that, we all worked. Young people should be encouraged to work. Work never did anyone any harm and it does most a great deal of good,' Jack's mother once said, setting out the classic Victorian creed of thrift and self-help.

Such an outlook was vital to cope with a tough environment in which money was scarce and the state provided little support. Cambridge may have once been a quiet East Anglian market town, dominated by the ancient university, but during the Victorian age it went through a tremendous upheaval caused by rapid growth, the arrival of the railways and the influence of industrialisation. Between 1830 and 1900, the size of the population almost quintupled to 53,000. By the time Hobbs's own father had been born in 1858, some quarters of the town were rife with overcrowding and destitution. A report in the *Cambridge Chronicle* for October 1850 expressed its shock that 'the dwellings of the poor are in the most disgraceful conditions'. Worst of all, said the paper's reporter, was a place called Falcon Yard. 'In one of the houses which I visited there were 13 families residing. In a room on one of the floors lived a man, his wife and 5 children. The eldest boy was 16 years of age, the oldest girl a little over 14, having been for several months a common prostitute.' The sanitary arrangements in Falcon Yard were pitiful, with over 300 people sharing just two lavatories. So inhabitants 'are in the habit of throwing all their refuse out of the window onto a large dung heap, the reeking steam from which is constantly penetrating the rooms'.

A mix of philanthropy and civic pride saw some improvements in the second half of the nineteenth century, such as the construction of a new sewage system, the introduction of street lighting, the provision of libraries, and the creation of better water supplies. But these were only limited palliatives. Life in the Cambridge of Jack's youth often remained a struggle for those outside the elevated circles of affluence, as was shown by the famous examination of the town conducted at the beginning of the twentieth century by the social reformer Eglantyne Jebb, who later founded the Save the Children Fund. Entitled 'Cambridge: A Brief Study in Social Questions', Jebb's survey used vivid language to expose the continuing hardship of the working class and paupers. 'In our streets we meet occasionally with pitiful caricatures of men and women, poor puny wastrels, starvelings and degenerates on whose faces the dull suffering of hopelessness has left an indelible stamp.' Jebb argued that the 'fundamental cause' of Cambridge's problems was the rapid expansion in population, which meant that there were 'a large number of persons living massed together in a narrow space' as well as vast disparities of wealth. Her report also found that the three biggest sources of occupation were the railways, service in the university and the construction industry, the initial occupation of Jack's father. But the wages in the building trade, she said, were low, amounting to just eight pence an hour on average.

Jack's home in Rivar Place was a classic of the type put up in the area for artisans and labourers in the 1870s, with two rooms on the ground floor and two on the first. The houses were made of brick and slate, with a tiled closet in the yard. According to an 1875 report by the Cambridge Medical Officer they had been 'designed with little regard to the health of the inmates'. Rents in the neighbourhood were around eleven pounds a year. A typically striking picture of this increasingly industrialised part of Cambridge was provided by Eglantyne Jebb's study. 'The whole place seems enmeshed in railway lines and the puffing of trains and screaming of engines break in upon the vibrating hum from the cement works,' read one passage. 'Wandering down these little streets you catch glimpses through an occasional gap between the houses of a wilderness of back gardens cramped between smoke-discoloured walls, store yards with stacks of wood or tiles or rusted iron, untidy heaps of debris, here a pile of old doors, there a mass of wheels, iron-roofed sheds with broken window panes, battered black palings and on every side the houses of sooty yellow,' read another.

Later in his life, Jack maintained that 'taking into account all the circumstances, I had a happy childhood'. Yet he admitted that he was also emotionally scarred by the physical surroundings of his formative years. 'I was always conscious of our humble circumstances. I detested the back road where we lived and I envied those who had big houses and who could hold their heads up in any company. Certainly I had the inferiority complex to a marked degree,' he wrote in his autobiography. In one sense, his upbringing in Cambridge presaged a key theme of his entire career. The conflict between town and gown, between poverty and privilege, was later to find its echo in the cricket world through the dichotomy between professional and amateur, between the paid servants and the aristocratic establishment. In the late-Victorian

Cambridge, not only was there serious poverty in the working class but the hostility between undergraduates and the townspeople could be ferocious. This strife sometimes flared up in explosive incidents like that in 1875 when a large student gang burnt an effigy of the Mayor in the main square, then proceeded to attack his house by smashing his windows and pulling down his fence, acts of hooliganism that were inspired by the Mayor's pledge to crack down on 'rowdyism'.

Yet Hobbs, just as he hardly ever rebelled against cricket's ruling elite, never showed any resentment towards the academic elite who made him feel inferior. On the contrary, he was proud of his hometown's link to the university and all his life was supportive of Cambridge students' sporting endeavours. His generous spirit always triumphed over any sense of grievance. At a dinner held in the Cambridge Guildhall in November 1925 to mark his conquest of W.G. Grace's record of centuries, Hobbs displayed his affection for the university. 'I can recall the old rivalry between town and gown but it is no matter of regret that there is very little of that old spirit, which was probably founded in class jealousy. Let us hope that this better spirit is but a sign of the times and indicates a general change of views upon this subject. I still have love for the old town, which includes our ancient seat of learning. I can still rejoice when our university beats Oxford in any branch of sport.'

Despite the straitened circumstances, Jack's mother ran a clean, well-ordered house. In typically Victorian fashion, she saw the maintenance of self-respect as a prime duty. 'She brought up all those children. There was never any spare money, but they never went without,' says Margaret Witt, who is married to one of Jack's surviving nephews, John Witt. 'She loved all her children but there was a lot made of the boys. My own mother always said that in the Hobbs house, the boys came first.' John Witt himself, the son of Jack's youngest sister Gwen, remembers as a child visiting his grandmother. 'She was a smallish lady but in command.' Indeed, because of the demands of child-rearing, Flora Hobbs had to be something of a matriarch, as she explained in a 1928 interview: 'Children must be made to mind if they are to grow up the best sort of men and women. They must learn to obey authority and put aside their own wishes when it is for the good of others. I always made my children mind what I said to them. From babies they knew that when I said a thing I meant it.' In the context of Jack's future fame, she made this interesting remark: 'Regularity of life in childhood helps

to form a strong character. It develops self-control, which is very necessary to young people destined to fill a big place in the world. A big
position often brings big temptations and the man who was made to
mind as a boy is much more likely to withstand them.' For all her stern-
ness, Flora Hobbs had one endearing eccentricity. During Jack's
boyhood, she kept a duck called Cyril as household pet, something that
Jack found 'most extraordinary'. According to Jack, 'Cyril followed its
mistress wherever she went. It behaved with all the dignity befitting its
position and answered Mother's call regularly and obediently. When
Cyril died of old age, she was much upset.'

Jack's father was a less dominant presence in the lives of the Hobbs
children than his mother, but he still exuded a natural authority. In his
autobiography, Jack described him as 'a reserved, quiet type, highly
popular with his fellow-townsmen. He was a great hero to me; from
childhood onwards I thought the world of him. He was strict, but kind
and just.' John Hobbs was a keen fisherman and also kept rabbits, but
the great passion of his life was cricket. By the 1870s the game was
significantly increasing in popularity thanks to a number of factors,
including the increase in leisure time for the working class, the expansion of the railways which facilitated county games, the personal influence
of the record-breaking W.G. Grace, and the public-school ethos of
'muscular Christianity' that held organised games to be part of a crusade
to strengthen Britain's moral character. Like much of the rest of England,
Cambridge was infected by the new enthusiasm for the sport, though
various forms of cricket had been played in the town since the beginning
of the eighteenth century. In the records of Trinity College there is a
reference from 1711 to 'impatient' undergraduates leaving their dinner
early to 'make a match at Foot-Ball or Cricket'. Competitive club and
university matches took place throughout the following decades, often
fuelled by heavy betting, but it was in the Victorian age that cricket really
gripped the public's imagination. Cricket flourished among school and
local teams, with Cambridge town becoming the dominant force in East
Anglian club cricket. New playing fields and recreation grounds were
opened. The Cambridgeshire county side, having played its first match
in 1832, reached a high standard, aided by the employment of a number
of professionals, including the father and grandfather of Tom Hayward,
the great Surrey and England batsman who was to become Jack's mentor
at the turn of the century. For all its success in the 1850s and 1860s, when

the side was accorded first-class status, Cambridgeshire was unable to sustain this quality and in 1869 reverted to minor counties level. But at the university first-class cricket was played continuously from 1820. The university club's first venue was Parker's Piece, a wide stretch of common land in the town's centre named after one of its owners in the distant past, an early seventeenth-century cook called Edward Parker. Fed up with having to share this large field with other cricket clubs and even football teams, the university moved in 1848 to a new site nearby leased by Francis Fenner, the Hampshire and former Cambridge town cricketer. The new ground brought a further rise in performances and, by the time Hobbs was born, the university could hold its own against the leading counties. Both Fenner's and Parker's Piece were to play a formative role in Hobbs's early life.

His father's devotion to the game was so deep that he was filled with an ambition to become a professional cricketer. In the 1880s, he and some fellow labourers started a cricket club at the pub they frequented, the Anchor. Soon the Anchor team had 'leapt into popularity' and was 'the talk of the town' because of its achievements, according to an account in the *Cambridge Chronicle*. Sadly, said the paper, 'this success was its undoing for its old members, who had founded the club, were driven to the wall to make room for the more showy members and eventually the club collapsed.' But the setback did not lessen John Hobbs's determination to make his living from the game. On the evidence of his fine work for the Anchor, he was offered a position as a professional at Fenner's, where his two main duties were bowling to the undergraduates and acting as a match umpire. He was now, effectively, one of Cambridge's large regiment of underpaid college servants, but at least he was involved in the game that he loved.

It was an obsession John soon passed on to his eldest son. 'Cricket is in my blood,' Hobbs once wrote. When he was just eighteen months old, his father took him to his first cricket match, as Cambridge University hosted the visiting 1884 Australian team at Fenner's. 'I am told that although I had not reached the dignity of trousers, or even knickerbockers, I was quick to recognise a big hit,' he said in a 1919 interview. Family legend had it that the infant Jack became so excited and yelled so loudly that he created a disturbance in the crowd, leading an Australian fielder on the boundary to remark to his father, 'Better make a cricketer of that kid, old man.' Rarely has any advice been more eagerly heeded. Almost as soon as he could walk, Jack showed a fascination with the game. Just as Don Bradman honed his reactions in childhood by hitting a golf ball with a cricket stump at the base of a water tank in his backyard, so Jack first learnt to play with equally primitive equipment. 'My first efforts in the summer game were halting enough and of the humblest character. Any old thing for a bat – a tennis racket for choice – a lamppost with three chalk marks on the wall for stumps and the street was my first playground, always with one eye on the ball and the other on the lookout for the policeman who in those days was our natural foe,' he told the Cambridge Guildhall dinner in 1925.

From the age of five, Jack attended the primary school connected to his family's local parish church of St Matthew's. A series of reforms in 1870 and 1880 had made elementary education compulsory in England for all children up to the age of ten, and Jack's was the first generation to experience the new, broader system, which reflected political concerns that Britain's place as the world's leading economic power was under threat from inadequate schooling. St Matthew's had about 250 pupils and charged no fees, its costs covered by the Anglican Church. As well as the basics of literacy and numeracy, its curriculum encompassed recitation, religious knowledge and even needlework, a subject whose mysteries Jack later admitted he could 'never fathom' despite his excellent hand–eye coordination. The school had just three classrooms situated in cold, damp buildings, though an official inspector's report for 1887 stated, in rather pejorative language, that 'the tone and discipline of this school are very good, considering the class of children attending'. One legacy of St Matthew's was Jack's elegant, neat handwriting, as recalled by a fellow Cambridge pupil T.F. Teversham, who kept up a lifelong correspondence with him. 'His writing, as with all of us who had been taught at an elementary school, was in the so-called Civil Service style, at an angle of seventy-five degrees – thin upstrokes, thick downstrokes; like his batting, void of careless or unfinished strokes; in short, technically perfect.' At the age of nine, Jack was sent to the neighbouring York Street Boys' School, where the fees were four pence a week. He was fortunate in that his headmaster, Mr Mallet, was keen on games, especially football and cricket, so there was a natural rapport between them. But Jack found the academic side more taxing. 'I cannot claim to have distinguished myself as a learner of the ordinary school lessons.' Luckily for Hobbs, there was plenty of time available for sports,

since the school hours were only from nine to twelve in the morning
and two until four in the afternoon.

Many of the traits that characterised Hobbs as an adult were conspic-
uous in his childhood. Just as he was a model sportsman, so he was
generally a well-behaved boy. His mother said that he did not give her
'a single day's unhappiness', while Jack himself declared that he never
threw stones or robbed orchards, 'probably because I was too scared of
the terrors of the law'. But, of course, no young boy is ever perfect. He
was once caned at York Street for illicitly swapping a tennis ball for
some snuff in the classroom, the teacher clambering over the desks in
his fury to reach him. It was, he wrote, 'the only real tanning I ever got'.
The playful enthusiasm for practical jokes was also evident, like ringing
the doorbell of the local vicarage with his mates before instantly scooting
'like hares'. Equally obvious was his innate gentleness. He was reduced
to tears when he lost a pet kitten and could not bear to steal from birds'
nests because 'I was too fond of birds'. More idiosyncratic was his chronic
seasickness, which was to make trips to Australia such a torment
throughout his career. When he was fourteen, his parents took him on
a day trip to Great Yarmouth, during which he went out in a boat off
the Norfolk coast. He was so violently ill that he collapsed, had to be
helped off the vessel and did not recover for two hours. Another trait,
the shyness that in adulthood made his public appearances such an
ordeal, was also on display in his youth. He hated to be the centre of
attention and several times he refused requests to be a Sunday school
teacher at St Matthew's church. 'I was always nervous of speaking to
any audience. I detested it and do to this day. I turn down hundreds
of invitations to functions of all kinds where speaking is involved. Never
have I tried to overcome this nervousness,' he wrote in 1935. Nor did
he ever lose the religious faith that had inspired him in his childhood.
Much of his early life outside the family and school revolved around
the Church and its organisations. He was a member of the St Matthew's
church choir, attending services and practice at least four times a week,
while he also went to Sunday school and Bible class. Other recreational
activities were provided by the local Temperance Society, whose youth
branch, known as the Band of Hope, organised board games, gymnastics,
boxing, talks and magic lantern shows, in which a story was told through
slide images projected onto a screen. There were also Temperance Society
day trips to East Anglian resorts, as well as cricket and football matches.

In adulthood Hobbs was never an evangelist about abstinence and indeed at various times in his life was happy to drink wine and champagne. But his youthful attachment to the Temperance movement led to an instinctive revulsion at overindulgence in alcohol, a feeling that was reinforced by living in a town notorious for its culture of heavy drinking. As Eglantyne Jebb's report pointed out, the average number of licensed premises in England was one per 230 persons, but in Cambridge that figure plunged to one per 138 persons. The study further found that on a single 800-yard stretch of the Newmarket Road, just north of Hobbs's home, there were no fewer than twenty-two public houses. 'The drink habit, so serious in its results, has a strong hold on the inhabitants of our town,' wrote Jebb, though she praised the work of the county's Band of Hope, which in 1900 had almost a thousand Cambridgeshire youths as members.

Jack's early experience of poverty left him with a sense of financial insecurity, which only began to lessen in the 1920s when he had achieved international fame. But there was another, more physical, consequence of his childhood lack of many home comforts. This was his love of traditional English food, especially roasts and desserts. When Jack was a child, the family's income was so limited that they could not afford to have any cake or decent meat during the week. Jack's younger brother Frank once confessed that his mother 'had a struggle' to feed her large family. Even an egg was a treat reserved for Sunday. On one occasion Jack and some friends were invited to tea by the choirmaster at St Matthew's. What impressed him most was the quality of the fare: 'never in my life have I tasted such delicious bread and butter and jam,' he wrote. Another time, when he was ten, he visited Fenner's to see the great Indian Prince Ranjitsinhji play but his greatest pleasure came from devouring 'a nice, hot pork pie' that his father bought for him. Gastronomic enthusiasm was to become a theme of his later life. On first moving to London as a young professional, he would be 'excited all day' if he knew he was 'going out to dine in the evening', while he was amazed that he could have an eight-course meal at the Hotel d'Italie in Soho for just half a crown. He never became a gourmand or a glutton, for moderation was always his byword, but as an established player he liked to eat well and, throughout his career, he commented regularly on catering arrangements, whether it be the excellence of his wife's full English breakfasts or the inadequacy of Australian dining cars. One of the reasons he liked the Oval so much, he explained to an Australian broadcaster, was because 'they gave us a grand lunch'. Yet the most opulent surroundings were no guarantee of fulfilment. 'I don't know why it is, but even in the most luxurious liners I have never yet been able to get a wholly satisfactory cup of tea,' he once complained in a BBC interview.

Jack's Cambridge upbringing was also imbued with the conventional racial outlook of late-Victorian England, when the British empire was at its peak and the conquest of Africa at its most exuberant. During his spell at York Street Boys' School, he once took part in a musical play in which, according to his own account, 'I appeared with a blackened face as a nigger boy and, holding a doll borrowed from a neighbour, I sang, "I'se a Little Alabama Coon".' The headmaster, Mr Mallet, was so pleased with Jack's performance that he came into the dressing room and gave him a threepenny bit. However innocent their intention, these stereo-typed attitudes lingered with Jack into adulthood, even into the 1930s, when the West Indies had been given Test status and nationalist, anti-colonial spirit was growing across the non-white parts of the Empire. In a revealing comment about the camaraderie of the England dressing room, he once praised Patsy Hendren's gift for humour and mimicry, explaining that the jokes his colleagues liked most were his 'nigger stories'. In the same vein, a passage in his 1935 autobiography described going to a 'Kaffir war-dance' near Johannesburg during the 1909/10 MCC tour, where he watched the black Africans 'all leaping about, banging their tom-toms and yelling like mad'. Again, in his defence, Hobbs was only adopting the language and mentality of his times. After all, Lord Hawke, the Yorkshire grandee, openly expressed his loathing in the 1920s for 'American nigger dances', while writers such as P.G. Wodehouse and Agatha Christie freely used the term 'nigger' in the 1930s. Yet Hobbs could appear progressive in other ways, as in his willingness to vote Liberal or in his reported support for the Suffragette movement before the First World War, even allegedly joining a march in favour of votes for women. On a personal level, he betrayed no shred of prejudice as his simple, innocent charm established friendly relations with Indian and Caribbean cricketers. 'I have always been a devotee of Jack Hobbs,' declared the West Indian all-rounder Learie Constantine.

With each passing year of his boyhood, Jack's love of cricket deepened. He took to the game naturally and always said that he 'never received an hour's coaching in my life'. But he was undoubtedly encouraged by

the example of his father, whose own professional career made a significant advance in 1889, when Jesus College appointed him groundsman
and umpire. It was an ideal job for John Hobbs. Not only was Jesus
near his home but also the college's cricket ground was one of the most
picturesque in the university, with a spacious thatched pavilion, rustic
in style though nineteenth century in construction, overlooking the
pitch. Moreover, no Cambridge college had embraced the late-Victorian
cult of games with more enthusiasm that Jesus, causing a contemporary
don to complain that its hearty, philistine atmosphere resembled that
of 'an ill-disciplined public school'. The 1889 edition of the Jesus magazine, for instance, devoted eighteen of its twenty-eight pages to cricket,
rowing and athletics, while the college Dean, E.H. Morgan, was described
as 'a glorified games master with an obsession for sport'. But academia's
loss was cricket's gain. Among the Jesus students who played on John
Hobbs's pitches were the brilliant Australian all-rounder Sammy Woods,
the Middlesex and England wicketkeeper Gregor Macgregor, and the
Nottinghamshire batsman Arthur Jones, later to be Jack Hobbs's first
Test captain. Judging by the quality of his wickets and the respect in
which he was held, John Hobbs was excellent at his job. The *Cambridge
Chronicle* wrote of him that 'he displayed such urbanity as a groundsman
as to win a good word from all with whom he was concerned'.

Just as importantly, the post at Jesus was invaluable for his son, who
spent much of his free time from school at the ground. By watching
the undergraduates in the nets or in matches, he absorbed the basic
principles of batsmanship, especially the need to move the left foot into
the drive. Sometimes he also had the chance to take part in makeshift
practice sessions at Jesus with a few college servants, using an old tennis
ball, a stump for a bat and a tennis post for the wicket. Hobbs later
wrote that these sessions laid 'a wonderful foundation, giving me a keen
eye and developing the wrist strokes which I had seen in the college
matches. Boy as I was, I tried to emulate the same strokes, and I was
surprised at the number of successful strokes I managed to make.' Hobbs
added that footwork came to him 'automatically and the practice became
a great source of enjoyment when I recognised how important everything was. The straight stump helped me to sense the importance of
the straight bat.'

Keenly aware of his status as a paid servant, John Hobbs felt that he
could not presume to exploit the excellent facilities at Jesus to coach his

son and Jack later recalled that he received direct instruction from his father in the nets only 'a couple of times at college'. What impressed him most on these occasions was his father's insistence that he should avoid stepping away to leg, a common habit of young players when confronted with high-quality bowling. 'Dad bowled to me without pads on,' Hobbs recounted in a BBC interview during his retirement. 'He had this spinner and it used to nip back. I could sense the break coming and, with no pads on, I drew away from the wicket a bit. I remember him trying to put me right.' Despite this early flaw, John Hobbs was deeply gratified by the progress of his son. With typical reticence, he did not express this admiration openly. 'He never spoke very freely to me about his hopes. This I regret, but it is a family trait,' wrote Hobbs in 1924. Yet a fascinating insight into his attitude towards Jack can be found in the interview that his wife Flora once gave, which contradicts Jack's claim that he received little coaching from his father. 'My husband trained him carefully since he was old enough to hold a bat. He always believed in the boy's ability. If his father was anxious to teach him, Jack was just as eager to learn.' At Jesus, she said, 'Jack often went as a little boy to bowl at the under- graduates. He used to follow cricket matches too, all over the county, and he knew all about cricket form. But he seldom talked cricket at home. From his conversation in the family circle, no one would ever have gathered that cricket was important to him but he used to discuss it seriously enough with his father and he practised every minute he could spare.' Crucially, said Flora Hobbs, her husband 'prophesied a great future for Jack, though not in front of him. He was too careful for that. But he did say to me, "That boy will be a great cricketer one day."'

It was at the Jesus ground that Jack Hobbs appeared in his very first game of organised cricket. At the age of just eleven he was roped into playing for the college choir XI when one of their regulars dropped out at the last moment. 'I was trembling like a leaf. Even in these early days, I took cricket very seriously indeed. I got one or two runs and was quite bucked about it,' he recalled. His next match was for the choir of St Matthew's against the Trinity College Choir XI, in which he scored three runs. 'I was not big enough to drive the ball but poked it through the slips.' From then on, the remainder of his schooldays and teenage years were dominated by cricket. He turned out for several sides, including the York Street Boys' School XI and the St Matthew's Choir XI, which he captained from the age of twelve. Later, when he had outgrown the choir, he and some of his friends started the Ivy Club, which played evening matches on Parker's Piece. He later recalled the pleasure that his involvement with the Ivy brought, though his innate shyness was again on display: 'We would meet on a Sunday night and talk of the past week's matches. Then on Monday morning we would meet in a little coffee tavern to pick the team for the next match. I was on the committee but I never dared say anything. Those were very, very happy days.' These initial games also taught him that even at the most junior level the Victorian rhetoric about cricket and fair play was not always translated into reality. In one match, after Jack had reached 30 not out, a prolonged dispute arose on the field over the run-out of his partner. 'In the middle of the argument, when we all gathered by the pitch, one of our opponents seized the ball and knocked my wicket down. Out I had to go after a wordy fight.' Soon afterwards, again batting for the Ivy, he had made 90 and was on the verge of his first century in cricket when he fell victim to a poor lbw decision by the umpire. Even at this early stage Jack's consistency had attracted his first follower, a young reporter on a local paper. This fan was even more outraged by the error than Jack was, and he had the power to do something about it. The scorecard that appeared in the next edition of the paper read: 'J. Hobbs, not out 90.' Jack admitted that he 'felt quite consoled' at this journalistic rewriting of the record. His father was even happier when he heard the news of the big score. 'He was as pleased as if he had come into a fortune,' wrote Hobbs. When he was not playing, Jack practised intensively on Parker's Piece, often rising at six o'clock in the morning to go the nets. At the other end of the day, he would carry on until darkness arrived. His mother Flora said of his fixation, 'I remember how, as a boy, when he had little jobs to do for me – an errand or two to run or something like that – he would come and say, "Mother, as soon as I'm finished may I go and play cricket on the Piece?" I can still see the delight on his face when I said "Yes" and he would hurry through his task to get away to the cricket field.'

The fruit of those long hours was later to be borne in Hobbs's superb, uncomplicated technique as a professional. Batting on the pitches of Parker's Piece, which were rougher than those he later encountered in the first-class game, undoubtedly honed his unique skill for playing on bad wickets. This expertise was a source of wonder to his colleagues, given that his home turf at Surrey was the batsman's paradise of the

Oval. As Wally Hammond, England's greatest batsman of the 1930s, later put it, 'How Jack Hobbs ever became a master of the turning ball on the Oval wicket of his day has always been a source of speculation among cricketers.' The likely answer was his training on Parker's Piece, something that the Australian Jack Fingleton sensed. 'The Piece must have had much to do with the correct moulding of Hobbs's technique. Provided a young batsman has inherent ability, there is no better place to build a solid defence than on turf that scoots, jumps and imparts abnormal break to the ball.' But what was really intriguing about Jack Hobbs's youthful cricket is that there was nothing freakish about it. He was good, far better than his Cambridge contemporaries, but he could not be described as a prodigy. No first-class teams tried to recruit him. No top coaches took an interest in his performances. John Arlott, the broadcaster and writer, argued that the failure of Jack to gain a place in county cricket in his teens was an injustice that reflected both the weakness of the youth development structure in Cambridgeshire cricket and the struggles of Hobbs's own background. Arlott might have had a point but the fact is that Hobbs's record as a teenage cricketer gave little hint of the feats that were to follow. Don Bradman scored his first century in competitive cricket when he was just twelve and by the age of seventeen had hit a triple-ton. Similarly, the Indian genius Sachin Tendulkar, who was regarded with awe when he was still at school, fulfilled his juvenile promise by scoring a century on his first-class debut at the age of just fifteen. It was hardly the same story with Hobbs, who was eighteen before he hit any kind of century. During the long summer days and evenings on Parker's Piece in the 1890s, Jack provoked admiration, but not amazement. Percy French, a cricketer who played with him at this time, told the *Cambridge Daily News* in 1962 that Jack 'hardly showed any promise in his early years at cricket' and that 'it was difficult to believe that he was one who was destined to become one of the greatest batsmen in the world'. This may have been an exaggeration, but it was a verdict with which his own mother largely agreed, saying that it was only when he became older that he started to be 'really unusual'.

Looking back on his career and his late arrival in county cricket, Jack himself, in a letter of October 1958 to the cricket historian David Frith, said, 'It seems to me that I matured late,' though he added there was one advantage of this. 'No doubt that was the reason I was able to go on so long.'

So, in his youth, there seemed no question of Jack pursuing a career in professional cricket. Once he left school at the age of twelve he had to earn his living in other ways. With typical diligence and filial concern, he had taken a part-time job to boost the family income in his final year at York Street Boys', working in domestic service at a private house in Cambridge where his duties were cleaning shoes and the silver, clearing and laying fires, and carrying coal, all for half a crown a week. He had to work early in the morning, before lessons started, and did a longer stint on Saturdays, when, to his delight, 'I got lunch thrown in'. On leaving school in 1895, he also took on a position as an errand boy for Simpson, a baker's in King Street, earning just two shillings and sixpence a week. But thanks to his father's connection with Jesus, he soon found more rewarding work in the summer months as a servant at the college. For seven shillings and sixpence a week, he had a variety of tasks connected to the college cricket team, including oiling bats, cleaning the pavilion, helping his father to prepare the wickets, putting up the nets and transporting the cricket gear by handcart to away fixtures. The job at Jesus, however enjoyable, offered Jack no prospect of permanent, long-term employment. He therefore had to learn a trade and so, at the age of sixteen, he was indentured as an apprentice gas fitter at the well-known Cambridge firm of John Vail. It was an occupation that offered steady work, since gas had become one of the prime sources of energy in the late nineteenth century. Street lamps, industry, and domestic heating and lighting all relied on gas, while gasometers, used for storage, were built in most major English towns. The most famous gasometer of them all, right beside the Oval, was put up in 1877, the very first year that Test cricket was played. With its lattice metal frame and huge drum, the feature became a treasured part of the ground's scenery, symbolic of the Oval's lack of pretension. It was perhaps appropriate that the former apprentice gas fitter should play so much of his career against this industrialised backdrop.

But the passion for cricket continued to burn within Hobbs. The experience of other work intensified his hunger for the game. As he moved towards adulthood, he was fired by the desire to follow his father's example and become a professional. 'It was my supreme ambition. It stuck out a mile beyond anything else,' he wrote. The dawn of a new century in England would bring the realisation of that goal, but only amidst profound personal heartache.

2

'The Darkest Spot in Jack's Career'

The cricket correspondent and MCC tour manager Colonel Philip Trevor, a man of strong, if sometimes erratic, opinions, once wrote: 'It is absolutely certain that without Tom Hayward there would have been no Jack Hobbs.' By this, he meant that Hayward, another Cambridge cricketer and the greatest English professional batsman at the turn of the century, was a crucial influence on Hobbs through his example and his 'careful tutelage'. In one respect, Trevor's statement was misleading. Hobbs always maintained that he was a self-made player and fiercely resented any claim that he had been reliant on coaching. 'I am a natural batsman, self-taught,' Hobbs wrote. He was uncharacteristically emphatic on this point, largely because of his justifiable pride at overcoming the obstacles of his background. His own career showed, he said, 'that those who have no great advantages, such as coaching, can hope for success, provided that they possess a certain amount of gumption and natural aptitude and, next, unlimited persistence and perseverance'. The 'popular belief' that Tom Hayward coached him was 'not correct', he concluded.

Yet this should not diminish the importance of Hayward as a key figure in the fulfilment of Hobbs's ambition to make his living from the game. During the 1890s, after he had first won fame at Surrey, Hayward was the hero to nearly all cricket-mad boys in Cambridge. It was an adulation sparked by his local connections to the town, for his father Daniel, grandfather and uncle had all played for Cambridgeshire. Daniel was also in charge of the nets and the upkeep of Parker's Piece, a huge responsibility given that more than forty cricket clubs played there during the summer.

Hobbs revered Tom Hayward as much as any of his mates did.

Whenever Surrey were playing, he used to run to the library to find out from the evening paper how many Hayward had made. Occasionally he had the chance to see Hayward batting against the University at Fenner's, and like so many others, marvelled at his strong defence and off-driving. Less orthodox was Hayward's open stance, with both shoulders almost facing the bowler. But it was not a style that inhibited his effectiveness. Having first signed as a professional for Surrey in 1891, Hayward had a career of unrivalled success up to the First World War, becoming only the second Englishman after W.G. Grace to score a hundred centuries. *Wisden* said of him that he combined 'unlimited patience and admirable judgement with remarkable powers of endurance'. Self-assured, sometimes curmudgeonly, he was keenly aware of his status as a skilled tradesman. Before the Oval Test of 1896, he joined a threatened strike by a group of England professionals in support of higher pay, though most of them backed down when their demand was rejected. With his heavy physique and large moustache, he exuded the air of a municipal dignitary, as the historian and academic Eric Midwinter wrote: 'There was something positively aldermanic in his perceived demeanour. It was as if he sat at the head of the council committee table, making prompt and expeditious assessments with solemn efficiency.' In later years, Hayward's solidity made him verge towards lethargy in the field. A useful medium pacer in his youth, he had it written into his Surrey contract that he would not be put on to bowl. There was also a match in which a temporary young amateur took charge of Surrey and sought Hayward's advice on placing his men. He replied wearily, 'I always stand there and the rest just spread out. They'll stop the ball right enough if it comes near them.' He remained a bachelor throughout his career until his retirement in 1914, when he married a woman who worked as a detective for the London and South Western Railway Company. After his playing days, he returned to his beloved Cambridge, where he was employed as the coach of the university cricket club at Fenner's. Rather bizarrely, for such a gruff, masculine figure, his favourite activity was to give massages to the students. 'He had a weakness for this emollient art and regarded it as a more integral part of the day than bowling off-breaks in the nets,' recalled Raymond Robertson-Glasgow.

It was in the summer of 1901 that Jack Hobbs, having hero-worshipped Hayward for years, first had the chance to play alongside him. The

opportunity arose because on reaching the age of eighteen Jack's batsmanship had dramatically improved. He was now a member of two
different local sides, the Ivy Club of his early teens having fallen into
decline. One side was Ainsworth, a team connected to his Bible class.
The other was the Cambridge Liberals, for whose football team he had
turned out in the winter of 1900/01, Jack's instinctive ball skills making
him a fair player at inside-right. He always stressed, however, that he
joined the Liberals purely for recreational purposes and had no interest
in their politics. During the early weeks of the cricket season, he alter-
nated between Ainsworth and the Liberals, impressing both of them
with his new confidence at the crease. Then the inevitable happened: a
fixture was arranged between the two sides. It was an indicator of Jack's
growing reputation that both desperately wanted to play him in a match
that attracted strong local interest. In the end, the two captains agreed
to toss a coin to settle the problem. Ainsworth won and Jack went in
to bat at number four. From the moment he arrived at the crease on
the fall of the second wicket, he scored freely against his former teammates. By the time he was out, he had made 102, the first century of
his life. 'The cheers that greeted me that day were the sweetest I have
ever heard. That day I would rather have been Jack Hobbs than W.G.
Grace himself,' he wrote. Over the next forty-two years, he was to score
another 244 centuries at all levels of the game. Invigorated by this
triumph, his good form continued, as he showed in an innings of 70
not out for Ainsworth against the Cambridge University Press.

This was the performance that helped ensure his participation in the
highlight of the summer. Every year, towards the end of the season,
Tom Hayward brought a team of professionals to play in a charity match
on Parker's Piece against Cambridge's best XI. Because of the high
standard of the visitors, the event always generated excitement in the
town and Jack was thrilled to be picked for the local side. The fact that
his father was one of the match umpires undoubtedly helped his selection. Local interest was all the greater because Hayward was then at the
peak of his powers, averaging over 50 for the season and a certainty for
the MCC tour of Australia that winter. Yet Jack was undaunted by the
pressure of playing against top professionals for the first time. For all
his shyness, he always possessed a wonderful temperament for cricket.
On this occasion, batting down the order, he made 26 not out and
seemed to be in little trouble against the high-quality opposition

bowling. Hayward, who had once taken over a hundred wickets in a first-class season, put himself on for a spell during Hobbs's innings but could not break his defence. In terms of runs, Jack's score was hardly significant, but in terms of promise, the innings was a breakthrough. He had demonstrated that he had the technique and mettle to compete with first-class cricketers. 'I walked on air for days after this,' he said. Sadly, on the next occasion that Hayward was to bring his side to Cambridge for a charity match, the cause was a response to a tragedy in the Hobbs family.

Hobbs's talent had caught the eye of other observers, leading to a further important step in his career. In the last weeks of the 1901 season he was asked to play as an amateur for Cambridgeshire, thereby marking his first appearance in minor counties cricket as well as his first mention in *Wisden*. He took part in one major partnership in the fixture against neighbouring Hertfordshire, when, batting at number nine, he made 30 not out and his fellow batsman A.J. Rich scored 92 in a substantial victory. But this was his only double-figure innings. Overall, he failed to translate the success of his charity and club appearances to the minor counties arena. *Wisden* revealed that 'Mr J. Hobbs averaged just 8.75 in four matches for the county'. But Hobbs refused to be downcast by this setback. The experience that summer of his first century and of playing against Hayward had only reinforced his determination to make his way in the game. So early in 1902, while he carried out his dreary job as a gas fitter, he applied for the position of assistant professional at Bedford School. On the strength of his performances in 1901, as well as character references from Cambridge club officials, he was appointed for the three months of the summer term. At last, he was about to become a professional cricketer.

In the grandeur of its imposing architecture and magnificence of its spacious grounds, Bedford School exhibited the apparent confidence of the British ruling class at the height of its power. Though the school was founded in the mid-sixteenth century, it really flourished in the late-Victorian age under the leadership of the headmaster James Surtees Phillpotts, an apostle of the creed of muscular Christianity. Designed to mould men for the armed forces and the empire, the school laid a strong emphasis on military training and sport. So effective were Phillpotts's methods that in 1891, due to the dramatic expansion of pupil rolls, the school relocated to its new site within Bedford, complete with Gothic red-brick buildings set on thirty-five acres of land. Particularly impressive were the cricket facilities. The school had no less than seven sets of nets, while the pitches, made of loamy soil, were 'nearly always excellent and reflected great credit on the professionals engaged on the ground', according to the 1901 edition of the school annual. Later these same grounds honed the youthful technique of Alastair Cook, the England batting hero of the 2010/11 Ashes tour. But amidst all this success, one shadow hung over the school in the early Edwardian period: the impact of the Boer War. As an institution that sent a large number of pupils to the military academies of Woolwich and Sandhurst, Bedford felt the consequences of this conflict more than most other schools. The first two years of the century saw a lengthening catalogue of fatal casualties among Old Bedfordians, and on Jack's arrival to start his job in May 1902, the fighting in South Africa was still continuing. On another level, the Boer War heightened anxieties about the threat to Britain's economic and imperial supremacy, for the bloody struggle by professional soldiers to defeat a group of Dutch farmers had exposed structural weaknesses in British society, especially in the inadequacy of living standards for a large section of the population. Remarkably, 40 per cent of potential recruits for the war, most of them from working-class backgrounds like Jack's, were rejected because they were physically unfit.

The experience at Bedford School was an unhappy one for Hobbs. Though he was now aged nineteen, he had led a sheltered life and had never lived away from home. Indeed, he had barely even ventured outside of Cambridgeshire except for the occasional day trip. Moreover, the exclusive public school surroundings fed what he admitted was his 'inferiority complex', just as in later life he said that he 'detested' Lord's, the home of the cricket establishment, so different to the comfortable base he had created at the Oval. Nor did he like his cricketing duties as much as he had expected. In the morning, he had to help the other groundsmen in preparing the pitches and mowing the grass. Then every afternoon, he had to bowl in the nets.

Hobbs was always a decent bowler, with a high action and a gift for making the ball swing away at medium-pace. In one match for Ainsworth during the 1901 season, he had taken eight wickets. But batting, as he put it in a 1930 interview, would 'always be my first concern and joy'. What made the task of net bowling all the more onerous was its repetitive nature. 'I found this work dreary, monotonous and fagging. You have to be as fresh and as keen and as instructive with the last comer as with the early arrivals,' he said. On the other hand, Hobbs accepted that the strong cricketing culture at Bedford assisted the development of his own game. The school had one of the country's strongest First XIs, led by the dashing all-round sportsman F.G. Brooks, who was Head of School and went on to play rugby for England. The Bedford annual for 1902 described him as 'the best bat the school has yet produced, very sound in defence'. The high standard partly reflected the influence of the cricket master, R.W. Rice, an Oxford blue who had played for Gloucestershire with W.G. Grace. 'I bowled to him occasionally and remember him as a very correct forward player,' wrote Hobbs. In a profile of Bedford School by the *Cricketer* in May 1933, Hobbs himself was recalled by one ex-Bedford pupil as 'a young player with a long nose who was a useful net-bowler and could make the 30 runs which was the maximum allowed in school games'. The *Cricketer* added, 'What a mercy it is for the game that Hobbs was rescued from becoming a cricket coach at a school for his natural career.' But, after his brief spell at Bedford, there was never any danger that he would remain in coaching. The only moment of real happiness he had at the school was when he accompanied the First XI on a trip to London to play St Paul's. After the match, he went with the First XI coach to a comedy at the Tivoli Theatre on the Strand and during the show, he laughed so hard that other members of the audience looked round at him, prompting further waves of laughter to run through auditorium. 'I have never forgotten that first visit to London, a big experience for a young lad from the provinces who had not seen much of life,' he wrote.

Hobbs's time at Bedford was cast further into gloom by a sudden decline in his father's health. Aged forty-five, John Hobbs contracted pneumonia, then a deadly illness before the invention of antibiotics. He was taken to Addenbrooke's, the renowned hospital in the centre of Cambridge, but the prognosis was bleak. His desperate condition meant an end to all cricket for him, but even while he was lying on his sickbed in late August, he was able to take one step to help advance his son's career. His close friend George Watts, the Cambridge wicketkeeper, had promised to organise a team from the market town of Royston for its local derby fixture against Hertfordshire Club and Ground, and together they agreed that Jack should be asked to play. The match was at the highest club level that Jack had yet reached, but more importantly, it was the first game in which he appeared as a professional, Royston offering him ten shillings plus expenses. The fee was certainly worth it. In front of a large crowd on Royston Heath, Hobbs hit 119 out of a home total of 299, 'a long and highly meritorious innings', declared the *Hertfordshire Mercury.* Hobbs, who already had a minor reputation in Cambridge, was now 'talked a lot about' in the town, to use his own words. 'In Cambridge, if you have done anything to make a fuss about, everybody knows you and points you out,' he said. His own family, usually so reserved, 'treated me as I were a victorious general'. Even his father, now extremely ill in hospital, was able to take delight in the news. Jack, it seems, had begun to live up to the prediction that his father had once whispered to Flora.

On 3 September 1902, exactly a week after the Royston innings, the harrowing blow fell as John Hobbs succumbed to pneumonia. His demise had been expected for weeks, but still hit Jack hard. His mother later said that the loss was 'the darkest spot in Jack's career. He died just when Jack was beginning to make a name in cricket.' Yet if there was any compensation for Jack in his grief, he found it in the astonishing outpouring of affection for his late father from the people of his hometown and the Cambridge cricket world. The heartfelt display of support was a tribute to the respect John Hobbs inspired and sympathy at the family's plight. Within days of his death, a committee was established to raise funds for the widow and her twelve children, these efforts inevitably focusing on cricket. Headed by W.F. Taylor, the proprietor of the *Cambridge Evening News,* the committee decided to hold a charity match on Parker's Piece on 27 September and soon Tom Hayward had agreed to bring a team up from London. His side could hardly have been stronger, featuring established Surrey stars like Tom Richardson, Bill Lockwood and Ernest Hayes. Generosity was also shown by local traders who provided timber stands round the ground free of charge. Indeed, everyone connected with the match gave their services voluntarily, from the two umpires to the members of the town's band, who played throughout the afternoon. The combination of celebrity players and exceptional organisation ensured a large crowd for the game, which was, fittingly enough, dominated by the batting of Tom Hayward. Jack Hobbs, still in mourning, was unable to take part but he was deeply touched by the response of the public, who filled the collection boxes to overflowing. The success of the event exceeded all expectations, as the *Cambridge Chronicle* enthused in an editorial: 'In the annals of Parker's Piece, this game must surely take a unique place. Never before has a team of cricketers of the first rank played in the town's best playground and the crowd of spectators was certainly the greatest ever assembled to witness a local match. All those who took part in the memorable game were animated by the noble desire to assist an afflicted family.' The final sum raised was just over £170, which was invested to provide Flora Hobbs with a small weekly pension. In addition, a collection at Jesus from staff and graduates brought in £35. In the face of loss, the family now had a degree of financial security, though circumstances were never easy: Flora carried on living in the cramped house at 4 Rivar Place until the end of her days.

For Jack, in his despondent state, the loss of his father had the paradoxical effect of intensifying his ambition to be a professional player. He knew he now had to be the breadwinner, and there was no other occupation he could contemplate. The charity match had not only shown him the extraordinary compassion of the cricket world but had also reinforced the attraction he felt for Surrey. He was in the club's debt, and he wanted to repay with his own service. During the winter of 1902/3, he took over his father's job as the groundsman at Jesus, and in this capacity he had several long talks about his future with F.C. Hutt, a college servant, who was also the cricket team scorer and had been his father's closest friend since the days of the Anchor pub team. Struck by Hobbs's dedication, Hutt resolved to take action. Using his Cambridge connections, he asked Tom Hayward to give Hobbs a trial with a view to Surrey offering him a place on the staff. Hayward agreed and, late in 1902, Hobbs was asked to present himself on Parker's Piece where his batsmanship would be tested by Hayward himself and another cricketer from Cambridge, Bill Reeves, who opened the bowling for Essex. 'They put me through it for twenty minutes and I batted pretty well. I had been advised beforehand not to be afraid but to go for the bowling,' recalled Hobbs. Hobbs's feeling that he had made a good impression seemed to be confirmed when Hayward muttered through his thick moustache a casual remark about 'getting a trial at the Oval next April'. At first Hobbs's spirits rose. But then followed months of silence. Hobbs sank into disquiet, unsure as to what Hayward had really meant. 'It was a dreadfully long winter,' he recalled. Even though he occasionally saw Hayward on the streets of Cambridge, he was too shy to approach him and ask what was happening at the Oval. 'I would no more have thought of going up to Tom Hayward than I would have thought of going to see the King,' he said. Hobbs poured out his troubles to Hutt, who, anxious to help the distressed young man, decided on a radical alternative to Surrey. He wrote a letter to the Essex County Cricket Club, setting out Jack's credentials and urging that he be given a trial. Essex, disinclined to take advice from a college servant, turned down the suggestion without even looking at Hobbs or giving a reason. With hindsight, this peremptory dismissal has to rank as a major blunder, akin to the rejection of the Beatles by Decca record executives in 1962: 'We don't like their sound and guitar music is on the way out.' If Essex had not been so negative, the history of English cricket might have been very different, for Hobbs, despite his fondness for Surrey, had nothing against joining the neighbouring county to Cambridgeshire. 'Had they offered me a job, I should probably be playing for Essex today,' he wrote in 1931.

Surrey were reprieved by Essex's indifference. In the spring of 1903, after his long, fretful wait, Hobbs was summoned to see Hayward, who told him the wonderful news that Surrey wanted him to report to the Oval on 23 April for a trial in the nets under the supervision of the county coach W.T. Graburn. Hobbs counted down the days with rising excitement until the fateful morning arrived. He was up at sunrise to make his way down to Cambridge station, proudly carrying his green carpet-bag, which contained his bat, pads and a pair of buckskin boots, the last item a present from his late father. On his arrival at Liverpool Street, he took the underground to the Oval, his first journey on such a train. 'I thought its speed remarkable,' he wrote. Such wonder, however, was not just another sign of his parochialism, for the tube was a relatively new experience for most Londoners. The first deep underground line powered by electricity had only been opened in 1890, running between the City and Stockwell, with the Oval as one of its six stations, and the comprehensive expansion of the network had just started.

Once Hobbs arrived at Surrey's ground, he encountered Graburn the coach and the rest of the aspiring young players who had been invited for the trial, some of them looking nervous, some cocky. He changed into his flannels, padded up and awaited his turn to bat in the nets. 'Come along, Hobbs,' a stentorian voice called out. Just as he had done at Parker's Piece the previous winter, Hobbs adopted an aggressive approach and quickly impressed. He was told he would be playing in a full trial match that afternoon. 'I was really to play at last on that classic ground,' he said. The two trialists' teams were led respectively by Jack Crawford, then a sixteen-year-old schoolboy at Repton but already a brilliant all-round talent, and Neville Knox, the pace bowler whom Hobbs once said was the 'best of my time'. Playing in Crawford's side, Hobbs batted well until, on 37, he mistimed a pull stroke and bottom-edged the ball into his stumps. The bowler was none other than Phil Mead, then a slow left-arm spinner on the Surrey ground staff before he went on to become one of the most prolific batsmen of his generation at Hampshire. Despite his disappointment at getting out when he was set, Hobbs's performance was good enough to win him inclusion in another trial the following day. That night he was put up in the Islington home of one of the Surrey professionals, and on the journey there he marvelled again at the speed of the tube. The two men went to a variety show at Sadler's Wells Theatre, but Hobbs was too preoccupied with thoughts of cricket to enjoy it. The next morning he was out for just 13, again bowled by Mead, but the number did not prove unlucky. At lunchtime the Secretary of Surrey, Charles Alcock, sent for him. The news could hardly have been more thrilling: Surrey offered him an engagement as a professional on the ground staff, with wages of 30 shillings (or £1 10 shillings) a week in summer plus match fees and a weekly retainer of one pound a week in the winter. The pay may sound meagre but this was an era when average full-time earnings only stood at 28 shillings per week, and some manual workers were even more badly rewarded: in 1906 a casual docker in the East End could be on less than a 10 shillings a week.

In any case, Hobbs cared far more about the position than the money. He was the only trialist from his cohort to have been selected. He had finally been given the opportunity to make it as a Surrey cricketer. 'I went back to Cambridge and, elated beyond measure, ran off to tell the news to Tom Hayward, who was highly pleased and congratulated me most warmly,' he wrote. Unbeknown to Hobbs, Hayward privately performed another kind deed on his behalf. Still mindful of the tragedy that had befallen the family the previous autumn, he persuaded Alcock to include in Hobbs's contract an additional bonus of £10 to be paid at the end of the 1903 season. It was an act that again displayed both Hayward's influence within the portals of the Oval and the compassion that lurked beneath a sometimes lugubrious exterior. There was, however, one major drawback to Hobbs's appointment to the Surrey staff. Under the strict rules which then operated in first-class cricket in England, a player who was not born in his chosen county could only qualify by residing there for a minimum of two years. The aim of this regulation was to ensure that the leading counties could not easily poach the best young players from anywhere in the country, though it had the effect of severely restricting the mobility of labour by professionals. Enforcement of the code was something of an obsession with Lord Harris, the overbearing Kent captain, MCC panjandrum, and Tory politician, who in 1898 had unsuccessfully tried to get the qualifying period raised to three years. Throughout his years at the heart of the establishment, Harris fought vigorously to protect this restrictive system, treating any dilution as a form of revolution. 'Bolshevism is rampant and seeks to abolish all rules,' he declared in 1922. It was an attitude that meant he was embroiled in regular disputes with the counties, most notably in the early 1920s over the case of Wally Hammond, whose right to play for Gloucestershire he challenged. 'May I congratulate Your Lordship on having buggered up the career of another young cricketer,' the President of Worcestershire Lord Deerhurst told him in the Long Room of Lord's during the height of the Hammond row. Later in life, Jack Hobbs shared this contempt for Harris. In one private letter he wrote: 'As for His Lordship, he is nothing but an old bore who thinks of nothing but Kent.' As with Hammond, the start of Hobbs's first-class career was significantly delayed, for he had to wait until the start of the 1905 season, when he was already twenty-two, before he was eligible to play for Surrey. At that age, figures like Denis Compton, Peter May and David Gower had already established themselves as major international stars.

But Hobbs's frustration was far outweighed by his excitement at joining the club he had followed eagerly since his early boyhood. Surrey was one of the great names of English cricket, its pedigree surpassed perhaps only by Yorkshire, its great northern rival. Indeed, the earliest written reference to cricket in English history came from Surrey, where a court case in 1598 over a plot of land in Guildford featured a statement from one witness that at 'the free schoole of Guildford' he 'did runne and play there at creckett'. More organised cricket appeared in Surrey in the eighteenth century, sometimes alongside other entertainment to heighten public interest. Notices for a pub fixture held at Walworth Common in June 1748 declared, 'After the match a Holland Smock will be run for by two women stark naked', not the sort of the diversion that the Surrey Committee of Hobbs's time would have dreamt of holding.

On a more elevated level, cricket clubs sprang up all over the county at this time, while a variety of teams, some representative, some merely village sides, played under the banner of Surrey. But it was not until 1845 that the county club was formerly established, when a group of enthusiasts agreed to lease a site at Kennington, south London, from the Duchy of Cornwall. Laid with 10,000 turves from Tooting Common, this field became the Oval cricket ground. Two professionals were hired, as well as four boys for practice days. After a few barren early years, Surrey became the leading team in the country during the 1850s, able to hold its own against even All-England XIs thanks to its great players like William Caffyn and Julius Caesar. Success on the field helped the club to prosper. By 1861 Surrey had over 1,000 members and an income of more than £2,000, enabling the committee to erect the Oval's first pavilion. The last decades of Queen Victoria's reign saw the county reach new heights. Under the leadership of John Shuter and then Kingsmill Key, Surrey won the county championship no fewer than seven times between 1887 and 1899. Their top players, like batsman Bobby Abel, all-rounder George Lohmann and fast bowlers Tom Richardson and Bill Lockwood, turned the club into the dominant force in English cricket. The Oval was the first ground to host a Test match in England, when the Australians were beaten in 1880, while phenomenal crowds flocked to see the county games. In 1892 63,775 paid over three days to watch Surrey playing Nottinghamshire and at the end of the century, the annual attendance totalled 400,000 spectators a season. This late-Victorian flowering partly reflected the growth of civic pride within the metropolis. The riches of London and its place at the heart of a vast global empire helped to make Surrey a wealthy and influential club, a process aided by a dynamic press that gave far more coverage to sport in the capital than elsewhere. By 1899, membership had increased to 4,000 and receipts from cricket alone totalled £13,593. Surrey's prestige was symbolised by the Oval's tall, elegant red-brick pavilion, which was built in 1897 at a cost of £40,000, four times the original estimate, and designed by Thomas Muirhead, the architect of a similar edifice at Lancashire's Old Trafford.

Yet for all its past glories, Surrey was in the doldrums when Jack Hobbs arrived at the Oval in 1903. The run of championships had ended. Attendances had shrunk. The great bowlers Richardson and Lockwood were in rapid decline thanks to a mixture of drinking and weight gain; both of them were to retire before Hobbs made his Surrey debut. Even more poignantly, the diminutive batsman Bobby Abel was afflicted by failing eyesight and forced to quit in 1904, becoming totally blind in his later years. So troubled was the club that in 1903, thirty-three different players were used in first-class games. Nor had a new captain emerged to halt the slump, with Surrey forced to rely on an array of inexperienced or ineffectual amateurs. A central reason for Surrey's troubles was the destructive control exerted by Viscount Alverstone, the Lord Chief Justice of England who also served as the club's president from 1895 until his death during the First World War. An earnest if uninspiring lawyer, he was a dogmatist in favour of amateur status to the exclusion of professionals, even arguing that the maintenance of amateurism was more important than the creation of a winning team. 'I should like, if possible, to arrange matters in the future so that at least three places in the eleven in all ordinary county matches should be filled by amateurs,' he told the Surrey committee in 1899. Ernest Hayes was one of the fine Surrey professional batsmen who found his career undermined by the judge's meddling. 'I felt very strongly about the way they were treating me,' he wrote privately.

Excluded by the rulebook rather than presidential fiat, Hobbs could exert no influence on Surrey's playing fortunes. But his two-year qualification period was not an empty one. Throughout the summer of 1903, he played regularly for the Surrey Colts and for the Club and Ground XI, made up of young professionals like himself as well as a few amateurs. Both sides had strong fixture lists against clubs and schools in London and the Home Counties, the standards high enough to serve as a thorough test for Hobbs. Just as he had done for much of his early life, he performed satisfactorily without doing anything startling. In his very first match for the Surrey Club and Ground, against Guy's Hospital, he hit 86, though he was less successful in his first appearance for the Colts. Opening the batting against Battersea, he was out for a duck. During the remainder of the summer, he made several useful scores, including 61 against Mitcham Wanderers and 52 against Epsom College. His medium-paced swing bowling also progressed, largely because his body had become stronger; in one match against the Sussex club of Heathfield, he took 6 for 41 in eighteen overs. In nineteen innings that season for the two Surrey teams, he scored 480 at an average of 34.29, while as a bowler he took nineteen wickets. The following summer saw a significant improvement as Hobbs grew in self-assurance and experience. 'I was no longer in a position like that of a new boy at school. I really belonged now to the Oval,' he wrote. Having graduated from the Colts, Hobbs played all his Surrey matches in the 1904 season for the Club and Ground team, averaging 43.9 in eleven innings. Twice he came close to scoring his first century for a Surrey side, hitting 96 against St Thomas's Hospital and 90 against Wimbledon. His burgeoning talent was just as apparent in the nets and practice sessions organised by the coach W.T. Graburn at the Oval, as recalled by Herbert Strudwick, then a young player on the Surrey staff, later to be a great England wicketkeeper and Hobbs's closest friend in cricket: 'As a boy of twenty, he showed exceptional promise and in the few games in which he was allowed to play for Surrey outside the ordinary county programme during his period of qualification he showed wonderful aptitude. I remember in those far-away days coming away from the nets with a coach whose job it was to teach the young members of the staff how things should be done. And this is what the coach said to me, "I don't know why they send that lad Hobbs here to be taught the game by me. I can't teach him anything. He knows so much already." I think the coach explained then the real secret of the success of Jack Hobbs. He was a born batsman. He did not need coaching. Right from the very first he had complete confidence in his own ability and that confidence was entirely justified.'

Hobbs's excellent record for Surrey Club and Ground also reignited the interest of his native Cambridgeshire, for whom he had briefly appeared without much success at the end of the 1901 season. Now, on his recall three years later, he proved a formidable batsman. The minor counties bowlers had little answer to his quick footwork, solid defence and wide range of attacking strokes. He made 92 against Norfolk, batting with Tom Hayward's brother Dan, and a 50 in each innings against Oxfordshire. But it was his two performances home and away to Hertfordshire that really showed his progress. Playing at Fenner's, he thrashed the Hertfordshire attack for 195, including twenty-four boundaries. It was an innings that prompted the *Evening Standard* in London to praise Surrey's new recruit. 'Cambridge, who furnished Tom Hayward for Surrey, has another likely batsman for Surrey in young Hobbs, who by next season will be qualified. This season he has been playing for Cambridge, and was yesterday seen to great advantage against Herts,' said the paper, adding that the display was 'quite one of the best played this year at Cambridge'. Ten days later, in the return match at Watford, Hobbs subjected the Hertfordshire bowlers to another battering, scoring 129 in quick time. One of those who was deeply impressed by Hobbs during 1904 was the Suffolk cricketer, the Reverend R.L. Hodgson, who served as the honorary secretary of the eastern county. As he later recounted in an article for the *Cricketer*, Hodgson turned up at Fenner's to play for Suffolk against Cambridgeshire when he met Tom Hayward at the gates. 'He was an old acquaintance and we talked of old times. Then he said, "There's a young fellow playing for Cambridgeshire I want you to notice."

'"Is he good?"

'"He's very good, and he's going to be great," Tom affirmed.

'"Batsman, bowler or all-rounder?" I queried.

'"He's a bit of a bowler, but it's his batting that's worth seeing. Just watch him!"

'I said I would. "And his name?"

'"Hobbs," said Tom, "Jack Hobbs. He's qualifying for Surrey."

'Cambridgeshire won the toss. I think J.B. Hobbs came in second or third wicket down. He was a quiet, modest-looking young man. He played very correctly and very carefully. Every ball seemed to be met with the middle of his bat.' Just before lunch, Hodgson was called up to the attack to deliver an over of leg-spin. 'For five balls, young Hobbs treated me as though I were a great bowler. He played each delivery gently back to me.' For the last ball, Hodgson decided to bowl a quicker one, but dragged it down short and Hobbs 'cut it prettily past point' for 3. As he walked in to lunch, the Suffolk vicar reflected on the wisdom of Hayward's words. Hobbs scored 45 runs that day at Fenner's, part of his total 696 aggregate for Cambridgeshire over thirteen innings at an average of 58. 'A new player in Hobbs rendered fine services as a batsman and came out with a remarkable average,' said *Wisden* in its review of the season.

One of the ironies of Hobbs's contribution to Cambridgeshire batting in 1904 was that he was not actually allowed to live in his hometown during these months, but instead could only make brief visits. This was because the rules on qualification were rigorously enforced, and a young player had to prove that he was residing permanently in his adopted county. Club officials even made regular inspections of his lodgings to check that that he was abiding by the regulations. Surprisingly, Hobbs, once the shy, provincial youth, did not find this demand oppressive. In fact, he relished life in the capital, revelling in his first experience of independence and the pulsating rhythms of the metropolis, such a contrast to his quiet upbringing. 'I was as interested in walking about London as in anything. The crowds, the shops and the traffic never failed to fascinate me,' he wrote in 1931. Sometimes in the evening he listened to a band in Hyde Park or went to a variety show. He saw all the great stars of the Edwardian music hall, including Sir Harry Lauder, reputedly the highest paid performer in the world, and Marie Lloyd, though his inherent innocence may have prevented him from grasping the louche double-entendres that were integral to her appeal.

Part of the excitement of living in London in this decade was the sense of being a witness to extraordinary social change. The streets were undergoing a revolution as the arrival of motorised vehicles and electric trams made horse-drawn transport increasingly obsolete; it was in 1904 that the very first petrol-driven bus appeared in London, operating the route between Peckham and Oxford Circus. This was also the period that saw the opening of the first cinemas in London, though they were primitive, malodorous places compared to the art-deco picture palaces of the interwar years. Other entertainment came through the major expansion in the number of West End theatres, reflected in the construction of huge arenas like the Hippodrome and the London Coliseum. Catering for London's masses was partly provided by the rapid growth of the Lyons chain of tea rooms and corner houses, which were renowned for their reliability and affordable prices, just the qualities that attracted temperate customers like Jack Hobbs. The sense of a vibrant new era was further reinforced by the advent of a new type of press, through the creation of the *Daily Mail,* the *Daily Mirror* and the *Daily Express* between 1896 and 1904. Lord Salisbury, the last prime minister of the nineteenth century, had sneered that the *Mail* was 'written by office boys for office boys', but in truth all three papers quickly acquired huge circulations through their mix of populism, hard news, jingoism and gossip. The market for everything from papers to Lyons cakes reflected both population growth and greater affluence in the new twentieth century, especially in the capital. With 6.5 million residents, London was by far the world's largest city in 1904, almost twice the size of Paris, prompting the American novelist Henry James to write of 'the brutal size of the place'. In almost every area, including the streets around the Oval cricket ground, there was constant housing development to meet rising public demand, though the living quarters of the poorest remained abject. Indeed, parts of south London were all too reminiscent of the squalor of Jack's Cambridge. Alexander Patterson, a teacher who lived there during Jack's early Surrey years, recorded in his diary how the very air around some tenement blocks stank of destitution. 'The vapour of the slum is so indefinable as to be more of an atmosphere than a smell. It is the constant reminder of poverty and grinding life, of shut windows and small, inadequate washing basins, of last week's rain, of crowded homes and long working hours.'

Fortunately Jack escaped the worst of this, living in digs at Fentiman Road, a terrace of smart nineteenth-century townhouses overlooking Vauxhall Park near the Oval. His fellow lodger was another member of the Surrey ground staff, Joe Bunyan, who was never destined to play first-class cricket but became an admired coach in Northern Ireland and then at King's College School in Wimbledon, where Jack's own brother Alfred served as groundsman. Bunyan remained 'a staunch friend' to Jack for the rest of his life, both men sharing similar person-alities and interests. Solid and dependable, neither of them indulged in any rebellious behaviour. 'There was no temptation for me in vice,' wrote Hobbs in rather biblical language, though such opportunities were certainly available since London was reputed to have more than 80,000 prostitutes at the start of Edwardian age. Nor did he succumb to other enticements. 'We never drank much and kept pretty good hours,' words that could have been an adage for the rest of his career. He and Bunyan joined a youth club in Camberwell known as the Cyprus, where they frequently played billiards. Hobbs also kept himself fit by long-distance walks and games of badminton. With an adult height of five feet, eight-and-a-half inches and a narrow thirty-four-inch chest,* he was conscious of his diminutive frame and so briefly experimented with a 'body-building' system, following the fad that had been imported from Germany. More importantly, Hobbs played football at centre forward for the Cyprus team that finished mid-table in the Dulwich

---

* Statistics taken from his RAF service record in 1919, National Archives.

League at the end of the 1903/4 season. Soccer also featured on some of his weekend visits to his family as he turned out for local club Cambridge St Mary's. Naturally athletic, he was an effective striker and in the 1905/6 season, he helped St Mary's win the Cambridge Football Association Senior Cup, the first of a cabinet-full of medals in his long career. But this was not his greatest achievement in football. In 1910, playing for Cambridge United, an amateur side that had no connection with the future professional club that went on to win league status in 1970, he led the frontline in a 2–1 victory over East Anglian rivals Lowestoft in one of the early rounds of the FA Cup. According to the *Cambridge Evening News,* Hobbs had to go for treatment in the dressing room but 'he cracked home the winner after he returned to the field', though later his injury meant 'he had to leave for the rest of the match'.

In later life Jack expressed regret that he had not been more productive with his time during his qualification period. 'Looking back now, I wish I had made more of it. It's what I ought to have done, you see, going to schools or something like that, but I did absolutely nothing in the winter.' Money was also tight because Jack had no form of employment outside the cricket season. Surrey, more enlightened and wealthier than most other clubs, had introduced the concept of winter pay for its professionals in 1895, but the retainer was only £1 a week. In October 1903, the committee carried out a survey of sixteen Oval staff, including Hobbs, which found that nearly all of them struggled to find winter jobs, largely because of the glut of unskilled labour on the London market. One of the respondents, the Surrey batsman Fred Holland, told the committee how 'the long closed season hangs terribly. This mode of living is not conducive to one's success at cricket. It amounts to saving as much money as possible in the summer and worrying whether it will carry you through the winter.' In response to the findings, C.W. Alcock, the Surrey Secretary, wrote to the Surrey members asking if some of them 'might assist the players who are engaged for the summer months to obtain employment in the winter'. Little came of the letter. Hobbs and most of his colleagues remained jobless during these months.

But the idleness was coming to an end. In the spring of 1905, having finally completed his two-year qualification, he was about to experience cricket at an entirely new level.

3

'He's Going to Be a Star'

Looking forward to the 1905 season, *Cricket* magazine reported, 'Hobbs, the promising young Cambridge player, is now qualified for Surrey. He is a batsman who may go a long way, for, with a variety of strokes, he plays with confidence and in an excellent and businesslike style.' But, despite his eligibility and his superb form in the previous summer, Hobbs had no guarantee of a place in the Surrey batting line-up. On the Oval staff, there were no fewer than twenty-two professionals, while eighteen amateurs were also available for selection. But Hobbs had one great advantage over other aspiring young players: the patronage of Tom Hayward, who had long recognised his potential for greatness and now had a crucial role in arranging Hobbs's first-class debut. Surrey's opening match of the season was at the Oval against the Gentleman of England, beginning on Easter Monday. To his joy, Hobbs saw his name in a squad of fourteen when the team list was posted on the board of the players' dressing room. In a departure from the usual convention of non-professional leadership, Tom Hayward was handed the captaincy for the match because of the absence of leading amateurs. Not only did Hayward ensure Hobbs's selection in the final XI, but he also chose to take the debutant with him to open the Surrey innings.

On a cold but sunny April morning, Hayward won the toss and decided to bat. The Gentlemen of England were a powerful, all-amateur side, their attack including Test players like fast bowler Walter Brearley and leg-spinner Charlie Townsend. Above all, their captain was by far the biggest name in cricket, W.G. Grace, then aged fifty-eight and in the darkening twilight of his career, though he remained a colossal presence on the field. There was a pleasing symmetry in the coincidence that Jack Hobbs should make his first-class debut in a match featuring the cricketer whom he ultimately succeeded as the world's greatest batsman, just as Jack's own last Ashes tour twenty-three years later marked the international debut of Don Bradman. A chain of continuity binds these three batting giants together over a span of eighty years.

Never one to be plagued by nerves, Hobbs was more excited than apprehensive as he went out to bat with Hayward. 'I felt keen, fit and happy,' he recalled, adding that he was relieved Hayward had chosen him to open. 'I looked upon it as a wonderful compliment. Moreover, it saved me the worry of sitting about, fretting for my time to go in.' In the first over, he got off the mark with a short single, something that was to become his trademark over the next thirty years. Just when he was beginning to build an innings, he was caught in the slips for 18 off a medium-paced outswinger from George Beldam, the type of delivery that would always give him the greatest trouble during his career. 'Hobbs has been more often missed and dismissed in the slips than any other batsman of his unquestioned class I have ever seen,' wrote Edward Sewell in 1933. A product of Bedford School and a fine amateur batsmen who played for the Gentlemen in this match, Sewell later became an acerbic sports journalist.

Hobbs's early dismissal prompted a dramatic collapse by the rest of the Surrey batsmen, who, on a difficult wicket, managed a total of just 86. The Gentlemen fared little better, reaching only 125. Hobbs and Hayward then had the prospect of a difficult hour's batting before the close. But they refused to be daunted by either the conditions or the deficit, their partnership remaining unbroken until stumps. Hobbs, in particular, went on the attack with an innings of 44 not out made in cavalier fashion. That evening, he was so pleased with his performance that, in order to celebrate, he took a hansom cab to the West End, where he went a variety show at the Tivoli Theatre on the Strand. As Hobbs queued up outside, a newspaper boy came down the street, selling copies of the *Star* evening paper. Hobbs eagerly bought one, just a halfpenny in price, and was thrilled to read a report of his 'admirable innings'. As he later remembered in a radio interview, 'The reports came in very quickly in those days. I was very pleased with myself. I may sound conceited but it wasn't conceit. My lowly upbringing guarded me from conceit.' The next morning he continued in the same commanding, easy style. At one stage he encountered the wiles of W.G., who bowled round-arm slow medium and was notorious for his sharp practice towards inexperienced players, as was demonstrated in one incident during Hobbs's innings. Having hit the ball towards cover, Hobbs was contemplating a quick single when Grace called out in his strange, squeaky voice, 'That's right, youngster, just tap it back here.' Perplexed by the high-pitched yet imperious order, Hobbs stopped immediately and did as the Grand Old Man told him. But, for all Grace's cunning intimidation, Hobbs was untroubled by his bowling. 'W.G. had a way of getting young batsmen out. I can't say I found him difficult, but I did not take any liberties with him, I must admit,' Hobbs told *The Times* in 1952. Grace himself, not one to lavish praise, was impressed enough by the young batsman to voice openly his admiration. Albert Lawton, a member of the Gentlemen's side, recalled that on the second morning, as Hayward and Hobbs came out to open, W.G. said, 'Just have a look at this fella coming in with Tom. Unless I'm very much mistaken, he's going to be a star.' Lawton agreed with that verdict. 'I remember thinking that this youngster Hobbs had no business being so good in his first match. No really, he had the stamp of class straight away.' Also playing in this match was Jack Crawford, who appeared for Surrey while still a Repton schoolboy: 'Hobbs was obviously such a perfect athlete in balance and timing. I remember old W.G. saying what a fine sticky wicket innings it was. One day, he said, that young fellow would be going in first for England. For me, Jack was the finest player I ever saw. His style was perfect and he could adapt himself to any conditions.' Within an hour, Hobbs had doubled his overnight score to 88. A century was in sight when he mistimed a short ball from Walter Brearley, pulling lamely to square leg. 'I would drop that stroke if I were you,' said Brearley as Hobbs passed him on the way back to the pavilion. But Hobbs never considered such a step. On the contrary, the pull remained one of the most lucrative strokes in his repertoire, its effectiveness founded on his uncanny ability to move into position quickly. Indeed, against all the tenets of traditional batting orthodoxy, Hobbs regularly pulled balls that were delivered well wide of the off-stump.

The match petered out into a rain-soaked draw, but the result could not dampen Hobbs's spirits at the emphatic success of his debut. At the close of play, he was summoned to the office of the Surrey Secretary C.W. Alcock, who warmly congratulated him. 'He told me that he was particularly pleased with the way I had faced W.G., who, he said "is very artful at getting out youngsters".' After producing the top score against the Gentlemen, Hobbs was assured of a place in Surrey's next match, their first county championship fixture of the season. The opponents were Essex, the club that had turned him down in 1903 without even giving him a trial. On this occasion, Surrey were led by their new permanent skipper Lord Dalmeny, who had agreed to take over the captaincy after a lengthening roll-call of amateurs had failed over the previous summers. Few figures encapsulated the nexus of wealth, breeding and influence at the summit of Edwardian cricket's structure more graphically than Dalmeny. He was the eldest son of the 5th Earl of Rosebery, the rich, clever but morose Liberal statesman whose disastrous premiership in 1894/5 had ended in a nervous break-down brought on by chronic insomnia and morphine. As the heir to the Rosebery title and fortune, Dalmeny occupied a prominent position in society, his authority illustrated by the way he persuaded King Edward VII, who was his godfather, to grant Surrey permission to use the Prince of Wales's feathers in the club crest. But Dalmeny had inherited neither his father's intellect nor his depressive nature. A bluff sportsman, racing enthusiast and officer in the Grenadier Guards, he had appeared occasionally for Middlesex and the MCC before deciding to play regularly for Surrey from 1904. An aggressive if inconsistent batsman, he proved an 'energetic and capable' leader, according to the Surrey historian Louis Palgrave. What Dalmeny also failed to inherit was the magnetic charm that had once made his father the darling of Liberal politics. At times he could behave like the worst sort of grandee towards the professionals, as the Warwickshire wicketkeeper Ernest 'Tiger' Smith recounted of a match against Surrey when Dalmeny came out to bat.

"'Good morning, Tiger," he said, as we met in the middle.

"'Good morning, my Lord," said I and then, encouraged by his mood, I said, "Just right for cricket," only to be stopped short with the words: "Twice a day, good morning and good night – that's enough for me!"'

Dalmeny could hardly have made a better start as Surrey captain, thanks to the batting of his young opener. Exacting a sweet revenge for his rejection of two years earlier, Hobbs hammered the Essex attack for 155 in the second innings at the Oval. With his daring pulls and elegant drives, he hit the runs in just three hours against a strong attack that included Bill Reeves and Claude Buckenham, who was reckoned to be one of the fastest bowlers of the Edwardian age. Made almost without error, his score included nineteen 4s, and a three 5s – until the law was changed in 1910, a clean hit over the boundary just counted as 5 and a 6 could only be made by hitting the ball right out of the ground. Essex then collapsed in the face of a difficult target, and Hobbs rounded off a superlative championship debut by holding the catch in the deep which brought Surrey victory. The Oval crowd cheered him all the way to the pavilion, where Lord Dalmeny, caught up in the excitement of the moment, awarded Hobbs his county cap. No Surrey professional had ever been given official recognition more quickly. The press also perceived that a significant new talent had been discovered, with *The Times*'s report full of praise: 'Hobbs had the satisfaction of making his first hundred for his county and, having accomplished this feat, he went on to add 50 more by powerful hitting. It was a masterful innings, including a variety of strokes and marred by only one chance, at 80. There should be a great future before Hobbs in the cricket world.' The weekly magazine *Cricket* was just as effusive, commenting favourably on his character as well as his batting: 'Hobbs, the new Surrey player, was quite the master of the situation . . . and there is really no reason why he should not become a great cricketer in a year or two. He can hit and he has a strong defence. He can keep his head and does not seem to be a man who will be ruined by the flattery which is the undoing of many young players.' Hobbs's century against Essex was even celebrated in verse by Albert Craig, the eccentric habitué of the Oval known to local cricket followers as 'The Surrey Poet'. A former post office clerk from Yorkshire, Craig had moved to London after he discovered there was a public appetite for copies of his poetic cricket commentaries. His verses, which mixed humour and invective in their colourful descriptions of matches, were printed on broadsheets and sold to the crowd for tuppence as he wandered round the ground. His poetry's topicality compensated for its dire lack of lyric quality or decent rhyme, as was shown by the doggerel he wrote in tribute to Hobbs's first century.

> Joy reigned in the Pavilion
> And gladness 'mongst his clan
> While thousands breathed good wishes round the ring;
> Admirers dubbed the youngster
> As Surrey's coming man;
> In Jack Hobbs's play they saw the genuine thing.

Hobbs's fine form continued in the following weeks, no matter how high the standard of the opposition. Against the might of the Australian visitors, whose side included the slinging fast bowler Albert 'Tibby' Cotter, Hobbs scored 94 before he was run out by a magnificent throw from square leg boundary by Clem Hill. Usually so phlegmatic, Hobbs was infuriated by this dismissal, partly because he was certain that he was well in, partly because he lost the chance of a substantial bonus, for it was the tradition to hold a collection for a batsman who reached a century. The sum raised could be as high as fifty pounds in a major match, a lot of money to Hobbs who, despite his elevation to the first team, was still on less than four pounds per week. But he found some comfort in another round of plaudits from the papers, such as this report in *Cricket* magazine: 'Making his first appearance against an Australian team, Hobbs played a wonderfully good innings. Unaccustomed to Australian methods, he at times was not seen quite at his best, but his innings, taken as a whole, left very little to be desired. He played with the coolness and resource of an experienced hand, and left no doubt in the minds of spectators and players alike that with ordinary good fortune he has a great career ahead of him.' Soon after his Australian triumph, he scored another century against Essex, this one in the return game at Leyton, further reminding the club what they had missed. As the *Cambridge Daily News* put it: 'The more Hobbs flourishes, the keener becomes the regret that he is lost to Cambridgeshire. The regret of Essex must be equally keen, for Hobbs at one time offered them his services, but they failed to discover his talent, and so lost a fine cricketer.'

One of the benefits for Hobbs at the beginning of his first-class career at the Oval was the quality of the pitches, which the groundsman of the time, Sam Apted, ensured were ideal for batting. Like his famous successor 'Bosser' Martin, Apted regarded a spicy wicket as an affront to his profession. Hobbs wrote of his perfectionism, 'Old Sam, we used to say, knew every blade of grass on the ground; we really believed he would miss one if it were plucked. He used to keep us professionals well away from the middle during practice time and used to shout at us in anything but moderate terms.'

Aided by the benign Oval turf, Hobbs carried his sparkling form into midsummer, scoring 58 in a second match against the Australians and a match-winning 75 not out against Middlesex in a heroic run-chase against the clock. But then his touch completely deserted him. The

brilliant feast of May turned into the famine of August. The flashing
strokes disappeared. Even moderate bowlers made him struggle. He
failed in innings and after innings. The transformation from dashing
self-confidence into hesitant introspection was remarkable. 'There were
times when I felt I could never get another run,' he confessed. In a
telling symbol of his downturn, when he returned to his native
Cambridge to play for Surrey against the University, he was caught
behind for a duck.

The reason for this sudden deterioration was simple: Hobbs was
feeling the physical strain of competitive cricket. Until the summer of
1905, he had never participated in any three-day matches; now he was
often playing them twice a week. Always a wiry but slight figure, his
physique not helped by his poor upbringing, Hobbs did not yet have
the stamina for the gruelling nature of the county championship. 'I
really needed a rest, and although I fancied I was sick of the sight of
cricket, it was just a matter of staleness and anxiety,' he recalled. Perhaps
the most surprising aspect of Hobbs's slump was the inadequacy of his
fielding. Positioned in the deep, he proved slow in the chase and weak
in his returns to the keeper, faults that would have seemed unthinkable
to those who saw Hobbs in his prime at cover-point, where he was
noted for his speed and powerful arm. Douglas Jardine, writing in 1949,
described him as 'one of the greatest if not the classic cover-point of
all time', while Henry Leveson Gower, another of his Surrey captains,
said that Hobbs 'set a standard of excellence that has not been surpassed
if it has been equalled. His fielding was in line with his personality,
without flourish but with positive certainty.' Yet in 1905 he displayed
none of this sharpness. At times his efforts could be so lumbering that
he attracted jeers from spectators at away games, a new experience that
he found deeply wounding and which only locked him more tightly
into the downward cycle of frustration. 'The crowd used to worry me.
It was a form of bullying me because I was young. I was very sensitive
and their remarks unsettled me and made me nervous,' he wrote. In
addition to fatigue and nerves, the ineffectiveness of Hobbs's fielding
was exacerbated by a shoulder injury. 'I had this bad arm fielding in
the outfield. I had thrown my arm out and it was agony to throw with
it,' he later revealed. But the cricket press made little allowance for such
factors. 'He is a cricketer of whom a great deal may be expected, but
he should endeavour to brighten up his fielding. Though a safe catch,

he is not at present very quick on his feet,' said *Wisden*. That was also the view of Andy Kempton, who was involved in Surrey cricket for almost fifty years and became one of Hobbs's closest friends, going into business with him after the First World War. 'He was a bashful lad, who was not too sure of himself and about the worst fieldsman I ever saw,' said Kempton in 1930.

As to his batting, *Wisden* was more generous in its verdict of his first summer, describing him as 'the best professional batsman Surrey have brought forward in recent seasons. Easy and finished in style, he is particularly strong on the on-side, scoring in front of short leg with great skill and certainty.' His play in the first weeks of 1905, said the almanac, was 'extraordinary', in contrast to his 'falling off' towards the end of the season, which *Wisden* ascribed not just to tiredness but also to Hobbs's increasing 'tendency to play too much with his legs'. Overall in 1905, Hobbs scored 1,004 runs for Surrey in the county championship at an average of 24.48, a sound if hardly electrifying start. In all first-class cricket he made 1,317 runs at 25.42, as well as taking six wickets with his fast-medium bowling. In another balanced assessment, *The Times* said: 'Although doing good work, he has not quite fulfilled expectations but there is no doubt that the Surrey season proved rather arduous for him. Anyhow, he showed that he was possessed of much ability and he should be of great service to the side for the future.'

As well as struggling with his form at times, Hobbs also came up against the nastier side of the dressing-room culture. Friction within teams has always been inevitable in first-class cricket, given the competitive nature of the sport and the amount of time players have to spend in each other's company. Success can lead to envy, failure to bitterness. Don Bradman, for instance, was intensely disliked by some of his Australian Test colleagues in the 1930s, and the level of Kevin Pietersen's popularity with his Nottinghamshire teammates was illustrated when his bag was hurled from the dressing-room balcony. For nearly all of Hobbs's career, however, his good humour, generosity of spirit and lack of self-importance enabled him to evade any such hostility. As his fellow England batsman Frank Woolley once said, 'A quieter, more modest chap than Jack Hobbs can seldom have played a big part in the cricket of the world. If he had been a conceited fellow, well, he would have had some justification! But his long-sustained success never spoiled Jack. He soon established himself as popular with his brother professionals and he remained so to his retirement.' Yet in his first season, someone within the club sought to undermine Hobbs by spreading malicious gossip about him. The first Hobbs knew of it was when he was given a rest for one of Surrey's non-championship matches. To his anguish, he found himself the victim of a scandalous rumour: that he had been dropped because he had got drunk and sworn at Lord Dalmeny. The story gained such credence that it even reached his family home in Cambridge but it was, of course, preposterous because in his earliest days as a professional he hardly drank at all and disliked the taste of alcohol. Fortunately for him, the only damage done was to his pride.

But, despite his sense of hurt over this slur, there was nothing priggish about Hobbs. The playfulness that was so much part of his character was on display in his first years at the Oval. Early in the 1905 season, the groundsman Sam Apted was the butt of one of his practical jokes. Batting in the nets at the Vauxhall End of the ground during a practice session, Hobbs spied a stranger wandering near the square. Mindful of Apted's ferocious, almost neurotic guardianship of his beloved turf, he called out, 'Hey, Sam, look at that chap over there.' Almost crimson with fury, Apted began to stride towards the offender, bawling curses at him. 'Be careful, Sam, it's Mr Raphael,' said Hobbs, invoking the name of a leading Surrey and Oxford University amateur who had captained the county side for a spell in 1904. Immediately Apted, all too aware of his position in the Surrey hierarchy, went into deferential mode. 'So sorry, sir. Didn't know it was you, sir – couldn't make you out at a distance, sir.' But as he drew closer, Apted realised he had been deceived by Hobbs. The figure was indeed a stranger and not Raphael at all, prompting the groundsman to ascend even greater heights of foulmouthed indignation. On another occasion, Hobbs's clowning almost landed him in trouble with his hero, Tom Hayward. During an away match against Sussex, when the Surrey team were staying at a hotel in Horsham, Hayward had retired to bed early, feeling unwell. But his attempts to drift off to sleep were ruined by the antics of Hobbs and some other junior professionals. 'The lads started running round the corridors making an awful row and I joined in,' recalled Bill Hitch, the young fast bowler who had been complaining earlier in the day of a sore leg. Suddenly Hayward's bedroom door opened and the veteran appeared in his nightshirt. Hobbs and the others fled but Hitch was caught. 'So that's your game. I thought you had a bad leg. I'll see your leg is better tomorrow. You'll bowl all day,' growled Hayward through his moustache. 'And I did. I could hardly walk that night,' concluded Hitch. For all his devotion to his fellow Cambridge batsman, Hobbs recognised that Hayward was 'a bit of an autocrat, the last of the Surrey professionals to be "the boss". His word was law with the other professionals and we had to be careful what we said and did. Cricket was a serious business with him.'

Hobbs had made a reasonable start to his first-class career, but he knew the real trial was to come the following season. The history of English cricket is littered with the wreckage of players who, like exploding fireworks, blaze for a moment, then fade and fall to earth. The second summer is often the hardest, once the bowlers have dissected a batsman's technique and focused on his weaknesses. Hobbs himself was only too aware of the syndrome. 'This was in reality the most critical time for me. My future depended on how I shaped. Was I just to be a one-season success, or could I keep it up?' he wrote. Throughout the winter, he practised vigorously both his batting and his fielding. He had one setback as a result of a visit to Cambridge, when he was cycling down a hill, lost control, went over the handlebars and suffered a deep gash in his knee as he landed. He was laid up for a month, but, apart from a lengthy scar that he had for the rest of his life, there was no permanent physical damage and he was back in the nets in the first months of 1906.

That summer all the hard work paid off as Hobbs's cricket showed a significant improvement. His fears about failing to live up to his promise proved unfounded. He began in the same manner as in 1905, making 85 against W.G. Grace's Gentlemen of England, but he maintained his consistency right through the summer. Four centuries came off his bat, including his highest score, a masterly 162 not out against Worcestershire at the Oval on the final afternoon when chasing a victory target of 286. The spectators were so thrilled by Hobbs's innings they held a spontaneous collection that brought in £30. Tom Hayward himself joined in the whip-round, leaning over the pavilion rails with a broad smile on his face and a cap in his hand to gather cash from the members. Another hundred was made in the return game at Worcester, where his 125 contained a 5 and twenty-one 4s, while Essex were given more cause to regret ignoring Hobbs as he hit 130 at Leyton, his third century in successive matches against this opponent. 'Hobbs, who usually scores very largely by strokes on the leg-side, practised the cut and the stroke beyond cover-point with great frequency,' said *The Times* reporter. The fourth hundred came against Middlesex in the last game of the season, scored in just one hour and three quarters. Having finished ninth in the Surrey batting averages for 1905, Hobbs climbed to second place with a championship aggregate of 1,751 from forty-seven innings at 41.69. He was, said *Wisden*, 'one of the best professional bats of the year . . . Good as he is, it is not in the least degree likely that he has reached the highest point. He has gained in all-round hitting but his chief strength lies in his on-side play.' Having criticised his fielding so severely the previous year, *Wisden* was also pleased to see progress in this facet of his game. 'It should be said that Hobbs improved out of all knowledge in the field, gaining so much in pace after the ball and smartness in picking it up at third man and in the deep field he could be compared to anyone.' In all first-class matches he scored 1,913 runs, and he told the *Daily Express* that he was 'disappointed' not to have reached the 2,000 mark. But the paper felt he had little cause for regret. 'There is plenty of time for Hobbs yet. He is in perfect health and any signs of weakness which at one time made it questionable whether he could stand the wear-and-tear of a full season's cricket have entirely disappeared.'

Perhaps the most significant feature of the season was the strengthening of his partnership with Tom Hayward, who had the most golden of summers in 1906. Combining the Edwardian orthodoxy of free-flowing drives with his own sure defence and immense powers of concentration, Hayward scored with unprecedented proficiency. His total aggregate of 3,518 runs would not be beaten until after the Second World War, and his thirteen centuries equalled the record of C.B. Fry in 1901. Neville Cardus described him as 'amongst the most precisely technical and most prolific batsmen of any time in the annals of cricket'. His alliance with Hobbs at Surrey, which lasted until 1914, was the first truly dominant opening partnership in English cricket, and he exerted a profound influence on Hobbs's approach to batting. 'I found him a great source of inspiration. He made the bowlers, especially the fast ones, look so simple. It gave me great confidence,' Hobbs told the BBC in 1930. In another interview, Hobbs explained how opening with Hayward taught him how to build an innings. 'After seeing Tom at the other end, I was an experienced player. I learnt to know what balls to leave alone and what to go for. I learnt the scoring strokes to improve and those to drop. Tom was one of the classics, Tom was, and I learnt a lot.'

There was, however, a less admirable aspect to Hayward's batting which Hobbs adopted, and that was his regular use of pads as a second line of defence. Indeed, he elevated pad play into an art form, much to the outrage of traditionalists who regarded this development as against the spirit of cricket. Hayward's attitude was summed up by his reproach to the young amateur Surrey batsman Donald Knight, who had been bowled by an off-spinner. 'Oh, where were your legs, sir?'

Hobbs was to become equally famous for his exploitation of the pre-1935 lbw law, which meant that a batsman could not be given out to any delivery pitching outside the off stump. Another renowned aspect of Hobbs's batting, his love of the quick single, had nothing to do with Hayward, who, by his mid-thirties, was inclined to heaviness and was reluctant to waste his energy. Yet there was no doubt about the importance of the bond that had been forged between the two Cambridge men, which helped Surrey to rise to third place in the county championship in 1906, their best position since the glorious days the 1890s. *Cricket* magazine made this observation on the partnership: 'To Hayward's active encouragement, Hobbs owes a good deal. In one respect, he has certainly profited by his mentor. His play generally has been moulded on the best possible standard, Hayward's to wit, and indeed many of his strokes are very suggestive of that model for young batsmen.' The 1906 season, said the magazine, augured well for Hobbs. 'As he is young and careful, he should have a great future before him.'

But, as always in high-class sport, success breeds its own controversies. The belief in cricket as a moralising force, a hangover from the Victorian age, led some purists to carp that Hobbs's recruitment by Surrey was a disturbing example of the increasing commercialisation and degradation of the game. Remarkable as it may seem now, Hobbs was regarded in some circles as a kind of mercenary whose ambition ran counter to the highest ethical principles of cricket. In a lengthy, rather sour, article, *The Times* commented in May 1906: 'Hobbs comes from Cambridgeshire and was invited to qualify by residence for Surrey. There is no doubt that the real intention of those who instituted the county championship was to see which county contained the best cricketers and not which county could collect the best cricketers. It is because Yorkshire adheres resolutely to the original spirit of the idea that they are justly the most popular of all counties.* It has been noted with some alarm that in this matter first-class cricket is imitating the unenviable methods of first-class professional football. The cricket missionary, who used to go out merely to impart what he knew, nowadays goes out only too often merely to collect. Surrey have long been addicted to the practice, which has lost them almost as many good men as it has gained them.' Such an argument was as unjust as it was absurd, for the logical conclusion was that Hobbs should be denied the chance to play first-class cricket simply because of an accident of birth.

Hobbs's success in 1906 only led to more criticism at the end of the season. *The Times* implied he had been given more chances than other young professionals because the Surrey committee wanted a return on its investment. 'Had the Surrey authorities treated other professionals on the principle on which they treated Hobbs, they might have been as successful with them as they have been with Hobbs. They specially procured Hobbs from a second-class county to play for them, and obviously an arrangement of that kind had to be justified.' This was equally specious. The reason Hobbs kept his place was because of his run-scoring rather than any notion of favouritism.

At the close of the 1906 season there was a dramatic change in Hobbs's personal life, one that must have come as a surprise to most of his Surrey teammates. For almost six years, he had been discreetly courting a young woman from Cambridge, Miss Ada Ellen Gates, the daughter of a local cobbler. It was typical of Jack's sober lifestyle that they had first met at St Matthew's Church after an evening service. Until then Jack had shown little outward interest in the opposite sex, largely because of his shyness and obsession with cricket. 'I was never very happy with girls, and they did not play any part in my early life. Games were everything,' he wrote of his boyhood. Indeed, after their first couple of encounters, Ada Gates found Jack so shy that she almost lost interest in him. Nor was the course of romance helped by passion for cricket. 'He was eighteen. I was seventeen. So crazy on cricket he was, I got so annoyed. "No good thinking about a girl when I've got to play cricket," he'd say,' she later recalled of their first steps into a relationship. But Jack, mixing chivalry with self-interest, felt that his

---

* Until the 1990s, only those born within the boundaries of Yorkshire were entitled to play for the club.

devotion to the game would help cement their love. Once they were courting, he wrote, 'I became even more keen to realise my ambition. I wanted to win her admiration, and it appeared to me that the more successful I was, the more she would look up to me.' The strategy worked. Whatever their first misunderstandings, they fell deeply in love.

Once Jack had become an established county player, he felt secure enough to propose. Ada accepted and, on 26 September 1906, the wedding was held at St Matthew's, Cambridge. In keeping with Jack's personality, it was a quiet affair. The best man was George Harding, his closest Cambridge friend stretching back to their days together as choir-boys, and the only two Surrey players invited were Bill Hitch, with whom Hobbs was then lodging, and Tom Rushby, another fast bowler. There was some surprise in Cambridge that Hobbs did not ask Tom Hayward but the decision reflected his continuing sense of diffidence towards his mentor, as he explained, 'The fact was that, although I had been associated with him for two cricket seasons, I had not lost that feeling of awe of him. I did not think that the wedding would be grand enough for him or that I should be able to accommodate him in the style that his position warranted.' But, given his burgeoning fame, Hobbs's wedding did not pass unnoticed in the cricket world. Telegrams from all over the country arrived at the church; the event was mentioned in the national press; and gifts were sent from the absent Surrey players, including a clock from Lord Dalmeny.

Afterwards, Jack and Ada went for a fortnight's honeymoon in the Sussex coastal resort of Hastings. 'We were ideally happy,' he recalled. It was the start of a long, successful marriage and they were to remain devoted to each other for the rest of their lives. 'If there is truth in the saying that a man never marries his first love, then we must be the exceptions,' Ada once said. The only real moments of sadness came whenever they were temporarily separated, mainly because of Jack's career. 'It was miserable sometimes when we were parted. But you try your best,' said Ada towards the end of her life.

Some cricketers revel in the amorous opportunities provided by their itinerant existences, especially on overseas trips. Denis Compton, the glamorous England star of the 1940s, admitted that 'the temptations were there' on tour. 'I was always one of the boys,' he said of his extra-marital liasons. Wally Hammond, with his keen eye for female talent, is alleged to have caught syphilis during the West Indies tour of 1925/6. But Jack, with his innate reserve, his Christian ethics and his abiding love for Ada, could never have been remotely like that. In many respects, he was an ideal husband: reliable, kind, warm and loyal, preferring to be at home rather than out for a drink with his mates. 'I am a rare home bird,' he once said, his domestic contentment enhanced by the arrival of four children, starting with Jack Junior in 1907, followed by Leonard in 1909, and Vera and Ivor in the two years before the First World War.

Warm-hearted, slightly plump, Ada had a strong maternal instinct which she regarded as more important than sensual femininity. Of the argument that wives should use 'paint and powder' to ensure their husbands continued to find them attractive, Mrs Hobbs was dismissive. 'Paint is more likely to drive away my husband than retain him and I should think that applies to most married men. My recipe for a contented – and therefore happy – husband is a comfortable home in which the husband can indulge those little foibles that most men possess and where the children are well looked after by the wife,' she said in an interview in 1925. Her nurturing qualities were described by the Reuters correspondent Gilbert Mant, who came to know her when she accompanied Jack to Australia for the 1932/3 Bodyline tour: 'She was a rather large and formidable-looking woman, but an absolute dear on closer acquaintance. Mrs Hobbs mothered all of us and was very popular.'

Through her husband, Ada developed a deep interest in cricket and, once their four children had grown up, regularly watched him in action. But she did occasionally voice regrets about his occupation. 'To be the wife of a popular man like Jack Hobbs is not easy. One must sacrifice many things that the average woman holds dear. My husband's career as a cricketer comes before everything else to me and I am proud to think that in a small measure I have helped him,' she told a *Daily Express* reporter in 1929. But, she continued, 'one thing I do not like about Jack's cricket is that we can never have a real summer holiday. When I see my friends going off to the seaside in August, how I envy them. During the whole of our married life we have had only one summer holiday . . . Nevertheless there are many compensations in being the wife of a great cricketer. You live in a kind of reflected glory which to most women is extremely pleasing.'

The glory days still lay ahead. In 1906, though he had established himself as a county cricketer, there was nothing affluent about Jack and his new bride. His pay as a capped Surrey player, including bonuses and the winter retainer, was around £275 a year, far beyond the dreams of his father, but hardly lavish for the mid-Edwardian era, especially because professional cricketers had to meet their own expenses like hotel bills, meals and travel. According to the extensive studies by Arthur Bowley, England's pioneering social statistician, the upper-middle class in this period could be classified as those with an annual income ranging between £1,000 and £5,000 a year, while the middle class were those living on anything between £300 and £1,000. Beneath these two divisions, Bowley placed the lower-middle class for those with incomes from £120 to £300, a level of earnings which he maintained left this group 'uncomfortably off'. This was the category into which most professional cricketers fell, though a few stars earned over £400 a year and also enjoyed lucrative benefits; in 1904 George Hirst, the Yorkshire all-rounder, made £3,703 in his benefit year, an unprecedented sum. Further down the scale were the artisans and clerks, many of them struggling on less than £100 a year, then the manual working class, and at the bottom those living in destitution or the workhouse. Like 90 per cent of the Edwardian population, Hobbs could not contemplate owning his own property, so in their first years of marriage, he and Ada had to live in modest rented accommodation and move frequently within south London. Their first marital home was 'a little flat in Denmark Hill', to use Jack's description, followed by brief spells in Brixton, Battersea and Mitcham before they were sufficiently wealthy to buy their own house in Clapham shortly before the First World War.

The wealth came largely through Hobbs's ascent into the ranks of international sporting stardom. That journey would begin at the end of the 1907 season.

4

'That Magical Message'

Lord's may have been the home of cricket but for most of Hobbs's early career he loathed the place. It brought out his keen sense of social inferiority through its intimidating atmosphere and its condescension towards professionals. To him, its very structure and facilities reeked of exclusivity, with the paid players treated almost as if they were trespassers in a gentlemen's private club. 'It used to seem to me uncomfortable as regards watching the game and the lunch served to us was very poor. I always felt at Lord's that a professional was looked down upon,' he wrote.

In its combination of loftiness and disdain, Lord's was emblematic of the great divide in English cricket between amateurs and professionals, then at its peak in Edwardian Britain. The period before the First World War may have become nostalgically known as 'The Golden Age' for its stylish, front-footed batsmanship epitomised by majestic amateurs like Archie MacLaren and Stanley Jackson, but this was also a time when institutionalised snobbery was woven into the fabric of the game, mirroring the concerns of wider society with exquisitely calibrated gradations of rank. Essentially, professionals were second-class citizens, their lower status reinforced by a wide range of practices. They had to use separate, usually inferior, dressing rooms, hotels, train carriages, meals and even entrances to the field of play. Amateurs had to be addressed as 'Sir' or 'Mister', while the professionals went by their surnames only. Scorecards and press reports usually maintained the rigid distinction by putting initials before the amateurs' names. Amateurs also tended to dress differently, often wearing multicoloured caps, blazers or ties. Only amateurs were allowed to captain Test or county sides, based on the theory that professionals would have neither the authority nor the inclination to give orders to their colleagues.

Joe Darling, the great Australian captain of the 'Golden Age', thought the culture of subservience was insulting. 'Some English captains speak to their professionals like dogs. No Australian would stand for it,' he said. A few outspoken English cricketers agreed. A.E. Knight, the Leicestershire professional who played three Tests against Australia during the 1903/04 tour, railed in 1906 against 'these miserable and hateful labels and distinctions which sicken most honest people by their unfairness'. Hobbs himself, usually so mild in his opinions, hated some of the elements of the system, especially the degrading use of separate gates onto the field for amateurs and professionals, which he described as 'ludicrous'. The cricket public, he wrote, 'resents the distinction still more than we do'.

The division may have been built on the determination to maintain social rank, reflecting the belief that no gentlemen should lower himself by earning his living from sport, but supporters of amateur status also argued that cricket was made more attractive by the presence of non-professionals, who could supposedly play with greater freedom because they were unburdened by any financial pressures or fear of failure. Yet there was little real evidence to support this claim, as was shown by Hobbs's own case. In the years before the First World War he played in a richly uninhibited fashion, always trying to go on the attack. Comparing his pre-1914 approach to that of the 1920s, Hobbs once said, 'I didn't know so much about defence and things, but I had more strokes and wasn't afraid to produce them, you see, when the occasion arose. I could hit all round the wicket and I suppose I hadn't the same fear of getting out.' Indeed, so polished and adventurous was Hobbs's pre-war approach that Plum Warner, the Middlesex captain, described him as 'a professional who batted like an amateur'. But there were many other professional batsmen of the era who shared Hobbs's aggressive outlook if not his prolificacy, such as Johnny Tyldesley of Lancashire, David Denton of Yorkshire and the elegant Frank Woolley of Kent. 'Lots of times I was out through forcing the game,' said Woolley, hardly the stereotype of dour professional caution.

Conversely, several leading amateurs exhibited little of the flamboyance that was allegedly the hallmark of their class. Johnny Douglas, the tough Essex all-rounder and Olympic boxer, regularly lived up to his nickname 'Johnny Won't Hit Today' with his wearisome batting, and C.B. Fry's success owed more to solidity than flair. 'A great factor in his large scores is his avoidance of risks, and herein he shows more self-restraint that any other batsman of modern times,' wrote the *Yorkshire Post* of Fry. But there was an even greater flaw in the contention that amateurs could be more dashing because of their financial independence. The reality was that many of them did in fact earn their living from cricket, but they were paid in a clandestine or indirect manner so they could maintain their privileges and social station. Some were given excessive expenses, others were provided with sinecures at their clubs. In the 1890s at the Oval, for instance, the batsman Walter Read was given the nominal post of Assistant Secretary, on an annual salary of £175 a year plus four guineas a match and expenses, to maintain the illusion of his amateur status. Similarly, in the 1900s Archie MacLaren earned twice as much as any professional at Lancashire, through his appointment to the titular posts of Assistant Secretary and Coach, a necessity for a self-regarding cricketer whose income never matched his extravagance. But by far the greatest exponent of 'shamateurism', as it was known, was W.G. Grace, who is estimated to have made over £120,000 from the game through testimonials and so-called expenses. For the 1891/2 tour of Australia alone, Grace was paid £3,000 and it was a rumour of his vast stipend of £50 per match that prompted several English players, including Tom Hayward, to threaten to go on strike in advance of the Oval test of 1896.

With hindsight, what is truly pitiful about all this deceit and class fixation is that there was nothing remotely shameful about cricket as a profession. Any occupation that attracted men of the moral calibre of Wilfred Rhodes and Herbert Strudwick could hardly be regarded as disreputable. Hobbs, in his gentle rectitude, had far more decency than the overbearing MacLaren, who might have been upright in his batting stance but certainly was not in his personal life, leaving a trail of debts and aggravation behind him. 'A spendthrift who got everything he could out of his tour,' was how the famous Australian scorer Bill Ferguson described MacLaren on an MCC trip, while the playwright Ben Travers found him 'pretty obnoxious'. Even some contemporary members of Edwardian high society felt the divide in cricket was ridiculous, especially the resort to 'shamateurism'. Writing in *Country Life* in 1903, R.H. Lyttelton argued that 'the calling of a professional is in every way an honourable and good one. What puzzles many of us is that, this being the case, so many should adopt the profession but deny the name.'

Yet the elitism of amateur status ran deep through English cricket in the Edwardian age and was to linger, anaemic, outdated but still defiant, until well after the Second World War before it finally expired in 1962. That was the year of the very last Gentleman versus Players match, the fixture that for more than 150 years had solemnised the split between the two groups of cricketers. When Hobbs first played for Surrey in the mid-1900s, the Gents v Players games were major events in the annual cricket calendar. There were usually three every summer, one at Lord's, another at the Oval, and the last at the end of season festival in Scarborough or Folkestone. With far fewer internationals played then, since only Australia and South Africa had Test status, the Gents v Players match at Lord's had the prestige of a major contest, a showcase for the nation's finest cricketers and the domestic game's 'high water mark', to use Hobbs's phrase. Though the professionals tended to prevail because of their greater all-round resources, the amateurs could put up a good fight; in 1906 the Gents won by 45 runs at Lord's and the other two matches were drawn.

It was in this arena that Jack Hobbs had his first taste of representative cricket, when he was chosen to appear for the Players at both Lord's and the Oval in July 1907. Hobbs owed his selection to a brilliant streak of form when, after a difficult start to the season, he began to bat with even greater assurance and more powerful off-side stroke-play than he had shown in the previous two years. Against Warwickshire in May, on a sticky wicket at Edgbaston that had the consistency of treacle, Hobbs held on for 60 not out, the first time he had carried his bat through an innings. Then in June, he and Tom Hayward had an astonishing burst of consistency, as they put on four century opening partnerships in the space of single week, an unprecedented feat that was never to be repeated in county cricket. This glut was followed by 150 in the home fixture against Warwickshire at the Oval, an innings described by *Wisden* as 'a splendid display, making no mistake until forcing the game after completing his hundred'. The performance led to his call-up by the MCC.

But Hobbs was quickly reminded of the toughness of competitive cricket. At Lord's he was twice dismissed for single-figure scores by the tearaway fast bowler Walter Brearley, who had got Hobbs out with a short ball on his debut for Surrey two years earlier. It was the same story in the first innings for the Players at Lord's. Having made just 2, Hobbs

attempted a full-blooded pull against Brearley, only to see the ball keep
low and crash into his stumps. In the second innings, after making 9,
Hobbs fell victim to the opposite problem: a delivery from Brearley
bounced more than he expected and he edged it to the keeper. Nor
did he do any better at the Oval, falling for 5 and 19. The bowler who
dismissed him in the first innings was Johnny Douglas, a master of
full-length, fast-medium swing. It was the start of a long duel between
them that lasted into the mid-1920s, with Douglas taking Hobbs's
wicket twenty-five times, a record unmatched by any other bowler. The
next was Colin Blythe, the Kent slow left-arm spinner, whose well-
flighted deliveries accounted for Hobbs seventeen times. Douglas,
though a heroic battler, lacked a yard in pace and could never be
described as one of the all-time great bowlers of English cricket; in
twenty-three Tests he took only forty-five wickets at an average of 33.
But in an article in the *Cricketer* in 1925 Hobbs explained why he found
Douglas 'the most difficult bowler to play'. The potency of his method,
wrote Hobbs, lay in the 'swing either way which only reveals itself at
the last moment', for there was 'nothing in the action' to indicate the
direction of the movement. No bowler, he continued, 'has given me
such tremors as Mr Douglas, whose bowling is fastish and so well-
pitched up that you are afraid to make a stroke as the ball either ducks
in or swings away. For a considerable time with the new ball you simply
dare not attempt to hit Mr Douglas through the covers. Caught in the
slips is the usual verdict.'

His failures for the Players reinforced criticism in some quarters that
Hobbs was too cavalier, too lacking in discretion. Extraordinary as it
may seem with hindsight, there were a few who believed that Hobbs
should rein in his strokes if he was to realise his potential. MacLaren,
in particular, was unimpressed. Despite such mutterings, Hobbs's generally good form for Surrey continued through the summer, as he hit
three further centuries, including 166 against Worcestershire at the Oval
in a seven-wicket win. Towards the end of the season, he also played
during the Scarborough Festival Week against the touring South
Africans, who had just completed their first Test series against England.
The South African attack was dominated by the spin quartet of Reggie
Schwarz, Gordon White, Ernie Vogler and Aubrey Faulkner, all of them
superbly exploiting the new art of googly bowling. In a grey summer
of damp wickets, they frequently proved unplayable, especially against

county sides. Though South Africa did not win any of the three Tests, the country was now established as a major force in the game. 'This new kind of bowling is a very great invention and it is possible it may completely alter cricket,' wrote Reginald 'Tip' Foster, the England captain of 1907. Even some great batsmen struggled against the South African googly merchants, but this was not true of Hobbs, whose quick footwork and excellent judgement made him a high-class player of spin. During this Scarborough match, he hit a fluent 78, the precursor of a host of authoritative innings against South Africa in the coming years that would crush the googly terror. In 1907 he passed 2,000 runs for the first time, one of only three batsmen to do so that summer, and for Surrey he was only just behind Hayward in both aggregate and average. 'No one among young professional batsmen looks to have such a bright future before him,' said *Wisden*. 'He has now far more strokes that when he came out for Surrey in 1905, having improved out of all knowledge on the off-side, while retaining all his power of scoring in front of leg.'

Long before the season was over, Hobbs was given the ultimate proof of his growing stature. On 7 August 1907 he received a letter from Francis Lacey, the long-serving Secretary of MCC: 'The committee of the MCC are sending an England team to Australia in September. I have been instructed to invite you to accompany the team. The terms of engagement are embodied in the agreement. If you accept the invitation, please sign and return the agreement.' The baldness of the official prose could not disguise the meaning of the words: Hobbs was on the verge of becoming an England cricketer. He was thrilled at what he called 'that magical message'. He later claimed that until the summer of 1907, the height of his ambition had been to secure a permanent place in the Surrey team. But then his exceptional batting with Hayward, combined with his call-up for the Players, sparked the idea that he might make it to the highest level. 'I will not deny that I had some sort of hope that I might be selected. There were hints in the press that I stood a chance of getting into the team for "down under",' he wrote. Hobbs recognised that his chances were boosted by the refusal of four professionals – Tom Hayward, Johnny Tyldesley, George Hirst and the Warwickshire wicketkeeper Dick Lilley – to go on the tour because they would not accept the MCC's terms, though the deal was hardly a mean one for the six-month trip. The players were offered a basic stipend of £300 and a first-class passage to Australia, plus 30 shillings per week for expenses during the sea voyage, going up to 40 shillings a week in Australia. In addition, all laundry bills and tips were to be met by the MCC.

Yet, for all his exhilaration at the letter, Hobbs hesitated over whether to sign the agreement. The difficulty was not money, for the offer represented far more than he had ever made in any season. No, the problem lay at home. Married for less than a year, Hobbs had become a father in July when his first son, Jack Douglas was born. Besides his fondness for his domestic life, he was concerned about leaving Ada and their young child alone for so long. These anxieties were not mere posturing. He was genuinely reluctant to accept, as was later recalled by Major Philip Trevor, the former army officer who had been appointed the manager of the tour. During a long conversation at the Oval, Hobbs told Trevor that 'his wife was ill at the time and he did not feel he could leave her. I strongly urged him to accept the invitation. I felt certain it would be the making of him . . . I pressed upon him my prediction of what he was likely to become in cricket if he went to Australia. Hobbs has no side on; he never had any and I much hope he will never have any. Doubtless he thought I was overestimating the probabilities of his cricket future. But I was convinced that what he needed was – I will put this quite frankly – to get away from people who were telling him to drop his strokes, when I pressed him to accept. I felt certain that he would establish himself at the very top. I wanted to give the reins to his own individuality.' After talking it over with Ada, he signed the offer, 'recognising that to go was to obey the call of duty,' as he put it. But Hobbs did not leave his young family on its own. Shortly before the MCC's departure, he took Ada and baby Jack up to Cambridge, where they could be looked after by her relatives.

On 20 September 1907, Hobbs travelled to St Pancras station, from where the MCC party would take the train to Tilbury to commence the long sea voyage to Australia. At the north London rail terminal there was an atmosphere of jubilation generated by the large crowd, which had gathered there to see off the team. With the steam from the locomotive wafting up to the curved roof, the concourse echoed to cheers and shouts from the well-wishers. Then the players climbed into their carriages. A loud hiss sounded and the wheels started to roll. As the train moved through the capital's outskirts and into Essex, the mood of celebration continued in the professionals' long saloon compartment.

But the joyousness was not universally shared, according to the vivid account left by Andy Kempton, the Surrey member, who, like some other supporters, accompanied the team to Tilbury. 'Everyone was happy and excited. And then I spotted one figure which was huddled up at the extreme end of the carriage. It was that of Jack Hobbs, and he was looking out the window with unseeing eyes; eyes from which tears were flowing. I put my arm around his shoulder and asked in a whisper, "What is wrong?" He told me of the parting from his wife and "day old" first-born and I'm not ashamed to admit that my eyes were not dry.'

Hobbs's anguish continued almost as soon as he was at sea aboard the SS *Ophir* of the Orient Line, a 6,814-ton vessel which had a capacity of 430 passengers. The trip should have been an exciting adventure for Hobbs, who had never been outside England before and, with endearing anticipation, had come prepared to enjoy it, buying deck shoes, summer suits, flannels and evening dress, all items that had not previously featured in his modest wardrobe. But throughout the voyage he barely left his cabin, which, by a cruel stroke, was at the front of the *Ophir* where he 'got the full benefit of the ship's motion', as he put it. Hobbs had first experienced his susceptibility to the ravages of seasickness as a child while on a pleasure cruise off Lowestoft. Now the condition returned with a vengeance. Almost as soon as the ship left the English channel he was gripped by extreme nausea, his only moments of relief coming when he could step onto dry land at various ports-of-call on the route, such as Naples and Colombo. Otherwise, he just lay in misery in his bed. So prolonged was his physical torment that the MCC manager Major Philip Trevor grew worried about him. 'I candidly admit that I was anxious about his health and not about his cricket for many days. I don't suppose he ever realised how thoroughly ill he really was, for it is a bad illness when you suffer in mind as well as body.'

His sickness was at its worst during the long crossing of the Indian Ocean, but at last, more than a month after leaving England, the SS *Ophir* reached the western Australian port of Fremantle, where most of the MCC party disembarked in advance of their first game, against the State side at Perth. But Hobbs, utterly debilitated, was unfit for any form of cricket and so, with several other players, stayed on board until the ship reached Adelaide. Relieved that his ordeal was finally over, he felt his spirits rise further on going ashore. 'The Australian climate, with its cloudless skies and brilliant sunshine, was a pleasant surprise to me, and it was a splendid experience to rest and revel in the sun after the trying time that I had gone through,' he wrote.

Hobbs was still too physically weak to participate in the next game, against South Australia at Adelaide, where the temperature reached 94 degrees Fahrenheit in the shade. Yet on his recovery, Hobbs was perplexed to find that he was given little chance to prove himself in the run-up to the first Test, playing in only two of MCC's six first-class fixtures. He felt the blame for his exclusion lay with the MCC captain Arthur Jones, the Notts skipper. A batsman whose impetuous style belied his ungainly stance, Jones was also a brilliant fielder who is reputed to have pioneered the position of gully in the 1880s while a schoolboy at Bedford Modern. Yet for all his gifts, he was an indecisive leader, often agonising over decisions until three in morning, while some also suspected him of bias towards his home side of Notts. Hobbs certainly believed that his captain did not treat him fairly. 'The impression was created in my mind that A.O. Jones had not the highest opinion of my capabilities and I could not help harbouring the thought that the right course would have been to play me. If I was worth sending, I was worth trying, to see how I shaped. Here was I, a youngster with my spurs to win; surely it would have been wise policy on the part of our captain to have "blooded" me at an early stage so that I could have adapted myself as quickly as possible to Australian wickets and conditions? How in all conscience could I be expected to come off in the Tests, if denied practice in the State games?'

In fairness to Jones, Hobbs did nothing outstanding to press his claims in the two games that he played, making just 3 and 26 against Victoria and 21 against Queensland. Like many England cricketers before and since, he initially found it difficult to adapt to the conditions of Australia, so different to those in English county cricket. As the *Sportsman* magazine wrote of the 1907/8 tour, 'Under the burning sun upon adamantine and terribly fast wickets, in the strange, glaring subtropical light, Englishmen possessing great names at home have often completely failed to reproduce the form which secured their invitation to tour.' On the other hand, any batsman who successfully made the adjustment could find the Australian pitches rewarding. Rock hard, they provided even bounce with little lateral movement. 'You only had to stick your tongue out and it's four,' joked Archie MacLaren. The key to these surfaces lay in the type of soil used at the top Australian grounds. The Melbourne wicket was made of Merri Creek soil, which was dark in colour and, in the baking heat, 'looked like polished ebony', to use the phrase of Arthur Gilligan, a future MCC captain. Sydney used Bulli soil, a fine clay that would set like marble after it had been well watered during preparation. The Atherstone soil at the Adelaide Oval produced perhaps the fastest wicket of all. One indicator of the firmness of the Australian turf was the difficulty that batsmen had in making their guard, as Reginald 'Tip' Foster recalled: 'It is impossible to make a block hole. You either scratch the ground with your boot sprigs or ruffle it.' Another feature of Australian cricket that was striking to visitors was its ferocious intensity, reflected in the high quality of fielding, the tough approach to captaincy and the aggressive nature of the bowling. 'The Australian is far ahead of us in bowling,' Arthur Jones himself confessed. 'Watch an Australian bowler: he is always doing something to the ball with his fingers and never bowls a ball down unless he has some object in view.' This outlook was bred partly by the demanding antipodean environment, with its high temperatures and hard pitches. But cricket was also a means of expressing national pride and unifying the continent. Though Australian Test teams had existed since 1877, it was only in 1901 that the nation of Australia had formally come into being through the confederation of the separate colonies; the newly created entity, with its population of just four million in the 1900s, was keen to assert itself against the mother country. Cricket was the ideal vehicle for that patriotism. 'Australia takes its cricket very seriously indeed,' Hobbs once said.

The strength of Australian cricket was all too obvious as the MCC struggled on the 1907/8 tour. On the eve of the first Test at Sydney, the English side suffered a serious blow when Jones became seriously ill with pneumonia. His place as skipper was taken by the Irish-born, Essex batsman Fred Fane. But despite Jones's absence there was still no room for Hobbs. The bespectacled amateur wicketkeeper Dick Young was asked to move up the order to open with Fane, much to Hobb's frustration. Even worse, the other player called up to fill the batting vacancy left by Jones was George Gunn of Nottinghamshire, who was not even a member of the original MCC party but had travelled to Australia for health reasons. Already aggrieved at his exclusion from most of the warm-up games, Hobbs was indignant at the way he had been treated.

'Surely a man who had been brought out as a member of the team should have been given the preference?' he wrote in 1924, though he felt no personal hostility towards Gunn. 'We were real friends throughout the tour,' he stressed. As it turned out, Gunn, a fearless, unorthodox batsman, gave a superlative performance on his Test debut, top-scoring in both England's innings with 119 and 78. Yet his robust hitting could not prevent Australia scraping home by two wickets, having been set a stiff target of 275.

Fane's captaincy proved unimaginative but the biggest culprit in England's defeat was Dick Young, who not only failed in both innings as an opener but also missed several crucial chances in Australia's tense run-chase. In his failure lay Jack Hobbs's opportunity. Fane decided that he needed a proper opener rather than a makeshift one for the second Test at Melbourne. Hobbs, who had scored well in the two games after the first Test, was the obvious choice. Just a few days after his twenty-fifth birthday, he was about to make his England debut. Considering the awesome feats he was to achieve in the international arena over the next two decades, it was a remarkably late start, illustrating both the awkward circumstances of his upbringing and the limited amount of Test cricket in the Edwardian era. At that same age, Sachin Tendulkar had hit already hit nineteen Test centuries. Nevertheless, Hobbs, who harboured a strong sense of ambition beneath his benign exterior, was thrilled at his selection. In his retirement, he described the emotions he felt on the eve of England matches. 'I really enjoyed the Tests. You approached them a little differently. You get that little flutter with the heart in a Test match. Some people called it nervousness. You are more keyed up and you want to do well. It is a bigger occasion. You know the eyes of the world are upon you.'

On New Year's Day 1908, Hobbs arrived at the Melbourne Cricket Ground with the rest of the England XI. Before the start, he was practising in front of the pavilion with a few colleagues when the Australian Clem Hill, one of the legendary names of the Golden Age, came up to him.

'So you're playing this time, Jack.'

'Yes, I am going to have a shot.'

'Hearty congratulations, then, and good luck.'

Such generosity of spirit has not always prevailed in Ashes contests. Hobbs's debut turned out to be one of the most thrilling matches in the history of cricket. Australia won the toss and batted first, making a modest 266 in the face of some fine medium-paced spin bowling by Hobbs's Surrey colleague Jack Crawford, who took 5 for 79. On the second morning, after the Australian tail had collapsed, Hobbs went in to open with Fred Fane against the new ball attack of Jack Saunders, who bowled left arm medium with a dubious action, and the paceman Albert 'Tibby' Cotter. In a BBC interview on his eightieth birthday, Hobbs described Cotter at the quickest Test bowler he ever faced: 'He was very fast indeed, he really was. He came bounding with energy and he slammed that ball down and it went by you just like a flash of lightning sometimes.' Yet Hobbs, adopting a more defensive approach than usual, proved resolute against this challenge. 'I was not exactly nervous, but I had the set idea of doing my very best and decided to take no risk, but to make them get me out.' He lost Fane when the score was 27 but continued to bat steadfastly until he had taken England's total to 160 for 2, when he was bowled by a snorting delivery from Cotter for 83. Altogether he batted for 182 minutes, hit eight 4s and gave just one sharp chance to square leg. It was an inspiring start to his Test career that put England in a strong position. 'Hobbs from start to finish played almost faultless cricket. He scored slowly, it is true, but his caution was amply justified for the Australian bowling never once got loose,' wrote the MCC manager Philip Trevor in his review of the tour. 'His was a distinctly fine performance for a young batsman in his first Test match. He was always really the master of the situation but he showed his good sense by not presuming on the fact. His forward strokes on the off-side were particularly good and his defensive back play was worthy of his master, Tom Hayward.'

Thanks to Hobbs's 83 and an elegant century from the Kent batsman Kenneth Hutchings, England gained a substantial lead, but the Australians responded well in their second innings. Most of their top order passed 50, including the sublime Victor Trumper, widely regarded as the greatest batsman of his times. In the field, Hobbs had the chance to view Trumper, then at the height of his powers, in typically scintillating action. 'He was a marvel. He didn't wait for the bad ball to come along. He took a delight in hitting the good ball for 4 too. I think Vic Trumper was a classic. He made all the strokes with perfect rhythm, and it was a treat to watch him,' said Hobbs in a radio broadcast to Australia in 1941. There were also elements of Trumper's character that were mirrored by Hobbs: his modesty, warmth and innate dignity. 'Trumper was a big personality as well as a cricketing genius. Everybody felt his charm,' said Hobbs.

Australia, all out for 397, set England a demanding target of 282 to win. This was a timeless Test, as were all such matches in Australia until the Second World War, and England's quest for victory began on the fifth morning. Hobbs and Fane gave England a good start, reaching 54 before Hobbs fell lbw to an off-break from Monty Noble. Though the score mounted slowly, England continued to lose wickets all day and the following morning until the last pair, Sydney Barnes and Arthur fielder, came together with 39 runs still needed. They were both fine bowlers but only moderate batsmen and the task seemed impossible. Yet they refused to crack, inching forward to the target run by run. Every single heightened up the nervous excitement among the spectators. 'There were men round the ground so breathless that they could not speak,' recorded the *Sydney Morning Herald*. The tension extended to the England players in their dressing room. In such circumstances, cricketers have always tended to be superstitious, refusing to move for fear of breaking the spell. 'There we stood, crowding, half-dressed at the windows with socks and shoes in our hands, not daring to stir a muscle lest the two batsmen out in the field were put off their game,' said Hobbs. Ernie Hayes, the Surrey batsman who was also a member of the MCC party, stood beside Hobbs as victory came agonisingly within England's grasp. 'Jack and I were standing on a form in the dressing room, looking out of the window. It was too exciting to be outside and I would not let Jack move in case he broke the luck,' recalled Hayes. A few more judicious strokes brought England level. With just one single needed, Barnes and Fielder met in the middle, where they agreed to run for anything, no matter where it was hit. Barnes then failed to make full contact with the next delivery and just tapped it a few yards on the off-side. It should have been a simple run-out. But the Australian cover Jerry Hazlitt was young and inexperienced. Overwhelmed by the pressure of the occasion, he threw wildly at the stumps and missed by yards, the ball flying past the keeper to the boundary. England had won by just one wicket. 'Jack and I fell off the form, shrieking for joy,' recalled Hayes.

In terms of wickets, the triumph was England's narrowest win in Ashes history. But it turned out to be the team's only Test victory on the tour. England were badly beaten in the third Test at Adelaide where Hobbs was hit in the stomach by the first ball he received from Saunders at the start of the second innings and had to retire hurt with severe bruising. He only returned at the fall of the sixth wicket, but despite some breezy hitting, could do nothing to prevent a defeat by 245 runs. It was the same story at Melbourne in the fourth Test, England losing by 308 runs. The one highlight was Hobbs's magnificent 57, made on a wicket that was badly affected by rain. His score represented more than half of England's first innings total of 105, for the other batsmen were completely unable to cope with the vicious movement achieved by Saunders and Noble. But Hobbs gave an early display of his unique ability to bat on sticky wickets, using his uncanny judgement of length, his swift footwork and his skill at playing the ball as late as possible. An Australian 'sticky', he found, was an even tougher challenge than an English one because of the hardness of the turf. 'A beast', he called it, where 'the ball kicks, flies, turns wickedly and does all that it shouldn't do.' In these exacting circumstances, Hobbs decided the most effective strategy was to go after the bowling, and in seventy minutes he hit no fewer than ten boundaries. The MCC manager Major Philip Trevor was euphoric. It was 'a quite remarkable innings', wrote the Major, in an interesting contemporary analysis of Hobbs's early style. 'He gave those who watched him bat a valuable lesson on the subject of how and when to run risks. His hitting was never wild or indiscriminate and the secret of his success – if indeed secret be the word to apply to it – lay in his recognition of the danger of playing forward on such a wicket. Much less did he feel for the ball. Others made both these mistakes and paid a quick penalty by making one or other of them. The short-pitched ball Hobbs punished not only with power but with certainty and he was not content merely to strike hard with the middle of the bat. He placed it at intervals skilfully between the fieldsmen on both sides of the wicket and he used his feet cleverly in getting to the ball which would have been awkward to play firm-footed.'

Despite his success in his initial Tests, Hobbs often felt miserable during the tour. He missed his wife dreadfully, and in the era before intercontinental phones, he could only communicate with her by letter. In his homesickness, he became close friends with Joe Hardstaff, the Nottinghamshire batsman who was exactly the same age as Hobbs and also had a wife and a young child back in England. 'Naturally, we chummed up and sympathised with one another, although the six months that were to pass before we saw England again seemed like a lifetime.' Away from the cricket, Hobbs has some memorable experiences on the tour to distract him from his melancholy, such as attending a concert given by the opera singer Dame Nellie Melba and visiting the gold mines of Bendigo, where he had to don a set of dungarees and crawl through a long tunnel network lit only by the flicker of his candle. He struggled, however, with some of the transport arrangements around Australia. The long railway journeys between cities often left him exhausted, especially when the catering facilities, always a deep concern of Hobbs's, were inadequate. On trips where there was no dining car, 'you clambered out of the long distance train at wayside stations and dined or breakfasted in a big hurry. They gave you hot soup or hot porridge and, depend upon it, almost before it was cool enough for your throat the five minutes' bell would ring you a warning to get back into the train.' Far more troubling was a trip to Tasmania, which brought on another virulent burst of nausea as soon as the ship left the harbour. But, once he had reached the island, he was captivated by his surroundings. 'The country is beautiful, far greener than Australia, with gorgeous mountain scenery,' he recalled.

By the last week of February 1908, the adventure was almost over, as the final Test took place at Sydney, always Hobbs's favourite venue in Australia with its picturesque stands, excellent playing area, famous hill and huge scoreboard, which provided far more match information than any such facility in England. In the very last newspaper article Hobbs ever wrote, in 1963, he spoke of his affection for the ground: 'Sydney had everything. Fielding was a delight because, no matter what your position, you could depend on the ball coming true.' The same applied to batting. 'The light was perfect from the angle of the batsman. Sydney was the pitch of pitches as I knew it – on which the fellow with the bat could do things to that ball, because the ball did what it should.' Hobbs proved the point by hitting 72 in his penultimate Test innings of the tour, but it was to no avail as England lost again. It had been a disappointing series for England, heavily beaten by a margin of 4–1. But, for Hobbs, it was personal triumph. He had proved that he could cope with the pressures of Test cricket. Despite his exclusion from the first Test, he finished second to George Gunn in the England batting averages, with 302 runs at 41.14. In all matches on tour he scored 934 runs at

42.45. 'It is quite possible that, some three or four years hence, expert opinion will select Hobbs as the very best professional batsman in England,' concluded his advocate Major Trevor. That eventuality would arrive even sooner than the MCC manager imagined.

5

'Very Nasty and Unsportsmanlike'

G nome-like in appearance, ebullient in manner, Henry Leveson
Gower liked to think of himself as something of a character. On
one occasion, during a late-Victorian tour to the West Indies, he bit
the arm of the Governor of British Guyana at an official banquet, just
to win a bet with another guest. Soon after the Second World War,
Plum Warner was entertaining the Prime Minister and passionate
cricket enthusiast Clement Attlee at Lord's when Leveson Gower leant
over from a neighbouring hospitality box and told the Labour leader
to 'play a straight bat' and abandon his policy of nationalisation. By
this stage of his life, he had already been a leading figure in the cricket
establishment for almost half a century, having been elected to both
the Surrey and the MCC Committees as long ago as 1898. It cannot
be said that the Leveson Gower, known as 'Shrimp' because of his
diminutive stature, owed his pre-eminence to his cricketing ability. A
moderate batsman, he averaged only 22.72 during a career of 277
first-class matches spread over thirty-eight years. Wealth and social
connections played their part in his rise, for the Dukedom of Sutherland
lay at the pinnacle of the wider Leveson Gower clan. But his effervescent, self-confident personality was also important. There was an air
of gaiety about him, like fizzing champagne, a trait that was reflected
in the light-hearted, holiday atmosphere of the Scarborough cricket
Festival that he helped to organise every year in September. He also
possessed a natural gift for leadership. Towards the end of the Edwardian
era, he was captain of both Surrey and England, as well as serving as
a Test selector, and through this trio of positions he was to have some
influence over the burgeoning career of Jack Hobbs.

Leveson Gower, once described by C.B. Fry as 'a pavilion magnate', took over the Surrey captaincy in 1908 from Lord Dalmeny, who had given up cricket because of his political career. Thanks to the prestige of his father's name, Dalmeny had been elected the MP for Midlothian in the Liberal landslide of 1906 but over the subsequent two seasons he found it increasingly difficult to reconcile the demands of the Oval with those of Westminster. In truth, he was not an effectual politician but he was hurt by criticism about missing votes in the Commons, so in 1907 he packed in the Surrey job. Leveson Gower soon proved a successful replacement, taking Surrey to third in the county championship, one place higher that they had finished in 1907. He was helped by Hobbs, who maintained his high batting standard despite the dampness of the 1908 summer.

Averaging over 40 in the county championship, Hobbs hit six centuries for Surrey, including a commanding innings of 161 in a big win over Hampshire at the Oval. But perhaps his best innings was in a losing cause when, at the end of July, he hit 106 in a defeat by Kent at Blackheath. Heavy rain, said Hobbs, turned 'the pitch into a gluepot – a dream wicket for the spin bowlers, where Kent had a great advantage, but to our batsmen a pig of a wicket.' He was up against Colin Blythe, the master of flight and subtle variations, but, according to *Wisden,* he 'played a truly superb innings'. The Surrey fast bowler Bill Hitch, who took part in that match, later said of this performance against Kent, 'To be at the opposite end to Jack that day was blinding. You realised your batting wasn't even the same job. The depressing thing was, he made it look so easy.' Blythe was the spinner that Hobbs always most admired, as he explained in an article for *Strand* magazine: 'The famous left-hander is easily the best slow bowler I have ever seen. He does indeed "bowl with his head" and is continually devising fresh traps full of guile for the discomfiture of the man behind the willow. Every ball he bowls is a study. His brain is working all the time, scheming and planning to send the batsman back to pavilion.' Hobbs's form, allied to his winter success, led to his selection for the Players against the Gents at Lord's, the most important representative game of the summer in the absence of any Test cricket that year. In contrast to his previous Players appearance, Hobbs was outstanding. In a brilliant innings of 81, he hit thirteen 4s, many of them with scorching drives. 'He played in beautiful style and hit with the utmost freedom. Hobbs's innings was perhaps the best of the day. He was always severe on the overtossed ball and to judge from his play yesterday, his Australian experience has greatly improved him,' wrote *The Times*. There was no fading in his form at the end of the summer. His very last match of 1908 saw him make 155 against Kent at the Oval. By the end of his fourth full season, Hobbs had proved himself one of the most reliable batsmen in the country.

His standing was confirmed the following spring when he was named as one of *Wisden*'s five cricketers of the year. 'Few batsmen in recent years have jumped into fame more quickly than Hobbs. In his case there was no waiting for recognition and no failure to show the skill he was known to possess,' said the annual in its tribute, going on to give this description of his style: 'Hobbs makes no secret of his indebtedness for good advice and encouragement to Hayward, on whose superb method his own style of batting has obviously been modelled. From the first, he was very strong on the on-side and though with increased experience he has naturally gained a variety of strokes, his skill in scoring off his legs remains perhaps the most striking feature of his play.' *Wisden* concluded: 'Very keen on the game and ambitious to reach the highest rank, he is the most likely man among the younger professional batsmen to play for England in Test matches at home in the immediate future.'

With the Australians defending the Ashes in 1909, Hobbs soon had the chance to make good that prediction. His remarkable burst of run-making in the opening months of the season ensured that he could not be ignored by the selectors, whose three-strong panel was made up of Lord Hawke, C.B. Fry and Leveson Gower. The first sign of his fecundity came at the beginning of May, when he enjoyed a phenomenal 371-run partnership for the second wicket with Ernie Hayes on a plumb Oval pitch against Hampshire, the runs coming at rapid pace in just two and a half hours. 'When Hayes joined Hobbs the fun really commenced and the Hampshire bowling was made to look very innocuous,' said the *Evening Standard*. Hobbs's final score, which featured a hundred before lunch, was 205, made in 225 minutes. It was the first double century of his career and prompted *Cricket* magazine to report that, 'Hobbs showed wonderful command over the ball and throughout his long innings did not make the slightest mistake, although he was always scoring fast. It was a very masterly display.' Every element of Hobbs's technique was now working in fluent synchronicity: the high backlift ready for the bat to begin its straight, downward swing; the sure defence primarily on the back foot; the perfect timing that gave such power to his shots without apparent effort; the powerful wrists and dancing footwork. The rich vein of form continued as Surrey took on Warwickshire at Edgbaston. Having just made his first double hundred, Hobbs now completed a century in each innings for the first time, hitting 160 and exactly 100. 'Everything else in this match was dwarfed by the batting of Hobbs,' said Wisden. Two days after the Birmingham game, he almost scored a third successive century when he reached 99 against Essex at the Oval but was then caught off Johnny Douglas's swing bowling.

As the first Test against Australia approached at the end of May, Hobbs had made certain he was in contention for a place in the England team. But his selection was by no means automatic. England's batting resources at the end of the Edwardian age could hardly have been richer and, in contrast to overseas tours, all the leading players were available. Hobbs was in competition with a host of more experienced batsmen such as Tom Hayward, Archie MacLaren, C.B. Fry, Johnny Tyldesley, Tip Foster, George Gunn, Kenneth Hutchings, Plum Warner, the volcanic Gloucestershire hitter Gilbert Jessop and the Lancashire stylist Reggie Spooner, names that still resonate more than a century after the Golden Age. He had two crucial advantages, however: his productive form and the support of Leveson Gower, who pressed the claims of his young Surrey colleague. The other two selectors, Hawke and Fry, accepted and Hobbs was named in a fifteen-strong squad, its very size indicative of the panel's indecision.

Flushed by his powers of persuasion, Leveson Gower wrote an effusive letter to Hobbs after the Warwickshire game informing him of his inclusion in the England squad. 'My dear Jack, Please be at Birmingham on Thursday to play if wanted for England. I am so pleased. No one deserves the honour more than you do. A thousand thanks for your wonderful innings last match. With very many congratulations.' Leveson Gower's next task was to secure Hobbs's place in the final eleven, but that would not be easy, given the weight attached to the opinions of the England captain Archie MacLaren, who in early 1909 was no admirer of Hobbs.

MacLaren was not the selectors' first choice as Test skipper for the summer. The job had initially been offered to Stanley Jackson, the leader in the triumphant 1905 Ashes series, but he had to decline because of

business commitments, so thirty-seven-year-old MacLaren, now in the
twilight of his career, was put in charge. With his magisterial batting
and demeanour, he was something of a cult hero to the Edwardian
cricketing public and press. But in truth he was a poor captain, prone
to moodiness and obstinacy. Given the resources he had at his command
during his sporadic spells in charge of England since 1897/8, his record
of leadership at Test level was a chequered one, not helped by his habit
of undermining team morale. 'Look what they've sent me,' was one of
his favourite lines in reference to the supposed idiocy of the selectors.
As the Eton master, cricket lover and litterateur George Lyttelton once
said, 'It is disillusioning to one of my youthful loyalties to realise that
the Majestic MacLaren was an extremely stupid, pig-headed and preju-
diced man.'

All his life, MacLaren oozed self-important grandeur. At Harrow, his
fag had been Winston Churchill, whom he dismissed as 'a snotty little
bugger'. His brusqueness to everyone from waiters to business partners
incurred embarrassment and animosity. Now, on the eve of the crucial
first Test, he appeared determine to leave out Hobbs. According to
Leveson Gower's account, 'MacLaren, to my surprise, opposed the young
batsman's inclusion, and it was only after considerable discussion that
he rather reluctantly gave his assent, saying that I was in a position to
know more about him than any other selector.'

MacLaren's own testimony, written in 1926, played down his opposition. 'I remember so well H.D.G. Leveson Gower, a member of the
Selection committee, coming to me and saying, prior to the first Test
played at Birmingham, that he was certain young Hobbs was a fine
batsman and that he felt sure I would be pleased with him, and that
he was anxious for him to be included in the England XI. I knew
nothing about him then, but I replied that it was good enough for
me, after listening to the Surrey skipper's description of this young
player.'

MacLaren's expression of unfamiliarity about Hobbs was absurd, for
he was extremely well informed about all aspects of English cricket; his
Wisden obituary in 1945 praised his 'expert knowledge, obtained by
careful study of every intricacy of the game'. By May 1909 Hobbs was
in his fifth season of first-class cricket, had successfully played in an
Ashes series in Australia, been named as one of the five *Wisden* cricketers
of the year, had appeared for the Players against the Gents and had

frequently been talked of in the press as a prospect for the 1909 tests. The idea that MacLaren knew 'nothing about him' could not have been less convincing. In reality, as Leveson Gower's account demonstrates, MacLaren was left uninspired by Hobbs's batting, not least because in ten innings for Surrey against Lancashire since 1905, Hobbs had made just one score over 50. But hindsight, touched by Hobbs's phenomenal record, meant that MacLaren was reluctant to admit his failure to recognise the incipient greatness in his midst, so he fell back on feigning ignorance.

With grudging acquiescence, MacLaren included Hobbs's name in the England XI. Ironically, the batsman to be left out from the original fifteen was none other than Tom Hayward, the guiding force behind Hobbs's rise to the top. The master had been succeeded by the pupil. Hayward was to play only one more Test, while Hobbs was still near the beginning of a career that would see him become England's biggest scorer in Ashes history, a record he still holds to this day. Yet his start in Test cricket at home could not have been more deflating. In damp conditions at Edgbaston, Australia batted first and, amidst frequent interruptions for rain and bad light, were dismissed for just 74. Colin Blythe, with 6 for 44, was the chief destroyer, backed up by the late swerve of George Hirst, who took 4 for 28. On the second morning, MacLaren marched out to open with Hobbs, who was feeling expectant rather than nervous. MacLaren took the first over which was sent down by Bill Whitty, the fast-medium left-armer whose gift for swinging the ball made him the Australian equivalent of George Hirst. The England captain safely negotiated a maiden. Then Hobbs prepared to face Charlie Macartney. Known as 'the Governor-General' because of his confident, aggressive batting, Macartney also bowled highly effective, orthodox left-arm spin, with a deadly quicker ball. Hobbs took guard for the first delivery and waited for the Australian, who took a surprisingly long run for a bowler of his pace. As Macartney's arm swung over, Hobbs made his usual movement back and across the crease, only to miss the ball and find himself plumb lbw. The umpire's finger went up immediately. In front of a large Birmingham crowd, he had been out for a golden duck on his home Test debut. Recalling his walk back to the pavilion, he wrote, 'I almost wished that the ground would open up to let me collapse into Australia.' With a degree of melodrama, he said that the feelings of anguish lingered long after his return to the dressing room. 'The rest of the day was a misery, to be followed by a night of wretchedness.' His mood was not improved by forthright press criticism of his dismissal. 'Hobbs has an evil habit, together with many other batsmen, of getting right in front of his wicket before he even moves his bat. It is a detestable habit which in this case met with the fate it thoroughly deserved,' argued *The Times*. Nor did Leveson Gower feel at ease after the failure of his protégé. 'I imagined that MacLaren's eye was on me!' he wrote.

England's bowling hero Colin Blythe, a highly sensitive, kind-hearted individual, tried to lift Hobbs's spirits by buying him a little statuette of a boy with a cricket bat in his hand. 'The Hope of His Side' was the inscription at the base of this souvenir. 'Here you are, Jack. Cheer up, this will bring you luck,' said Blythe. Sentimental though this innocent gesture may have been, it seemed to have its effect on Hobbs. After Australia had been bowled out in their second innings for 151, Blythe and Hirst again doing all the damage, England had been set a target of 105. With typical gloominess, MacLaren was pessimistic about England's chances on a pitch that still strongly favoured the bowlers. But then he was approached by C.B. Fry, who, just like Hobbs, had been out first ball to Macartney. 'I asked him to let Jack Hobbs and me go in first to bustle our pairs of spectacles. After sucking his pencil, Archie agreed,' recalled Fry. 'Go and see what you can do,' said the England skipper.

The change in the batting order worked to perfection. Hobbs overcame the lingering anxieties from his first innings flop in the very first over he faced, which was delivered by the big Australian all-rounder Warwick Armstrong. 'I shall always remember how I cracked Warwick Armstrong to the boundary from the third ball he bowled to me and the confidence I felt from that moment until we made the winning hit,' he recalled. As the England score increased, he went after every Australian bowler; at one stage Macartney was pulled for three successive fours through mid-wicket. For much of this whirlwind innings, C.B. Fry was almost a bystander at the other end but this left him time to admire Hobbs's technique and temperament. In his autobiography, *Life Worth Living*, Fry described Hobbs's performance: 'as great an innings as I ever saw played by any batsman in any Test match or any other match.' The flow of runs was reminiscent of Ranji, said Fry: 'Jack Hobbs, on a diffi-cult wicket, took complete charge of the good Australian bowling, carted it to every point of the compass and never made the shred of a mistake. His quickness with his bat and his skill in forcing the direction of his strokes made me feel like a fledgling.' By the time England reached their target without the loss of a wicket, Hobbs was on 62 compared to Fry's 35.

Amid scenes of jubilation at England's ten-wicket victory, more than 10,000 spectators rushed onto the field and gathered in front of the pavilion. Bashful as ever, Hobbs was embarrassed to be ushered onto the balcony to acknowledge the sustained cheering. 'I felt overwhelmed and was so absolutely excited that I just managed to stand there three seconds, waved my cap and dashed back to the professionals' dressing room. I much preferred the ordeal of facing Australian bowling to that of facing a jubilant English crowd,' he wrote in 1935. Meanwhile, Leveson Gower could hardly contain his satisfaction, as MacLaren recalled. 'After the innings was over, the Surrey skipper, beaming all over, asked me what I thought of Hobbs and I replied, "Strongly as you advocated his claims, you did not paint him in sufficiently strong colours."' MacLaren was also keen to take the credit for the decision to open with Fry and Hobbs. 'I threw them in at the deep end and how delighted I was to see them keep their heads above water,' he told the *Evening Standard* years later.

With the cheers of the England supporters still ringing in his ears, Hobbs was brought down to earth when he returned home to Mitcham, where he rented a house from Bert Strudick, the Surrey wicketkeeper. 'I thought to myself how delighted my wife would be, how she would be standing by the door to welcome me as a hero returning from the battlefield,' he wrote. But to his disappointment, Ada was out shopping. Moreover, when she returned, he found she knew nothing about his innings. The absence of radio and telephones, combined with the limited coverage given then by the evening papers to cricket, meant that she had heard nothing about England's triumph. 'As far as she was concerned, I might just as well have not played,' he said. Ada, however, now had other things on her mind. Her role as mother was busier than ever, following the birth of their second child, Leonard Edward, in mid-February 1909. As she explained in a 1925 interview with the *Weekly Dispatch*, the rearing of their children 'gave me plenty of home occupation during the early years of my husband's cricketing career'. At the same time, Hobbs also experienced mild disappointment on the professional front. His second innings in the Birmingham Test had brought his total runs in May to 919, so he was just 81 short of equalling W.G. Grace's unprecedented achievement of 1895 in scoring 1,000 runs in May. There was only one day left in the month when Surrey embarked on their fixture against Nottinghamshire at Trent Bridge. Unfortunately, Notts won the toss and batted all day, with the result that Hobbs had no chance to reach the landmark. For the remainder of his career, he was never to come close again to scoring 1000 in May. Yet this setback was only the precursor to several months of frustration, injury and controversy for Hobbs. At both Test and county level, the blazing start to the season gave way to despair.

After the comfortable win at Edgbaston, England should have felt confident for the second Test, which began at Lord's in mid-June. The preparations were thrown into turmoil, however, by a shambolic selection policy that saw five changes made to the side. Blythe, always highly strung, had to withdraw on doctor's orders after a nervous attack, and Fry was unavailable because he had to appear in court in a fraud case involving his brother-in-law. But the problem of these enforced absences was disastrously compounded by the selectors' decision to opt for a weak, inexperienced attack on a quick wicket. Bizarrely, no fast bowler was chosen, even though Walter Brearley had been in the Edgbaston squad, while Wilfred Rhodes was also dropped. Normally so restrained, *Wisden* denounced the 'extraordinary blundering' by the selectors. 'How these gentlemen came to make such a muddle of the business no one has ever been able to understand.' The disarray boosted the mood in the Australian camp. 'When the names of the XI for the second Test were published, Armstrong and I agreed that if we could not beat this team, we had better sell our kits,' recorded Monty Noble. The result was all too predictable, as England crashed to a nine-wicket defeat. While the bowlers toiled in the field against the Australian batsmen, the embittered, well-lubricated figure of Walter Brearley could be found just under Leveson Gower's box in the Clock Stand, loudly proclaiming his own talents. 'I often get six wickets in an innings, usually the leading batsmen. I don't always trust the fielders, so I clean bo-o-o-wl them,' he kept bellowing until he was asked to move along by the police. England's batting did not fare much better than the bowling, Hobbs sharing in the collective failure. In the first innings he was out for 19, caught behind off an outswinger from Frank Laver. The second saw him fall to Warwick Armstrong for just 9, the first wicket in a dismal procession.

Perhaps the saddest aspect of the Lord's Test for Hobbs was that it represented the end of Tom Hayward's international career. Struggling with an injured leg, he fielded poorly and was cheaply dismissed in both innings. 'What a splendid player Tom had been ... He was perhaps the last of the old-school pros. Among the other members of our county team he was like a monarch,' wrote Hobbs.

England never recovered from the self-inflicted fiasco of Lord's. They suffered another heavy defeat at Leeds, where Hobbs was embroiled in an explosive controversy over his dismissal in England's first innings. Having reached 12, he vigorously pulled a ball from Macartney through square leg but in the process of starting to run he slipped and dislodged the bails. Immediately, he thought he was out 'hit wicket' and began to walk back to the pavilion. But after taking a few strides, he had second thoughts; perhaps he had completed his stroke before his foot knocked off the bails. So he stopped walking and instead appealed to the umpire, who immediately gave him 'not out'.

The Australians were furious at this decision. They gathered in the middle to discuss the umpire's verdict and denounce Hobbs. Foul language filled the air. Protests were made to the officials. Angry fingers pointed at the batsman. 'The chief offender was Warwick Armstrong who got very nasty and unsportsmanlike, refusing to accept the umpire's decision,' said Hobbs. But there was nothing the Australians could do. Hobbs was allowed to continue with his innings.

Then there followed a strange occurrence. Two balls later, Macartney sent down a straight delivery on middle stump. Like someone in a trance, Hobbs hardly even attempted to play it but instead just let it bowl him. It seemed an inexplicable move but some took this as an example of Hobbs's high ethical standards. Writing in *Cricket* magazine, the Reverend R.S. Holmes gave this description: 'As I watched him through a powerful glass from the Press Box he appeared to me to allow himself to be bowled; he evidently thought he ought to have been given out the previous ball [*sic*]. I wondered whether for the moment he had lost his nerve or was his action dictated by a magnanimous refusal to take advantage of what in his judgement was a wrong decision?' The Australian captain Monty Noble shared this view. 'My

impression of the incident at the time was and still is that, believing
himself to be legally out, he deliberately allowed himself to be bowled.
It is a very difficult thing to allow yourself to be bowled without
betraying the fact to the bowler or someone fielding near the wicket.
It was a match of small scores and the loss of a player of Hobbs's ability
probably had a determining influence on the success of Australia. Yet
that was cricket in excelsis.'

But Noble and the reverend were giving too much credit to Hobbs.
The fact was that Hobbs was the one who had asked for the umpire's
verdict. If he had really felt he was out, he would have carried on walking
back to the pavilion instead of asking for a decision. The truth, as he
later admitted, was that he was temporarily disconcerted by the
Australians' remonstrance, which meant that his concentration was shot
to pieces. 'I did not know whether I was standing on my head or my
heels, with the consequence that two balls later, I let one go,' he said in
one account. 'I lost my grip,' he wrote in another. In a sense, Warwick
Armstrong, the raging bull of Australian cricket, had achieved his goal.
But Hobbs never forgot or forgave. 'I still bear this incident in mind
against Armstrong,' he wrote in 1924. Hobbs fared a little better in
England's second innings, reaching 30 before he was bowled by one of
Tibby Cotter's expresses. This turned out to be the top score in a sorry
England collapse to 87 all out, with the middle order blown away by
Cotter.

Hobbs's troubles continued after the Headingley Test. In his first
county game, against Lancashire at Old Trafford, he almost tore off
a fingernail while trying to make a catch in the deep from a fierce
hit by Walter Brearley. He was out for five weeks with this painful
injury, and missed the last two Tests of the summer, which were both
drawn, enabling Australia to retain the Ashes. Apart from his innings
at Edgbaston, it had been a disappointing first domestic Test series
for Hobbs. He averaged just 26, and had failed to establish a stable
opening partnership for England. On his return to the Surrey team
in mid-August, he also struggled, scoring only one century in his
remaining twenty-four innings of the season. Altogether in first-class
games during 1909, Hobbs scored 2,114 runs at 40.65, but considering
almost half that total came before the end of May, he had not displayed
his usual consistency.

Part of the cause of his fluctuating form was the internal strife that gripped Surrey during these months, largely as a result of the autocratic outlook of the club's President Lord Alverstone. At one stage, the lively Australian batsman Alan Marshal, who had qualified by residence for Surrey in 1906 and had become a close friend of Hobbs's, was suspended from the team over a trivial incident during an away fixture at Derbyshire, when he and some other players, while walking back to their hotel in Chesterfield, were fooling around with a child's ball that they had bought in a street market. Hobbs, then at the Headingley Test, was not among them, though such a kickaround was precisely the sort of innocent fun he enjoyed with his mates. But it did not seem so innocent to an officious police constable, who stopped the players and demanded Marshal's name. Feeling that no crime had been committed, Marshal refused to give it. He was then arrested and taken down to the station. In support of Marshal, the other players followed. Fortunately, when the Derbyshire Chief Constable learnt about the episode he ordered that no further action be taken. The Surrey Committee, however, did not taken such a broad-minded view and Marshal was given a hefty ban for 'insubordination'.

Even worse friction followed soon afterwards because of Lord Alverstone's insistence on the inclusion of certain amateurs at the expense of key professionals. Jack Crawford, who took over the Surrey captaincy during the frequent absences of Leveson Gower on business and selectorial duties, was incensed by this policy and, after he had been told to leave out the opening bowler Tom Rushby for a tour match against the Australians, simply refused to lead the team. Alverstone was furious at this challenge. To his discredit but all too predictably, Leveson Gower took the president's side, banning Crawford from the Scarborough Festival and warning him that he would have no place in the future county team. 'Either you or I must give up playing for Surrey,' Leveson Gower told him with all the menace that his tiny frame could muster. Together, Leveson Gower and Alverstone ensured that the committee passed a resolution declaring that Crawford should never be invited to play for Surrey again. Having been 'practically branded a criminal', as he put it in *Cricket* magazine, Crawford, one of the finest young cricketers in the country, abandoned the English game to take up a teaching post in Australia. Equally sickened by the whole affair, Rushby left Surrey to play for Accrington in the Lancashire League.

Hobbs, never keen on club politics, avoided any involvement in this saga, yet the turmoil must have discomfited the professionals' dressing room. By the end of the 1909 season, his own career seemed in danger of stagnating. He was now advancing towards his late twenties and had not yet emerged as a dominant force in world cricket. But all that was to change in the winter of 1909/10, when he took part in the MCC South African tour led by Leveson Gower. It was a trip that would transform his reputation.

6

'You Could Always
Trust Wilfred'

As he contemplated winter in South Africa, Hobbs dreaded the twin
scourges of a lengthy absence from his young family and the chronic
seasickness of the long voyage. But this time, unlike the MCC tour to
Australia in 1907/8, Hobbs had no hesitation in accepting, partly because
the journey was much shorter than that to the Antipodes and partly
because his domestic responsibilities meant that he could not forgo the
fee. 'The tour was a paying proposition and I was glad to go. Really, I
am a home bird, but one cannot refuse these tours,' he wrote in 1924.
In the era before the First World War, an England trip to South Africa
had nothing like the prestige of one to Australia, as was illustrated by
the unrepresentative nature of the MCC side. The captain Leveson
Gower would never have come close to a place in an Ashes series and
indeed played his only Test cricket on this tour. Many of the top English
cricketers, particularly the leading amateur batsmen, stayed at home,
though there was a core of high-class professionals, including Hobbs,
Rhodes, Woolley, Strudwick, Blythe and Denton. Perhaps the most
intriguing selection was that of George Simpson-Hayward of
Worcestershire, who bowled underarm lobs that spun sharply from the
off. Despite his unorthodox method, he enjoyed considerable success
in the South Africa Tests. But this was the last appearance of underarm
bowling at international level until the infamous incident at a one-day
game in 1981, when the Australian Trevor Chappell gently rolled the
ball along the ground to prevent the possibility of the New Zealand
batsman hitting the 6 needed for victory off the last delivery.

Yet for all its inferior status, the 1909/10 South African Test series
represented a titanic challenge for England's batsmen, because of both

the alien conditions and the quality of the opposition spin bowling. South Africa had a completely different cricket environment to that of England. The pitches consisted of matting stretched over turf or soil, while the outfields were almost bare of grass. Hobbs's Surrey colleague Ernie Hayes, who had coached in South Africa, left this description of the Wanderers ground in Johannesburg: 'The playing field is a monotonous study of brick red, broken only by the strip of greenish-brown matting spread over the wicket. After a few overs, the ball takes on the colour of the outfield and players unused to these conditions find it difficult, especially if a dusty wind is blowing, to follow its flight.' Extravagant turn and bounce could be achieved on matting surfaces, prompting Leveson Gower to write that it was like batting on 'a sort of fast sticky wicket'. South Africa had just the bowlers to exploit these advantages through their celebrated quartet of googly experts: Reggie Schwarz, Ernie Vogler, Gordon White and Aubrey Faulkner.

Googly bowling was the sensation of Edwardian cricket, exposing the weakness of traditional batting techniques and adding a revolutionary weapon to the arsenal of spin. The invention of this new delivery has usually been ascribed to Bernard Bosanquet, the Middlesex all-rounder who discovered a way of sending down an off-break with the classical leg-break action. At first he deployed the innovation mainly as a party piece to amuse his teammates, but he developed it sufficiently to use in county and even Test cricket, spreading bewilderment among batsman. The very first time he tried a googly in a Test, during the 1903/4 tour of Australia, he knocked back the middle stump of Victor Trumper, who, expecting the normal leg-break, had played down the wrong line. Yet Hobbs himself cast doubt on the claim that Bosanquet was the first cricketer to bowl the googly. In his 1935 autobiography, he revealed that he once received a letter from Kingsmill Key, the former Surrey captain, who stated the googly was actually invented at Oxford in the mid-1880s by an undergraduate called Herbert Page. According to the testimony of Key, who was at Oxford at the same time, Page 'used to bowl it constantly when a wicket fell, while waiting for the next man to come in'. But Page never dared try it in a first-class match so, whatever the truth about his skill, the fact is that Bosanquet was the man who perfected the googly at the highest level, and this had huge implications for South African cricket. For among Bosanquet's teammates at Middlesex was a young, rather ordinary bowler called Reggie

Schwarz. Having failed to achieve much success in the county game, he emigrated to South Africa in 1901. But Schwarz returned to England with the South African tourists in 1904, when he renewed his friendship with Bosanquet and learnt the art of the googly. Within a few months, Schwarz had been turned from a mediocrity into a world-beater. On his arrival back in South Africa, he taught the new craft to his three colleagues, Faulkner, White and Vogler, and the four had soon created the most lethal spin attack in Test cricket. This was the difficult prospect that Hobbs and the rest of the MCC team now faced. 'Everybody talked about the deadliness of the Africans at home, especially those who had been out there on the tour previous to my first,' Hobbs wrote. Many fine batsmen had been reduced to impotence by the googly, including Tom Hayward who, in Hobbs's words, 'couldn't make head nor tail of it. But, for Hobbs himself, the threat would bring out his best.

Leveson Gower's MCC party left for South Africa in November 1909. For Hobbs, the beginning of the journey was tangled up in logistical difficulties, which showed not only how modestly professionals lived before the First World War but also that antiquated transport persisted in London well into the twentieth century. He and his next-door neighbour in Mitcham, Bert Strudwick, who also happened to be his landlord, departed early in the morning with the intention of meeting the rest of the side at Waterloo. They had already sent on their heavy luggage and each of them carried a single suitcase. But they could not find a cab in their street, so, with time running short, they decided to catch a tram to Tooting Junction railway station. To their consternation, no tram arrived. They began to walk by foot, but their pace was slowed down by the weight of their cases. 'Suddenly a donkey barrow came round the corner, and the man agreed with us to transport the suitcases to Tooting station. We walked briskly behind, and this undignified process was the start of our trip to one of the Empire's great dominions,' he recalled. At Waterloo, there was a large crowd to cheer the players as they left by train for Southampton, where they boarded the RMS *Saxon*, a 12,385-ton vessel belonging to the Union Castle line.

In his biography of Frank Woolley, the cricketer and writer Ian Peebles, who had personal experience of travelling to South Africa with the Union Castle line, gave this vivid description of the ship. She was, he said, 'a typical Edwardian mail steamer. Her grey-painted hull began with an uncompromising stern and ended with a graceful counter stern.

She had two very tall red funnels and rather stiff upper-works. The general impression was of a trim, firm but benevolent nanny.' Most of the cabins had bunks rather than beds and in the dining saloon the chairs were fixed in position. 'When the sea rose to a gentle swell the whole fabric would groan and creak so that knowing travellers would nod sagely and say she was a good ship.'

Sadly, some of the groaning also came from Hobbs who had to endure his usual seasickness, especially during the crossing of the Bay of Biscay. But once the *Saxon* had reached calmer waters off the west coast of Africa, Hobbs felt well enough to venture out of his cabin and even join in some batting practice on board. With the kind of foresight that he had not always shown in England team selection during the previous summer, Leveson Gower had arranged for a net to be brought from Lord's. On the teak deck sailors then laid down a matting wicket and stretched it taut in its four corners, which provided a true surface similar to the pitches that would soon be encountered in South Africa, though it had the one disadvantage of sloping slightly from leg to off. The players also practised their fielding using a slip catching cradle, as well as keeping fit by taking walks around the upper deck or playing games like quoits, at which Hobbs, with his instinctive coordination, excelled.

After seventeen days at sea, the *Saxon* arrived at Cape Town, where the players were given a civic reception and then taken to the Newlands ground, lying beneath the vast plateau of Table mountain. Here they had their first net session on dry land, watched by the local press. A reporter from the *Cape Times* was not too impressed with his initial sight of the Surrey batsman. 'Hobbs might just as well go back. He will never be any good on matting wickets.' But Hobbs soon proved his critic wrong by scoring successive centuries in the first two games. The reality was that, in the absence of so many stars like MacLaren, Fry, Foster and Tyldesley, Hobbs was the premier England batsmen on the tour and he appeared to thrive on his promotion. There was another major step forward for Hobbs which radically improved his game. For the first time in Test cricket he was part of a stable opening partnership. In his seven Tests so far, he had opened with no fewer than five different partners, Fane, Gunn, MacLaren, Fry and Hayward, hardly a recipe for consistency. But now the tough Yorkshireman Wilfred Rhodes was asked by Leveson Gower to take on the job for the South African series. So began a profitable association that would serve England up to the First World War and establish records that have lasted to this day.

The rise of Rhodes to the top of the England batting order was a remarkable tribute to his pertinacity, for he had begun his Test career a decade earlier as a bowler who batted at number ten. Yet for all his talent as an orthodox slow left-armer, batting was the discipline that Rhodes really enjoyed. 'I hope that some day I shall be played for England for my batting,' he told his Yorkshire captain Lord Hawke early in his career. Hawke had given little support to this ambition since, as he explained, 'I always feared that the development of his batting powers, which from the first were quite evident, would check his skill with ball.' Hawke was right. By the end of the Edwardian age, Rhodes had become an opening batsman who bowled occasionally. In the 1909/10 series, for instance, he sent down just fifty-seven overs in five Tests, taking only two wickets. His batting, however, prospered dramatically in league with Hobbs. In many respects, they were different personalities. Where Jack was cheerful, sensitive, affable and kind-hearted, his warmth epitomised by his wide smile and fondness for practical jokes, Rhodes was a taciturn, cautious, detached individual. 'He was a damned uncooperative old bugger,' recalled one of his Yorkshire captains. 'Wilfred never bought himself a packet of cigarettes in his life,' said the Yorkshire bowler Schofield Haigh. Yet he was also a man of granite-like integrity, who inspired deep respect throughout the cricket world. 'You could always trust Wilfred,' said Hobbs.

Like Hobbs, Rhodes came from a poor background. Born on a farm in Kirkheaton, he remembered the area where he grew up as 'very mucky' because of the smells and fumes from the dyeworks at Huddersfield. His first job was as an apprentice on the railways, but, with a natural gift for finger spin, he could not resist the lure of cricket and soon found work as a professional in Scotland before graduating to the Yorkshire XI. He shared with Hobbs an enduring pride in his occupation as a professional cricketer and was fastidious about his appearance. His biographer Sidney Rogerson recalled, as a child, finding himself in a railway carriage opposite Rhodes in around 1908. 'He was wearing a well-cut flannel suit. His brown shoes shone with much polishing.' With his 'deeply tanned face', he reminded Rogerson of a 'young captain' in the army on leave from military service in India.

Just as in their characters, Rhodes was much less expansive than

Hobbs in his batting style. Predominantly a defensive player, he had a very open stance with both shoulders square to the bowler and largely eschewed the flamboyant strokes that were central to Hobbs's pre-war repertoire. The long-serving Middlesex professional Harry Lee left this description of Rhodes at the crease: 'The bat became as broad as a Yorkshire barn door, and it was a very slippy bowler who could get one past our Wilfred. Characteristically, most of his runs were scored by deflections past slip or to the leg-side. I rarely saw him drive or hook.' For all his attacking limitations, Rhodes was highly aggressive in one area of his game: running between the wickets. The quick single was one of the hallmarks of his association with Hobbs, who regarded Rhodes as the best runner out of all the partners he had in his long career. Between them, there was an instinctive harmony and a complete faith in one another. The baronet and cricket historian Sir Home Gordon, who saw them numerous times in action, wrote that 'the wonderful running between the wickets of Hobbs and Rhodes in Test cricket has never been surpassed. Oddly enough, they never called one another but made an almost imperceptible sign, the raising of one finger in a batting glove.' The Yorkshire cricket writer A.A. Thomson felt that the key to their running was 'their superb individual judgement. Hobbs and Rhodes could time a short run, without hesitation or haste, to a fraction of a foot or a fraction of a second.' Rhodes himself, in a BBC radio interview, had this to say about his partner: 'Before he made any stroke he always positioned his back foot, went on to his back foot and positioned it. And I think this was a great secret of his success, cos it made him have more time to see the ball and I think he used to play the ball slightly later than most of English cricketers. He was a very fine judge of a run and also he was very quick between the wickets, a fast runner. I thought he was a fine natural cricketer who had a lot of strokes.' The admiration was mutual, as Hobbs explained to John Arlott: 'Wilfred would always come. He wasn't a sprinter but he was always backing up a yard or two and we knew each other so well that, just a nod – or nothing at all – we went. You could say he ran better for me than I did for him because, while I often started almost before I had finished my stroke, he was not so quickly away, but we hardly ever had a run-out. We trusted each other completely. You wouldn't call Wilfred a great batsman – not as good as Tom Hayward or Herbert Sutcliffe

– but he was so sound; he never attempted anything he couldn't do; the other side had to get him out.'

The new partnership proved itself in the first Test at Johannesburg. In front of a crowd of 15,000 at the Wanderers, Rhodes and Hobbs went out to open in the late afternoon of the first day in response to a poor South Africa total of 208. After Rhodes played out a maiden from Vogler, he and Hobbs met in the middle to discuss how to handle the next over, to be delivered by the tall South African captain Tip Snooke, who could get alarming bounce off the matting wicket. They agreed to take a single off his first ball. Snooke roared in, Hobbs made his customary move across his stumps and then played a dead bat stroke, dropping the ball in front of silly point. Before any fielder had time to move, Hobbs and Rhodes had crossed for a run. They continued to do the same to Snooke in the next few overs until the big South African lost his composure and took himself off. The quick running set the tone for the batting that evening. By the close of play they had achieved an unbroken stand of 147 in just 105 minutes, with Hobbs on 77 not out and Rhodes on 57 not out. Unfortunately, neither of them was able to continue long the next morning, with Rhodes falling to Vogler for 66 and Hobbs caught behind off the same bowler for 89. When Hobbs was out, England were 190 for 2 but they failed to capitalise on their strong position and ended up losing by 19 runs in a nerve-shredding, second innings run-chase. Again Hobbs was dismissed by Vogler, this time for 35, but he had coped far better than any other England player against the googly.

The Hobbs–Rhodes partnership performed well in the second Test at Durban, with stands of 94 and 48. Hobbs, growing in confidence against the spinners, top-scored in both innings with 53 and 70. Simpson-Hayward's underarm bowling also proved strangely effective, accounting for seven wickets in this match to go with the eight he took in the first Test. 'He used to spin the ball as if it belonged to the billiard table; I believe it was by manipulating a billiard ball that he learnt his job. You could hear the click of his fingers as he let the ball loose,' recalled Hobbs. They were the two most celebrated England cricketers in Durban, as the *Daily Mirror* reported: 'The town is full of Hobbs and Simpson-Hayward, and I hear that a new brand of whisky is coming out to be called Hobbslobbs whisky.'

Once more, however, neither Hobbs's runs nor Simpson-Hayward's lobs could compensate for a weak middle order that struggled badly against the googly bowlers, and England lost by 95 runs. 'The topic of conversation is the damage done by the googly in the last Test match again and some of the players are wondering where this googly will end,' said the *Mirror*, though the paper did not apply this criticism to Hobbs. 'If the batsmen could only imitate his style what a future there would be.' There was, in fact, no great mystery about Hobbs's success against the googly. His skill depended on the two cardinal virtues of batsmanship against spin: either moving right forward to smother the turn or going right back to play the ball off the pitch. What made him unique among his England contemporaries was the combination of his perfect judgement of length and his swift footwork to get himself in the correct position. The key, said Hobbs, was for the batsman to be decisive in his movements in going forward or back: 'The worst thing is to be caught between two minds. "He who hesitates is lost" every time to the googly bowler, but the man who acts with decision has the googly man more than half beaten before he takes his guard against him,' Hobbs wrote in the *Strand* magazine in 1912. He also argued, in a departure from his usual pre-war method, that caution rather than aggression was vital against this type of bowling. 'The "hit out or get out" policy is not the least use. If you try to knock a googly bowler off, he will be much obliged to you. Be content to put as much willow as you can in the way of the good ones and those which are just a little faulty tap with care for a single or a couple. Depend upon it, the strain of bowling real googlies must tell, and when the stuff begins to lose its twist and length then is the time to lay on the wood with a vengeance, for there is no easier bowling to flog than the tired googlies.' When he first went to South Africa, Hobbs could not easily detect the googly at the point of delivery, so he relied largely on instinct and perception of length to combat it. But experience, allied to his acute eyesight, taught him to read the spin before the ball pitched, either from its flight through the air or from the bowler's wrist action. As a result, this type of bowling lost all its sting for him. 'I don't believe anyone could send me down a googly without my spotting it,' he later wrote.

The South African bowlers of 1909/10 varied in their style. Reggie Schwarz, the mentor of the quartet, bowled nothing but googlies, so in effect he was really an off-spinner, though his medium pace made an awkward opponent. Vogler and White cleverly mixed their googlies among their orthodox leg-breaks, and Hobbs found White's googly the hardest to detect. But he thought that Aubrey Faulkner was the best of the lot because of the big amount of turn either way. Despite Hobbs's admission that he could not always detect the spin during the tour, other members of the MCC side marvelled at his ease against the South Africans. 'Personally, I very seldom saw him in difficulty when facing the googly bowlers,' said his skipper Leveson Gower, while Bert Strudwick said that Hobbs 'played the googly better than any other batsman I know'. In fact, Hobbs's skill was so pronounced that he led the South Africans to think that he could pick them all the time. Years later, Faulkner recalled in a radio interview with Hobbs how dispirited he had become during one of the England opener's long innings in South Africa: 'Well, I only bowled that one googly, Jack, and as you hit it for four, I realised you had spotted it and wouldn't risk it again.' Hobbs was genuinely surprised at this confession, and explained that he had merely 'watched the ball off the wicket and decided it was a ball to be hit'. But Hobbs's expertise could also arouse the envy of some of his fellow professionals. In May 1910, following his return from South Africa, Hobbs was playing for Surrey at Fenner's against Cambridge University, whose attack included the Scottish-born leg-spinner John Bruce-Lockhart. Hobbs went back to one of Bruce-Lockhart's deliveries, which pitched far outside the off-stump. Initially he planned to pull it but then, aware of a packed leg-side field, he decided to leave it, only to watch the ball turn in wickedly and bowl him behind his pads. 'Jack is showing us how to play the googly,' said Hayward sarcastically on Hobbs's return to the pavilion.

Hobbs's judgement proved sounder in the second innings of the third Test at Johannesburg, where his magnificent batting brought England victory. In the first innings he had dropped right down the order to number seven, having suffered badly from sunstroke while fielding. Still feeling poorly, he was bowled by Faulkner for just 11. He had not recovered when England began their run-chase of a target of 221 and therefore batted at number five, the only time in his entire career that he did not open in either innings of a Test match. England's prospects looked hopeless when the sixth wicket fell at 93, but the new batsman Morice Bird, a young amateur at Surrey, stuck with Hobbs who, after a uncertain start, was playing with iron resolution. 'Dashing was out of the question; I set my teeth and decided to play carefully,' he wrote. Bird and

Hobbs put on 95 for the seventh wicket to bring England close to their target. As the score mounted, Hobbs grew in aggression, regularly piercing the field with his cuts and drives. Then, after Bird had been dismissed, Leveson Gower stayed with Hobbs to see England through by three wickets. 'I shall always remember the end. We wanted 1 to tie and 2 to win. I played one to cover and ran 1. Gordon White fumbled the ball and I never hesitated but turned and ran another. The match was ours,' said Hobbs, who finished on 93 not out, his innings lasting 130 minutes and containing ten 4s. The spectators swarmed onto the field, many of them England supporters, and Hobbs was carried aloft back to the pavilion. In another tribute, £90 was raised from the public through a collection held at the ground. 'It was a great personal triumph for Hobbs, and he deserved all the eulogy that he got at the end of a memorable match,' said the *Daily Express*. There were fewer plaudits at the end of the fourth Test at Cape Town, when Hobbs, restored to the opening position alongside Rhodes, failed disastrously in each innings. He made just 0 and 1, the closest he ever came to making a pair in first-class cricket and the only time in Tests he did not reach double figures in either innings. Without runs from their top batsman, England were badly handicapped. They lost by four wickets and South Africa took the series with one match still to play.

While he was Cape Town, Hobbs shared a hotel room with Strudwick, who was not only his landlord in Mitcham but also his closest friend in cricket. They were very similar men: quiet, genial, conscientious and honourable. They were both practising Christians and, when Surrey played away, they usually went the local Anglican church together. In fact, Strudwick was even more devout than Hobbs; during his early career, he would not even eat a hot meal on a Sunday because of his Sabbatarian principles. He was also a more strict teetotaller than Hobbs, who until the 1920s took the occasional glass of wine. Once, however, Strudwick inadvertently consumed some alcohol at the end of play when he accidentally picked up a glass of ginger beer mixed with gin, which was intended for the Surrey fast bowler Tom Richardson. When informed of his mistake, he said with a smile, 'Well, that is a funny thing, because I was just thinking that was the best drop of ginger beer I ever tasted.'

The friendship between Hobbs and Strudwick deepened on the South African tour, particularly because they went through so many varied experiences together. There were long hot train journeys by day and uncomfortable hotel stays by night. Their Cape Town room was so filthy that it was overrun by ants, and their only solution to the problem was to place apple cores and sweets in the fireplace to attract the insects away from their beds. There were often long hours of boredom in the evenings, filled by games of cards or walks through dusty streets. But Hobbs and Strudwick also had other, more interesting moments, like their visits to the famous Kimberley diamond mines and the battlefield sites of the Boer War, which had first impinged on Hobbs as a coach at Bedford School eight years earlier. Struggling in the heat and the barren terrain, Hobbs was amazed to think that British troops, with their heavy uniforms and kit, had fought in such conditions.

Perhaps the highlight of the tour, from the viewpoint of relaxation, was the hospitality shown at Groote Schuur, once the home of Empire builder Cecil Rhodes, now the official Government residence in the Cape Colony. 'I spent many hours there, lying in a hammock, and very much did I appreciate the food there after hotel living for so long,' said Hobbs, showing his usual concern about nutrition. While the players were at Groote Schuur, a lioness gave birth to a pair of cubs in the zoo attached to the residence's grounds; they were immediately named 'Hobbs' and 'Strudwick'.

It was on the South African trip that Hobbs played his first ever round of golf, a sport that was to give him great pleasure right up to the end of his life. Strudwick, already an experienced player, took him for a round on a course at Port Elizabeth, though the session was ruined after only a few holes by a ferocious thunderstorm. Just as they were running for the clubhouse through the torrential rain, a bolt of lightning struck a flagpole and sent it crashing to the ground in front of the two cricketers. 'We did not feel much like golf after that,' said Hobbs.

To his mild embarrassment, he also attracted some female attention on the tour. Though he always took pride in his sartorial appearance, he was far too bashful to have the slightest vanity about his looks. But, according to a gossipy report in the *Daily Mirror*, his tanned face and dark brown eyes did not go unnoticed when the professionals went to a skating rink in Durban. Hobbs did not join his teammates on the ice but instead watched the action from a stand. 'Hobbs was wearing such pretty socks, and some of the rinking ladies asked who was the good-looking fellow with the pretty socks,' said the *Mirror*. Yet, despite his modesty, there was one aspect of physiognomy that intrigued Hobbs. As he explained in an article in the *Star*, written in the context of the 1933 West Indian tour, he had an eccentric theory about eye colour and batsmanship. 'It may only be my own fancy but I have the idea that the majority of great batsmen are dark-eyed. A little quiet examination will, I think, bear out my contention that, compared with dark-eyed players, there have been comparatively few with blue eyes.' There was one big flaw in his argument: Don Bradman had blue eyes.

By the second week in March 1910, England were preparing for the final Test of the series, to be played again at Newlands in Cape Town. It was a game in which Hobbs dominated with the bat, but also contributed with the ball. In the absence of a strong pace attack, Hobbs had already opened the bowling in the first two Tests, delivering a total of nineteen overs. In this match he gained his only wicket in Test cricket, having Reggie Swarz caught by Morice Bird in South Africa's second innings during a spell of 1 for 19 off eight overs. Altogether, Hobbs bowled 62.4 overs in Test cricket and had an average of 145, hardly impressive figures. There were, however, many fine judges who thought that Hobbs, with his whippy, sideways-on action, could have made a useful all-rounder if he had not concentrated on his batting so intensively. 'He bowled really well, keeping a nice length and making the ball swerve a little from leg and then come quickly off the ground,' said Plum Warner. The cricket historian Sir Home Gordon believed that 'if Hobbs had not been the greatest bat of his time, he would have been one of the finest bowlers'. To support this claim, Sir Home cited a match at Leyton in 1920, when one of the Surrey bowlers turned up late and Hobbs had to take the new ball. On a 'perfect' batting pitch, Hobbs ripped through the top order, taking 4 for 36, including the wicket of the opener, the Reverend Frank Gillingham, who scored over 10,000 runs for Essex during his career. 'The crack Essex run-getters literally could not "look at" him and Parson Frank Gillingham will recollect coming back to the pavilion to remark, "Jack sent down absolutely the best ball I ever tried to put my bat against,"' wrote Sir Home. The same season Hobbs also took 5 for 21 against Warwickshire at Edgbaston, all of them batsmen in the top seven of the order, and his seventeen wickets at 11.82 saw him head the Surrey bowling averages. The best bowling of his career came in 1911 at the Parks against Oxford University, when he took 7 for 56 with an extravagant swing in overcast conditions.

Remarkably, five catches were dropped off his bowling that day. 'He was medium-paced, delivering the ball from a hand unusually high and employing a baffling swerve,' said his county captain Leveson Gower. But Surrey, like England, were reluctant to use him much as a bowler for fear of prejudicing his batsmanship. As the career of Wilfred Rhodes demonstrated, this was no empty concern, though later in his life Hobbs sometimes expressed regret over the way his bowling was disregarded. 'If a second innings of life were granted me, I should certainly make more of my bowling and I would look for greater encouragement to do so than I have actually received,' he told the *Evening News* in 1930.

His bowling in South Africa was just a minor bonus. It was his batting that made his name. In the fifth Test, which was his twelfth match for England, he far surpassed anything he had previously achieved in Test cricket. Going in to open after England had won the toss, he and Rhodes put on no less than 221 for the first wicket, then a world record. Throughout the mammoth stand, Hobbs scored quickly, reaching a chanceless 91 not out at lunch. Steady as ever, Rhodes was on 47 not out. 'As a first-wicket partner, I just love to go in with Rhodes. His influence is great and he is such a splendid runner,' Hobbs told the *Cape Times*. Rhodes fell on 77 in the afternoon, but Hobbs carried on until he reached 187, when he was out hit wicket after knocking his stumps with his boot, the only time he suffered this mode of dismissal in his sixty-one Tests. Altogether, in a performance described by *Wisden* as one of 'brilliancy', he batted for 225 minutes, hit twenty-three 4s and his innings enabled England to post a big enough first innings total to win by nine wickets. In the wake of this victory, Hobbs had pushed himself to the front rank of international batsmen. When the South African press interviewed the top Australian batsman Syd Gregory, who was passing through Cape Town on his way home, he told them, 'I believe Hobbs to be just about the finest bat in the world today. Moreover, he is the prettiest to watch.' In all games on the tour, Hobbs scored 1294 runs at an average of 58, while his average in the five Tests rose to 67 from 538 runs. No other England player came near to this record, as *Wisden* commented: 'The feature of the trip was the superb batting of Hobbs, who easily adapted to the matting wickets and scored from the famous googly bowlers with amazing skill and facility.'

But the sweet taste of triumph in the final Test was diluted by two controversies, which led to a sense of angry grievance among the England professionals. The first arose at a dinner hosted by Sir Abe Bailey, the diamond tycoon, financier, politician, art collector and patron of South African cricket. During the course of a post-prandial speech, Sir Abe turned to Morice Bird and said, 'This is the type of man we want out here as coach, not the professional cricketer.' The England professionals, seated at their own table further down the room, were outraged. 'That was a nasty remark,' said Hobbs. 'Professionals are not accustomed to being unfavourably compared with amateurs, nor is there any justifica-tion for a comparison of that kind.' What made the comment all the more wounding for Hobbs was that, on the basis of his success in the early Tests, he had actually been offered a job as a professional in the Natal colony. It is unlikely he could have taken it, given his commitments to Surrey, England and his family, but the implication of the comment from Sir Abe, who wielded enormous influence in South African cricket, was that men like Hobbs should not be given such employment. Even greater friction followed, this time within the England camp, when the MCC announced that two extra matches had been hastily arranged in Rhodesia, after the official end of the tour in Cape Town. The consequence of this move was a potential three-week extension of the tour with no additional pay, a burden that the profes-sionals regarded as intolerable, given that they had already been away from home for more than four months. They also harboured suspicions that the new fixtures had been organised, not for the purposes of cricket, but primarily to allow the amateurs to see Victoria Falls and indulge in some big-game shooting. A particular target of the professionals' wrath was Major Teddy Wynward, the Hampshire batsman, who had already incurred a mix of unpopularity and derision with his high-handed manners. In one incident early in the tour he had posted in the professionals' dressing room a list of the players that he required to bowl at him in the nets on a certain afternoon. Having put on his batting gear, he waited confidently for the named bowlers to arrive. None of them did so. In umbrage, he marched back to the dressing room, where he found that his notice had been screwed up and thrown in the waste-paper basket. Wilfred Rhodes, the senior professional, called Wynward 'the villain of the piece' and argued that he was in South Africa 'more or less on a joy-ride'.

With Rhodes exuding the same kind of resistance that he showed at the wicket, the rest of the professionals, including Hobbs, refused to agree to the new arrangement. Effectively they went on strike, demanding that the terms of their contract be respected. Like most of his colleagues, Hobbs was no radical or rebel but nor was he a pushover when it came to his status as a professional, as he later proved in the 1920s when he laid down his conditions for participation in MCC tours. In the case of the 1909/10 tour, Hobbs and their colleagues won their point through their tough stance. They were allowed to return home on the scheduled day of departure. The amateurs went on alone to Rhodesia. Later, when news about the strike leaked out, the professionals came in for some criticism in parts of the press, typified by this outburst from sports paper the *Winning Post* which, in the form of an open letter to Rhodes, accused them of disloyalty and moaning. 'Not everybody is aware that the professionals in Mr Leveson Gower's team in Africa went in for a little strike on their own . . . Presumably you and your professional comrades had had enough travelling and cricket, alleging that your contract ended with the fifth Test match. It is not a very pretty tale though probably you all thought you were in the right.'

The voyage back was the calmest of Hobbs's international career, and he did not suffer his usual bout of prolonged seasickness. But he was still desperate to get home. On the night before the ship arrived at Southampton, Hobbs was so eager to catch his first glimpse of England in months that he did not go to bed. At the docks, Ada and the other wives had gathered to greet their returning husbands and there was another enthusiastic welcome from friends when the train pulled into Waterloo. But it was already early April, just a few weeks before the start of another cricket season. Expectations of Hobbs had never been higher.

7

'The Perfect Batsman'

The batting technique of Jack Hobbs had withstood its stiffest examination. Against a radically new type of bowling, he had proved himself to be in a different class to any of his fellow England cricketers. He was, beyond dispute, seen as the finest batsman in the country, especially now that the generation of MacLaren, Hayward, Jessop and Jackson was in decline. There were two remarkable aspects to his achievement. First, despite some guidance from his father, Hobbs was largely self-taught and in his formative years had not been involved in intensive competition. He therefore had to grasp the principles of batsmanship himself, which points to a high degree of natural talent and cricket intelligence. Second, Hobbs came on the first-class scene just as the art of bowling was undergoing major change, not only through the advent of the googly but also through the development of controlled swing. Bowlers had, of course, always swung a cricket ball, which by the very nature of its composition will inevitably move in the air. But it was only in the Edwardian age that bowlers, led by George Hirst of Yorkshire, really learnt how to command the swerve with lateness and accuracy. When he was in form, George Hirst could bowl an inswinger that was described as spearing into the batsman like a throw from cover-point. Yet Hobbs, having never encountered these bowling methods during his Cambridge upbringing, mastered them far more successfully than his contemporaries.

To that most lyrical of cricket writers, Sir Neville Cardus, this was the essence of Hobbs's greatness before the First World War. In a 1954 article in the popular weekly *Everybody's Journal*, Cardus wrote that Hobbs was 'brought up as a batsman in the Victorian school', so he learnt his cricket at 'a period in which fast bowlers pitched the ball on or outside the off-stump; when slow left-handers wanted two slips at least, and would have retired from the field insulted if a short-leg had been set for them.' At the beginning of Hobbs's career with Surrey, continued Cardus, 'the general style of attack was much the same as Grace had known', yet soon after his baptism 'a revolution occurred in cricket, the most far-reaching since bowlers were allowed to raise the arm above the shoulder. Googly and swerve developed everywhere. The established "classical" batsmen, with a few exceptions, were at a loss. The graceful thrust of the front leg down the pitch, the confident rhythmical swing of the bat to the ball – these devices were no use against the mysterious and seemingly illogical spin of the 'wrong 'un'. It was as though cricket had suddenly been flung into another dimension. Hobbs adapted himself to the changed scene and procedure. He showed how the googly and the late swing could be countered by delayed strokes, legs and pads covering the wicket, bat held loosely, so that if a vicious ball made a positive hit too dangerous, the spin might be rendered as null and void as if it had collided with a sandbag.'

Hobbs's technique was supremely effective, but it was also aesthetically pleasing. There was a poise and fluency about his movements; nothing was ever ugly or angular. 'I never saw him reduced to undignified pokes, prods or pushes. I never saw him make a crude stroke,' wrote Cardus in another of his elegiac tributes, this one written in the *Listener*. In defence Hobbs never seemed panicky, in attack never brutal. The distinguished cricket historian David Frith, who has watched more vintage footage than any other expert, says that film of Hobbs shows how 'he was really quite elegant. You can see how he could fit into any age. He was a very easy mover with strokes all around the wicket. The only stroke he didn't have was the reverse sweep. He never looked as if he was putting himself out. There was no violence in his batting.' One of Hobbs's early critics, Archie MacLaren was so won over by Hobbs's batting from 1909 that he even wrote a book about him entitled *The Perfect Batsman*, based on a set of pre-war photographs that displayed Hobbs practising a wide range of batting strokes at the Oval. In his commentary, MacLaren described Hobbs as 'the most perfect model of what a batsman should be'. Anyone examining the action photographs, said the former England captain, could not fail 'to notice his footwork, the grace of his style, and his perfect balance in all his strokes, to say nothing of his delightful follow-through at the very end of his strokes.

Hobbs possesses the athletic figure so essential for the game, the loosest of loose shoulders, as his delightfully free shoulder-swing shows, a pair of wrists that any batsman might well envy, perfect temperament and a thorough knowledge of all that is possible in batting.' The foundation of Hobbs's method was a relaxed stance at the crease, with his feet quite close together, his bat face turned slightly inwards, his weight evenly distributed and his left foot pointing towards cover. Some classical purists thought he was a little too open-chested or 'two-eyed' to use the misleading contemporary phrase, though when he moved into any off-side stroke he rapidly swung his left shoulder and elbow into the line of the ball. 'One never sees Hobbs showing his chest to the bowler in any of his forward play or driving,' wrote MacLaren. Hobbs generally took his guard on leg stump because, as he explained in the 1925 manual *The Game of Cricket As It Should be Played,* 'I can get a truer sight of the direction of the ball and be in the best position to deal with all sorts of ball.'

The bats Hobbs used weighed between two pounds five ounces and two pounds six ounces, but his chief concern was that they should have the right balance. He also took an interest in the type of wood. 'As a general rule, narrow-grained wood is best for driving power and a broad grain for durability.' Hobbs's gracefulness was captured in his smooth, high backlift, similar to that employed later by those West Indian greats Brian Lara and Garry Sobers, but his bat came down straight in line with the stumps rather than at an angle from point. At the moment of delivery his instinctive response, what modern coaches would call his 'trigger' movement, was to shift back and across his stumps, creating a strong platform from which to play the ball. Hobbs was renowned for his ability to hit all round the wicket off either foot; there was no finer sight in pre-war cricket than his dance down the wicket to loft a spinner straight back over his head. But in contrast to the orthodoxy of the early 1900s, with its emphasis on front-foot play, Hobbs favoured the back foot because he felt this gave him more time and control. As he later explained in a BBC interview, 'I think I'm right in saying that you should always play back if you can because you can watch the ball right onto the bat. When you play forward there must be a split second when you lose sight of the ball. If I was in trouble I had a tendency to play back.'

Hobbs was classically orthodox in the straightness of his bat when defending or driving, yet he was also superb at the cut and the pull. The veteran scorer Fred Boyington, who watched every Surrey First XI game for forty-three years between 1882 and 1925, believed that Hobbs's forceful play through the leg-side was one of the most attractive parts of his game. 'Jack Hobbs is very fine at the pulling stroke and will often pull a ball from a foot outside the off-stump for 4,' said Boyington in a rare press interview. Against fast bowling, Hobbs was also adept at the hook, though he used it judiciously, as his greatest admirer John Arlott noted: 'Jack Hobbs played the hook coolly but selectively, only if he was certain of doing so safely. Often he left the decision late and if he decided not to play it swayed inside the line of the ball.' Wiry and slim, Hobbs did not exude physical strength at the crease. Instead, his domination of bowling attacks came from his gifts of timing and place-ment. 'The secret of power and hitting is not so much muscular force as ease of swing and perfect timing,' wrote Hobbs, who was an expert at finding the gaps in the field. His first England manager, Major Philip Trevor, said of him: 'In the common acceptance of the word, Hobbs is not a hitter, hard as he may actually hit the ball. As a placer, however, he has never had his equal among professional batsmen.' Gubby Allen, the England captain on the 1930s, had this insight: 'Technically he was perhaps the greatest batsman of my lifetime. Jack always seemed to get his feet in the right place, which is the hallmark of the great player . . . He was a very good placer of the ball. I said to him once, "You always beat the fielder, Jack." His reply was simple: "Well, that's one of the arts of batting, isn't it?" And, of course, he was right.'

The keynote of Hobbs's batting before the First World War was his attacking intent, a big difference from the approach he adopted after 1918. In his later years, though still capable of brilliance, he was more of a consolidator and an accumulator, not only because of his age but also because of the pressures bred by his own prolificacy. 'I honestly believe that I played a better game in those years before the First World War,' said Hobbs in a 1954 interview. 'I didn't have over my head the burden of this or that record which I was expected to beat. I wasn't then being pursued by the press, who meant well but they chased me insistently. As a result, I got the obsession that it was my duty to create new achievements in cricket. In those pre-1914 days, I could go in to bat and just enjoy myself; and, too, with the joy of my eyesight at its keenest.' It was a change noticed by his contemporaries, both observers and players. Sir Home Gordon wrote that 'with advancing years, Hobbs ceased to indulge in the grand strokes to the ropes and patted dexterously placed singles, being more careful to remain at the wicket, less venturesome in lashing out'. Similarly, the Yorkshire cricket writer A.A. Thomson said that after the war Hobbs was 'still to be the world's greatest batsman, in certain ways greater, certainly a more complete artist, but the sheer lightness of heart was no longer there'. Plum Warner, who played throughout the pre-war era, was once asked to describe Hobbs's early style and, perhaps surprisingly, said it was similar to that of Denis Compton, who was so adored by the 1940s cricket public for his cavalier spirit. This sentiment was echoed by Frank Woolley, an England player alongside Hobbs in every domestic Test series from 1909 to 1930. In his 1936 autobiography, Woolley wrote: 'As regards Jack's cricket, I feel I am going to run counter to popular opinion in what I have to say about it. There were two Jacks, the Pre- and the Post-War Jack. The *real* one was the Pre-War. Those of my readers who have seen only the Post-War one . . . have little idea of what the genuine article was like. Some batsman!'

The long-serving Warwickshire wicketkeeper E.J. 'Tiger' Smith, whose first-class career almost ran in parallel with Hobbs's, regarded him as 'the greatest all-round batsman I've seen, season in, season out, on all types of wickets.' He too witnessed the change in Hobbs's style over the span of the war: 'Before, he was as brilliant as Victor Trumper, with plenty of lofted drives and dazzling footwork. Afterwards he played the ball more on the ground and developed his masterful style.' Tiger Smith also revealed an intriguing, little-known fact about Hobbs's cricket, which makes his achievements all the more remarkable. 'Considering he suffered badly from migraine throughout his life, his career was magnificent. Many a time Jack would turn to me at the crease and ask if I had any pills for a headache but he never let people know how much he suffered.' Indeed, Hobbs, who had a powerful streak of Victorian reticence, hardly ever complained about this problem, though he did once ruefully admit towards the end of his playing days: 'All my life I have suffered a great deal from severe headaches and sometimes I have taken the field or batted when I hardly knew how to hold up my head.' But, for Smith, his admiration of Hobbs was only increased by the ailment. 'He was so cool, so masterful and relaxed, even though I've seen him totter at the crease many times because he was suffering from migraine.' Throughout his career Hobbs was never the most robust of players. His vulnerability was, perhaps, a legacy of his upbringing. Lacking great stamina, he regularly complained of fatigue at the end of a long innings or towards the close of a season, while heaviness of the county schedule was one of his strongest complaints about the life of a professional English cricketer. Migraines were just another factor in his occasional bouts of exhaustion.

It was perhaps a sense of staleness after his South African tour, as well as the appalling weather, that contributed to a disappointing summer for him in 1910. In all first-class games he scored 1,982 runs at 33.03, the lowest average of his career apart from his debut season. 'The wet weather was against him, and perhaps he felt the change from matting to turf wickets,' pronounced *Wisden* sympathetically. But Hobbs was fortified by a long break that winter, during which he took up golf seriously for the first time, his interest having been sparked by that first abortive round in South Africa with Strudwick. He came to adore the sport and played regularly with Strudwick well into his late seventies. The two men's annual post-season golfing holiday became a fixed ritual in their lives. In a private letter to a friend written in 1934, Hobbs explained the sport's appeal. 'It is a grand game. I am playing poorly at the present time but before long I shall be coming home after a round thinking I know all about the game and have nothing more to learn until I play again. The beauty of the game is that one can always play a perfect hole or two during a round even if one is playing badly.' In the winter he also played billiards, table tennis, squash and badminton, the last of them a sport that Ada also enjoyed. Now almost thirty, happily married with two young children, he was the personification of domestic contentment. He and Ada led quiet lives centred on their home in Mitcham but that was the way Hobbs liked it. His serenity in his personal sphere was symbolised by his fondness for his pipe, which he once described as 'a great consoler. Many a time when I have failed and when the bottom seems to have fallen out of the world, it has brought back peace to me.' Still the devoted son despite his fame, Hobbs continued to visit his mother and siblings in Cambridge, as John Witt, the son of Jack's youngest sister, recalls: 'My mother Gwen always said what a gentle person he was. She thought the world of him. She said he was ever so good to his mother. He would come down to Cambridge and give her a present or some money. We might be talking about a ten-bob note or five shillings.' Hobbs remained close to his sisters but there was more distance between him and some of his brothers. Sydney, who later ran a sports shop in Cambridge, had 'a chip on his shoulder' about all the adulation that Jack received, according to John Witt. In the same vein, when Frank, who served in the army and then worked for the local gas company, was interviewed by the local paper about his elder brother, he said brusquely, 'We knew he made a name for himself but we didn't think much of it.' The gap in fraternal relationships was to widen during the First World War and its aftermath.

Following his disappointing season in 1910, Hobbs's form improved significantly in 1911, helped by much better weather. 'This was undoubtedly the driest season for many, many years. Hardly a match was spoilt by rain and the heat at times was quite tropical,' wrote Ernie Hayes in his scrapbook. Hobbs's average in all-first-class games rose to 41.68 from 2,376 runs, including four centuries, and it was telling that some of his best innings were made in the biggest games, another reflection of his cool temperament. This was the first season that the cricket authorities held Test trials in England, representative games that supposedly would help the selectors to choose the national sides. But Hobbs felt that the trial matches were pointless because they were far too artificial to provide any real indicator of talent. The stable cricketer, he wrote, 'is playing against his own colleagues and it is impossible to get the Test match atmosphere'. A much more competitive contest, he believed, was the annual Gentlemen v Players at Lord's, which in 1911 resulted in an easy win for the amateurs despite an epic innings from Hobbs. The Players were set 423 to win, but on a lively pitch against an excellent Gents attack that included Johnny Douglas and the Warwickshire quick left-armer Frank Foster, they all failed to reach 50 except Hobbs, who carried his bat for 154 not out. He gave one chance to short leg on 94, but otherwise his innings was 'a wonderful feat', according to *Wisden* and 'worthy of a place among those that can legitimately be called great,' in the view of *The Times*. No fewer that 18,000 people paid to watch the match over three days, an indicator of the fixture's continuing appeal, but the pinnacle for any top player was still the Ashes. Indeed, with the growth of the popular press, Test cricket was becoming more important than ever in the second decade of the twentieth century, so there was tremendous interest in the MCC's prospects for their tour of Australia in the winter of 1911/12.

The team was captained by Plum Warner, the second time he had been handed the Ashes leadership, and had a strong batting line-up headed by Hobbs, Rhodes and Woolley. Previewing the tour, the former Australian captain Harry Trott predicted that Hobbs would prove the key figure at the top of the order: 'He is my ideal of what a perfect batsman should be, for he watches every ball carefully, his placing is perfection and, being a firm believer in keeping every ball "along the carpet", he rarely gives the fieldsman a chance of catching him. He has lovely strokes all round the wicket and can force the pace well when the ground is on the soft side.'

But England's bowling was just as powerful. In addition to Douglas, the most senior bowlers were Sydney Barnes and Frank Foster, two of the most unconventional individuals ever to have played for England. With his unique ability to spin the ball either way at above medium pace, Barnes was one of the greatest bowlers in history, with an astonishing record of 189 wickets in just twenty-seven matches. But he was also a ferociously independent, stubborn cricketer who felt that professionals were undervalued in the first-class game. He therefore largely plied his trade in the Lancashire League, one reason that Hobbs hardly ever faced him except in highly controversial circumstances during the First World War.

Frank Foster could not have been more different. A swashbuckling all-rounder and amateur, he had led Warwickshire to their first championship title in the summer of 1911, his deadly swing contributing enormously to this triumph. Rare in a quick left-armer, he tended to bowl round the wicket, and what made him so dangerous was his combination of movement, accuracy and pace off the wicket. For all his success at this time, he was an ultimately tragic figure whose life went rapidly downhill after a motorbike accident in the First World War that finished his playing career. Sinking into alcoholism, he grew increasingly eccentric, and was involved in a bizarre murder case in which a woman was found dead in his bed, though he was eventually cleared of any crime. He spent his last days in a lunatic asylum.

Long tours overseas were always difficult for Hobbs, given the wrench from his family and the apprehension of seasickness. Such a mood of anxiety explained why, for such a well-ordered and neat man, he could sometimes be rather flustered at the moment of departure. On the day of leaving for the 1909/10 tour of South Africa, he and Strudwick were reduced to sweating consternation by their failure to order a cab. Now, in September 1911, he was plunged into another state of panic when he did not realise that his watch was half an hour slow and he only made it onto the train with seconds to spare. Unfortunately he was in such a rush that, in the scramble to find his carriage, he lost sight of the porter with his suitcase. As the train rolled out of Victoria station, he could only watch in despair as the bewildered porter walked up and down the platform. The suitcase had to be sent on later, and did not reach him until his ship made a stop in its journey through the Mediterranean. In the meantime, Hobbs had to cope as best he could by borrowing items from Strudwick. The two men did not actually join the MCC party until Marseilles, for Hobbs, determined to avoid the rough passage through the Bay of Biscay, had arranged for them both to travel overland by rail through France. Just before the MCC left England, Hobbs had bet his Surrey colleague Bill Hitch, the junior paceman in Warner's team, that he would be seasick before the ship left the Bay of Biscay. Sturdy and self-confident, Hitch had happily accepted the wager. As Hobbs boarded the MCC's ship at Marseilles, Hitch greeted him with a forlorn grin and slipped half-a-crown into his hand.

The ship carrying the MCC was the 12,000-ton RMS *Orvieto*, a coal-fired liner built in 1909 in Belfast for the Orient Line. But the vessel's modernity could not prevent Hobbs suffering his usual crippling malady once he was at sea. 'I thought it impossible to go on living,' he wrote in his account of the tour. Nor was the voyage without other troubles. The players had looked forward to a stop in Naples but then found they could not go ashore because of a severe outbreak of cholera in the city. When the *Orvieto* reached the Bay of Taranto on Italy's southern coast, it was again prevented from docking, this time because the harbour had been laid with mines by the Italian navy as a precaution against any incursions by Turkish forces. In a harbinger of the conflict that would soon engulf the whole of Europe, Italy and Turkey had embarked on war in September 1911 as a result of a bitter dispute over colonial territories in North Africa. Attempting to compensate for the inconvenience caused to the passengers of the *Orvieto*, which had to remain offshore while supplies and mail were brought onboard, the Italians sent out a small boat carrying a brass band to provide some entertainment. As the musicians played, several of the England professionals, by now thoroughly bored with the whole episode, chucked pennies and small fruit down the ends of the large brass instruments. Hobbs, who had temporarily emerged from his cabin now that the *Orvieto* was anchored in a static position, joined in the barrage, for this was precisely the sort of silly prank that appealed to him. Once restocked, the *Orvieto* was allowed to creep through the dangerous waters, escorted by Italian torpedo boats, until the open sea was reached. Despite the disruptions and Hobbs's incapacity, the team spirit was excellent in the MCC party. 'I didn't hear one cross word pass between any of the players from October until April . . . and I spent many happy hours talking cricket with players of great knowledge,' recalled the wicketkeeper Tiger Smith. Again, as in previous MCC tours, the professionals were relatively well paid for the trip, each receiving £300 plus thirty shillings a week in expenses.

In the third week of October, the *Orvieto* finally arrived at Colombo, where Hobbs was grateful to step onto dry land but soon found he was confronted by the challenge of the intense heat in Ceylon. 'It was so hot that steam was rising from the ground,' remembered Frank Foster. In the sweltering conditions, the MCC visitors had to wear enormous khaki-coloured topees, the classic headgear of the Raj, when they played a one-day match on a slow wicket against the Colombo cricket club. Despite his physical weakness after the journey from England, Hobbs was the top scorer with 43 in a winning total of 213, showing his 'best form', according to the skipper Plum Warner. No fewer than 5,000 spectators gathered to watch the game, a reflection of the huge popularity of cricket on the island which would ultimately lead to Test status for Sri Lanka seventy years later. By an odd coincidence, the organiser of the match and the hospitality for the MCC was an official called E.O. Mackwood, whom Hobbs had coached in the nets at Bedford School in 1902.

After this pleasant interlude, the MCC travelled on to Australia, arriving there at the end of October. On reaching Adelaide, where they were to play their opening match, they were greeted by Jack Crawford, Hobbs's former teammate from the Oval who was now a schoolmaster in the city following his explosive fall-out with Leveson Gower and the Surrey Committee. The MCC's fixture at Adelaide was a personal triumph for Warner, who hit 151 in an easy victory over South Australia. Unfortunately for him, it was his first and last innings of the tour, for

soon afterwards he developed a serious stomach ulcer and was too ill
to play again. From his sickbed he instructed that Johnny Douglas should
take charge of the team. The only alternative leader would have been
Frank Foster, the gregarious Warwickshire captain, but Douglas was
preferred, said Warner, because he was 'senior in both age and experience', as well as being 'a great fighting man'. Hobbs was relieved at the
choice. He was sorry for Warner, whom he regarded as 'a fine skipper',
but Douglas was a cricketer he hugely admired. Indeed, during his career,
the only amateur he respected as much was his own post-war county
captain Percy Fender. In an interview with the *Sunday Dispatch* in June
1931, Hobbs explained his attachment to Douglas: 'It would have been
impossible to have a leader who was a keener fighter, a more dour and
determined performer with bat and ball. An uncompromising battler,
he was not popular with everyone but with those who knew him best
few men were more loved. What a fine fellow was Johnny Douglas. He
would stick with them through thick and thin to the end.' Tiger Smith
was also glad that Douglas had taken over the reins. 'Where Warner
always wanted the pros to look up to him and let them realise he was
the boss, Johnny was as straight as a gun barrel. There was none of this
"Mr Douglas" nonsense with him. He let you know where you stood
with him. He was one of us, more of a professional amateur than an
amateur of the old school. We all respected him greatly for his strong
qualities and his honesty.' There was another side of Douglas that
appealed to Hobbs: the new England skipper was a poor public speaker
and loathed the diplomatic circuit. 'I hate speeches,' he said during the
tour. Hobbs, with his inferiority complex and his terror of oratory, felt
nothing but empathy.

Despite all the support from his team, Douglas got off to a disastrous
start when the series began at the Sydney Cricket Ground in mid-
December. In the run-up to the first Test, several England batsmen had
struggled with their form, including Hobbs who had been afflicted by
sunstroke during a trip to Queensland, his condition later exacerbated
by the long train journey from Brisbane to Sydney. The carriages, wrote
Hobbs, 'were like furnaces during the whole twenty-seven and a half
hours we were travelling'. The form of Wilfred Rhodes was even worse.
Before the Test, he averaged just 14, with a top score of only 34, so he
was dropped down the order at Sydney and the debutant, Septimus
Kinneir of Warwickshire, was asked to open with Hobbs. But the bowling

rather than the batting was the real problem in the Test, and Douglas was accused of making a grievous error on the very first morning when he took the new ball himself alongside Frank Foster rather than giving it to Barnes. Not one endowed with either reticence or a low estimation of his own talent, Barnes openly expressed his fury at Douglas's decision. 'What does he think I am – a bloody change bowler?' he yelled across to Frank Woolley fielding nearby. 'Never mind, Syd, he's just going to take the shine off for you,' Woolley responded. Boiling in resentment, Barnes was not amused. The troubled start for England in the field allowed Australia to build an intimidating total of 447, with Victor Trumper hitting his final century in Test cricket. Going in on the afternoon of the second day, Hobbs and Kinneir made a reasonable start and put on 45 before Kinneir fell to Charlie Kellaway. Hobbs remained until the close, but he never felt on top of the bowling and edged through the slips several times. 'I was very slow and, until I got into the twenties, I couldn't time the ball a bit,' he wrote in his account of the tour. The next morning, he was out almost immediately, caught at forward short leg for 63. England fell badly behind and never recovered. In England's second innings, Hobbs started a sorry procession when he was out for 22, caught behind off a ball he tried to cut, as Australia cruised to victory by 146 runs.

The recriminations started quickly. So fierce were the attacks on Douglas's leadership that he invited all three of the senior professionals, Hobbs, Strudwick and Rhodes, to set down in writing their thoughts on where he had gone wrong in the Test. They all agreed that he should have put on Barnes first. But that was not the end of the matter. Plum Warner, still in his sickbed in a sanatorium but continuing to exert a powerful influence, felt that the issue of the captaincy had to be resolved before it became a crisis. So he called in the leading professionals, including Hobbs, to his bedside for a council of war. Crucially, Douglas himself was not invited to the meeting, an indicator of how sensitive the subject was. A number of players felt that Douglas had to go, but Hobbs held the opposite view. As a youth, he had been too shy to contribute to the meetings of the Ivy Club, and all his life he retained this diffidence. But he now felt a duty to speak out on behalf of a man he deeply admired. His remarks, all the more weighty because Hobbs rarely held forth with his views, were decisive. The majority voted in favour of keeping Douglas. Years later, Hobbs wrote, 'I have never regretted being on his side for he was always a cricketer and a man who had my admiration and respect: he was also a good friend.'

It turned out to be a wise decision. Douglas had learnt his lesson about the attack and, on the first morning of the second Test at Melbourne, he handed the new ball to Barnes. The proud, temperamental figure proved his point in the most emphatic style. On a perfect batting wicket, he produced the most lethal opening spell in Ashes history as Australia's top-order found him completely unplayable. At one stage, the hosts were 11 for 4, Barnes having taken the wickets of Charlie Kelleway, Warren Bardsley, Clem Hill and Warwick Armstrong. The England team could hardly believe what had happened. Bill Hitch ran over to Hobbs and, in his excitement, whispered, 'Jack, we've won the match.' Hitch was a little premature, for Australia staged something of a recovery to 184, but then England built up a substantial lead and had a final target of 219 to win. Hobbs, who had failed in the first innings, again caught behind off Cotter, was utterly dominant in the run-chase. His opening partner was Rhodes, now restored to his usual place, and together they put on 57 for the first wicket. Hobbs did not falter for a moment once Rhodes fell, but carried on driving, cutting and pulling all round the Melbourne ground. He was particularly hard on the leg-break and googly bowling of Dr H.V. Hordern, a dentist universally known as 'Ranji' because of his dark complexion. With his accuracy and cunningly disguised spin, Hordern was singled out by Hobbs as the biggest threat to England before the series began. 'He keeps a fine length – somewhat rare with a googly bowler – and makes the ball turn a good deal both ways without altering in the slightest degree his delivery. This great bowler is likely to do more for Australia in the Tests than any other two men,' Hobbs told the *Daily Mirror,* an opinion that was confirmed when Hordern took twelve wickets in the Australian win at Sydney. But in the second innings at Melbourne he had no answer to Hobbs's mastery and went for more than four runs an over. By the time the victory target had been reached for the loss of just two wickets, Hobbs had made 126 not out, his first century against Australia. Plum Warner, who had been watching from the stands, penned a generous tribute: 'It was a truly magnificent and faultless innings. He may have played more brilliantly in the past but never more finely. When he first went in, he restrained his natural desire to have a "go" at Cotter's off ball – a stroke that brought his downfall in the first innings and also in the Sydney Test match; but once he had got his eye in, his cutting was simply delightful, whether square or late, while he was also very strong in the off-drive and in playing to leg. Only once, indeed, did he make a faulty stroke and his crisp, wristy method of execution left nothing to be desired. He played Hordern either right back or jumped out and hit him.'

The ebb and flow of the series was generating unprecedented public enthusiasm for cricket in Australia. More than 96,000 people attended the Melbourne Test, easily a record. The vibrant nature of Hobbs's batting had helped to fuel this surge in popularity and in the next Test, at the Adelaide Oval, he continued in the same manner. Again Australia were bowled out cheaply, this time Foster acting as the destroyer with 5 for 36. Then Hobbs and Rhodes ruthlessly built on England's advantage with a stand of 147 for the first wicket. Once Rhodes had gone, Hobbs continued elegantly towards his second chanceless century in a row, his placement of the ball reducing the Australian captain Clem Hill to despair, as Tiger Smith recalled: 'Clem Hill tried to frustrate Jack by putting a man deep to block his square drive and square cut. But Jack didn't trouble – he kept placing his shots down the field and running an easy two.' After he had passed the hundred mark, Hobbs played with ever greater daring as he hit a stream of boundaries. But the intense heat also began to take its toll on him towards the end of the second day; it was 109 degrees Fahrenheit in the shade at some moments during the Adelaide Test. 'The weather was very hot and dry, without a breath of wind,' wrote Hobbs. One spectator had actually died from heat exhaustion on the previous day. As Hobbs fatigued, he began to make mistakes. The Australians missed him three times before he was eventually dismissed for 187, having batted for five and a half hours. 'I was so very tired that I was not at all sorry to get out,' he wrote. But he knew his achievement had put England in a wonderfully strong position. 'The story of yesterday's play practically surrounds Jack Hobbs,' said the *Manchester Guardian*. 'It is very evident from the scoring done by the England team in the last two matches that the terrorising "googly" has been fathomed . . . The Surrey man batted magnificently and his work received unstinted applause from the Adelaide crowd.' England eventually made 501, and though Australia fought a tough rearguard action in their second innings, it was not enough to prevent a defeat by seven wickets.

During the rest day of the Adelaide Test, Douglas's team had been invited for lunch at the residence of the Governor-General of South Australia, Admiral Sir Day Bosanquet. The weather was again roasting and as the team's convoy of motorcars headed towards Government House, the players noticed dense clouds of heavy smoke in the distance. Once they reached the entrance and parked their cars, they realised a bush fire was raging nearby, all the time coming closer to the Governor-General's house. The crackle of burning wood filled the air, sparks flew upwards and flames could be seen through the thick smoke. One group of players decided to drive back as fast as they could to central Adelaide, but Hobbs and his band pressed on by foot. 'Shielding our faces with our arms, we dashed along the narrow road, cut through a forest. Flames were bursting out on either side, and the smoke was blinding and suffocating. Dead chickens lay in the road, scorched to death. Many of the trees were pillars of flaming fire.' They made it through the inferno and reached the official residence, where they found Admiral Bosanquet and his staff fighting frantically to save the building. In the searing temperatures, windows cracked and timbers buckled. But the rescue operation, now ably assisted by the brawn of the England players, managed to hold back and eventually defeat the fire through the use of chains of men passing buckets of water from one to another. 'We had earned our lunch,' said Hobbs.

The heatwave continued across southern Australia after the Adelaide Test was over. The MCC's game against Victoria shortly before the fourth Test took place in a cauldron at Melbourne. Hardened farmers had sunstroke. Iron foundries had to close down because the tools were too hot for men to use. One train driver told Hobbs that if the oppressive heat continued 'some of us will be reduced to grease spots'. The mood at the top of Australian cricket had also reached boiling point, as a result of violent acrimony between the senior players, including Clem Hill, Warwick Armstrong and Victor Trumper, and the Australian Board of Control. The friction revolved around the appointment of the manager for the forthcoming tour of England in the summer of 1912, though this was really a symptom of a deeper power struggle between the key players and the administrative establishment. Shortly before the fourth Test, this discord came to a head at a meeting when Clem Hill reacted to some disparaging comments from Peter McAlister, the Chairman of the Selectors, by striking him in the face. 'You've been asking for a punch in the jaw all night and I'll give you one,' Hill is reported to have said as he swung his fist at McAlister. A twenty-minute brawl between the two men ensued before Hill was prised away and dragged out of the room by some colleagues. After shouting 'You coward!' at Hill as the door was closed, the bloodied and bruised figure of McAlister then returned to his seat at the table, where, with amazing aplomb, he resumed the meeting. But the combustible quarrel did nothing to restore the morale of a beleaguered Australian team already behind in the series.

On the eve of the fourth Test, the heatwave finally broke and Victoria was engulfed in a huge thunderstorm. After weeks of playing in parched surroundings, the players suddenly found themselves in much damper conditions. So when Douglas won the toss, he decided to take the field. For the third time in a row Barnes and Foster were irrepressible, bowling out the Australians for just 191. Yet the wicket seemed so much easier when Hobbs and Rhodes opened in the late afternoon. Ominously for Australia, they were still together at stumps, their unbroken partnership worth 54. The following day, in perfect batting conditions with blue skies overhead, the two stalwart professionals batted themselves into the record books with a colossal partnership of 323. As they continued to build the England total, the Australian attack was reduced to complete impotence. At one stage in the early afternoon, a large advertising balloon floated down and landed near the pitch, which prompted one wag in the crowd to yell out, 'There's another bowler for you, Clem.' Others in the 32,000 crowd were more forthright, with one barracker telling Hill, 'If you don't get them out, we'll shoot them.' Some of the Australian press, exasperated by the apparent invincibility of Hobbs and Rhodes, took to complaining about their supposed dourness. 'To call it playing a game is a misuse of words. They never smiled nor took risks,' said the *Melbourne Age*. But this was an unjustifiable charge. In fact, Hobbs scored at his usual rapid pace, reaching his century in just 133 minutes. His innings was almost without error until that milestone; then he hit out with more abandon, giving three chances before he was caught behind off Hordern for 178. Altogether, he made his runs in just four and a half hours and hit twenty-two 4s, a large number of them with the square cut. His triple-century stand with Rhodes was by far the biggest for the first wicket by an England pair in Test matches until then, and it remains an Ashes record to this day.

In contrast to the *Age*, most commentators were full of praise for their batting. 'They helped themselves to runs almost as they pleased;

the weakness of the Australian attack was completely and mercilessly exposed,' said the *Argus*. Tom Horan, the former Test cricketer, was even more rhapsodic in his column in the *Australasian* weekly paper: 'In the centre of the arena were two English batsmen, Hobbs and Rhodes, holding their positions hour after hour with a grim tenacity of purpose which made us feel proud of them as our kith and kin of the good old British stock.' The other England players were equally full of admiration, not just at the batting but also the running between the wickets, as Strudwick recalled: 'This was a most wonderful performance! What I saw was a glorious display of all strokes, beautifully timed and placed, while Hobbs and Rhodes running between the wickets was an education in itself.' Tiger Smith similarly felt privileged to have witnessed a master-class. 'I learnt more about the art of run-getting that day than before or since. Their command was effortless – Jack all graceful strokes and calmness, Wilfred, stiff-legged and sensible, working the ball away to his heart's content. Their running between the wickets was a joy. They avoided the fine fielders like Trumper and picked out poor Hordern. They kept playing the ball to his left hand at point and running singles. Once either moved they were off – no "yes" or "no" was needed.'

Hobbs himself once elaborated on the unique nature of his relation-ship with Rhodes: 'Many have firmly believed that there was some sort of telepathy between Rhodes and me; that our running between the wickets, particularly for the short single, had some magic thought-link about it. Actually, it was all based on simple, unbounded confidence in each other. Wilfred backed up so well that he was ready to run whenever I called. Whichever of us was the non-striking batsman would say no immediately, or simply run.' More sensitive than might be imagined from his genial, calm exterior, Hobbs later admitted that he was highly emotional after this historic innings. 'I have my moods. The reaction after success sometimes disturbs my sleep. When Rhodes and I got 323 for the first wicket I was really excited. That was my third century in succession and I was hot and feverish and when I got to bed I played all the strokes all over again,' he told the *Evening News* in 1925.

Their partnership helped England achieve a formidable total of 589, another Test record at the time. Broken by their ordeal in the field, Australia collapsed to 173 all out. It was appropriate that the skipper Johnny Douglas should use the occasion to take his first five-wicket haul of the series, for England's massive victory by an innings and 225

runs ensured that his team had won back the Ashes. Amid the celebrations in front of the Melbourne pavilion, Clem Hill made a gracious
speech in which he singled out the batting of Hobbs as a vital factor
in England's recovery of the famous urn. In the team hotel that evening,
the players enjoyed a special seven-course dinner with dishes named in
honour of the players, featuring such delights as Saddle Woolley Lamb
and Hobbled Asparagus, all rounded off with Ashes on Toast.

In addition to his astonishingly productive batting, Hobbs had also
driven England's victory charge with his exceptional fielding at cover.
Long gone were the memories of those early days with Surrey, when
he fielded in the deep and was roundly criticised for his clumsiness and
slowness. Under Leveson Gower's captaincy at Surrey, Hobbs had moved
from the outfield to the covers and in this new position he flourished.
The lumbering carthorse was transformed into a menacing panther.
Batsmen became mesmerised by the sleek figure of Hobbs patrolling
the off-side. Booming drives were blocked almost with insouciance.
Quick singles were full of danger. Apparently safe runs were suddenly
turned into desperate lunges over the line as Hobbs, in one flowing
movement, pounced on the ball and then hurled it at the keeper or the
stumps. 'I never saw – and never hope to see – a finer cover than Jack
Hobbs; even when there was cut on the ball, which so often happens
to take it away to the left, he hardly ever fumbled, and his throw-in was
perfect,' wrote the long-serving *Daily Express* cricket correspondent
William Pollock. Hobbs later explained that the early criticism of his
fielding had stung him into striving for improvement: 'In my early days
I was often told that I was a bad fieldsman – told by my captain, my
colleagues and the press. So it must be true, and I certainly came to
believe it. This was a reproach that I was determined to remove and I
studied the methods of the players who were admittedly good, and
where I could imitate them I did. Very soon I noted the beneficial effects.
And as soon I took a real pleasure in straining after perfection in this
department, I may claim that in time I became quite adept,' he wrote
in 1926.

Hobbs's prowess in the covers was based on a number of attributes.
First, although he did not have a long throw, he certainly had a fast and
accurate one. Contemporaries found it uncanny the way he could hit
the stumps or the keeper's gloves from almost any angle, a skill that
reflected the same unerring spatial judgement that he brought to his

batting. Again, as in his strokeplay, there was a perfect sense of timing in his arm action that helped to make his returns so swift. 'The only similar speed I've experienced was when I first kept to Harold Larwood,' said Strudwick of Hobbs's throwing. Hobbs's unique batting talent also gave him an instinctive sense of anticipation as a fielder. In a perceptive passage in a coaching manual, the Somerset cricketer Dar Lyon argued that this was the key to Hobbs's brilliance: 'Why was Hobbs the greatest cover in the game in modern times? It was because from his knowledge of batting he could tell by the way the batsman shaped for his stroke, by the movement of his feet, in what direction the ball was coming. He could judge at once whether the batsman was going to play the ball gently to cover or hard. If the former, Hobbs took two or three more quick steps in, so that the batsman would at least have to scamper like a frightened rabbit if he was to steal a short run. Again, he could usually tell, by watching the batsman's position, if the coming stroke would send the ball to cover's left or to his right.' Another factor was Hobbs's capacity for deception, a gift that mirrored the playful, mischievous side of his character. He loved to surprise batsmen by sudden changes of pace in his movements or by deliberately straying out of position. A vivid description of Hobbs's cunning art was provided by the *Daily Telegraph*'s Jim Swanton after witnessing him in action for Surrey: 'He would walk about in an innocent, preoccupied sort of way, hands often in pockets in between times. If the ball were pushed wide of him and the batsmen made to run, he would usually move at quite a leisurely speed to cut it off. Then suddenly an apparently identical stroke would be repeated and this time the relaxed figure would sprint into action with cat-like swiftness – there was a dart, a swoop, and the swiftest of flicks at the stumps, with the batsman pounding to the crease, as if for dear life.' All these skills were on display on the 1911/12 series, when he developed a fearsome reputation among the Australians for his dexterity and speed. During all matches on the tour he was estimated to have run out fifteen batsmen and it was said that in the Australian dressing room batsmen were instructed not to take a run to him. 'In Hobbs we had a cover-point the equal of any fieldsman in that position I have ever seen,' said Plum Warner.

England rounded off a tour of unprecedented success with victory by 70 runs in the fifth Test at Sydney. It was the first time they had ever won four Tests in a series against Australia. After scaling the heights of a trio of centuries in successive matches, Hobbs came down to earth with innings of 32 and 45, dismissed both times by Hordern, though he and Rhodes put together a stand of 76 in their last Test partnership of the series, almost exactly the same as England's margin of victory. It was perhaps appropriate that the last Australian wicket to fall was through a run-out by Hobbs, when Hordern tried to snatch a single only to have the stumps broken by a fast throw from cover. Hobbs's final record in the series was 662 runs at an average of 82.75, his aggregate of runs a Test record until it was beaten by Herbert Sutcliffe in the 1924/5 series. His former colleague Jack Crawford, who had recognised Hobbs's greatness from his first days at Surrey, said of him in this series: 'When he came to Australia in 1911/12 he was a far more mature – almost assertive – batsman. You could say that he simply did not have a weakness. He was never off balance and he was so quick without ever having to hurry. He seemed to flow through the strokes, yet he sometimes left the ball so late that you thought it was through, when he hit it for four.'

Hobbs and the MCC team returned home as national heroes and had a triumphant reception on their arrival in London. Later a banquet was organised in his honour in his hometown of Cambridge, where he was given an illuminated address as well as prolonged cheering. In his speech, Hobbs was, as usual, far too modest to say much about his own contribution but instead gave the credit to the spirit in the MCC party. 'The reason for our team's great success was that we were such a happy family. We had not a cross word with each other from the start to the finish of the tour.' The contrast with the Australian team could hardly have been greater, as the season of 1912 would prove.

8

'The Innings of a Great Master'

A mood of apprehension descended on Britain in 1912. The sinking of the *Titanic* in April could almost be seen as a metaphor for Britain's fading pre-eminence. The self-confidence and imperial splendour of the late-Victorian age had long evaporated, replaced by deepening concern about national decline. On every front, conflict seemed to be looming. Throughout industry and transport, strikes were rife. In March almost one million coalminers took industrial action, and in May more than 100,000 London dockers walked out. The country's economy suffered from intensifying global competition, especially from the USA and Germany. For the first time since the seventeenth century, there was a real danger of civil war on British soil, as the Liberal Government's attempts to assuage resurgent nationalism in Ireland by offering a measure of Home Rule were countered by the threat of armed rebellion from the overwhelming unionist north. Within Parliament, there was the permanent stench of corruption and crisis. The exhausted Prime Minister H.H. Asquith began to sink into alcoholism. Several of his ministers, including the Chancellor Lloyd George, were embroiled in a major scandal over insider trading of shares in the Marconi company. On the seas, Britain was engaged in a draining naval arms race against the German Empire, now under the neurotic but belligerent leadership of Kaiser Wilhelm II.

Hostility also reigned between the sexes in 1912. The Suffragettes, led by the redoubtable Emmeline Pankhurst, were becoming more militant in their campaign for women's voting rights in Westminster elections*. Hunger strikes, arson attacks and vandalism were amongst their tactics;

---

* Female ratepayers already had the vote in municipal elections.

one group of Suffragettes even tried to cause an explosion in Manchester using a mix of gunpowder and benzine, though the bomb caused only minimal damage. In response, the state became ever more authoritarian in its determination to weaken the movement. The leaders were frequently arrested and their offices raided. Women on hunger strike at Holloway prison were subjected to brutal force-feeding. 'Holloway became a place of horror and torment. Sickening scenes of violence took place almost every day, as the doctors went from cell to cell performing their hideous office,' wrote Pankhurst, who was herself incarcerated and force-fed in March 1912. The harsh treatment of the Suffragettes undoubtedly raised public sympathy, though the majority of men remained against an extension of the vote.

Yet it would be wrong to exaggerate the strength of masculine opposition. There was a sizeable group of men, including politicians such as the Labour leader Keir Hardie and the senior Tory Lord Robert Cecil, who backed the Suffragettes. Some of these campaigners even formed their own organisation, the Men's League for Women's Suffrage. One of the League's founders, the intellectual, author and playwright Laurence Housman, brother of the poet A.E. Housman, later wrote in his memoirs of the broadness of male support for the Suffragettes. As an indicator of this, he made the singular claim that Jack Hobbs himself was involved: 'More and more it became difficult to belittle a movement which could hold up the traffic in London with processions two or three miles long and decked from end to end with hundreds of banners, some of them of vast size, while in the ranks the most unexpected people were to be seen testifying their support of the movement. I think it was Jack Hobbs who one day startled the clubs of Piccadilly by joining the men's section in one of the big processions. When the hated cause had enlisted the support of a famous cricketer, matters indeed were becoming serious.'

On the surface this seems an unlikely statement. Throughout his life, Hobbs tried to avoid controversy and disliked large public gatherings. Even the cheers of cricket crowds left him embarrassed. Nor does there seem to be any evidence from press reports or archival material to back up Housman's claim. But perhaps Hobbs's involvement is not so fanciful. After all, he was the very opposite of a male chauvinist. Devoted to his mother, he was closer to his sisters than his brothers, and could hardly have been more solicitous to his wife Ada. During the 1920s he put his

England place at risk because of the priority that he attached to her happiness. Moreover, he was no diehard reactionary or political hermit. In 1925 he revealed that he had voted for both the Liberal and the Conservative parties in past General Elections, and he did occasionally give his backing to certain causes. During the Spanish Civil War, for instance, he condemned the deliberate bombing of civilians, while on two other occasions he argued against increased government taxation of businesses. Whatever the truth, Housman's image of Hobbs causing the members of clubland to splutter into their glasses of port is a compelling one.

The climate of conflict in 1912 also badly affected Australian cricket. The quarrel that had resulted in a punch-up between Clem Hill and Peter McAlister now led to a boycott by six top players of the England tour that summer. Along with Hill, five others – Armstrong, Trumper, Cotter, wicketkeeper Hanson Carter and the popular left-handed batsman Vernon Ransford – declined invitations on the grounds that the Australian Board of Control had imposed its own manager rather than accepting Frank Laver, the former Test all-rounder, who was the players' choice. Without the 'Big Six', as the boycotters were known, the Australians were a desperately weakened team. Led by the forty-two-year-old Syd Gregory, who had not played Test cricket the previous winter, they were described by Tiger Smith as 'the worst Australian side ever to reach England'.

The purpose of their visit was not another full-scale Ashes series but participation in the Triangular Tournament, a three-way Test competition with England and South Africa that was meant to cement the bonds of imperial cricket and raise the international profile of the game. The contest was the brainchild of the South African magnate and colonial dreamer Sir Abe Bailey, who had been the driving force behind the creation of the Imperial Cricket Conference as Test cricket's governing body. But his grand project of the Triangular Tournament turned out to be a disastrous flop, providing neither memorable cricket nor big crowds. The mediocrity of the emasculated Australians was one problem. Another was the decline in the quality of the South African side since their victory over England in 1909/10, partly because most of their players were far more used to playing on matting than on turf. An even bigger factor was the appalling weather that plagued England throughout the summer; the rainfall in June, July and August was twice the national

Jack Hobbs in his golden season of 1925, displaying the broad grin that so epitomised his spirit. 'No sportsman more truly deserved the hero-worship that Hobbs attained,' said one of his England captains.

(*Left*) The modest terraced home in Rivar Place, Cambridge, in which Jack was brought up in the late Victorian age.
(*Below*) The bleak Cambridge streets around his home.
'I detested the back road where we lived,' he once wrote.

Hobbs runs back to the Oval pavilion
at the end of a superb innings of 88
on his first-class debut in 1905.

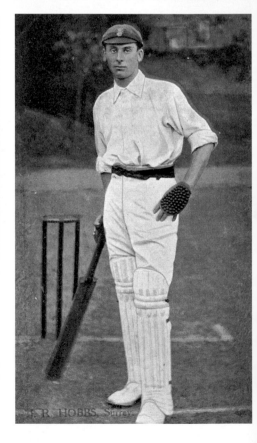

Hobbs at the crease after his first,
highly successful, Ashes tour, 1907/08.

Hobbs batting against the South Africans before the First World War: (*above*) at the rustic but picturesque Cape Town ground on the 1909/10 MCC tour and (*below*) at the Oval during the ill-fated 1912 Triangular Tournament.

Hobbs going out to bat in 1910 with his great Surrey opening partner, Tom Hayward.

Doughty Yorkshireman, Wilfred Rhodes, Hobbs's most successful England opening partner before the First World War. Their stand of 323 in the Melbourne Test of 1911/12 is still an England record in the Ashes.

Hobbs leaping down in the wicket. His pre-war
style was renowned for its sense of adventure.
(*Below*) The Yorkshire autocrat Lord Hawke.
His accusation that Hobbs was involved in
"scandalous behaviour" during the First World
War sparked a long feud between them.
(*Right*) The Surrey captain Percy Fender,
who was hugely admired by Hobbs

Hobbs at indoor net practice, completing the follow-through of a classical straight drive.

(*Below left*) Hobbs in a contemplative mood. 'I am very sensitive to criticism,' he once said. (*Below*) Hobbs in Italy during the trip out to Australia for the 1920/21 Ashes series. Also enjoying some sight-seeing are (left to right) Wilfred Rhodes, Frank Woolley and Herbert Strudwick

Hobbs on the balcony
at the Headingley Test,
1921. He was a very sick
man at the time and
was about to undergo
emergency surgery.

Hobbs batting
against South
Africa in the
Edgbaston
Test of 1924

The moment Hobbs brought
the nation to a standstill, equalling
W.G.Grace's record of 126
first-class centuries, Taunton, 1925

Hobbs, a teetotaller in the mid-
1920s, raises a glass of ginger
ale to mark his achievement
and toast the capacity crowd.

average. Above all, cricket followers became bored with a tournament that dragged on too long and featured too many rain-affected games where England had no involvement. As the *Daily Telegraph* put it, 'Nine tests provided a surfeit of cricket, and contests between Australia and South Africa are not a great attraction to the British public.' Against this troubled backdrop and the wider sense of malaise within the nation, England's dominance in the tournament provided nothing like the satisfaction that usually accompanied an Ashes triumph.

One of the few bright points in a bleak Test summer was the batting of Hobbs. If he was not quite the all-conquering figure of the winter Australian tour, he was still easily the finest batsman in the tournament. His form had been erratic at the start of the season, and in fourteen innings before England's first game in June, he had scored only one century, a knock of 104 against Nottinghamshire at Trent Bridge. The inconsistency continued in England's opening Test, against South Africa at Lord's, when he was bowled out in his first over by the left-arm medium-pacer Dave Nurse for just 4. As he later recorded, 'I played one on to my wicket in the first over, having hit a full toss past cover for 4. I tried to hit another; the ball swung a trifle and I got it on the edge of the bat.'

Except for Hobbs's pride, the dismissal mattered little. England thrashed South Africa by an innings and 62 runs. During South Africa's failing struggle to save the game in their second innings, the England captain C.B. Fry gave Hobbs an extended bowl after Frank Foster had suffered an injury to his hand, ironically caused by one of Hobbs's bullet-like returns from cover. 'We had the situation in hand in this match. I tried to produce Jack Hobbs as a fast bowler. My experiment did not win the approval of the critics. Jack Hobbs was a batsman, therefore he could not possibly be a bowler. All the same, but for his innate modesty, I would have made one of him,' explained Fry. It was the first home Test in which Hobbs had bowled but the venture achieved nothing dramatic. In eleven unthreatening overs, Hobbs went for 36 runs without taking a wicket.

As a batsman Hobbs fared much better in his next Test, against Australia at Lord's. The match itself was a rain-interrupted draw, with only three and a half hours' play possible on the first day and just twenty minutes' on the second. But this still provided enough time for Hobbs to give an exhibition of his unrivalled skill on a sticky wicket. Fry won the toss and decided to bat; Hobbs and Rhodes went out to open under grey skies. After less than two overs, the rain began to fall heavily, sending the players back into the pavilion until after the lunch interval. In the afternoon, the openers played with supreme judgement and restraint against the ball sometimes moving violently on a damp pitch which became all the more awkward once it started to dry. Their running between the wickets, as so often before, disheartened the fielders and captivated the spectators. 'Such perfect unison in running between the wickets I have never seen elsewhere. Neither called or made a sign,' wrote E.H.D. Sewell. Rhodes fell for 59 when the score was 112, but Hobbs went on to make 107, his first century at home against Australia. 'Very rarely has he shown finer cricket on a difficult wicket. Without being at all rash, he seemed to seize every opportunity for scoring,' said *Wisden,* while *Cricket* magazine declared that 'his innings of 107 must be ranked with the historic efforts in Tests for the pitch, without being exceptionally difficult, was never easy. It was ever a pitch on which nothing could be taken for granted; the ball was always turning and its pace and rise from the pitch varied.'

In this gloomy, damp summer, centuries were a rarity. In fact, Hobbs's was the only one made by an England player in the tournament. But though he failed to reach three figures again, he continued to perform solidly, hitting 55 against South Africa at Leeds and 68 against them at the Oval on what he called 'a slow, rain-sodden wicket'. The latter was a typically skilful innings in conditions so treacherous that no other batsman passed 42 in the match and South Africa were twice bowled out for under 100.

Once again *Wisden* enthused about his performance: 'Considering the state of the ground, this was very remarkable batting. Few batsmen could have played so well on such a wicket, his driving and pulling being superb.' In another tribute, *The Times* said that 'it was the innings of a great master'. As the cricket historian Clive Porter pointed out in his study of Hobbs's Test career, this was the first time in print that the Surrey batsman had been given the accolade. Later, in the golden summers of his long ascendancy during the 1920s, Hobbs would be widely known by the honorary title of 'The Master'.

The South Africans were confounded by the endless dankness that enveloped the tournament and soundly lost all three of their matches to England. The Australians struggled almost as badly. Their second

Test against England, at Old Trafford, ended in the same manner as the first, as heavy rain throughout the three days prevented much play. In England's only innings, Hobbs fell for 19, bowled by a full inswinger from the left-armer Bill Whitty. The mode of dismissal prompted the writer E.H.D. Sewell, always an outspoken, nostalgically minded critic, to complain about Hobbs's reluctance to go on the front foot in the manner of the classical heroes of the early Golden Age. Hobbs, he wrote, had been 'properly punished for his slavery to back play'. But Hobbs once again proved the strength of his technique with another invaluable innings in the final Test against Australia at the Oval. Because the outcome of the tournament was still undecided, this match was a timeless Test to be played to a finish.

England were on top from the start, thanks to another century opening stand from Hobbs and Rhodes. They would have put on even more than their 107 runs had it not been for a soaked outfield that prevented many of Hobbs pulls and drives reaching the boundary. Having given no chance, he was eventually out for 66, but his innings helped England build a big enough total to win the game by 244 runs. In Australia's disastrous second innings, when they were bundled out for just 65, Hobbs again demonstrated that adroitness in the field which had so shaken them during the previous winter's Ashes tour. Batting at number four, Warren Bardsley cut a ball to point and started to trot through for what he thought was an easy single. But he had not counted on Hobbs, who swooped down on the ball, and, in a single movement, turned and threw down the stumps at the bowler's end. Up went the umpire's finger, followed by an explosion of cheering from the Oval crowd. 'It was a magnificent bit of fielding, perfect from start to finish,' recalled Frank Woolley. Bardsley was so stunned that he refused to believe he was out and, in Hobbs's own words, 'remained at the wicket as if challenging the decision'. But the umpire, Jack Moss, confirmed his ruling: Bardsley had to go. There was a huge controversy about the incident, not so much over Bardsley's show of dissent, but over the correctness of Moss's verdict. The flames of the row burned all the more fiercely when two distinguished spectators in the pavilion, Ranji and Warner, publicly sided with Bardsley. But Hobbs felt this was nonsense, for the fielding side were in a much better position to see what had happened. 'Barnes, who was bowling, was quite clear that the batsman was out,' he wrote.

Australia's heavy defeat ensured England were the victors of the tournament, having won five of their six matches. For Hobbs, the twin series were confirmation of his international pre-eminence as a batsman. During the final game at the Oval, he passed 2,000 runs in Test cricket, the first Englishman to reach a landmark that had already been attained by Clem Hill and Victor Trumper. The summer also provided further proof of his temperament for the big occasion, since he batted much more productively for England than for Surrey. Altogether he hit just 1,012 runs at an average of 36.14 in the county championship, with only two centuries. What was noticeable about his appearances for Surrey was how much more carefree he had become. Compared to his adhesive performances for England, full of concentration and correct strokeplay, Hobbs at times seemed gloriously impetuous in his determination to go on the offensive. 'When I was young I thought I could do it all – and I tried to. You see, I enjoyed it so much and I was making runs all the time – and that was my living. I never took such risks after the war because I didn't feel I could,' he once said. It was a style that could electrify the crowds at county games but also, as *Wisden* pointed out, lead to 'more failures than one would have expected'. *Cricket* magazine worried about the downside of his 'new game', as the weekly described it. 'Whether Hobbs's batting will benefit in the end by this new game, or rather by the habitual adoption of daring, forcing methods, is a question apart. Hobbs's new game tends towards recklessness; while it exhilarates the spectator, it is apt to intoxicate the batsman.'

Interestingly, the word 'reckless' was used by Hobbs himself to describe his innings that summer for Players against the Gents at Lord's, when he blazed away to 94 before he was stumped trying to hit the six that would bring him his century. He was even more flamboyant in the Players v Gents game at the Oval. After being bowled out for a duck by Frank Foster in the first innings, Hobbs went on the rampage in the second innings, smashing 54 in just twenty minutes. The bowler that suffered most was Bill Greswell, the Somerset slow-medium pacer whose gentle inswingers kept disappearing over the leg-side boundary until Hobbs played one daring stroke too many and was caught. Not everyone was delighted by Hobbs's exhibition. Soon after the match he received this letter, which must have been written by a schoolboy: 'Swanker – You thought yourself very clever for getting a few fours off Greswell and you only did it to pander to the Oval mob, which you are always doing.

They applaud anything Surrey do there, even if Hobbs Esq. misfields a ball! You had not so much side on Friday when Foster bowled you for a duck! England would fall to pieces without you – I don't think.'

Remarkably, the summer of 1912 was the last time Hobbs was to bat for England in a home Test for the next twelve years, this long, barren spell resulting from a mixture of war, illness and the limited number of Test matches in the early twentieth century. For the next two seasons, England did not play any Test series at home and the entire focus of the English cricket world was on the county championship. Nor was there any major tour in the winter of 1912/13. The MCC sent a first-class party to the West Indies, but it contained only one Test cricketer, the Sussex all-rounder Albert Relf.

Often prone to weariness, Hobbs was grateful for the break. 'After the strenuous season, which had followed a tour of Australia, which in its turn had been preceded by a full summer's cricket, it was a treat to be able to be lazy,' said Hobbs. But he was hardly lazy in the off-season. Always keen to attain financial security, he accepted a post in 1913 as a private cricket coach to the son of Friedrich Eckstein, a South African who had made his fortune in gold mining and built a magnificent stately home at Ottershaw Park in Surrey.

Like many top players, Hobbs was never a great cricket coach, largely because the sport came so naturally to him. His own first cricket book, a batting manual entitled *How to Make a Century*, was published in 1913 by Adam and Charles Black but provided few real insights into his craft. The essential narrative was to take the reader through the construction of an innings, from the first delivery, through the growing sense of command until the hundred was attained. But the impact of the book was undermined by both the stagey, posed photographs and the ghostwritten text, archaic even for the time and filled with phrases such as 'upon my word' and 'beastly severe'. One interesting point, however, was that Hobbs reiterated his belief in back-foot play, despite the criticism he received from purists. 'Forward play must never be allowed to dominate a man's batting to the exclusion of everything else or it will do a great deal more harm than good. For preference, if the argument is pushed to an extreme, I would rather have a man play "all back" than "all forward" and I do not mind how many coaches of the old school shake their heads at that remark,' he wrote.

Aside from private coaching, Hobbs was going through a time of upheaval in his own private life. After almost seven years of moving from one rented home to another, he and Ada finally bought their own house, 17 Englewood Road beside Clapham Common. Built in the 1890s, it was a classic late-Victorian terraced property, with a mock-tudor timbered gable over the bay windows and an attractive arched entrance. This was a very different home to the cramped one in which he had been raised at Rivar Place. The journey from the back streets of Cambridge to prosperous south London suburbia was a graphic illustration of Hobbs's own growing stature, as well as the rising status of the professional cricketer. By 1913, Hobbs's Surrey contract was worth around £375, excluding talent money, bonuses and England fees. This put him in the same comfortable bracket as much of the outer London middle-class. In exactly the same year, Noël Coward, another figure who, like Hobbs, was to become an English cultural icon during the interwar years, also moved to a house by Clapham Common.

Coward was only a boy of fourteen then but he had vivid memories of the area, which he later recounted: 'Clapham Common was a nice place to live. There was a pond opposite the house in which Father used to indulge his passion for sailing a model yacht . . . We used to take our tea out under the trees during the summer and play bat-and-ball afterwards. There were pleasant walks in Clapham along tree-shaded roads, neatly spaced with refined suburban houses, secure in small prosperity with their conservatories and stained-glass windows and croquet lawns.' One of the less attractive features that Coward remembered was the City and South London Railway, later part of the Northern Line on the London underground network and a line that Hobbs regularly used for the Oval. 'It was unique in uncomfortable charm. The trains were smaller than any of the other tubes and rattled alarmingly, and over it all brooded a peculiar pungent stink which will live somewhere in the back of my nostrils forever.' Whatever the aromatic drawbacks of the transport system, Hobbs and Ada enjoyed living in Englewood Road, especially because of its convenience and tranquillity. Their family was also growing in size: their third child, Vera, the inadvertent source of much domestic anguish in their twilight years, was born in April 1913 and she was followed in August 1914 by their fourth and last child Ivor.

Refreshed by a winter devoid of competitive cricket, increasingly mature because of his experience and family responsibilities, Hobbs enjoyed one of the most successful domestic seasons of his career in

1913. Now aged thirty, he managed to fuse the two sides of his game – the exuberant and the correct – into one devastating whole. Unlike in 1912, there was no air of recklessness in his Surrey appearances, just masterful authority. Altogether, he averaged 52 for his club and hit eight centuries, while in all first-class matches in 1913 he made 2,605 runs at 50.09, putting him in second place in the national batting averages just behind Phil Mead. Twice against Gloucestershire, both home and away, he hit a hundred before lunch on the first day, while he also stroked his way to a century against Hampshire at Southampton in exactly one hundred minutes. His opening partnership with the veteran Tom Hayward, now in the penultimate season of his career, was more impregnable than ever. In one of their most towering performances, they put on 313 runs for the first wicket in just 190 minutes against Worcestershire, Hobbs hitting the bowling all round the wicket for 184. 1913 was also the season when Hayward, moustache bristling more triumphantly than ever, became the first cricketer since W.G. Grace to hit a hundred centuries in a career. The milestone was reached at the Oval against Somerset and Hobbs, with genuine appreciation, expressed his 'supreme delight' at the achievement. 'I well remember Tom's wonderful reception, and the crowd cheering for several minutes.' But Hobbs's finest innings involved neither a century nor Surrey. On the final afternoon of the annual Gents against the Players match at Lord's, Hobbs led a thrilling run-chase of a target of 123 runs in 105 minutes. On a rain-affected wicket, he and Rhodes made a meteoric start, scoring 87 runs in sixty-five minutes before Rhodes was dismissed. The professionals then fell behind the clock, thanks to some tight bowling and fielding by the amateurs before Hobbs managed to bring the scores level. Then, in the penultimate over, Hobbs cut Jessop to the boundary to achieve the win and bring his own score up to 72 not out. The innings was another reflection of his supremacy in English cricket. In its annual review of the 1913 season, *Wisden* paid its most lavish tribute yet: 'For a batsman who attempts so much, he was wonderfully consistent, keeping up his form to the end of the season. The remarkable thing about Hobbs is that he is great on all sorts of wickets. No player now before the public in England could have played as well as he did on the soft ground in the Triangular Tournament of 1912 and in 1911, on a crumbled pitch at Lord's, he scored 154 not out against the Gentlemen. Over and above his brilliant doings in England he has found himself as much at home on the matting wickets of South Africa as on the billiard-table pitches of Sydney and Melbourne. Highly tried under all conditions, he has come out as incontestably one of the greatest bats of his generation. Last season he was at his best for Surrey, and was beyond question the chief attraction to the public at the Oval. When he was getting runs there was no idle talk about cricket having become dull or uninteresting. Perfection of footwork is, of course, one of the main causes of his success. No one else can, quite so quickly, get into the right position for every sort of hit. Hence his surprising adaptability to varying conditions of ground.'

That winter Hobbs went as the star batsman in the strongest side the MCC had yet sent to South Africa. Led by Johnny Douglas, the team's professionals included Strudwick, Rhodes, Relf, Woolley, Mead, the young Yorkshire all-rounder Major Booth* and, above all, Sydney Barnes, whose bowling on matting wickets was almost impossible to play. Hobbs himself was now renowned for his skill on all types of wickets and South Africa cricket followers were glad to welcome such a distinguished but modest celebrity, as the *Cape Town Times* recorded: 'He first of all lays us under an obligation by showing us the greatest of all batting, without ever being in danger of requiring bigger-sized headgear. That's why we like you and your pals, Mr Hobbs.'

The challenge of the South African matting wickets was unique because of the bounce, pace and capacity for turn yet, as Hobbs pointed out, they also offered a truer surface than many of the soft, damp pitches in England. 'A ball never rears up or does unexpected things on a matting pitch but I should say that as a rule it comes a little higher on to the bat,' Hobbs wrote in the *Strand* magazine in 1912. 'They are fast too, those matting pitches, often a good bit faster than even what is called a fast wicket at home. The bowler has plenty of scope on them, as the surface holds together quite well enough to enable the breaking ball to get in its bite and come twisting off the pitch in a way that gives full value for every atom of spin. But the leather does nothing more or less than this on a matting pitch – there are none of those little accidental effects which can surprise both batsman and bowler on a turf wicket.'

More relaxed than ever in his home life and his cricket, Hobbs went through none of the logistical anxieties that preceded his two most

---

* 'Major' was his Christian name and had nothing to do with military service.

recent tours. He called a cab, made sure that his watch was set correctly, and reached Waterloo with time to spare. But he could not avoid suffering his usual seasickness during parts of a voyage that lasted eighteen days, though the waters became calmer once the ship reached the south Atlantic.

On their arrival, the MCC team found that the immediate pre-war mood of conflict extended to South Africa. As in Britain, there was widespread industrial strife, with lengthy disputes crippling the railways and the mines. In Johannesburg, a general strike began in January 1914, which prompted the government to declare martial law, intern the trade union leaders and impose a strict curfew across the region. 'We had to get permits to go about and every night we were obliged to be in the hotel by nine o'clock. Anybody in the street after that hour was arrested by the military patrols, and night after night we heard the tramp of those patrols outside our windows,' recalled Hobbs. At a match in the city of Benoni, east of Johannesburg, the MCC played in a completely empty ground, because the military authorities had banned all public gatherings for fear of trouble.

The hostility between the Afrikaners and the British, a legacy of the Boer War, also impinged on the MCC at times. In one incident, the MCC team arrived at the railway station in Bloemfontein, in the heart of Boer territory, where the mayor and other civic dignitaries had organised an official reception. Unfortunately the players, having alighted from the train feeling tired, did not realise that the crowd that they saw standing at the far end of the platform was a municipal welcome party, so when their motor coach drew up at an entrance nearby, they just walked through an open gate and climbed on board without much thought. But the mayor of Bloemfontein and his colleagues were furious. They felt they had been the victims of a deliberate snub. The episode was reported in the press. Furious editorials were written. Social functions were called off. A trip to the local Boer battlefield was cancelled. All too aware of the frostiness, the MCC ensured their match at Bloemfontein was over as quickly as possible. Barnes and Rhodes, wrote Tiger Smith, 'decided that we weren't going to hang around there too long. They bowled the opposition out twice in a day and we left in a hurry.'

In addition, the England team had serious difficulties with their manager. The South African Cricket Association had to meet all the costs of the trip, including the £200 fee for each player, and therefore insisted not only on restricting the size of the MCC side to just thirteen, but also on appointing its own manager, Ivor Difford, a former Transvaal player. The relationship between Difford and the Englishmen was fraught. They regarded him as untrustworthy, hypocritical and stingy, and were particularly incensed when they believed he was responsible for spreading rumours that they were a gang of heavy drinkers, a ridiculous piece of gossip given that most of the players, like Hobbs, rarely touched alcohol. What made this insinuation all the more insulting was that they felt Difford himself was abusing the hospitality allowance. The aggravation was compounded at the end of the tour as Difford tried to reduce some of the players' fees on the most trivial or unjust grounds: Mead had five pounds deducted for supposedly being unfit, while Tiger Smith had no less than fifty pounds taken from his payout because he had only played in a few matches. 'There was a hell of a rumpus. Johnny Douglas argued with Difford, made sure I got my two hundred pounds and all the other lads got their full whack as well,' recalled Smith.

Hobbs had a few of his own troubles on the tour. He was disturbed to find out that, during his stay in Kimberley, the capital of the northern Cape, he was a victim of impersonation by an audacious fraudster. In the days before television and news photography, Hobbs's deeds were well known around the British Empire, but his face was not, a fact exploited by the criminal to indulge himself. One day at the cricket a local South African fell into conversation with a member of the MCC team.

'Queer chap, Hobbs, isn't he?' said the South African.

The MCC player was puzzled. 'Hobbs is all right. Why do you call him queer?'

'Well, he was in a hotel last night and asked if anybody was going to buy him a drink, after which he borrowed a couple of pounds.' The player laughed at the absurdity of this tale. The idea of the abstemious, prudent Jack Hobbs borrowing money to pay for drinks in a public bar was ridiculous. He said that there must have been some mistake, but the South African did not seem convinced. The next morning the extent of the fraud became more apparent. First Hobbs received a bill for three bottles of champagne from a hotel he had never visited. Then, just as Hobbs in his bewilderment was showing this bill to some of his team-mates, a man strode up to him.

'Good morning, Mr Hobbs, and thank you so much for placing that order at my shop yesterday.' The grateful stranger turned out to be a tailor. Hobbs later wrote, 'I had never seen his shop and it became obvious that someone was going round the town impersonating me. We took steps to find out who he was but he disappeared.' Fortunately, Hobbs did not have to pay any of the bills, and in later years he expressed his amusement at the saga, which was, in an indirect way, a tribute to his international fame.

A far more serious incident occurred when Hobbs and two colleagues were making a road trip to Amanzimtoti, a seaside resort south of Durban. It was the moment when Hobbs came closest to death during his early career as a professional, and only by amazing good fortune did he escape serious injury. During the rest day of the Durban Test, he, Strudwick and Booth were in a car being driven by a chauffeur, who assured them he was fully competent, though motoring was still something of a novelty before the First World War. As the three men enjoyed the coastal scenery, the vehicle approached a narrow railway bridge. Ahead on the road was a slow-moving horse and trap. The driver decided he could overtake the trap before he reached the bridge so he stepped on the accelerator. But, to his horror, just as the road narrowed he found he had no room to pass. In his desperation, he slammed on the brakes. Amidst the sound of screeching tyres, the car skidded off the road, went out of control, and smashed through a gate. Just as the car's front end dug into the ground, causing the vehicle to begin a somersault, Hobbs was hurled over the windscreen and Strudwick was thrown out the side. 'The next thing I remember was picking myself up in the road, while feeling myself all over to see if I was still intact,' wrote Strudwick. He was. So too, miraculously, was Hobbs, who had suffered no more than minor grazes. The two men stared at each other in relief and shock, then they heard a muffled scream from beneath the overturned, crumpled vehicle. Together, they managed to lift it off the ground just enough for Booth and the driver to crawl out. Like the other two, Booth was almost uninjured, but the driver was covered in blood and badly hurt. Yet he refused all offers of help and instead slipped away from the scene. Following a police investigation into the incident, it emerged that he was working without a licence. Shaken but grateful to be so unharmed, the English trio managed to get a lift back to the team hotel in Durban, where they took some rest in their rooms before

venturing downstairs in the evening. By now, news of the accident
had reached Johnny Douglas, who had gone on a separate trip that
day. As is so often the way with reports that are filtered through several
sources, Douglas was informed that half his team 'had been killed in
a terrible accident'. Panic-stricken, he rushed back to the hotel, only
to find Hobbs, Strudwick and Booth chatting happily on the veranda.
'His relief was great,' wrote Hobbs with typical understatement.

The social side of the tour was not by any means entirely negative.
Hobbs took up fishing for the first time, played some football, and,
along with the rest of the team, enjoyed the hospitality of several wealthy
cricket patrons such as Sir George Farrar, the mining tycoon, politician
and soldier. One memorable Sunday the MCC squad were invited to
the estate that Farrar had created at Bedford Farm near Johannesburg.
'We were lavishly entertained,' wrote Hobbs, 'driving out in cars, croquet
and tennis, lunch and tea; altogether a happy day.' In spite of all the
political troubles and hair-raising personal experiences, Hobbs said that
he had 'a real good time on this tour. I knew the ropes and was meeting
friends I had made on my last visit.'

Successful cricket added to his pleasure. England were utterly
dominant in the Test series, winning four of the five matches and
drawing the other. Almost all the South African batsmen were helpless
against the bowling of Sydney Barnes, who took forty-nine wickets, still
a world record. The only exception was the South African captain,
Herbie Taylor. His elegant method, which enabled him to play Barnes
with confidence and score 508 runs at 50.80 in the series, often drew
comparisons with Hobbs, as Ian Peebles once wrote: 'Both founded an
impeccable defence and a great array of strokes, on a fundamental but
rare quality of batsmanship. When they played forward, they played at
the maximum range of front foot and top hand, and when they played
back it was as close to the stumps as practical considerations would
permit. It was not easy for a bowler to drop away on a spot where he
could not be smothered or conveniently be seen and met from the
pitch.'

As if to prove the point, Hobbs had just as good a series as Taylor.
He scored slightly fewer runs, 443, but at the significantly higher average
of 63.28. In the whole tour, he made 1,596 runs at 63, leading *Wisden*
to hail him as 'an absolute master on matting wickets. It was said that
he was not quite so brilliant as in England, but, judging by results, he

did wonders.' Surprisingly, he did not score a century in the series, though he came close on three occasions, hitting 82 in the first Test, 92 in the third and 97 in the fourth, the last an innings that guaranteed England a draw on the final afternoon. Some critics pointed out that he did not play with the same freedom that he employed with Surrey, but again this just emphasised Hobbs's temperament for Test cricket. As he himself wrote, he felt that when playing for England 'my value to my side was more apparent to me and I felt my duty and responsibility'. The other key aspect of England's batting during the series was the continuing sureness of Hobbs's opening partnership with Rhodes, as they put on two century stands and another worth 92. Oddly, in the second Test at Johannesburg, Hobbs was dropped down the order to number three, since Douglas choose to open the innings with Rhodes and Albert Relf because of his unusual theory that the Sussex all-rounder should be batted into form by being given more responsibility. The stratagem worked well for Relf, who made 63, but was not so fruitful for Hobbs, who scored only 23. In the third Test, Hobbs was restored to his rightful position alongside Rhodes. Altogether, their partnership averaged 68, following averages of 42 in the Triangular Tournament and 90 on the 1911/12 tour Australia. In terms of style, Rhodes may not have been a great batsman, but he was one of pillars of Hobbs's greatness in the pre-war years. 'I had a very happy association with Wilfred,' Hobbs once said.

Soon after England's return from South Africa, the 1914 season began. Hobbs was now at his zenith, his batting a rich synthesis of daring and consistency. He was the benevolent monarch of English cricket, wielding his unparalleled influence with a smile. 'Hobbs stands forth on his own, the most remarkable batsman of his time,' declared *Cricket Chat* in its opening edition for the season. Archie MacLaren, once one of Hobbs's strongest critics, demonstrated the heights of his admiration in *The World of Cricket*, the new threepenny magazine that he now edited. In an article headlined 'The Surrey Super-Batsman', the weekly trumpeted: 'Great is John Hobbs! If a poll could be taken at the present time among all who follow cricket the wide world over, as to who is the first among the batsmen of the day, it is probable that 90 per cent of the vote would be given to John Berry Hobbs.' The magazine then extolled the virtues of his style: 'No bowler can tie him up for very long'; he 'often makes quite good bowling look easy'; 'he has in his repertoire strokes that are beyond the ken of the merely good batsmen'. *The World of Cricket* concluded: 'He was a good batsman in 1905, a great batsman in the making. Now he is the great batsman made.'

The Surrey Committee shared in this appreciation of his greatness by awarding him a benefit in 1914 in recognition of his tenth season of service with the club. In this era, benefits were seen by professionals as a mixed blessing. On one hand they could be extremely lucrative in the right circumstances, as George Hirst discovered in 1904 when he made £3,703. On the other hand, they were subject to the vagaries of fate, the player's form and the weather. A benefit match, always a crucial element of the fundraising, might be a washout or over in a day, thus dramatically reducing the gate money. It was precisely to avoid the injustice of chance that in 1911 Surrey, more enlightened than most other counties, introduced a system whereby the beneficiary would be guaranteed £500, the club making up any shortfall between this sum and the actual total of donations, subscriptions and takings. Surrey also promised to give every beneficiary a grant of £50 to start off the public appeal. But the club could afford to be generous as it was by far the wealthiest in England. During the two decades before the First World War, Surrey made an annual average profit of £1,005, compared to Yorkshire's £550 a year. Most other counties struggled to break even or made losses. Surrey's munificence also came with the key condition that the club would hold on to the beneficiary's money to ensure that it was invested wisely rather than squandered. This practice, followed by most other counties, was seen as the worst sort of condescending paternalism by professionals like Wilfred Rhodes, who considered it 'a scandal' that proceeds of a benefit were not the property of the player. As it turned out, however, Surrey's protective attitude would rescue Hobbs later in the summer when the gathering storm clouds of war threatened to eclipse his benefit completely.

The club's First XI was under new leadership in 1914 after Morice Bird had given up the captaincy because of business commitments. The new skipper was Cyril Wilkinson, a gifted lawyer who went on to become the Registrar of the Probate and Divorce Registry for twenty-three years. He was also a fine athlete, later winning a gold medal in hockey at the 1920 Antwerp Olympics. As a cricketer, he was a neat, sound batsman, far more competent than many of the amateur figureheads who graced the county circuit. Wilkinson brought no great tactical nous to his captaincy, but he was a firm leader, respected by his players, and in 1914 the team flourished under him after years of failing to live up to expectations. Another ingredient in Surrey's improvement was the arrival of the effervescent, unorthodox all-rounder Percy Fender, who, after two years with Sussex, returned to the county of his birth.

But by far the greatest factor was the phenomenal batting of Hobbs. After a patchy start, he truly struck form in the match at the end of May against Yorkshire at Bradford Park Avenue. On a soft wicket in the first innings, against an attack made up of Rhodes, Hirst, Booth and the left-armer Alonzo Drake, Hobbs hit a blistering century in just seventy-five minutes with no fewer than five 6s. In the second innings, Hobbs was almost as scintillating, even though the wicket had deteriorated. One of his towering blows, hit off a ball from Drake, sailed straight into a clock on top of the pavilion and drove the hands back half an hour. 'Well, Jack, tha' should have knocked the ruddy thing to half-past six, and then we'd be rid of thee,' said Drake. Hobbs's score of 75 was easily the highest in a total of 179, which was sufficient to give Surrey a victory by 28 runs in a thrilling contest.

After this, Hobbs was almost unstoppable. In Surrey's next match, in an innings victory at the Oval against Warwickshire, he made 183. Then, in mid-June, against Essex at Leyton, he showed his unrivalled brilliance by hitting 215 not out in four hours, an extraordinary achievement given that no other Surrey batsman made more than 27. 'His cricket was perfect and his hitting often exceptionally brilliant,' said *Wisden*. It was the highest score of his career to date, and it was followed a week later by 163 against Hampshire at the Oval. Hobbs maintained the run feast in July, with centuries for Surrey against Lancashire at the Oval and against Kent at Blackheath, where he and Hayward put on 234 for the first wicket in just 175 minutes. The leg-spinner Douglas Carr, who had played for England in the 1909 Ashes series, was punished so severely that he completely lost his line and length and never played first-class cricket again. It was not just Surrey that gained from Hobbs's batting. In early July, for the Players against the Gents at the Oval, he scored 156, twice as many as any other batsman in the match.

But all this profuse midsummer batting took place against the backdrop of the slide towards war. The animosities between the great imperial powers of Europe, crackling for more than a decade, now exploded into open belligerence. On 28 June, as Hobbs fielded for Surrey in their

county championship match against Middlesex at the Oval, far away in
the Bosnian capital of Sarajevo, Archduke Franz Ferdinand, heir to the
throne of the Austro-Hungarian Empire, was shot dead by a Serbian
nationalist, Gavrilo Princip. The assassination sparked an incendiary
chain reaction that soon had the flames of conflict spreading across
Europe. In retaliation for the murder of the Archduke, Austria threatened
to attack Serbia, an action for which Kaiser Wilhelm II pledged the full
support of his military forces. Russia and France responded by promising
to back Serbia. Full-scale war was now inevitable, and, because of her
allegiance to France, it was difficult for Britain to avoid being dragged
into the conflagration, especially after the Kaiser issued a bellicose ulti-
matum to neutral Belgium demanding passage for the German armies
through her territory. The menace shown by the Second Reich towards
Belgium united most of Asquith's Liberal Cabinet in favour of military
action. The home fleet, already on summer manoeuvres, was partly
mobilised in late July. A Council of War was held in Downing Street on
3 August, at which it was agreed to put through the orders for the full
mobilisation of the remainder of the Royal Navy and the entire British
Army, including the reserves and the territorials. In an atmosphere of
growing tension, huge crowds gathered around Whitehall and Buckingham
Palace, desperate for news or a sense of solidarity with others in this
hour of crisis. The next day, 4 August, the last flickering hopes for peace
were extinguished as the might of the Reich launched its invasion of
Belgium. The British Government warned that it would fight alongside
France. By 11 p.m. that night, the country was at war with Germany.

'The lamps are going out all over Europe. We shall not see them lit
again in our time,' the Liberal Foreign Secretary Sir Edward Grey
famously remarked on the eve of the war's declaration, though even
he could not have imagined the scale of the horrors that would follow
over the next four years. Yet, in the midst of the encircling gloom, the
attitude of the nation in the first week of August could almost be
described as schizophrenic. Alongside the deep apprehension and fear,
there was a willingness to suspend reality, a determination to enjoy the
summer whatever was happening on the continent. Excellent, almost
sultry, weather and the Bank Holiday on 3 August exacerbated this
dichotomy, which was reflected in packed beaches at the seaside and in
large attendances at cricket matches. On the Bank Holiday Monday,
the Oval was almost full to see the start of Surrey's game against

Nottinghamshire, with 15,000 people in the ground. A fascinating description of the scene was later provided by Andy Kempton, the Surrey member and close friend of Hobbs, his account also illustrating the profound sense of obligation that Hobbs felt towards the cricket public. 'I shall never forget the August Bank Holiday of 1914. In the morning I was parading on Whitehall, where thousands of others, like me, were awaiting with anxiety the declaration of war with Germany. I realised that nothing mattered when compared with the likelihood of this huge European conflict. No news leaked out, and just before noon I arrived at the Oval, fully prepared to be told that the Surrey v Notts match would not be commenced. Cricket is an extraordinary game, for while outside the Oval the world was in a state of great tension, I was amazed to find a vast crowd of several thousands concerned only with the likelihood of Hobbs getting another century. Surrey had won the toss! What mattered if we did have a silly old war, so long as Jack Hobbs gave us something worth looking at?' Kempton went into the Surrey dressing room to have a word with his friend, only to find Hobbs in agony from one of his migraine headaches.

'You cannot play in that state,' said Kempton, disturbed at how ill Hobbs seemed.

Hobbs rose to his feet and pointed to the waiting crowd. 'Do you see those thousands to whom a fine Bank Holiday is rare? They've come to see Surrey and expect me to do something big.'

A few minutes later, Hobbs staggered out the door to face the Nottinghamshire attack, which was led by the young tearaway fast bowler Fred Barratt, later an England cricketer. 'He was a sick man but he thought only of those who had come to see him and he gave of his best,' wrote Kempton. Hobbs survived through to lunch, then came back to the dressing room and lay on a bench. Eventually he was dismissed in the late afternoon – for 226, now his highest first-class score. 'From first to last he batted with wonderful skill and judgement, making runs all round the wicket in masterly fashion and giving no chance,' said *Wisden*.

But cricket could not keep out the realities of war for long. During the Notts game, Hobbs was summoned to see the Secretary of the Surrey Committee, William Findlay. 'I'm afraid I have some bad news for you. The military authorities have commandeered the Oval,' said Findlay. Only the day before, 3 August, Findlay had been informed by

the War Office that the army needed the Oval for the training of the
territorials. This was potentially a disaster for Hobbs, since his benefit
match was due to be played against Kent starting on 10 August. Findlay
tried to lessen the blow's impact by explaining that the committee had
arranged with the MCC for Surrey's next two home games against
Kent and Yorkshire to be played at Lord's. The committee recognised,
however, that the takings at Lord's would be nothing like the money
Hobbs would make on his own ground, especially because Lord's had
a ban on collections within its premises. So Findlay offered Hobbs a
choice: he could postpone his benefit game until after the war or he
could proceed at Lord's. Hobbs, mindful that he was guaranteed at
least £500 by the Surrey Committee, decided to go ahead. But given
the unusual circumstances, he also asked the committee to give him a
guarantee of £200 towards his collection at Lord's. The Surrey
Committee considered this plea at its meeting on 6 August. As the
minutes recorded: 'It was decided to take no action at present but the
Secretary was instructed to inform Hobbs that the committee would
do its best to ensure that he should not suffer as a consequence of the
war crisis.' Eventually, the Surrey Committee reached a compromise
with the MCC whereby the normal rules were waived and collecting
boxes were allowed in certain parts of the ground. In the days before
10 August, while the news continued to be dominated by the war, some
of Hobbs's supporters tried to raise public interest in his benefit, urging
either attendance at Lord's for the Kent game, where the daily admission was sixpence, or at least a subscription to his appeal. In the
fashionable society magazine *Tatler,* the indefatigable Sir Home Gordon
wrote plaintively: 'None will grudge 6d a day, but if they neither pay
it nor subscribe they are in no way helping the beneficiary. And I feel
sure everyone with his mite desires to assist in testifying to Hobbs the
enormous pleasure derived from his great cricket. Hobbs is the only
professional batsman I know who enters the charmed and charming
circle of superbly delightful batsmen . . . That Hobbs is the most
glorious professional bat of this or any other time I have no manner
of doubt. He plays the game as a game, and is the finest run-getter
today in the whole world.'

Sir Home's entreaties seemed to have little effect. The worst fears
of Hobbs and the committee were realised. At a poorly attended game,
which resulted in a Surrey victory within less than two days, the

collection for Hobbs was pitiful. On the first day, just twenty-four pounds was donated, an insulting sum for England's top cricketer. Altogether, Hobbs's 1914 benefit raised only £657 from all sources, a sum much lower than the average for a county cricketer in the pre-war era. Long-serving professionals could generally expect to receive between £800 and £2,000, while at Yorkshire five benefits in the Edwardian decade averaged £2,344, boosted, of course, by Hirst's unique year. It is a tribute to the esteem in which Hobbs was held at his own club that Surrey decided that he had to be rewarded properly after this unjust financial failure brought about by the war. At its meeting on 3 September, the committee agreed to a motion put forward by Sir Jeremiah Colman, a scion of the Norwich mustard family, that Hobbs should be given another benefit either the following year or when the war was finished. In addition, Surrey agreed to keep open the subscription lists until the next benefit, a gesture that is unlikely to have been extended to any other professional. Another sign of the committee's admiration for Hobbs lay in its relaxation of its normal rules about controlling all of the investment of benefit monies. At a meeting in November 1914, it was agreed to purchase on Hobbs's behalf £550 of debenture stock in the Canadian Northern Railway company. The shares were equivalent to his £500 guarantee plus the £50 grant, but, crucially, the committee also 'decided to hand over to Hobbs the balance of the money subscribed towards his benefit, £107'. Hobbs expressed no hurt about the fickleness of the public, only his affection for the Surrey administrators. 'They have always acted towards me most handsomely and my relations with them, individually and as a body, have always been cordial and happy,' he wrote in 1924.

The war inevitably continued to overshadow the season long after the sorry episode of Hobbs's benefit game. The government returned the Oval to Surrey at the end of August, enabling the team to play its final fixture at home against Gloucestershire. With an innings of 141 in another easy victory, Hobbs scored his tenth century for Surrey and his eleventh in all first-class games. But by now the diversionary enthusiasm of the Bank Holiday mood had long since passed and most of the nation was grimly focused on war. There was mounting public feeling against the continuation of first-class cricket while men of the British Expeditionary Force were fighting in France, this sense of antipathy fuelled by a recruiting speech from the famous retired commander Lord Roberts, who singled out cricketers for criticism in his rallying cry for a greater show of patriotic spirit. Similarly, W.G. Grace wrote to the *Sportsman* newspaper calling for a suspension in the county cricket schedule for the duration of the war. 'It is not fitting that able bodied men should be playing day by day,' thundered the Grand Old Man in one of the last declarations of his life.

Surrey bowed to public opinion. At a special meeting on 31 August, the club agreed to cancel its last two remaining fixtures. But there was a brighter side to this move, for the MCC announced that, in a truncated season, Surrey should be crowned county champions. It was a fair decision, since Surrey were so far ahead of their rivals and, with Hobbs at the head of the order, they had played much the best cricket in 1914. This was Surrey's first title since 1899, and it was to be the only one of Hobbs's career. With his free-scoring method, he had dazzled in a way that he was never to do again. For Surrey he hit 2499 runs at an average of 62.77, with three double hundreds, and in all first-class games his aggregate was 2,697. For all the difficulties over his benefit, his tenth season had ended on a high note. Now aged thirty-one, he was at the peak of his powers, with 27,000 first-class runs and sixty-five centuries to his name. But during the next year, as Europe sank into the bloody quagmire of war, Hobbs was to be pulled into the most bitter controversy of his life.

9
'A Most Unfortunate State of Affairs'

There are two persistent myths about public attitudes at the outbreak of the First World War. The first is the belief that most people thought it would be a short war, reflected in the slogan: 'It will be all over by Christmas.' In reality, such optimism was rare and in fact there was a widespread sense of foreboding, a fear that the war would be bloodier and longer than anything previously experienced in the history of mankind, particularly because of the development of new technology. Typical of this anxiety was the entry that middle-class Kensington housewife Ada Reece made in her diary, 'All are agreed that the war will be more terrible than any previous war with all the horrible engines of destruction that science has been perfecting through a hundred years of peace.'

The second myth is that the country was swept by a wave of hysterical jingoism that brought cheering multitudes out onto the streets and galvanised recruitment into the armed forces. 'Your Country Needs You', proclaimed Lord Kitchener, the new War Secretary, in the famous 1914 poster that was supposed to symbolise this national mood of patriotic enthusiasm and sacrifice. But the truth was much more complex than this image of martial euphoria. Unlike continental nations, Britain had never possessed a large standing army and so suspicion of militarism was widespread. The Bradford-born writer J.B. Priestley, who volunteered for service out of a sense of duty and a determination to test himself, captured this nuanced outlook: 'I was not hot with patriotic feeling. I did not believe that Britain was in any real danger. The legend of Kitchener, who pointed at us from every hoarding, never captured me. I was not under any pressure from public opinion, which had not got to work on young men as early as that.' Nor was there any spirit of triumphalism, as the *Manchester Guardian* commented when surveying the quiet, orderly crowds gathered in the city centres: 'What appeared almost unanimous was that no one seemed to want war.'

There were certainly a few who tried to whip up a pro-war frenzy such as the retired naval officer Admiral Charles Fitzgerald, who created the Order of the White Feather in August 1914. Made up almost entirely of women, his organisation used moral blackmail to coerce men into joining up by giving non-volunteers a white feather, the traditional emblem of cowardice. But Fitzgerald's outfit was regarded as a bunch of cranks and was unrepresentative of mainstream public opinion, which held that if men were bullied into military service against their will, then they were not really volunteers at all. The novelist Compton Mackenzie, who was serving as a soldier, thought the Order was full of 'idiotic young women using white feathers to get rid of boyfriends of whom they were tired.'

Though the spirit of volunteering for military service was by no means universal in the male population, there were certain groups in which it was more prevalent. One was ex-public schoolboys, another was university graduates, a third was top-flight sportsmen. It has been estimated that around 40 per cent of all professional footballers in Britain joined up, while the rate for first-class cricketers was even higher. Lord Hawke, himself an adjutant in the West Riding Volunteers, claimed at the MCC's annual meeting in April 1915 that '75 per cent of first-class cricketers are serving in the army and navy'. This figure is borne out by the fact that during the 1914–18 war, 210 first-class cricketers enlisted, roughly three-quarters of the playing staffs at the sixteen counties. Hawke ensured that the contracted players at Yorkshire knew where their duty lay by stipulating that 'a strict condition of their continued engagement would be participation in war work'. But there was little need for such pressure, since the mood in the cricket world ran heavily in favour of service, a legacy of the Victorian ethos of 'playing the game' where sport was imbued with a sense of moral purpose and honour. The Secretary of Hampshire, Francis Bacon, who was in the Royal Naval Reserve, suggested that this mentality should be used to form a corps of professional cricketers, though in November 1914 *Athletic News* reported that 'it was not possible to form a battalion of cricketers because so many had volunteered already'. At the Oval, there was a strong commitment to the military drive. As the Surrey Committee reported with an air of satisfaction in October 1914, there had been a rush to the colours among the leading players: Ernie Hayes, Percy Fender, Bill Hitch, Donald Knight, Cyril Wilkinson, Morice Bird and the youthful batsman Andy Sandham all signed up, most of them in the Royal Fusiliers.

But Jack Hobbs was one of the notable figures who did not enlist voluntarily. Instead, at some stage during the first two years of the war, he joined a munitions firm in south London, though he was always rather vague about the timing of his appointment and the nature of his job. 'For a time I worked on munitions in a factory,' he wrote in his 1935 autobiography. The Surrey off-spinner 'Razor' Smith and the keeper Herbert Strudwick also performed munitions work, as did Hobbs's England opener Wilfred Rhodes, who, with typical dedication to a craft, soon immersed himself in the intricacies of thread-milling machines, though he inevitably grumbled about his pay of two pounds a week. Despite his munitions job, Hobbs was only too aware of mutterings that, as the nation's leading cricketer, he had not set a good example by failing to volunteer. 'A few nasty things have been said that I did not join up straight away,' he wrote in 1924. Some wild, utterly fabricated rumours were even spread about him, as revealed in a letter sent by the Australian cricket writer Jack Pollard to the historian David Frith: 'What do you know about Jack Hobbs being taken to court for illegally dodging the call-up for military service in World War 1?' asked Pollard. This was speculative nonsense, for there was no conscription at all until 1916 and Hobbs did his duty when he was required.

Hobbs's reasons for not enlisting in 1914 were two-fold. First of all, he said that he had not grasped the full consequences of the conflict at its start, a fair explanation given that Britain had never been plunged into the concept of total war before; all previous campaigns had been fought abroad by professional soldiers or sailors with little direct impact on the public. 'Like many others, I did not at once realise how grave the situation was; it was many months before I came to realise it.' Secondly Hobbs argued that he had extensive duties to his family which barred him from military service. 'I was just on thirty-two, married with four young children; I had a widowed mother to whom I had certain obligations and my financial position left room for improvement. I do not wish to make excuses, I merely explain my circumstances,' he wrote. Again, at the start of the war, there was widespread sympathy for married men who were regarded as belonging to a different category from bachelors. Even *John Bull* magazine, famous for its tub-thumping patriotism, carried an editorial which argued that the domestic support provided by family men amounted to its own form of war service: 'The men who have women and children dependent on them, who have established homes, who have taken upon themselves the full burden of citizenship may, in the last resort, be compelled to defend their country, but that time, I submit, has most emphatically not come, so long as men without responsibilities or family ties are at liberty to waste their time at football matches and picture palaces.' But this generally tolerant attitude began to evaporate as the death toll mounted and reports of the horror of the trenches emerged.

Work in the munitions plants could be tough, even dangerous, because of the long hours and the risk of explosions. Peggy Hamilton, who spent most of the war in various factories, gave this description of a scene in one in Birmingham: 'The working conditions were frightful: dark, airless grimy buildings without any kind of heating.' Another woman, Jenny Johnston, found nothing to enjoy in her factory: 'You didn't do anything apart from work. It was a miserable existence. It wasn't worth having.' Perhaps because of his embarrassment at not immediately enlisting, Hobbs himself never gave any details of his employment in the munitions industry, neither the dates he served nor the tasks he performed. It may be that he worked on one of the production lines. However, investigative research into the personnel records of the south London munitions plants during the war throws up another intriguing possibility. Lodged in the National Archives is the staff list of 1916 for the Nine Elms factory, which was conveniently situated between Vauxhall and Battersea, not far from Hobbs's Clapham home. At the raw materials depot of the plant, a worker by the name of 'J. Hobbs' is listed against code 130. Throughout the munitions industry, each member of the establishment was given a code relative to their occupation. Code 130 stood for registration clerk so it appears that Mr J. Hobbs had some sort of clerical job, a less physically demanding role than one on the machines. There is no certainty that this was Jack Hobbs himself, but the location and timescale make it likely. Moreover, his neat hand-writing and well-organised, reliable personality would have made him an efficient clerk.

There is one other, indirect, piece of evidence. The shop floor factory workers had to put in hours that now seem incredible. In her memoir, Peggy Hamilton said that, during one peak of production in 1915, she was on an eighty-four-hour week, excluding travelling time. But Hobbs, if employed as a clerk, would have had nothing like this burden. Tellingly, he seems to have had plenty of time to take on other paid employment, something that would have been impos-sible if he was slaving over a lathe. Hobbs certainly remained on the Surrey professional staff during the initial year of the war and, in the absence of any county programme, he appears to have been expected to carry out some duties on the ground, like coaching or bowling to members. But, always concerned about financial security, he was on the lookout for other work, particularly in cricket. In March 1915 he found just the post he wanted as the cricket coach at the famous public school of Westminster in central London. Because of his status as a professional, he had to ask Surrey for permission to take up the post. The committee raised no objection. The minutes of its meeting on 15 April 1915 recorded: 'An application from J. B. Hobbs, asking the committee to allow him to leave the Oval early on certain days in order to enable him to coach at Westminster School, was granted.' Again, the impression is that Hobbs was hardly over-extended at the munitions plant. Indeed, with his Westminster and Oval duties, it is hard to see how Hobbs was working in munitions at all in the spring of 1915 except on a casual basis. It may be that he did not actually go into the industry until the autumn. That possi-bility is reinforced by a curiously light-hearted interview he gave to a local reporter from the *Bradford Daily Telegraph* during a visit to Yorkshire in May, when he made no mention of any war work but instead talked about his job at Westminster, as the subsequent article noted. 'There is nothing stand-offish about the Surrey man. He was as ready to chat with anybody and everyone as if he had been a nobody! Hobbs, at the present time, is coaching at Westminster School – lucky boys to have such a mentor – but his duties are of a very light character, an hour or two in the nets in the evening and a bit of match practice on Wednesday afternoons. On Saturday the boys play their matches, in which Hobbs services are not required and thus he is free.' If Hobbs was a munitions employee at this time, what makes the relaxed tone of this interview so extraordinary is that May 1915 was precisely the month when the industry was gripped by its darkest crisis of the war, after the British Commander-in-Chief Sir John French privately complained that shell shortages had contributed to the failure of the Allied offensive at Neuve Chappelle in March. French's views, leaked to the public by *The Times*, created a huge political scandal so serious that the increasingly discredited Prime Minister H.H. Asquith had to dissolve his Liberal Government and create a national Coalition, with David Lloyd George taking on the crucial position of Minister of Munitions to clear the bottlenecks in the industry. Meanwhile, in the factories, the production schedules reached new heights to satisfy the demand at the front and most of them had to operate seven days a week.

But none of this seems to have touched Hobbs. His detachment from the war in the early summer of 1915 became even more apparent when he agreed to play on Saturdays as a professional in the Bradford League, a decision that would plunge him into a ferocious public dispute. The very continuation of the League in 1915 was the source of some controversy, since all other competitive cricket had been suspended at the beginning of the war. But John Booth, the President of the League, took the opposite stance to other administrators. Despite complaints that the cricket was a distraction to war workers and a threat to recruitment, Booth strongly maintained that the League actually assisted the war effort by raising spirits. 'Those who had done personal and national duty during the week should be allowed two or three hours of manly and recreative sport,' he said. Booth's willingness to challenge the collective wisdom of the other cricket authorities reflected his own strong-minded, maverick character. The son of an agent for the Liberal Unionist party,* Booth ran a wholesale pharmacy business but cricket was his passion. As the driving force behind the Bradford League, he was regarded by some as authoritarian but by

---

* A movement that split away from the mainstream Liberal Party in 1886 over William Gladstone's attempts to introduce Home Rule for Ireland. The Liberal Unionists formed a coalition with the Tories in 1895 and the two parties were formally merged in 1912.

others as a charismatic leader who brought higher standards and bigger crowds. The League itself reflected some of Booth's fierce independence. Founded in 1903, it had built on the popularity of limited-overs weekend cricket that had developed among clubs in Bradford in the mid-Victorian age, encouraged by the Factory Acts that gave the working classes free Saturday afternoons for the first time. The atmosphere of this instant version, with its emphasis on big hitting, was entirely different to the three-day game and, as the academic Tony Barker wrote in his history of Bradford League cricket, 'played over a few hours close to where people lived, it was well suited to the working rhythms of manufacturing society'. The Bradford clubs had been so popular that, from the 1870s, they had been able to recruit professionals and by the end of the Edwardian age, some of the League's clubs had no fewer than five paid players in their ranks. Partly because of its success, the Bradford League was viewed with suspicion by Yorkshire County Cricket Club, whose autocratic boss Lord Hawke saw Booth's upstart outfit as a threat to the traditional fabric of the game, as well as a rival market for professional talent and crowds.

The refusal to integrate into the wider structure of Yorkshire cricket meant that Booth felt no compunction about urging the League to continue along its own, self-reliant path in wartime. His organisation would play by its own rules, including the hire of top-class professionals to give spectators the entertainment they deserved. Following Booth's lead, Saltaire, one of the Bradford League's foremost clubs, announced in December 1914 that it would employ three professionals next summer, but few guessed at the extent of its ambition. Then, in April 1915, Saltaire revealed its star signing, none other than Sydney Barnes, universally acknowledged, to quote Hobbs's own phrase, as 'the greatest orthodox bowler in the world'. Despite the increasingly gloomy news about the progress of the war, the Bradford public was captivated by the signing of Barnes. On his debut for Saltaire, a crowd of 6,400 people paid £176 to watch him and he fully lived up to expectations by taking eight wickets for 8 runs in just five overs against Bowling Old Lane, the newest club in the League. In the next game he was just as unplayable as he took 10 for 14. The breathtaking start by Barnes could not be ignored by Idle, one of Saltaire's biggest rivals and the native village of John Booth. Determined to match Saltaire's audacity in signing the world's greatest bowler, Idle decided to recruit the world's greatest batsman. So in May 1915 the club wrote to Jack Hobbs with an offer to hire him as a professional on terms of five pounds per match plus two pounds travelling expenses, reportedly double the sum that Barnes was earning. Hobbs accepted with some eagerness, as he explained to the *Bradford Evening Telegraph*: 'In all circumstances, he was not sorry to come to terms with Idle. He loves the game and did not fancy a summer without serious cricket. He declared himself in fairly good practice, but he vastly prefers match practice to that at the nets which, of course, is practically all the cricket he has had this season.'

Given that he would only be required to appear for Idle on Saturday afternoons, it was feasible, if tiring, for him to stay in Clapham and make a round trip by railway for each appearance. But the logistics of Hobbs's employment were a matter of supreme indifference to Bradford cricket supporters. They were only too happy to have such an icon playing in their league. His outstanding reputation led to a series of adulatory profiles in the local press. 'Jack Hobbs: Idle's sensational capture', proclaimed the *Bradford Daily Telegraph*, which gave full praise to his character as well as his cricket. 'He possesses a great personality in addition to all else, the personality which has played almost as important a part as his actual performances in securing for him worldwide popularity. Even Sydney Barnes himself possesses no greater fascination for a cricket crowd.' The *Shipley Times and Express* was even more lavish in its plaudits, describing him as 'the world's greatest batsman: a cricket genius for Idle'. The paper went on to predict great success for Hobbs in the league: 'Hobbs's style makes him eminently suitable for Saturday afternoon cricket, where time is of great importance, for he is essentially a brilliant batsman, a man who takes great risks to achieve great results. There is no more attractive batsman in the world than he. He could hardly be dull even if he tried to be. Without being in any senses a "slogger", he has such a wonderful command of strokes, such supple wrists, such a wonderful eye that it is well nigh impossible for any bowler to keep him quiet.' With some prescience, the paper also forecast that he would also prove a useful bowler: 'Though he has taken comparatively few wickets in first-class cricket, he could yet have made a fine bowler had he not been so great with the bat that he has been persistently kept away from the ball. There are so few who can make better use of the leather when it is still shiny and the seams stand out boldly.' *The Times and Express* concluded with a tribute to his fielding: 'He is unsurpassed in this or any other country as a fieldsman. At cover-point he is absolutely brilliant, while he is fast, clean and clever in any other position.'

After all the hype, Hobbs's beginning with Idle was something of a disappointment. His debut at the village of Eccleshill was so badly hit by rain that he never got the chance to bat. But he did reasonably well in the next match against Bingley, scoring 39 in an Idle total of 127 that was large enough to secure an easy win. In front of a crowd of 2,500, he had made a scratchy start to his innings against the pace bowling of Albert Judson, who was to play for Yorkshire after the war, but then he began to employ the strokes that the cricket world knew so well. 'It was a glimpse of the real Hobbs which the crowd got. His powerful drive called forth admiration, the crowd rewarding him time after time with round after round of applause,' said the specialist local sports paper the *Bradford Cricket Argus*.

But there were others who were far less enamoured of Idle's new recruit, viewing cricket as a frivolity at a time of national emergency. The progress of the war was now at a critical stage, not only because of the shell crisis, but also because of the rising intensity of the conflict across the globe. May was the month that saw the sinking of the ocean liner, the *Lusitania*, by a German U-boat, with the loss of almost 1,200 lives, while the Allied landings at Gallipoli, overseen by Winston Churchill, were faltering badly. One of those who died in this savage campaign was Hobbs's former Surrey colleague, the Australian batsman Alan Marshal. Brooding on the Allies' struggle, Lord Hawke grew increasingly furious at the conduct of the Bradford League and John Booth, particularly because he had barred his own Yorkshire professionals from playing for any league. At a meeting of the Yorkshire County Cricket Club on 2 June 1915, he gave full vent to his wrath. As the *Bradford Daily Telegraph* reported, 'Lord Hawke gave it as his opinion that this engagement of Hobbs and Barnes by Bradford clubs in the present circumstances was scandalous. He objected it to it very strongly and thought it a most unfortunate state of affairs, considering the present crisis.' Hawke even claimed that the excitement generated by the arrival of Hobbs had interfered with military recruitment in Yorkshire.

The scene was now set for a blazing row between Hawke and the League. As soon as he read the reports of Hawke's speech, Booth exploded with anger and sent Hawke a telegram, demanding a meeting with His Lordship and asking for confirmation that he had really used the word 'scandalous' about the signing of the League's two new stars. In reply, Booth received the following message from Hawke: 'Thoroughly disapprove of any cricketer of military age being engaged by Yorkshire clubs. Telephone Toone, who will give you the views of the committee.' This was a reference to Frederick Toone, the highly regarded Secretary of Yorkshire and later a popular manager of the MCC's three tours to Australia in the 1920s. Still seething, Booth rang Toone and began to harangue him about the use of the word 'scandalous'. As he explained later, he told Toone that it was 'a very serious thing because if any of their clubs were doing anything scandalous it was time the league took steps to clean their stables and they could do that without the interference of Lord Hawke'. In response, Toone admitted that 'neither he nor Hawke had any right to object to what the clubs had done, but they were of the opinion that players should not be brought in from outside to create a sensation'. Toone further contended that the decision to hire Hobbs and Barnes 'was driving people away from the main business of the nation and was detrimental to recruiting'. But in an attempt at mollification, Toone claimed that he could not remember Hawke using the word 'scandalous', adding, in that classic stratagem of evasion, that His Lordship had been misquoted. Toone 'blamed the reporters for putting in a word that was not used'. Booth responded that if there had really been a misquotation, then the press reports 'should be publicly repudiated' by Lord Hawke. The conversation ended there, and Hawke and Toone made no further contribution to the row. But the idea that Hawke had been misquoted was strongly denied by one of the journalists who had heard his speech to the Yorkshire CCC. Burns Campell, a well-known correspondent from Sheffield, wrote to the *Bradford Daily Telegraph* to say that 'Mr Toone is wrong. There were several pressmen present when Lord Hawke talked over the matter and when first His Lordship stated that he had a very strong objection to the engagement of famous professionals for spectacular league cricket at the present time, he was asked whether he had any objection to his views being published. His reply was, "Certainly not. I think it scandalous and I don't mind you saying so" – or words to that effect. In any case, the word scandalous was used.' Campbell felt Toone should now apologise to the press, though the Yorkshire Secretary had no intention of doing so.

Booth and the League then called a special meeting of the Bradford League's committee to discuss Hawke's remarks. The President of Idle, Mr H. Dawson, opened the proceedings by confessing to be 'very sore' about the whole affair. He wanted the full approval of the committee 'on the engagement of Hobbs by his club'. But other representatives felt that, since their clubs had done nothing to be ashamed of, they should not dignify Hawke's statement with any further response. Summing up the mood, Booth made a bullish defence of the League's policy of continuing to play cricket, which brought 'about relief from the nightmare of war'. The League, he continued, 'is catering for a centre where people are working night and day on government work, and they have a right to recreation on a Saturday afternoon. I consider that the Yorkshire County Cricket Club are pursuing a dog in a manger policy, based on the success we are achieving, and if the word scandalous can be used at all it can be applied to the criticism which has been levelled at us.' Booth also strongly denied that the hiring of Hobbs had been detrimental to recruiting. 'The League could put figures before Lord Hawke to prove that he was wrong. Why the very week that Hobbs was engaged, the official figures for recruiting in Bradford showed 700 men, a clear record for the city for the year.' After further debate, the meeting agreed to the following resolution, that 'the action of the Idle and Saltaire clubs in engaging Hobbs and Barnes requires no confirmation by this committee, as the clubs have acted strictly within the League rules in so doing'. But the motion did not bring the row to an end. It continued to cast a shadow over the rest of the 1915 season, causing divisions within Yorkshire cricket and society. Even Booth's own family was divided. In August, the *Bradford Cricket Argus* published a remarkable letter from Sergeant William Booth, a soldier in the King's Own Yorkshire Light Infantry who was being held as a prisoner-of-war in Germany. In a thinly veiled attack on his own brother and professionals like Hobbs, Sergeant Booth wrote: 'How any man can play cricket or spend time running cricket organisations or how men can have the hard neck to watch matches when the fate of the country hangs in the balance is quite beyond me. They cannot have any idea what the Expeditionary Force has had to face or care little what the soldier has to face daily. After what I have gone through and after the anxiety we are experiencing over here, it pains me to think the people take things so easily. It is no use saying all is well in England. If so, why all this delay? Patriotism is not the mere wearing of a khaki tie, and I think that all the cricket fields and tennis courts ought to be turned into drill grounds and the players made into recruits.'

Hobbs never made any public comment about the controversy, though it may have exacerbated his reticence about the war. One certain legacy was a chill in his relations with Lord Hawke, who provoked a number of further public rows with Hobbs in the 1920s and 1930s. In private, Hobbs described Hawke as 'a silly old fool' who had 'never had a kind thing to say about me'. In public, he adopted a puzzled tone: 'I wonder why Lord Hawke so often attacks me. Almost every year he has a go,' Hobbs complained in the *News Chronicle* in 1933. It is likely that the answer lay in the events at Bradford in May 1915. But, for all the bitterness, neither Hobbs nor Idle had any intention of changing course. He carried on playing most Saturdays through the summer of 1915, and occasionally ran up useful scores, such as 60 against Lidget Green and 79 not out against Windmill, 'a masterly display to the delight of the large crowd of spectators' said the *Shipley Times and Express*. But overall, his performances were nothing like as good as the Idle administrators had expected. Typical was his comparative failure in the crucial match in early July against Saltaire, when he faced Barnes for the first time. Though Idle won by three wickets, Hobbs made only 17 before he became one of Barnes's victims. By the end of the season, his average was a modest 36.63, far lower than in any of his recent Test series. 'There is no getting away from the fact that Hobbs has not reached his real form in local cricket and many people think he has been taking league trundlers much too cheaply,' said the *Shipley Times and Express*. Hobbs himself admitted to the same paper that complacency had played its part in his poor record, along with some other factors. 'Hobbs told the writer that the main reasons for his low scoring were that he had not played sufficiently to keep at the top of his form and that he had tried to please the crowd too much instead of playing his own game. The great cricketer further observed that he had found the bowling in the Bradford League of a quality not to be despised and he had tried to score off it too quickly.' Such language is very different to that he used in his 1924 memoirs when he referred to appearing in an 'occasional afternoon league game' during the war. 'The standard of play is not very high; a side may have a couple of good bowlers and two or three decent batsmen, but the teams are no better than those fielded by good class clubs in London.'

With all cricket over at Idle, the Oval and Westminster at the end of the 1915 season, Hobbs had to concentrate on munitions work through the autumn and winter. Yet he still found time to do some business for John Booth, for he was instrumental in the recruitment of Frank Woolley for the Bradford League. In late November 1915, he wrote to Booth to urge that one of the clubs hire Woolley, then also working in munitions. 'It may help you to know that Woolley tried to enlist sometime last winter but was rejected – something wrong with his feet or toes, I forget which,' he said, the implication being that Woolley would not soon be disappearing on military service. Thanks partly to Hobbs's intervention, the Kent player eventually joined the Keighley club. Despite his own disappointing season, Idle were keen to renew Hobbs's contract, since he had dramatically boosted the club's income. According to Idle's treasurer, the club would have made a £50 loss rather than a £6 profit in 1915 without him. Hobbs was just as keen to play in 1916. The Westminster coaching job had ended, the Oval had reduced its professional staff to just four employees and, in Hobbs's own words, 'I was not making much at munitions.' There were, he said, no difficulties about playing regularly in the League in 1916, since 'Saturdays were half-days at the munitions factory' and Hobbs was given special leave in the mornings to travel up to Bradford. Yet the generous treatment shown by the authorities towards Hobbs caused some friction within his own family. Four of his five brothers had enlisted in the armed forces, the exception being Sydney who had been born with a bad limp. Two of them were badly wounded: Alfred in a gas attack, and Harry by shrapnel from an exploding grenade which took out one of his eyes. According to Harry's grandson Mark, there was some resentment over the apparent favouritism towards Jack. 'I picked up a feeling that the rest of the family were not impressed. When Harry was in the trenches and thinking his luck was bound to run out, it must have gone through his mind about Jack, who didn't serve then just because he'd got a certain ability. Human nature being human nature, I think there was animosity.' Mark Hobbs is emphatic on this point. 'The animosity comes from the fact that other people in the family were expected to serve in the First World War and Jack wasn't because of his position as a cricketer. I heard from my father's mother that there was an unspoken belief that he was someone who was selected not to serve.' Much of this would have been unjust, since there was no military conscription before 1916 and therefore there were no special exemptions. But it is true that Hobbs for the first two years of the war had a much less traumatic experience than four of his brothers. When asked about Jack's explanation that he had to look after his family, Mark Hobbs says, 'So did thousands of others who served. The animosity carried on after the war.'

But Hobbs did not allow any discord to interfere with his cricket for Idle in 1916. He had learnt his lessons from the previous summer and was now more focused, less imprudent. He not only showed his true quality as a batsman but was also one of Idle's leading bowlers, his movement and pace too much for many opposition teams. His status as a genuine all-rounder at league level was proved in his two titanic clashes with Barnes's Saltaire side. In the first, on 26 May in front of a crowd of 5,000, he scored only 24 in a disappointing Idle total of 73, but this was to prove more than adequate as he ripped through the Saltaire batting order with a spell of 7 for 24, including the wicket of Barnes. Even more emphatically, in the return fixture at Idle, he cut and drove his way to 87, then put in a sensational bowling performance to take 9 for 39, with Saltaire bundled out in less than an hour. 'From the start Hobbs, who opened the bowling with the setting sun behind him, had the nerves of the batsmen. He was distinctly fiery, the ball sometimes rearing in alarming fashion,' reported the *Shipley Times and Express*. The large crowd showed its appreciation by holding a collection for him which brought ten pounds fifteen shillings, almost half the sum that was collected for him on the first day of his benefit at Lord's in 1914. During the whole season, Hobbs scored 790 runs at 52.6, including big centuries against Windmill and Keighley. 'He had played glorious cricket, using almost every known stroke with equal grace and ability,' reported the *Bradford Cricket Argus* of the latter innings. His bowling figures were even more dramatic: 65 wickets at just 6.27 runs. Thanks to his all-round performance, Idle stormed to take the Bradford League title. In the celebrations after the last game, when Idle was formally presented with the trophy and winners' medals by Mabel Booth, the wife of the League President, Hobbs was showered with congratulations, expressions of gratitude and an illuminated address. With his usual modesty, Hobbs said that he was 'far happier wielding the willow than speech-making', but spoke of his deep appreciation for all the kindness he had been shown in Bradford. 'I could not pay a greater compliment than to say you are first-class sportsmen, all of you,' he told the rest of the Idle team. In the celebratory atmosphere, John Booth responded by declaring that 'they had never had in the Bradford League a player who had become more popular, not only on account of his cricket but because of his gentlemanliness'. That was a sentiment echoed by the Idle wicketkeeper Harry Plowright, who said that 'when the history of the Idle club came to be written, the name of Jack Hobbs would figure prominently and that brilliant cricketer could not be better described in that history than as "John Berry Hobbs: Gentleman"'.

Amidst all the mutual affection, which Hobbs so often generated wherever he went in the cricket world, there was one disappointing announcement for Idle followers. Hobbs explained that the final game of the 1916 season would 'probably be the last match I will play in the Bradford League'. The reason was simple: Hobbs had been conscripted into the armed forces and had been instructed to join the Royal Flying Corps in the autumn. Asquith's Government had resisted compulsory military enrolment for as long as possible, believing that such a measure was against the British tradition of liberty. But the voluntary supply of manpower could not keep up with the appalling level of casualties; by the end of 1915, more than 500,000 men had been killed and another 200,000 wounded. In January 1916 the Coalition therefore introduced the Military Service Act, which required all single men aged between eighteen and forty-one to serve in the forces. From May 1916, conscription was extended to cover all married men in this age bracket, with the new recruits given no choice over which service they joined. In a sense Hobbs was lucky to have avoided both the army, then bogged down in the quagmire of the trenches, and the Royal Navy, which would have been

physically nauseating for him, whereas the RFC, founded in 1911, was
Britain's newest and most glamorous service. It also had the advantage
that a significant part of its operations were devoted to home defence.
Conscripted as an air mechanic, whose job was to maintain and repair
the biplanes, Hobbs entered the Royal Flying Corps on 12 October
1916. After his initial training, he served at airfields in west London
and Norfolk, though he still got some time off to play cricket in a
few RFC and charity games in the summer of 1917.

Hobbs was even able to reverse his prediction about not appearing
in the Bradford League again. In July and August 1917 he turned out
infrequently for Idle, most notably in a cup tie against Saltaire. More
than 8,000 people gathered to witness another round in the duel
between Barnes and Hobbs. On this occasion there was no doubt
about the winner, as Hobbs hit 132 in an innings that included twenty
4s. Many of these boundaries flew straight into the crowd or even
out of Idle's ground, but there were at the time no sixes in the
Bradford League. As a cricket correspondent based in Bradford, the
writer Leslie Duckworth remembered the innings as one of the highlights of his youth: 'Barnes's face got blacker and blacker and I was
torn between suffering with him and exulting in such batting as I
had never seen before in my young life.' One shot from Hobbs, wrote
Duckworth, went 'through a bedroom window' of an adjoining house.
Another spectator, Ronald Mather of Low Moor, later wrote of the
innings: 'Barnes was putting all he knew into his bowling that day
but Hobbs was unmerciful. When Barnes was running up to the
wicket Hobbs was walking up to the crease to meet him and it was
a four nearly every ball. Those roof tops round the Idle ground –
there must have been a lot of cracked slates that afternoon.' Sadly
for Idle, Hobbs was able to make only two other appearances that
summer due to his RFC commitments and the club slid down the
table in his absence.

In November 1917 Hobbs was sent to the newly formed 110
Squadron, based first at Rendcombe in Gloucestershire, then later at
Sedgeford near King's Lynn in Norfolk. Initially, the RFC planned to
send this squadron to France in early 1918, but, fortunately for Hobbs,
it was kept in England and used as a training unit right through the
spring and summer. One of the perks of the Sedgeford base was its
proximity to the home of Mrs Emma Drewery, a farmer's wife who

loved to have the young, often homesick, airmen round to generous meals in her white-washed cottage. She became so well known that she was nicknamed 'the Mother' of the local aircrews. 'Another of my old boys is Jack Hobbs the cricketer, who has had many a supper around the kitchen table,' she said in an interview in 1939, again revealing the priority that Hobbs always attached to his nourishment.

Hobbs was also fortunate that interest in cricket was beginning to reawaken by mid-1918. With the war almost four years old and the weary public eager for entertainment, the cricket authorities took a more relaxed stance towards holding matches. Due to the influence of Plum Warner, a number of high-quality exhibition games were arranged at Lord's, and Hobbs, who was stationed from mid-June at the south London airfield of Kenley, was able to play in several of them. At the beginning of August, he turned out for an England XI versus a Dominions XI, made up of servicemen from South Africa and Australia. The crowd of 9,265, which raised nearly £1,000 for the Red Cross, showed the extent of the yearning for cricket. Hobbs failed in this match but he did much better for Warner's XI in a match against Colonel Stanley Jackson's XI towards the end of the month, when he hit 86. 'Those present had the pleasure of seeing Hobbs bat in his very best form. By general consent his 86 was the finest display of the season,' said *Wisden*. Even the previous hostility from the establishment towards the Bradford League was forgotten, as Warner arranged for his team, including 'Air Mechanic J.B. Hobbs' to play against a composite league side at Bradford. Facing a strong league attack that was led by Cecil Parkin of Lancashire, Hobbs scored 70 and 22, a performance which 'easily outshone all the other batsmen', according to *Wisden*.

The continuing excellence of Hobbs's form, despite the absence of any real competition, was witnessed by Bert Oldfield, then serving in the Australian army and later to be a chivalrous opponent of Hobbs throughout the 1920s. On one occasion, having been given a day's leave, Oldfield and his army pals decided to take a bus out to Uxbridge and then roam through the countryside nearby to enjoy some fresh air. After walking for several miles, they came across an air force camp, where a cricket match was in progress. 'As we watched the game there was one player who stood out on account of his undoubted batting ability. Not only did he appeal to us because of his cricketing skill, but his immaculate appearance in his flannels – the hallmark of many an international – gave him a striking distinction. Never at any stage did he look like losing his wicket as he seemed to do just what he liked with the bowling and certainly thrilled the meagre collection of khaki-clad onlookers. We learnt to our surprise and delight that it was none other than the renowned Jack Hobbs. Imagine our excitement seeing such an international cricketer in action during the war days in one of the most secluded and prettiest settings to be imagined.'

By the end of the summer of 1918, the Allies, reinforced by a surge of troops from the United States, finally had victory in their sights. The German lines were broken. The Austro-Hungarian Government was crumbling. But Hobbs's war suddenly threatened to reach a new level of intensity. In April, the RFC had been merged with the Royal Naval Air Service to create the RAF under the leadership of Hugh Trenchard, a passionate believer in the destructive capability of air power. As part of this aggressive new mood, 110 Squadron was mobilised for service in France and equipped with the latest type of light bomber, the Airco DH9A, colloquially known as the 'Ninak'. At the beginning of September, the squadron, complete with all its support crews, was sent to Picardy, northern France, where it established its base at the airfield of Bettencourt. According to No. 110's official history, filed in the National Archives, the main duties in France were 'long-distance day bombing with an occasional single machine for photographic reconnaissance'. A few daring raids into Germany were mounted, including one to Frankfurt, 160 miles from the aerodrome, and altogether ten and a half tons of bombs were dropped. The official history had some praise for the work of the mechanics: 'It is also noteworthy that, so far as has been ascertained, on no occasion was a machine obliged to land on the German side owing to engine failure.' But Hobbs never referred to any of this work. As with his munitions job, he was always reticent about his RAF service. In fact, the only mention he ever made of going to France was in his 1924 memoirs, where he recalled playing some RAF matches at Kenley before 'we were mobilised for overseas'. Not only does his spell in the air force contradict any idea that he was a shirker, a word that first gained currency in 1914, but his near silence on the issue demonstrates his innate modesty, though Mark Hobbs says that this did little to lessen the apparent acrimony in his family. 'When Jack was serving in the RAF, the war was really all over. It was party time then,' he says.

The war really was all over on 11 November 1918, when Germany, shattered and in retreat, signed the armistice with the Allies. It was little more than two months since 110 Squadron had arrived at Bettencourt, but Hobbs was not released from RAF service immediately. The Government, now led by Lloyd George, drew out the process of demobilisation in order to avoid a sudden increase in unemployment. Men were discharged from 9 December 1918, priority given to those with long service or with jobs vital to the economy. Each ex-serviceman received a railway warrant, a ration book, a clothes allowance and a small payment, but such handouts could not compensate for the growing frustration at the delays. In January 1919, nearly 5,000 men at a camp near Calais started a riot over their demand for immediate release, chaotic scenes that prompted the British Commander-in-Chief Field Marshal Douglas Haig to demand the execution of the ring leaders. But the War Secretary Winston Churchill refused to approve this drastic request and instead speeded up demobilisation. It was not, however, until 26 February 1919 that Jack Hobbs was finally discharged from 110 Squadron.

He returned home to a nation exhausted and traumatised by the experience of the previous four years, which had seen the deaths of 750,000 Britons. Cricket had its own tragic part in this toll. Sixty first-class cricketers had lost their lives, including Hobbs's England teammates Colin Blythe, Kenneth Hutchings and Major Booth. The agony was over, but the wounds would never properly heal. The Britain of Hobbs's first decade at Surrey had vanished for ever.

10

'This Tremendous Feat'

In the 1919 edition of *Wisden*, published in February, the editor Sydney Pardon previewed the forthcoming season. 'The long nightmare of the war has come to an end and in the coming summer first-class cricket will again be in full swing.' But Pardon then expressed his disapproval of a controversial experiment that was to be tried with the county championship, namely the introduction of two-day matches for the first time in England. The primary aim of this bold move was to take advantage of the longer hours in the summer evenings that resulted from the continuation of the government's wartime 'daylight saving' scheme. With each day's play scheduled to last until 7.30 p.m., the supporters of the change argued that the clubs would attract more after-work spectators. Opponents of the experiment warned of exhaustion among the players and a rise in the number of drawn games. The Surrey Committee was strongly opposed to the move on financial grounds, pointing out that the loss of the third day in 1914 would have cost the club thousands of pounds. But at the MCC's Advisory Committee, Surrey's objections were overruled by eleven votes to five, and it was agreed to proceed with the change. In his editorial notes, Pardon expressed the fear that 'a grave mistake has been made in not letting the game alone. The restriction of all county matches to two days strikes me as being a sad blunder.'

Pardon turned out to be right. The 1919 season should have been a glorious success after years of sporting famine. The weather was hot for weeks on end. As all the pent-up emotion of the war years was released, there was a huge public appetite for escapist entertainment and crowds flocked to the opening games. But the weaknesses of two-day cricket soon became apparent. The exceptionally dry summer that produced excellent batting surfaces also made it difficult to achieve results in the shortened timescale. Out of 126 county matches in the championship, no fewer than 56 were drawn. Typical was the experience of the Surrey team which drew half of its twenty games. Gradually, both the public and players grew bored with the endless round of stalemates. This problem was exacerbated by deepening fatigue among the cricketers, who not only had to endure long hours but then often had to travel through the night for their next fixture. 'Cricketers grew more and more tired as the season progressed,' recalled the Middlesex professional Harry Lee. Much to his annoyance, Wilfred Rhodes regularly found himself at Penistone Junction in the middle of the night waiting for a connection. Even home games could be difficult. 'It was hard work,' said Hobbs, 'and both players and public soon got fed up with the new arrangement. After a 7.30 finish, by the time one had dressed and dined, it was too late to go anywhere.'

Hobbs was now thirty-six, an age when many professional sportsmen begin to think about retirement. But, after the late start to his first-class career and losing four years to the war, he had no intention of leaving the stage. Indeed, with his talent and ambition undiminished, he was about to enter the most productive period of his career. Rather than reducing his capacity for run making, his maturity led to a further evolution of his batting style as he gradually reined in the exuberance of his pre-war years and replaced it with a majestic new solidity. It was during these post-war years that the legend of 'The Master' was really born, though Hobbs occasionally expressed his wistful regret at the disappearance of the cavalier. 'I was only half the player after the first war that I was before,' he once told John Arlott, despite his astonishing record in the fifteen years after 1918.

As soon as the new season began, Hobbs showed that his faculties remained as keen as ever. In an early trial match at the Oval, he hit a century in each innings, the second coming in just eighty minutes. 'Hobbs is without doubt England's greatest batsman. Yesterday he made good bowling look very poor stuff, his driving and pulling to leg being exceptional,' said the *Daily Mirror*, whose reporter singled out one particular shot as 'a great inspiration. The ball pitched well outside the off-stump but Hobbs got it away to the boundary past square leg.' Apart from one brief spell of comparative failure in late May when he fell lbw a number of times trying to play straight balls to leg, he kept up this superb form

throughout the summer, scoring 2,594 runs in all first-class matches at
an average of 60.32, and including eight hundreds. Among his many
dominant innings was a double century for Surrey against the Australian
Imperial Forces side, then carrying out a tour of England before its
members were demobilised. The leading fast bowler in the AIF side was
Jack Gregory, who gave a foretaste of his deadly pace at Test level by
striking a couple of blows on Hobbs's body, though he could not stop
the Surrey batsman regularly driving his fuller deliveries through the
covers. Hobbs also made a trio of centuries against the Gents in the
games at the Oval, Lord's and the Scarborough Festival, and in his final
match of the season at the Oval he hit 101 in two hours for the Rest of
England against the Champion County, Yorkshire, batting 'brilliantly' in
'characteristic fashion', according to the *Daily Express*. Hobbs was just
as prolific in the county championship, making centuries home and
away to Lancashire and giving a further demonstration of his unrivalled
skill on a rain-affected wicket with 102 in a defeat by Kent at Blackheath,
Surrey's most unlucky ground. 'The task was too heavy, but Hobbs made
a magnificent effort. His batting on a drying pitch was beyond praise,'
said *Wisden*.

There were several intriguing developments in Surrey cricket during
the 1919 season, all of which were to have a major impact on Hobbs's
later career. One was the decision by the committee to ask him to act
as a temporary captain during a championship game, the first time
Hobbs had led a side in first-class cricket. Like all other counties, Surrey
clung to the tradition of amateur leadership and Cyril Wilkinson, the
skipper of the 1914 championship-winning side, still held the job. But
he was not always available and his natural deputy, Percy Fender, had
been so badly wounded in the war that he was still on crutches during
the 1919 season. The other amateur contender for the role was Donald
Knight, a stylish young batsman who had played for Surrey before the
war while still a schoolboy at Malvern. Following his war service,
however, Knight was now a student at Oxford so could only play when
the university term was over. At times, therefore, Surrey had to field an
all-professional XI, as happened at the beginning of June when they
played Warwickshire at the Oval, the game for which Hobbs was asked
to take charge. It was another sign of the respect in which he was held
by the committee that he was given this duty. He performed well enough,
making 88 in Surrey's first innings and leading his side to victory by

seven wickets, though the *Daily Express* felt the leadership affected his performance with the bat. 'He was hardly as aggressive as usual. As acting captain, he had more responsibility on his shoulders than ever,' said the paper.

There was some truth in this observation. As a shy individual, sensitive to criticism, Hobbs never relished the burden of leadership. One of the recurrent themes of his later career was his frequent complaint about the pressures of responsibility as a batsman who was constantly expected to make runs for his county and England. In an essay for the 1924 *Empire Cricket Annual* he revealed that the toughest aspect of his life as a cricketer was 'a great feeling of responsibility and anxiety. Fancy when you fail to make a satisfactory score. Fancy when you are out for a blob.' His dislike of decision-making was captured by the fast bowler Maurice Allom, who occasionally led Surrey towards the end of Hobbs's career. 'In general Jack was very reluctant to bring any influence to bear on a skipper. I don't recall him suggesting anything – be it about bowling changes, fielding positions or tactics in general when I was captaining the side.' Once, after a week when Surrey had been left drained by several long days in the field, Allom had to decide whether to enforce the follow-on in a match against Lancashire, with just three hours left to the close of play. 'I had been out with a serious illness earlier in the season and was not yet restored to full health. I said to him, "Jack, our lads look absolutely whacked. I don't feel at all fit myself. Would it be an awful thing if we were to bat again?" It was the only time I asked him, but he wouldn't commit himself. Jack would not give me an answer, one way or the other. Extraordinary really, with the wealth of experience at his disposal. Anyway, we did bat again, and, I recall, I was hounded afterwards in the press.' In June 1919, after his brief experience of leading Surrey against Warwickshire, Hobbs was relieved to hand over the reins to the veteran Ernie Hayes for the next game, then Cyril Wilkinson returned. But, despite Hobbs's reluctance, the captaincy issue rumbled on for the rest of his career, at one stage provoking another serious row with his old adversary Lord Hawke.

A further key step in 1919 was the start of his long association with the Surrey batsman Andy Sandham, who succeeded to the role of Hobbs's opening partner upon the retirement of Tom Hayward. Though Sandham, known in the Surrey dressing room as 'Sandy', had played occasionally before the war and reached the age of thirty during the

1919 season, he was still severely lacking in first-class experience, which
meant that his initial stands with Hobbs in May and June had only
limited success. For much of the later summer, Knight rather than
Sandham opened with Hobbs. Nevertheless, in the seasons that followed,
it was Sandham who became a fixture at the top of the Surrey batting
order alongside 'The Master'. Theirs was the third and longest of the
great opening partnerships of Hobbs's career, after the ones with Tom
Hayward and Wilfred Rhodes, and it lasted right up to 1934, yielding
sixty-six century stands. Undemonstrative and reliable, Sandham was
the perfect foil for Hobbs. In physique, he was even shorter than Hobbs,
though slightly stockier, and, like many small men, he was a nimble,
quick mover on his feet because of his low centre of gravity. Born in
Streatham in 1890, the son of a gardener, he was, like Hobbs, an entirely
self-taught cricketer whose technique adhered to the timeless, basic
principles of batsmanship. Assured in defence, he was a fine cutter and
hooker of pace bowling, but what really distinguished his attacking play
was the delicacy of his deflections and glances. 'In almost any other
county he would have been the hero, the cynosure. I know he was quite
capable of such a position; I am not quite sure he was desirous of it.
His style of batting, like his talk, was quiet, neat and crisp,' said the
Oxford and Somerset bowler Raymond Robertson-Glasgow. One of
Sandham's last captains at Surrey, Errol Holmes, called him 'a combination of efficiency and elegance' and left this description of his style:
'His stance at the wicket was the essence of perfection, being natural
and easy, with the weight, if anything, slightly on the right foot; the
arms were almost straight without being stiff and the left shoulder
pointed up the wicket towards the bowler. His shots were executed with
confidence and a sort of finality . . . It has been said that Sandy was
the greatest exponent of the late cut, and I have certainly never seen
anyone play it later or more gracefully, but he was almost equally good
at the leg-glance and, in fact, I doubt if there has ever been a greater
player of the deflection strokes.' Writing in 1927, Patsy Hendren, known
as one of England's greatest fielders, revealed that Sandham's skill with
the cut sometimes made him more difficult to anticipate than Hobbs.
To deal with the stroke, said Hendren, 'I have to place myself square to
stop Jack Hobbs. But Andy Sandham leads me "up the garden". If I put
myself square he makes the cut so fine that I cannot reach it, and if I
get fine he cuts it square. Hobbs doesn't leave his stroke so late as Andy.

Therefore I find him a trifle easier to field to as a rule. This is about the only time I can get upsides with the master bat of our time.'

As in the partnership with Rhodes, Hobbs and Sandham were renowned for their smooth running between the wickets and their judgement of quick singles. Sandham once said of their method: 'We never called; we looked and went. I knew Jack wanted a run as soon as he shaped for his push on the off-side and I was a yard or so down wicket as soon as the ball was bowled.' Though in August 1926 he complained, perhaps only half-jokingly, of Hobbs's predilection: 'The only time I get cross with Jack is when he makes me run some short singles. But, bless you, he only laughs at my black looks.' Despite such occasional exasperation, Sandham was a deep admirer of Hobbs's technique. 'He could bat on both kinds of wickets, and some of the hundreds he made on bad wickets were marvellous, you know, because the man was so brilliant,' Sandham once told the BBC. 'He picked up the ball quickly, his footwork was so good and of course a lot of it was a little bit unorthodox. Jack could do it because he was Jack. I've seen him hit balls a foot outside the stump round the square rig, you know, by putting his right foot over quickly and hooking. Well, not so many of them can do that, you know, and he's got a wonderful pair of wrists. He didn't like anyone to bowl a maiden to him because he contrived to get a single out of something even if it was a good length one, you know, that sort of thing. He hated to be kept quiet.'

Even-tempered and unselfish, Sandham was generally philosophical about playing in the shadow of his more famous partner, though at times he was wryly amused at the disproportionate coverage that Hobbs received. 'It is a curious experience. The attention of the crowd is centred entirely on Hobbs. I feel that from the moment I leave the pavilion. The runs I score are hardly noticed,' he said in 1925. In one match at the Oval, Hobbs was out first ball, while Sandham went on to score a chanceless century. For once, thought Sandham to himself, he might receive top billing in the press, but as he walked out of the ground, he glanced at the news placards, which read, 'Hobbs out for o at the Oval'. Later Sandham said, 'Well, I suppose you've got to be a pretty good player to merit a contents bill when you've got a duck.' Far from resenting Hobbs, he revered him for his modesty. 'He's a fine chap. If he'd been at all swollen-headed he would have been unbearable because at the time, you know, the newspapers were all Jack Hobbs this, that and the other. But he was a grand fellow. Now I've grown older, I realise how fat-headed he could have been if he had been that way inclined. But he was nice to everybody,' said Sandham in his BBC interview.

What really aggravated Sandham was not his subordinate role to Hobbs, but his lack of recognition from the cricket authorities. Despite a record that including over a hundred centuries and more than 40,000 runs in his career, he won only fourteen England caps and, in his own words, 'I was never considered good enough to play for the Players at Lord's.' Of the official attitude towards his partnership with Hobbs, he commented bitterly, 'It seemed as though they wanted us to confine this to county matches.' Much of this neglect was due, of course, to the presence of Herbert Sutcliffe, the consummate Yorkshire opener who made his first-class debut in 1919, but still, Sandham could have batted down the order. On the cricket field, Sandham appeared more solemn than the genial Hobbs, as was shown in this vivid portrait by Ronald Mason, the writer and devoted Surrey supporter: 'Sandham was blessed with a curiously Mongolian cast of countenance; under the shady peak of his cap his eyes hooded themselves watchfully, never blinking, always alert, a little mysterious, inscrutable. Unlike his partner, who had at rare moments a slow and rather appealing grin, Sandham was not seen to smile; it disturbed his methodical concentration. Instead, he sported a thoughtful frown, preoccupied and absorbed, advertising a purposeful determination that he put resolutely into practice.' Yet this severe demeanour at the crease disguised the reality that Sandham was actually more of an extrovert than Hobbs. With the social status of professional cricketers rising dramatically in the interwar years, he revelled in the perks of fame and comparative wealth, including cars, holidays abroad, the cocktail circuit and even expensive property. It is telling that in the 1930s Sandham bought a fashionable apartment in the ultra modernist, art deco block of Du Cane Court* in Balham, one of most prestigious and largest private developments in the capital. Inhabited by film stars and other celebrities, it had its own glamorous social club and restaurant. 'It was a wonderful place and the flats even had sockets for television sets,' says Sandham's daughter Johnnie, a sprightly

---

* It has often been claimed that the Nazi party planned to use Du Cane Court as their London headquarters if they had successfully occupied Britain in 1940, though there is no documentary evidence to support this.

nonagenarian. She also has memories of her father's attitude towards Hobbs: 'Daddy thought the world of Jack. He learnt so much from him. Whatever he said about Jack was always respectful and he would never hear a word against him. But they were not close. That may have been because of the difference in their personalities. My father was more outgoing and Jack was reserved.'

Sandham was batting at number four for Surrey rather than opening when Hobbs produced his most celebrated innings of the 1919 season. This performance, which was remembered by Surrey fans long after Hobbs had retired, did not involve a century or even a fifty, but only the modest score of 47 not out. Yet the circumstances of the match made it a truly memorable achievement. Towards the end of August, Surrey hosted Kent at the Oval and, like so many other games that summer, the game appeared to be heading towards a tame draw at six o'clock on the final afternoon, when Kent were almost 100 ahead with three wickets still in hand. Even when Bill Hitch ripped through the tail, a result seemed impossible, for Surrey were left needing 95 in just forty-five minutes. But Donald Knight, who was the Surrey captain in this game due to another absence from Wilkinson, decided the target should be chased. Having opened with Hobbs in the first innings, Knight dropped himself down the order and instead sent in the more aggressive Jack Crawford, who had returned to England from Australia, patched up his differences with the Surrey Committee now that Lord Alverstone was dead, and agreed to appear whenever he could. As he and Hobbs walked out to bat, light drizzle started to fall. In the deepening gloom, the cause seemed more hopeless than ever. But the Surrey opening pair was undaunted and immediately went on the attack against the two Kent bowlers, the off-spinner Bill Fairservice and the slow left-armer Frank Woolley. At first, Crawford was the more pugnacious. Refusing to allow himself to be inhibited by either the dankness of the atmosphere or the moisture dripping off his spectacles, he regularly danced down the wicket to smack the bowling to all parts of the ground. In just fourteen minutes, 35 runs were scored, Crawford hitting 27 of them. Then Hobbs, who up to this moment had largely been dealing in singles, accelerated dramatically with his trademark pulls and drives. In the next seven minutes, 25 runs were made, most of them from Hobbs's bat. The pair's confident running between the wickets further heightened the pressure on Kent, whose confidence began to fall apart.

At one point, a drive by Hobbs brought 7 runs thanks to a wild over-
throw. Their chase was not a slog but strokeplay of the highest quality.
In a desperate last attempt to calm the whirlwind, Kent brought on the
fine leg-spinner Alfred 'Tich' Freeman. But he quickly disappeared for
11 runs in his first over. With fifteen minutes still to go, Hobbs made
the winning hit off Freeman. Hobbs was on 47, Crawford 48. As the
ball raced over the boundary, the huge, sodden crowd poured onto the
field. 'There was a terrific scene at the close. I was lifted up and carried
along, being finally deposited over the pavilion rails. My damp flannels
were black where the enthusiasts had patted me. The thumb was all
that was left of one of my batting gloves,' Hobbs recalled. The cheering
lasted long after the players had disappeared inside the pavilion. 'It is
doubtful whether any other two players in England than Mr Crawford
and Hobbs could have accomplished this tremendous feat,' said the
Manchester Guardian. But credit also had to be given to the generous
sportsmanship of the Kent team, who managed to bowl 12.1 overs in
just half an hour, an expeditious rate that would be unthinkable in the
modern age.

What made this victory all the more satisfying for Hobbs was that
it took place in his benefit match, the Surrey Committee having kept
its promise to give him another game after the sorry failure in 1914. In
the happier circumstances of 1919, the event was far more successful,
raising just over £1,670, a decent sum given the hardship that the public
had endured through the war. The Committee further showed its generosity not only by keeping the subscription lists open since 1914, but also
by giving a direct grant of £100 to the fund 'in recognition of his exceptional services to Surrey cricket during 1914 and 1919'. Hobbs now had
a comfortable salary, since in May 1919 Surrey had given him a five-year
contract worth a basic £400 a year, excluding talent money and bonuses.
But as he craved long-term financial security and independence he
decided to invest the proceeds of his benefit in a sports shop in central
London to provide his family with an alternative income to cricket.
Because the Surrey Committee usually looked after the investment of
benefit funds, he had to ask for the balance to be advanced to him but,
given his high standing with the club, this was no problem. Hobbs's
partner in the venture was his close friend Andy Kempton, who had
made his money in the construction industry and supplied some of the
additional capital needed for the business. One of Kempton's other

confidants in the cricket world was Jack MacBryan, the Somerset opener, who later revealed that a formal, legal contract over the financing of the shop was not required because the two men so deeply trusted each other. 'No single word of an agreement was drawn up. Simply that they shared 50/50 in the profits!' In some respects, Hobbs was following a path well trodden by previous professional cricketers; former England players like Arthur Shrewsbury, William Gunn, Alfred Shaw and Frank Sugg had all opened and successfully run sports stores. But Hobbs was also taking a risk. He had no experience of commerce and a limited education. His only previous work in retail had been as a baker's errand boy in Cambridge in the 1890s. He had no knowledge of bookkeeping, accounts or sales. Moreover, the economy was in poor shape after the ravages of war. But Hobbs never lacked courage or ambition. In the winter of 1919/20, having turned down a well-paid coaching job in South Africa, he pressed ahead and opened 'Jack Hobbs Limited' at 59 Fleet Street. He worked hard to ensure a successful start, often putting in six days a week at the shop, though he was assisted by two other managers: Douglas Brown, a sound organiser who stayed with the firm until his untimely death in 1940; and his brother Sydney Hobbs, who worked alongside Jack until he opened his own sports shop in Cambridge in 1937.

A lifelong bachelor with a crusty air, Sydney could be an awkward character, as Jack's nephew John Witt recalls. 'He was a strange chap, my Uncle Sydney. To be honest I was a bit frightened of him, and I think most of his brothers and sisters were. A lot of people would say of Sydney, "He's a miserable old bugger." Sydney looked very like Jack in appearance but he could be abrupt whereas Jack always had very good manners. He always seemed to have this chip on his shoulder, I suppose from Jack being so famous, and he grew fed up working in Jack's shop, especially going down to London from Cambridge every day. That's why he opened up a shop here.'

Despite this occasional friction, the shop soon proved a prosperous enterprise. Many clients were obviously attracted at first by the appeal of Hobbs's reputation, but fame alone would not have been able to sustain the company. Hobbs succeeded by providing a courteous service and good quality merchandise at fair prices. He also gained from the growing popularity of cricket in the 1920s, with increasing number of boys taking up the game and major local authorities like the London

County Council expanding their provision of facilities. He was further helped by his contacts in the cricket world. The Surrey minutes show regular purchases of equipment, some of them significant, by the Oval from his shop, transactions that some more puritan souls might regard as representing a conflict of interest. Thus the records of the Finance Committee on May 1924 record that 'the account to Jack Hobbs Ltd of £120 and 10 shillings be paid in full', while in April 1928 a bill for £102 had to be settled. The fact that Hobbs could end up being owed large sums by his own employer was another graphic indicator of how the status of the professional cricketer had risen in the 1920s.

Hobbs always said that he made more money from his shop than he ever made from cricket. His sense of satisfaction was obvious from the start. In January 1920, only a couple of months after the Fleet Street store had opened, the *Daily Mirror's* gossip column reported, 'Jack Hobbs tells me that he has taken quite kindly to business life – he is now an athletic outfitter – and that he is doing very nicely thank you. His many admirers will be pleased to hear it.' His pride in the shop is clear in this advertisement he placed in the *Cricketer* in 1924: 'When not playing cricket I devote all the time in attending to the business and select all cricket bats to make sure supplying the best possible; should a customer specially want my personal attention, I give it with pleasure. My business is mostly by recommendation but a catalogue will be sent to you post free on application.'

From April 1920, however, Hobbs could not give the personal service he wanted, for he was facing a hectic year of cricket, with the forthcoming English season followed by an Ashes tour in the winter. To the relief of most first-class cricketers, the MCC abandoned the experiment of two-day games and switched back to the traditional three-day format for the summer of 1920. A few critics feared that Hobbs's new shop would distract him from his other business of making runs but they could not have been more wrong. In fact, he enjoyed one of his finest seasons, scoring 2,827 runs in all first-class matches at 58.59 and finishing second in the national averages behind Patsy Hendren.

Right from the start of the summer, he was in superlative form. In the very first match, against Northamptonshire at the Oval, he hit a century and ten more followed, including a double hundred for the Rest of England against Middlesex, the champion county that year. Of this innings, *Wisden* wrote: 'Making his biggest score of the year, Hobbs was for the most part astonishingly brilliant. At one point in his innings he became reckless, and seemed as if he wanted to get out, but the hope of making 200 steadied him and he played as well as ever. Except for a possible chance in the slips there was no flaw in his cricket during the first 100 runs.' He also made a big hundred against Hampshire in Phil Mead's benefit game at Southampton in early July, taking 169 off an attack that was led by the accurate fast-medium seam of Jack Newman and Alec Kennedy, two of the finest bowlers on the county circuit in the 1920s. Kennedy later gave his insight into the experience of bowling to Hobbs: 'There never was a better batsman than Jack Hobbs and everyone who ever played with him knows that. It was not just that he was a textbook player; he was so much more than that. Once, just after the war, I started a match against him and the first ball I bowled was a late outswinger. It moved from about middle to off-stump and he stepped across and hit it to square leg for four and – before I could say anything – he looked down the pitch and grinned and said, "I shouldn't have done that, should I? – I was a bit lucky." That is how good he was; he was so sure of the ball; it was always hitting the middle of the bat. You used to feel he knew what you would do before you knew it yourself.' Newman concluded: 'He was the one batsman I never really thought I would beat and get out. I just used to keep on bowling and hope he would get himself out; he did that sometimes when he was tired or it all seemed too easy; but if he set out to stay in, you never had a chance or at least I never did.'

Hobbs enjoyed one remarkable patch in mid-June 1920, when he hit four centuries in successive innings, beginning with 110 against Sussex, followed by 134 at Leicester and 101 against Warwickshire at Edgbaston. The fourth came in Surrey's first innings against mighty Yorkshire at Sheffield, the home attack including Test bowlers Wilfred Rhodes, Abe Waddington, Roy Kilner and George Macaulay. 'As usual, his cricket was very attractive to watch,' said the *Daily Mirror*. In the second innings, Hobbs looked likely to score a fifth successive century, but when he was on 70 his old batting partner Rhodes came on and immediately tempted him into a mistimed drive that lobbed up to mid-off. 'There have been times when I have considered 70 a good score, but that day was not one of them,' Hobbs wrote ruefully. He felt that the best of the quartet of centuries was the one against Leicestershire, partly because it was made so quickly, in just sixty-five minutes, and partly because the pitch was so difficult. 'His driving, cutting and pulling were really wonderful. What made the innings more brilliant was that the wicket was a really bad one, not wet but very fast and fiery,' recalled Herbert Strudwick. In addition to batting, Hobbs had to take over the captaincy in the field at Leicester when Percy Fender was called away to London on business. Again, for all his dislike of responsibility, he did a good job, leading Surrey to a big innings victory. One of his ruses worked well when he kidded the brawny young amateur pace bowler Gilly Reay into increasing his speed. Reay had thought he was bowling quickly, but, after a couple of overs, Hobbs came over to him and said, 'Why, you're only supposed to be a slow bowler – see if you can bowl a few faster balls.' In the next two overs, Reay clean bowled three Leicestershire batsmen. Less successful was Hobbs's decision to give a liquid reward to Tom Rushby for a penetrating spell of 7 for 32 in Leicestershire's first innings.

'Well bowled, Tom. Will you have a drink?' asked Hobbs.

'Yes please. I'll have a double Scotch,' replied Rushby.

Soon afterwards, Rushby was out again on the field at the start of Leicestershire's second innings. Before he had completed one over, Rusby had to make a swift return to the pavilion with a stomach upset.

Idiosyncratic leadership was the hallmark of Percy Fender, who took over the Surrey captaincy in 1920 as Wilkinson retired from full-time cricket to pursue his legal career – as well as a gold medal for hockey at the Antwerp Olympics. By now, Fender had recovered from his war wounds, and he quickly proved himself an inspirational leader on the field, full of original ideas and innovative tactics. The son of a London businessman who ran a firm of wholesale stationers, Fender had attended St Paul's school, where he was a contemporary of that other unconventional leader Bernard Montgomery, the victor of El Alamein. Having intended to become a barrister, Fender entered the wine trade, which he found gave him enough time and money to support his amateur cricket career. His natural flair for captaincy was sorely needed at the Oval in the 1920s, for Surrey were badly hampered throughout the decade by a weak bowling attack. It was only through his constant scheming and man-management that they became serious contenders for honours. Douglas Jardine wrote that Fender possessed 'the ablest, the quickest and most enterprising cricket brain' he had known, while the fast bowler Alf Gover said that Fender was 'worshipped by the whole team'. Among the measures he introduced at the start of his long reign were special absorbent underwear for players, a cap with a bigger peak to shield eyes from the sun and the recruitment of a baseball coach to improve the team's throwing. In another challenge to orthodoxy, he broke down the barriers between professionals and amateurs to ensure that Surrey played as a unit. He abolished separate lunches and teas at the Oval, and also led his team onto the field through one gate, a move that prompted the outrage of some traditionalist diehards. 'We had several bad shocks to our sense of the solemnities of cricket,' said one shaken visitor to the Oval after attending a county match there in 1924. 'We saw Fender, the Surrey Captain, lead the "gentlemen" of his team to the professionals' headquarters and bring his team out into the field in a body, just for all the world as though they were all flesh and blood. It was a painful sight and many of us closed our eyes rather than look upon it. We felt that Bolshevism had invaded our sanctuary at last.' But, interestingly, it was the professionals, led by Hobbs, who stopped Fender going as far as he would have liked in this direction. Fender had suggested that the whole team should share a single dressing room but Hobbs told him, 'With respect, Mr Fender, we like to talk about you and laugh at what you're going to do next.' Such a remark should not be taken as any sign of a lack of respect from Hobbs towards Fender. Just the opposite is true. He wholeheartedly shared his team's admiration for their skipper and believed that Fender should have been given the England captaincy. 'I know I speak for 90 per cent of cricketers, by whom I mean both players and public, when I say that Mr Fender is a finer and more inspiring captain than any man now playing,' he wrote in 1924.

Hobbs never got his wish that Fender be elevated to the Test leadership. This was largely because of hostility towards him within the MCC establishment, provoked not only by Fender's disdain for the divide between amateurs and professionals, but also because of the belief that he was too eager to stretch the rules. 'He had a reputation for gamesmanship and I saw a bit of that,' said Freddie Brown, later an England captain himself. He was not above time wasting, discreetly scuffing up the wicket or intimidating the opposition. Even as hard a cricketer as Tiger Smith, who became an umpire after his retirement from playing, regretted the atmosphere that Fender created: 'Surrey weren't a pleasant side to umpire in those days. Fender liked his own way and the air was blue from the amateurs when things weren't going right. Like the

Australians of recent years they'd take the mickey out of the batsmen to upset them.' There was another reason for Fender's failure to gain the England captaincy: he had a poor relationship with Leveson Gower, who regularly served as Chairman of the Selectors throughout the 1920s. The main source of this discord, said Fender, was his refusal to play in the Surrey side the kind of amateurs that Leveson Gower favoured. 'I had a lot of problems with Shrimp over the question of team selection,' recalled Fender. 'Shrimp, who made his living acting as a contact man, suggested that I should include two young cricketers, who were sons of some of his business friends, when they had been barely good enough to get into their college side at university. I said I wasn't willing to accommodate them.'

With his trademark long sweater, thick moustache, round glasses and crinkly black hair, Fender was a caricaturists' dream, his unique image firmly imprinted on the public consciousness in the 1920s. But his awkward looks could not hide the reality that he was fine all-round player. As a fielder, he was one of the finest slips in the country, while his leg-spin bowling, like his captaincy, was full of wiles and novel variations, though Hobbs once complained of his methods, 'The only criticism I could offer is that he occasionally gives away too many runs in order to carry out some deep-laid scheme to trap a batsman.' His batting was unorthodox but highly effective. He was one of the fiercest hitters in county cricket and at Northampton in 1920 he hit the fastest century in the history of first-class cricket in just thirty-five minutes.

This was part of an excellent season for him that ensured his selection, alongside Hobbs, for the MCC tour of Australia that winter under the captaincy of Johnny Douglas and the management of the Yorkshire Secretary Frederick Toone. Because of the responsibilities of his shop, Hobbs initially hesitated about agreeing to the trip when he first received the invitation in July, but at the beginning of August, having reassured himself that the business was in capable hands, he accepted. 'Everybody is pleased that Jack Hobbs will, after all, go to Australia. All obstacles have, apparently, been overcome,' proclaimed the *Daily Mirror*. The MCC side was, on paper, reasonably strong in batting, with Hobbs supported by Woolley, Rhodes, Hendren and J.W. Hearne, but the bowling smacked of inexperience and weakness, with only Johnny Douglas having any sort of Test record and he was now thirty-eight. Sadly for England, Sydney Barnes, still one of the world's finest bowlers, had turned down a place on the tour because the MCC would not allow him to bring his wife, a decision that only reinforced his contempt for the establishment, not least because the captain, Johnny Douglas was accompanied by his entire family, including both parents. One particularly odd selection was that of the forty-one-year-old leg-spinner Rockley Wilson, whose long career as a Winchester schoolmaster had severely restricted his playing opportunities. Wilson's place in the side grew even more controversial as the tour progressed because he was contracted by the *Daily Express* to provide match reports, a role that led to some anger in Australia and embarrassment to the MCC.

As he had done on his last trip to Australia, Hobbs tried to reduce his amount of time at sea by travelling through France, then picking up the MCC's liner, the 12,000 ton SS *Osterley* of the Orient Line, at the Mediterranean port of Toulon. He was accompanied on this Gallic section of the journey by his Surrey teammate Strudwick and the Lancashire bowler Cecil 'Ciss' Parkin, a popular, maverick character whose two favourite activities off the field were performing magicians' tricks and aggravating the cricket authorities. It is a reflection of how far Hobbs was from teetotalism at this stage in his life that between Dover and Paris the trio consumed two bottles of champagne, which were bought for them by well-wishers. Inevitably, the voyage across the waters was far less pleasant for Hobbs. 'Even with the weather at its very best and the sea at its smoothest, I never felt really well,' he told the *Evening Star*. That discomfort was worsened during the usual stop in Colombo to play a Ceylonese cricket team. He and several other players made the mistake of having prawns for lunch, just as Graham Gooch's team famously did in Madras during the disastrous 1992/3 tour of India. 'In the morning eight of us were very ill. The attacks lasted a couple of days and we suffered excruciating pain,' recalled Hobbs.

After this trauma, he also had a bizarre experience while sailing across the Pacific when he decided one night to sleep on the deck because of the intense heat in his cabin. As he recounted in an article for the *Star*, 'I had a nightmare and awakened with a feeling of not being too clever. While in this state, I heard a gurgle and a groan, which apparently came from another part of the deck, some ten or twelve yards away. I peered into the darkness and saw something white which moved, while all the time it gave periodical groans and gurgles.' Disturbed by this ghostly apparition, Hobbs got to his feet and groped around until he found a

cricket ball attached to a rope, this device used by the MCC for practising on the deck. 'I threw the ball, as I often throw from cover-point,
straight at the object. I scored a hit; the figure jumped up with a yell
and both of us fled – in different directions.' The next morning at
breakfast Hobbs 'noted a fellow passenger with a bruised cheek. Why
he did not say anything about the previous night's adventure beats me.'
It was a strange incident, which illustrated the innocent, almost child-
like, side of Hobbs's personality, both in his fear that he had seen a
ghost and in his willingness to be frank about it, when other, more
cynical middle-aged men might have kept quiet to avoid looking foolish.

On the *Osterley's* arrival at the western port of Fremantle, there was
more hassle for the MCC party as they were taken into quarantine
because one member of the ship's crew had died from typhoid fever.
For a week, Hobbs and his colleagues were housed in a group of army
huts at a station near Perth. They were able to get in a little practice as
some coconut matting was laid on the rough ground, though this was
nothing like as satisfactory as proper nets. Away from the cricket, Hobbs
enlivened the mood at the base with his fondness for practical jokes.
One day, the young fast bowler Harry Howell found a dead iguana and
brought it into Hobbs's hut. Knowing of Parkin's dislike of snakes and
lizards, Hobbs quietly placed the reptilian corpse under some clothing
on Parkin's bed, and then retired for the night. According to the account
left by Patsy Hendren, when Parkin discovered the dead creature he 'did
a correct imitation of a rising rocket! He never suspected Hobbs. I
reckon the Grand Old Man's century record would still be standing if
Jack had not been sleeping.'

Once the players had passed all their medical tests after a week in
quarantine, they finally were allowed to travel on to Adelaide. Just before
they left Fremantle, Ernest Jones, the former Australian fast bowler
and now the Customs Officer at the port, called out, 'I'll lay five to one
you don't win a Test,' to which Hobbs nonchalantly told Parkin, 'Every
trip we've been on he has told the same tale.' But this time Jones was
right. England suffered by far their worst humiliation on an Ashes tour
in the twentieth century. As on Andrew Flintoff's disastrous trip in
2006/7, every single Test was lost, all of them by big margins. In all
three disciplines of the game, England were completely outplayed, their
fielding being particularly poor. Even Hobbs, never one for strident
judgements, admitted at the end of the tour that 'the slip catching of

the team has been execrable'. Up against a formidable Australian batting line-up, England's already inadequate attack inevitably grew disheartened at the lack of support in the field. The fact that Percy Fender topped the bowling averages with only 12 wickets at 34 runs was a sign of the bowlers' impotence. The batting was slightly better, but Rhodes, Woolley and Hendren disappointed, while Hearne was able to play only two innings because of injury.

The total eclipse led to a predictable and anguished debate in England about the causes of this overwhelming inferiority. Some blamed the decline of the amateur. Others said that the real problem was the new obsession with googly and swerve bowling, which meant that the old virtues of line and length had disappeared. Certain pessimists said that batsmen were too square on or were playing too much on the back foot. But by far the favourite explanation was that English cricket was simply exhausted after four years of war, and had insufficiently recovered. There was an element of truth in this, especially on the bowling front, just as after the Second World War England's bowling was desperately weak. Yet this reasoning, which gave some comfort to England followers because it both emphasised heroic sacrifices and lessened the responsibility of the team for failure, slid over the reality that Australia had been through the same ordeal. Many of the Australian stars of the 1920/21 series had served in the armed forces, including Herbie Collins, Johnny Taylor, Clarrie 'Nip' Pellew and Jack Gregory. Indeed, the writer E.H.D. Sewell, felt that references to war fatigue encouraged complacency among England supporters who should 'dismiss from their minds once and for ever the fallacy that Australian cricket did not suffer so much from the war as did English cricket. Proportionately to the respective number of cricketers in the two countries, Australia suffered more than England did in the war.'

A more convincing explanation for Australia's superiority lay, not in deep structural faults within the English game, but in the fact that the home side had unearthed a trinity of truly great bowlers in the two pacemen, Jack Gregory and Ted McDonald, and the leg-spinner Arthur Mailey. The history of the Ashes shows that overwhelming victories are always won by irresistible bowling attacks, whether it be Tyson and Statham in 1954/5, Lillee and Thomson in 1974/5 or McGrath and Warne at the end of the 1990s. Even Hutton, Compton, Washbrook and Edrich could not cope with Lindwall and Miller in 1948; it is often forgotten that Len Hutton was actually dropped in the middle of this series because he was perceived by the selectors as insufficiently robust in the face of the Australian attack.

Yet against the Australians' destructive power of the 1920/21 series, Jack Hobbs's maintained his reputation as a great batsman. He was the one England player who could cope with the searing pace of the quick bowlers and the unpredictable turn of Mailey. In his ten innings in the series, he scored 505 runs at an average of 50.5, far ahead of the next placed England batsman, Johnny Douglas, who averaged 39. On the fast, bouncy wickets of Australia, Hobbs was masterly in both attack and defence, particularly at judging which rising deliveries to leave from Gregory and McDonald, as the wicketkeeper Bert Oldfield recalled in this passage about Hobbs's technique: 'Both these bowlers made the ball fly high and disconcertingly. To balls pitched on or outside the off-stump, I observed that Hobbs appeared to play at them with the bat held high. It amazed me that I found continually taking these balls, which I thought he would be sure to cover. I discovered that it was all part of his general-ship, for at the very last fraction of a second he would draw his bat away from the line of the ball just sufficiently to avoid the possibility of being caught behind or in the slips – a splendid example of his supreme confidence and natural skill.' With his talent for playing the ball as late as possible, Hobbs was just as effective against the spin of Mailey, who later recalled, 'As a batsman pure and simple, I found Jack Hobbs one of the most interesting I had bowled against. I knew after my first over to him that he was going to be a great source of annoyance as well as of interest. I was never quite sure whether he could pick the "wrong 'un"; but I knew, as when bowling against Trumper, that Jack's great talent would not allow him to be fooled too often. My experience against him taught me a good deal about the finer science of slow bowling. We all recognised it as a feat to have Hobbs out before lunch.'

The supremacy of the Australian bowling was apparent from the opening Test at Sydney in mid-December 1920. England made a decent start, dismissing Australia for 267, to which Hobbs at cover contributed both a run-out and a catch. According to Mailey, Hobbs's fielding had barely declined since the war, despite his reaching the age of thirty-eight. 'Many of the Australians had never played against Hobbs. When they saw him lazily mooching around the covers they came to the conclusion that a shot in Hobbs's direction meant an easy run. He ran so many batsmen out and gave so many a shock that halfway through the season the Australians held a caucus meeting in the dressing room and adopted the slogan, "No runs when the ball goes to Jack Hobbs.'" But the Australian total would have been much smaller if more of England's fielders had been as dexterous as Hobbs, for a number of crucial chances were missed.

When England went in to bat, Hobbs opened with a new partner, Jack Russell of Essex who, unlike Rhodes, had been in good form in the warm-up games. Russell failed badly, however, falling first ball, and this set the tone for both the innings and the rest of the series. In an England effort of just 190, Hobbs top-scored with 49 but even he was out in uncustomary fashion, bowled behind his legs by Gregory. As Fender recorded in his account of the tour: 'Hobbs said afterwards that it seemed to him a plain straight ball and he was obviously surprised to find himself bowled. He seemed to think that somehow just for that ball he must have taken a wrong guard. If so, it seems an extraordinary error, especially as Hobbs had been batting for over an hour, during his time he had hit four 4s.' Australia then exploited their advantage with a mammoth total of 581 in their second innings, the twenty-one-stone colossus of Warwick Armstrong hitting 158, a performance that brutally symbolised his psychological dominance over England. The target of 659 to win was far too high a mountain to climb, and England were all out for 281, Hobbs again top-scoring with 59.

It was the same pattern in the second Test at Melbourne, with England hopelessly outplayed but Hobbs restoring some pride with his exceptional batsmanship. Replying to Australia's first innings of 499, England were caught on a rain-affected wicket which became vicious as it dried under the hot sun. 'The ball was jumping about from the first over bowled, some being simply short balls which bumped clean over the batsman's head or good length ones which went over the wicketkeeper's head,' wrote Fender. At one point late in England's innings, Strudwick was hit three times over the heart by balls that reared from Gregory. Yet it was on this damp minefield that Hobbs managed to score a chanceless century, many of his runs from nine 4s coming from drives through the covers and straight. Eventually he was out for 122, made in three and a half hours. Strudwick called his innings 'splendid'; *Wisden* said it was 'from the English point of view, the finest innings of the tour' and Hobbs himself, with his usual modest understatement, said that it was 'an innings I number among my best'. But it was not enough to prevent England following-on and losing the Test by an innings and 91 runs.

Just as had happened on the 1911/12, a crisis meeting was called with the senior professionals to discuss the captaincy of Douglas, who had been in poor form with bat and ball. The manager Frederick Toone felt that the energy of Fender, who had yet to play a Test in the series, might revive England. In contrast to his support for Douglas in 1911/12, Hobbs now backed his own Surrey captain, not just out of county loyalty but also because he felt that Douglas had been too distracted from his cricket by travelling with his family. Woolley, another of the senior pros, supported the position of Toone and Hobbs, but Rhodes was more equivocal, having little knowledge of Fender as either player or captain. Moreover, Rhodes never had much faith in Toone, his own county secretary. 'I don't like him and if I wished him well, I should be telling a lie, so I'm saying nowt,' declared Rhodes later in the decade when asked why he refused to congratulate Toone on his knighthood for services to cricket.

With the leading professionals so divided, the scheme to change captains went nowhere. Always a fighter, Douglas absolutely refused to stand down when Toone put the suggestion to him and remained in charge for the rest of the series. Though Douglas's batting improved in the last three Tests, he could do nothing to halt Australia's progress towards the first whitewash in an Ashes series. Nor did the inclusion of Fender dramatically help England, though he bowled some useful, if expensive, spells. One of the few sources of consolation for England amidst this embarrassment was the batting of Hobbs. In the third Test at Adelaide, he scored 123 in the second innings, his sixth century against Australia, as England unsuccessfully chased a distant target of 489. As a result of this innings, Hobbs was summoned during the final lunch interval to see the governor of South Australia, Sir Archibald Weignall, who presented him with an oval tiepin as a tribute to his batting. Cecil Parkin, having taken 5 for 60 in Australia's first innings, was also sent for, but according to his account, all he received amidst much hand-shaking were three words of congratulation, 'Well bowled, Parkin.' When he returned to the dressing room, Parkin complained to everyone that he had 'got nowt', to which Hobbs apparently replied, 'Well, Ciss, you would be a bowler. I can't help it.'

Sadly, Hobbs's once prolific opening partnership with Rhodes was now barely functioning, due to the Yorkshireman's collapse in form. In the second and third Tests, their stands only totalled 101 runs at an average of 25. It was the same sorry story in the fourth Test at Melbourne, where they put on only 18 and 32 together, with Hobbs failing in both innings for once. He should not have played in the final Test at Sydney, having torn a thigh muscle while fielding in the state game against New South Wales. 'My injury was very painful and I should have had at least a month's rest,' he wrote. But Douglas, having seen Hobbs bat effectively if a little gingerly in the nets on the eve of the Test, begged him to remain in the side. Somewhat reluctantly, but following his usual conscientiousness, Hobbs agreed. It was a decision that was to spark a remarkable chain of events that culminated in a moving display of the Australian public's affection for Hobbs. When England batted first, his mobility was restricted but not sufficiently to prevent him making a solid 40 and putting on his first fifty stand of the series with Rhodes. In the field, however, his lameness was more of a problem. Hobbling badly, he could not take up his usual position at cover and at one stage, as he limped after the ball from a stroke by Charlie Kelleway, the batsmen were able to run two when there should only have been a single. Ignorant of Hobbs's injury, some of the spectators loudly hooted and jeered at him. At the end of the over, Kelleway was so embarrassed that he apologised to Hobbs and told him, 'Sorry, I forgot about your injury. I would not have taken that second run had I remembered.' But the incident was blown up into a huge controversy when Fender and Rockley Wilson, who were reporting on the match for the English papers as well as participating in it, sent cables to their news desks in London that contained strident criticism of the crowd's abuse of Hobbs. Immediately these reports were relayed back to Australia, where the cricket public reacted furiously. During England's second innings, for which Hobbs was too handicapped to open, Rockley Wilson marched out to bat at number four, only to be met by a crescendo of boos, the noise increasing in volume with each stride he took towards the middle. His stay was a short one, as he was stumped off Mailey for just 5. Hobbs, waiting to go in next, was shocked at the vehemence of the crowd's animosity towards Wilson: 'When he got out they hooted again, even the members joined in as he reached the pavilion. Wilson was naturally amazed that the pavilion people should have done such a thing. He simply pulled up and coolly stood at attention, raising his cap. Several people made as though they would attack him, but fortunately nothing happened.'

Just before Hobbs walked out of the pavilion, he was taken to one side by the former Australian captain Monty Noble, who sensed that Hobbs was shaken by the scene. 'Don't let it worry you,' Noble reassured him. Hobbs was grateful for the support. Then an extraordinary thing happened. 'The moment I appeared at the door of the pavilion, the spectators rose from their seats and cheered liked mad, shouting, "Good old, Hobbs!" They even sang, "For He's a Jolly Good Fellow". This was undoubtedly intended to make it clear to me that any chaff directed at my fielding had been due to ignorance of my injured leg; they had never meant to be unfair to one of their favourites,' he wrote in his 1935 autobiography. The cheering continued as he reached the wicket. 'I felt a bit wobbly, but showed no emotion. Not even did I acknowledge the cheers by raising my cap.' He pulled himself together sufficiently to make 34 before he fell to Mailey.

England's second innings total of 280 was too small to prevent the fifth Australian victory in a row, this one by eight wickets. For the team, the series could not have ended on a lower note. But for Hobbs, the memory of the warm demonstration by the crowd lived with him for the rest of his life, 'an unparalleled scene in my career as a cricketer'.

11

'You Would Never Have Reached London'

As Hobbs sat down in his train carriage, the pain worsened. Throughout the previous days, he had felt a dull ache in his stomach but with the third Test coming up at Headingley, he had hoped it would fade away with the help of some medicine prescribed by his doctor. The medication made no difference. Now, accompanied by Ada on the journey from London to Leeds, he feared that the problem might be more serious. Every movement was uncomfortable. His skin grew pale and beads of perspiration formed on his forehead. He tried to look at the passing countryside or read the paper, but could not be distracted from the pain. Ada, sitting beside him, could do nothing except worry.

When they arrived at Leeds, they were met by their friend Seth Pilley, a schoolmaster at whose Calverley home they often stayed during any visits to Yorkshire. Pilley was disturbed by Hobbs's wan appearance and immediately expressed his concern. Hobbs, not wanting to make a fuss, said he was just feeling 'a little seedy' and was certain a night's sleep would put him right. But the next morning, Saturday 2 July 1921, he was even worse. Nevertheless, he travelled with his cricket gear to the ground, where England were due to play Warwick Armstrong's rampant Australians who had already won the first two Tests of that summer. As soon as he reached Headingley, he was summoned to a meeting with the England selectors to discuss which bowler to leave out of the squad for the final XI.

'First of all, I don't feel very well myself,' he told them, going on to outline his difficulty.

The selectors looked anxiously at each other. Then their chairman Harry Foster, the elder brother of the former England captain 'Tip'

Foster, said to Hobbs, 'If you can stand the risk of playing, we'll stand the risk of playing you.'

Hobbs reluctantly agreed, still hoping that the medicine might take effect.

Australia won the toss and batted. As Armstrong's men built up another big total, Hobbs grew sicker during the afternoon. After the tea interval, he was too ill to return to the field or bat in England's reply. With concern mounting in the England camp, he was examined by a doctor who could not locate the cause of the pain but ordered Hobbs to return immediately to Pilley's house and go to bed. On the Sunday, following a more restful night, Hobbs felt a little better and even began to contemplate batting for England when the match resumed. But on Monday, the ache was more severe than ever. The same doctor who had seen him on Saturday now absolutely refused to give him permission to play, though his medical diagnosis remained vague. Hobbs was relieved. In his condition, he could not face Gregory and McDonald. When he turned up at Headingly to give the England selectors this grim news, Harry Foster took one look at the pallid, ailing figure and urged Hobbs to return to London as soon as possible for treatment.

Before the war, Hobbs had been involved in that dangerous road accident in South Africa which could have cost him his life. But he came even closer to death on this occasion. If he had followed the chairman's advice, he might well have died before he even reached London. By a stroke of good luck, just before Hobbs left, someone in the dressing room mentioned that one of England's most eminent surgeons, Sir Berkeley Moynihan, was based in Leeds. Desperate for a remedy, Hobbs quickly changed his plans, and hurried off in a taxi to Sir Berkeley's private nursing home. As soon as the news that the great cricketer was on the premises reached him, Sir Berkeley came out of his operating theatre. He shook Hobbs by the hand, felt his torso, and, with the assurance borne of years of expertise, instantly diagnosed acute appendicitis.

'You must be operated on today. If you go to London, I tell you emphatically that you will go at your own risk. Moreover, if you go, the operation must be done today. Remember that.'

Sensing the urgency of the issue, Hobbs then asked: 'If I decide to have it done here, will you operate on me yourself?'

'Delighted,' replied Sir Berkeley.

In response Hobbs explained that he would have to return to Headingley to consult his wife. As solicitous as he was confident, Sir Berkeley said that he would make the arrangements to have Ada brought to the nursing home. Once she had arrived, Jack immediately secured her agreement for the operation to proceed. Within moments, he was anaesthetised and lying on the table in the theatre, ready for the surgeon's scalpel.

Sir Berkeley's talent lay not so much in advancement of clinical knowledge as in his outstanding surgical proficiency. Regarded by many as an artist and by some critics as a showman, he regularly practised his manual dexterity through exercises such as knotting and unknotting a piece of string with the fingers of one hand. Hobbs was relieved to be in the care of such a skilful practitioner: 'Had I been the king, I could not have been better cared for,' he later remarked. The operation was a complete success, though the speed with which it was performed only emphasised the physical danger Hobbs had been in. This was a point dramatically made to Hobbs when Sir Berkeley came to his bedside the next morning.

'That was the best day's work you ever did. It was a bad case – worse than I thought. You would never have reached London. You could not have lived for another five hours,' he said.

Hobbs knew he owed his survival to the surgeon and always remained in his debt. As a token of his appreciation, he sent an autographed bat to Sir Berkeley's fifteen-year-old son Patrick, then a pupil at Westminster, while he also gave Sir Berkeley an inscribed gold fountain pen. In turn, Sir Berkeley said it had been an honour 'to have rendered a service to England's greatest cricketer'. Unlike Hobbs, Sir Berkeley, who was elevated to the House of Lords a year after the operation, was not heavily endowed with the virtue of modesty and as his gift in response, he sent Hobbs a signed photograph of himself with the inscription: 'In memory of a good innings and a great score.'

Hobbs had been spared, but what was so odd about the episode was that the other doctor had so badly failed to diagnose appendicitis. Yet this oversight may have reflected Hobbs's stoicism in the face of pain, the quality that he showed in coping with his migraines. As Hobbs himself later explained, 'The doctor who attended me first told me later that he could not understand how my appendix could have been in such a state without my rolling in agony but the pain was really very severe.'

On leaving Sir Berkeley's nursing home in early July, Hobbs recognised that his season was already over. A long period of recuperation lay ahead. But this was not the first medical setback in what turned out to be a

calamitous summer for him. He had returned from Australia in April
with his reputation intact and his record stronger than ever. A laudatory
profile in the newly launched *Cricketer* magazine, edited by Plum Warner,
reflected on Hobbs's status at the end of the tour. Describing him as 'the
best batsman in the world today', the article continued: 'He possesses a
keen eye and his natural style has the mark of inborn genius . . . It may
truly be said of him that he is equally at home on any pitch and against
any bowling. Moreover his batting is never in the least dull; he is always
making the most of every opportunity and his quickness of foot enables
him to get into position in plenty of time for his stroke. Quite apart
from his superb batsmanship, his name will live on as a cover-point.
Quick on his feet, he swoops on the ball, gathers it with lightning-like
rapidity and in a flash it is in the bowler's or wicketkeeper's hands. A
very safe catch, he has the sort of hands which act like a magnet to the
ball. He has a peculiar shrug of the shoulders when fielding or batting
but he is neat and crisp in all his movements and gives the impression
of thoroughly enjoying every ball of a match. "Go it, Jack!" is a familiar
cry at the Oval and he deserves his popularity, for in spite of his many
successes, he is not in the least spoilt. He has a nice figure and a pleasant
face and his flannels sit well on him.'

As the new season began, Hobbs appeared to have recovered from
the torn thigh muscle that ruined his last Test in Australia. At the end
of April, he took part in a Surrey trial match, in which his contribution
was noteworthy not for his moderate score of 26 but for his bizarre
mode of dismissal, for he fell to a high lob delivered by the Cambridge
undergraduate Trevor Molony, who went on to take three other wickets
in the trial. Molony's unorthodox style, bowling slow underarm to a
packed leg-side field, appealed to the eccentric in Percy Fender who
picked him for three of Surrey's early games. Apart from one burst of
3 for 11 against Notts, Moloney accomplished little and was hit with
such ferocity that he became a greater danger to his own fielders than
to the opposition. Despite his failure, he earned a place in the record
books as the last ever lob bowler to have played county cricket.

After the interlude of the Surrey trial, Hobbs had his first real match
of the 1921 season when he agreed to play for Lionel Robinson's XI against
the visiting Australians. Robinson was another of those fantastically
wealthy colonial patrons of cricket who crop up regularly in Hobbs's saga.
Born in Ceylon and raised in Melbourne, he had made his money in

stockbroking and used part of his fortune to buy a 2,000-acre estate in the Suffolk village of Old Buckenham, where he built his own country house and laid out a cricket ground complete with turf imported from Australia. Though never fully embraced by the establishment because of his aggressive manner, Robinson had sufficient influence to attract first-class cricket to his domain, and no match played there was ever more prestigious than the one that started on 4 May between Warwick Armstrong's feared Australians and his own invitation team that featured several Test stars including Fender, Hendren and Douglas as well as Hobbs.

In front of a crowd of 12,000 people, the match began in bleak, damp weather, worsened by a blustery wind sweeping across the ground. In such conditions, with the ball moving about extravagantly, it was no surprise that the Australians were all out for 136. There seemed little chance that, against the pace of Gregory and McDonald on a difficult wicket, Robinson's XI would fare much better and indeed Donald Knight was soon out lbw for 1. But, just as in the winter, Hobbs showed his class and courage. He was hit a few times by rising deliveries, but never flinched. His technique remained masterly as he showed precise judgement in leaving the ball, playing a dead bat or going on the attack. Batting with the Northants all-rounder Vallance Jupp, Hobbs ensured that his team began to approach the Australian total with just one wicket down. So faultless was his strokeplay, so sure was his defence, so strong was the opposition attack that, in later years, Hobbs declared this to be the finest innings of his life, out of all his long catalogue of great achievements. 'I was playing at my best form. I always think that I hit the real height of my abilities. Everything came off. There were some good bowlers and all my shots I kept middling, everything in the middle of the bat,' he told *The Times* in 1952. Then shortly before the close of the first day, with Hobbs just 15 runs short of an almost perfect century, disaster struck. Hobbs stroked the ball into the off-side and called Jupp for a characteristic quick single. Just as they crossed in the middle, Hobbs's vulnerable thigh muscle suddenly went. The tissue gave out so violently that Jupp later swore he had heard it snap as he passed. Hobbs immediately pulled up in agony, limped to the other end and then was helped back to the pavilion. The injury from Australia had returned with a vengeance.

Hobbs was so concerned about his leg that he feared he might have to undergo surgery on it. But having consulted a specialist, he was sent to be examined by Dr George Murray Levick, a man of wide-ranging talents who, in addition to his medical work, had been a biologist, writer, explorer and Royal Navy hero. In one expedition to Antarctica in 1912/13, after his party was prevented by the frozen wastes from reaching their ship, he had to spend the entire, miserable winter on an inhospitable island, living for months in an ice cave and supplementing his rations with seal blubber. So the challenge of a troublesome thigh muscle was not too daunting for him. Over several weeks he gave Hobbs a course in physiotherapy, including massage and electric stimulation. This worked even better than Hobbs could have imagined and he had fully recovered by late June. The injury, however, meant that he was forced to miss the summer's first two Tests, in which England were predictably crushed by Armstrong's juggernaut. As England staggered from one crisis to another, Hobbs's batting was sorely missed. 'The inability of Jack Hobbs to play is a calamity,' said the *Daily Mirror,* while in the *Cricketer* Archie MacLaren bewailed the effect that Hobbs's absence had on the England line-up at Lord's. 'There was a total absence of headwork on the part of our batsmen who had no correct model to watch such as Hobbs.'

When Hobbs returned for Surrey in the third week of June, the selectors were desperate for him to prove his form and fitness sufficiently to warrant an immediate recall to the Test side. On the very ground where the third Test would be played at the start of July, Hobbs fulfilled all their hopes by making 172 against Yorkshire in his first county championship match of the season. It seemed that he had been able to carry on where he had left off in the match at Buckenham, hitting twenty 4s in a chanceless innings that lasted 220 minutes. After that, his place at the top of the England order was an inevitability.

The Leeds Test turned into the most ill-fated, painful match of his career. Yet, even in the midst of the near fatal collapse of his health, there were a number of positive side-effects of the episode. One was the spontaneous outpouring of affection towards him from the public. Hobbs might have still been just a cricketer in 1921 but he was already on the path to becoming a national icon, a status he would achieve over the next four years. During his stay at Sir Berkeley's private nursing home at Leeds, he was deluged with letters, cards and telegrams like this one from west London: 'Eight hundred working men at Rowton lodging house,* Hammersmith, wish you a speedy recovery', a cable that indicated the breadth of Hobbs's appeal. His illness also sparked more generosity from the Surrey Committee, which now held him in the highest respect. As the minutes show, the club not only paid Sir Berkeley Moynian's bill in full, which amounted to £115, but agreed 'to make Hobbs a special grant of £200 in consideration of the loss and disappointment from his illness in 1921'.

Perhaps even more satisfying, in terms of his family, was the fact that Hobbs was able to take a summer holiday with his wife and children for the first time since he married. A few weeks' convalescence by the coast was exactly what he needed and the press helped to ensure that he was left in peace. 'J.B. Hobbs is making a good but somewhat slow recovery. The secret of his seaside retreat is jealously guarded, lest he be overwhelmed by well-intentioned but misguided admirers,' reported the *Star*. In fact, Hobbs and the family were staying in a hotel in Margate in Kent, an unpretentious but attractive resort that they visited regularly over the coming years. It was, he wrote later, 'a wonderful, health-restoring' break. While he was in Margate, Surrey kept him informed of all the latest reports and scores from the cricket scene by sending him daily telegrams, the only means by which such news could be swiftly communicated since the radio was still in its infancy and the BBC was not created until the following year.

By the middle of August, Hobbs had recovered sufficiently to travel up from Kent to the Oval to watch the fifth Test, in which England, having lost the series, earned a creditable draw thanks to a massive 182 not out by the Hampshire batsman Phil Mead, then a record in a home Ashes Test. Almost twenty years earlier, Mead had lost his place on the Surrey ground staff due to the arrival of Hobbs from Cambridge. Buoyed by the spirit that England had demonstrated at the Oval, Hobbs now overestimated the extent of his recovery. As had become an end-of-season tradition for him, he organised a team to play a charity match in Wimbledon to raise money for the local hospital. This time Hobbs had no intention of playing, but even the strain of the event proved too much for his delicate state, as he recorded: 'There was a continuous

---

* Rowton Houses were a chain of cheap hostels built across London by the Montague William Lowry-Corry, 1st Baron Rowton, the philanthropist and former private secretary to Benjamin Disraeli.

demand on the ground for my autograph and I signed willingly at first, because it brought coins to the fund, but it nearly caused me to collapse, and, after a time, I had to quit the ground and come back to the pavilion by another entrance, to avoid being overwhelmed by the friendly auto-graph hunters.' He was relieved to get home to Clapham that evening. There was no more involvement in cricket until the following year.

During Hobbs's lengthy period of convalescence in the 1921 season, rumours circulated that he was considering retiring from first-class cricket because of his health. Some of the press even claimed that he had plans to make money in the less demanding environment of the Lancashire League, following the examples of Sydney Barnes and Cecil Parkin, who regularly turned out for Rochdale. Indeed, it was Parkin's decision to concentrate on playing for Lancashire in 1922 that had opened up a vacancy at Rochdale for a top professional, prompting a report in the *Pall Mall Gazette* on 21 July that Hobbs might fill the place. 'An official of the Rochdale club informed me this morning that a representative of the club will meet Hobbs at Manchester next week with a view to him becoming Parkin's successor next season. He stated that Hobbs's recent illness had made him decide to leave county cricket for less strenuous club cricket.' But this report was completely unfounded, as Hobbs soon made clear when he confirmed that his future lay in Surrey and denied that there had been any negotiations with Rochdale. 'I have not had any offer from Rochdale and I intend to rejoin the Surrey team as soon as I am fit,' he told the *Daily Herald*.

During a restful winter, Hobbs regained that fitness with lengthy walks around Clapham Park and some games of badminton, often with Ada, who was a useful player. 'I am almost as keen on badminton, and each of us has achieved some success in the league competitions of the game that flourish around London. I verily believe my husband gets more excited about his badminton prospects and games than he does even over his cricket,' she once said with a degree of exaggeration.

He quickly demonstrated his fitness once the 1922 season arrived. Prolific all summer, he raised the spirits of cricket followers after the recent Ashes disasters, as Sydney Pardon wrote in his notes for the *Wisden* annual: 'It may have been due to the fact that Hobbs was back in the field, getting hundreds in his inimitable way, but I think English cricket as a whole was appreciably better than in 1921.' From the opening matches in May, Hobbs showed that he had lost none of his technical skill. A century against Essex at the Oval was followed by another against Gloucestershire at Bristol, an innings that led the *Daily Mirror* to declare: 'The Surrey crack was very aggressive and treated the bowling with scant respect.' The runs continued to flow in June and July, with four big hundreds for Surrey. His score of 168 against Warwickshire at Edgbaston was the ninety-fifth hundred of his first-class career, passing the total of ninety-four made by C.B. Fry and putting him third on the all-time list of centurions behind Hayward and Grace. It was, said the *Daily Express*, a 'brilliant innings. Nothing disturbed the Surrey star batsman, who scored with delightful ease all round the wicket.'

Appearing as captain of the Players against the Gents for the first time at Lord's, by far the biggest match of the 1922 season in the absence of any Tests, he also made 140 against accurate bowling and a well-set field, though the *Cricketer* struck a slightly critical note in its report: 'It was not the Hobbs we are used to watching when well set for a century. He was comparatively never really at his ease . . . He was always fighting for his runs and a tough struggle he had.' Yet such stern words illustrated the incredibly high standards by which Hobbs was now judged compared to his contemporaries. The Players' century at Lord's was the ninety-sixth of his career and it seemed that, if he maintained his form, he was likely to reach the milestone of the hundredth hundred before the end of the 1922 season.

For all its faults, this hundred also revealed the deepening imperturbability and determination that the advancing years had brought to Hobbs. In the pre-war era, he would have tried to hit his way out of the tight fielding net. But verve was now giving way to accumulation. The dashing cavalier was consolidating his position as The Master, revered by the public for his relentless march through the record books. The writer Ronald Mason, a devoted follower of Surrey in his youth, put it well in his 1960 portrait of Hobbs: 'He himself, now nearing forty, was ripe for veneration; he had assumed an avuncular maturity which the rather shy, wide-eyed diffidence of his youth could never have compassed. He moved with all the old grace and with an added assurance; his eyes had retired behind humorous and contemplative wrinkles, his pale, slightly feminine features had tanned and weathered to an alert liveliness, he looked about him with an air of amused anticipation. If he was aware that he was the centre of idolatrous hero-worship, and he could hardly have escaped noticing something of what was going on, he never showed it.'

Hobbs just failed to reach the landmark as he hit another three centuries in August and September, leaving him with a tally of ninety-nine. But his overall form faded slightly as tiredness set in towards the end of the season. The reality was that he had not entirely recovered from the previous year's operation. In fact, Hobbs believed that physically he was never quite the same player after the traumatic experience of 1921. Always lacking in robustness, he felt that his stamina had been significantly reduced by his illness. 'After reaching about 70 I began to feel fagged and I do not believe that I ever quite got over it. I advise any cricketer who contemplates having a severe operation to have it earlier in life than I did, say about the age of twenty-five, when one's recuperative powers are greater.' *Wisden*, in its review of the season, agreed with that verdict: 'His illness of 1921 had left him rather weak and he seldom played a long innings without showing distinct signs of fatigue. Several times he seemed anxious to get out as soon as he passed the hundred.' Yet Hobbs still finished second in the national averages, just behind Patsy Hendren, with 2,552 runs at 62.24, and ten centuries, the last of which was scored in late September at the Oval for the Rest of England against Yorkshire, the champion county.

September also witnessed an intriguing moment in Hobbs's later batting career, though few could have seen its significance at the time. Playing at the Scarborough festival for an XI run by the flamboyant erstwhile Cambridge and Middlesex amateur Charles Thornton, Hobbs opened with the twenty-seven-year-old Yorkshire batsman Herbert Sutcliffe, who had made his first-class debut just after the war and was fast gaining a reputation as a cricketer with an unruffled temperament for the big occasion. In an augury of their later fruitful association, they put on 120 for the first wicket, Hobbs scoring 45 and Sutcliffe progressing smoothly to a century.

That winter, Hobbs declined a place in the MCC party to South Africa under the leadership of the forceful Middlesex captain Frank Mann. It was the first time in his career that he turned down an England tour, though his decision was not regarded as unusual because MCC teams to South Africa were never fully representative until 1938/9. Hobbs's decision was based not only on his determination to pay more attention to his Fleet Street shop but also on his concern to give his body more time to recover. 'Too much cricket obviously makes a player stale, whereas, after a winter's rest, you come back to the game fresh and keen,' he wrote. Having reached the age of forty in December 1922, Hobbs embarked on the 1923 season hoping to pass the rare milestone of a hundred centuries. He did not have long to wait. For their second match of the summer, Surrey travelled down to Bath to play against Somerset, whose attack included the left-arm spinner Jack White and the veteran medium pacer Ernie Robson, now aged fifty-three but still a fine exponent of away swing, always the type of bowling that Hobbs feared most. 'It may surprise you that Ernie Robson gave me as much trouble as anybody,' Hobbs once told the *Evening News*. Robson himself was well aware of this small chink in Hobbs's armour. 'I always felt you had some chance against Jack Hobbs early in his innings. But let him get started and you will live to regret it,' he once said.

Robson proved his point right at the start of the play on the second day, the first having been almost completely lost to heavy rain. In overcast conditions, he ran in for his first ball, sent down a good length delivery just outside the off-stump and Hobbs stepped onto the front foot to push it for a quick single, his habitual method of getting off the mark. But to his frustration, the ball stopped slightly on the damp pitch. As Hobbs went through with the stroke, it flew in the air towards extra cover, where the Somerset captain John Daniell dashed in and pulled off a superb catch. 'I went back sadly to the pavilion, sick with the world in general,' recalled Hobbs in an account of the match he wrote for the *Sunday Express*.

Sandham also fell to Robson for a duck and Surrey collapsed to 91 all out. In the wet conditions, Somerset also struggled but gained a narrow lead of 49 before they were bowled out for 140. Hobbs and Sandham then had a few overs to survive that second evening, always an awkward period for an opening pair. Though Sandham was dismissed cheaply again, this time by White, Hobbs appeared untroubled, striking four 4s before the close.

In a relaxed mood, he went off to the theatre that evening in Bath to see the play *The Sign on the Door*, a popular 1920s thriller by the American writer Channing Pollock.* The final day of the Somerset v Surrey match was certainly a thriller. Within the first half-hour, Surrey were in deep trouble thanks to two run-outs, with Hobbs, normally so

---

* In 1929 the play was made into a Hollywood movie under the title *The Locked Door*, providing Barbara Stanwyck with her first talking role.

sharp between the wickets, involved in both. First, Andy Ducat had his
wicket thrown down by a direct hit from third man after Hobbs had
sent him back. Then, the slightly lumbering figure of Tom Shepherd
failed to respond swiftly enough to one of Hobbs's calls for a quick
single and was beaten by a throw from cover. 'Sandham or Hitch would
have walked it, but Shepherd was a bit slow,' said Hobbs, who confessed
that he felt 'very sick and almost inclined to chuck up the sponge'. The
ebullient skipper Percy Fender now came in. Hobbs walked up to him
to apologise for running out Shepherd. 'Can't be helped,' replied the
captain briskly. Then, after yet another run-out scare, Fender fell to
Robson and Surrey, still behind with four wickets down, looked doomed.
But Bill Hitch, the Surrey all-rounder, quickly began to change the
complexion of the game with some breezy hitting as well as some
outrageous good fortune as the ball regularly shaved his stumps. He
and Hobbs were still together at lunch, each with more than 50 to his
name. After lunch, against tight, accurate bowling, they kept going,
Hitch swinging wildly, Hobbs concentrating on his sure defence with
the occasional elegant stroke. Gradually, his own and Surrey's total
mounted. Yet remarkably, Hobbs claimed that the thought of his
hundredth century did not enter his head until he was almost near
three figures, partly because the primitive Bath scoreboard did not give
the individual batsman's scores. Only when he reached 94 did he realise
how close he was. 'I really did not know what I had made till, after
hitting Mr White for 6 and 4 in one over, Strudwick, who was standing
by the scoring tent, held up six fingers. Then I suddenly grasped the
astonishing position. I became anxious – desperately anxious. It is not
just six runs between 94 and 100. It is a terribly long journey, believe
me. I could feel the spectators knew the position. They were keenly
watching every ball. I had been very slow, but they realised before I did
that I was on the verge of making my hundredth hundred.'

Three singles took Hobbs to 97. Then he hit a ball from Robson to
cover and went for another quick run. The fielder threw at the stumps,
missed and saw the ball go for two overthrows. Hobbs had made it,
eighteen years almost to the day since he had scored his maiden century
against Essex in 1905. 'A terrific crash of cheering and high above it I
could hear the yell from my fellow county-men. I felt ready to laugh
and cry,' said Hobbs in his *Express* article, adding with quiet satisfaction,
'even if it was not one of my best centuries, I have never had to work

so hard to get one. It needed concentration the whole time and every ball wanted playing. The outfield was heavy and the ball would not travel – but I got it!' As he came off the field at the end of his innings, with the adulation of the crowd echoing again in his ears, his joy was tinged with sadness. 'I thought of my old dad, to whom I owe so much, who encouraged me in every way when I started, but who never lived to see me fulfil all his cherished hopes.'

Strangely, it was his first hundred against Somerset. His score contributed to a nerve-shredding Surrey victory, for Fender declared soon after Hobbs reached his ton and then Somerset were bowled out for 157, just 10 short of the winning target. But the excitement of the narrow win was lost in the exhilaration at Hobbs's achievement. Once again, the flood of letters and telegrams demonstrated the special place he occupied in the affections of the public, this spirit captured by a tribute from the *Daily News*: 'There is no batsman in the world whose score of a hundred hundreds could give more unalloyed pleasure than Hobbs. He is delightful to watch making runs for the very reason that he never seems to be thinking how many runs he can score or worrying about his average . . . This well-graced actor expresses in his style and in his general attitude to the game the true spirit of cricket. He remains the perfect model for professionals and amateurs alike.' In the *Cricketer* Archie MacLaren called him 'one of the greatest masters of batting the world has ever seen' and went into a paean about his batting method. 'Jack Hobbs is possessed of the most perfect loose shoulders imaginable and when we add to this accurate timing and quick footwork, it can be understandable that, on a perfect wicket, no ball could be bowled which he could not drive or cut for four whilst his onside play on slow or difficult wickets was grand always. A cool head and a quiet brain, with true batting spirit such as his, make for a very rare combination.' The Surrey Committee, increasingly his benefactor as well as his employer, gave him a gift of a hundred guineas 'in recognition of his feat' and then, rather shame-facedly, awarded the same sum retrospectively to Tom Hayward, who had been given no such memorial when he reached his hundredth century in 1913.

The rest of the 1923 season was something of an anti-climax. Amidst poor weather, Hobbs only sporadically showed his true form and suffered a higher number of failures than usual, bringing down his first-class average to 37.94. Nor did he make any major score in either of the Players v Gents matches at the Oval and Lord's, in which he again served as captain despite his dislike of responsibility. 'He had not the physical strength that was his before his operation and illness in 1921. It struck one that not infrequently he lost his innings through his old fault of overeagerness to turn the straight ball to leg without waiting to get the pace of the wicket,' said *Wisden*. But it would be wrong to exaggerate the extent of his deterioration. He still averaged over 40 in championship matches for Surrey and hit four other first-class centuries after the one at Bath.

After making 104 at the Oval against Lancashire, the *Daily Mail* published this study, which gives a vivid picture of Hobbs in action that season: 'The peak of his dark blue England cap pulled well down over his wonderful brown eyes, Hobbs is watching the bowling with catlike intentness. A sharp-featured, rather slim-built, loosely made man, who is not so tall that he has to stoop over his bat or so short that a bumping ball threatens to brain him; you can feel the personality of Hobbs at the wicket without the misfortune to be out in the field helping to chase his hits.' The *Mail* article then described his idiosyncrasies at the crease which became so well known to the cricketing public during the 1920s: 'After each delivery he steps out of the ground, looks minutely at the spot where the ball pitched and administers a reproving tap to the turf – "gardening", as the cricketers' phrase goes – but all the time he looks as if no one can get him out – no one but himself. After each ball he twirls his bat round several times in his strong, supple, sun-browned hands but there is no fidgeting in his play. He is always perfectly calm, always in position for the next ball, his bat well up long before it flashes into execution. Footwork and eyework are the great Hobbs secrets. He sees the ball with exceptionally quick sight, makes up his mind about it at once and has placed himself to drive, to cut, to hook, to glide or just to pat it down long before it gets to him.' The *Mail* concluded, 'It looks so very simple to make a hundred the way Hobbs does it.'

There would be plenty more of them in the years to come. Now in his early forties, Hobbs was still barely past the halfway mark of his lifetime total of centuries.

12

'No Greater Pair
of Opening Batsmen'

Immaculate in appearance, cool in manner, Herbert Sutcliffe was the silken revolutionary of interwar cricket. His explicit aim, to be achieved by his own personal example, was to see that the professionals gained full equality with amateurs in cricket's hierarchy. His goal was encapsulated in the words he used on one occasion to the young Yorkshire fast bowler Bill Bowes, who had neglected to put on a blazer for lunch. Telling Bowes to change, he said: 'Remember, as a Yorkshire pro, you have to do everything better than an amateur. Your manners must be better and, if possible, you must speak and dress better too.'

This was a very different attitude to that of Jack Hobbs, whose deferential nature more easily accepted the divide between the amateurs and the professionals. Hobbs had a key part in raising the status of the paid player during his career, but this was due not to an intentional act of will, but to the influence of his benign character and respect for his unique achievements. Sutcliffe was a much more deliberate radical. He saw himself as leading the vanguard for change, consciously showing by all his actions that the professionals could not be treated as second-class citizens, that they were just as much gentlemen as any amateurs. So he dressed in well-tailored suits, drove a Rolls-Royce, and even carried his cricket flannels in a briefcase so they would not be creased. Whereas Hobbs generally kept to tradition by calling amateurs 'sir', Sutcliffe caused some surprise by his habit of addressing them by their Christian names. Whilst Hobbs retained the soft Cambridgeshire accent of his youth, Sutcliffe taught himself to speak with the clipped tones of the southern upper-middle class. So convincing was his adopted voice that the author and scientist C.P. Snow once said to him, 'You would never

know you had not been to public school or Cambridge.' Again, unlike
Hobbs, Sutcliffe had no fear of public speaking and possessed such
eloquent confidence on the public stage that he was sometimes nicknamed 'the Mayor of Pudsey', a reference to the Yorkshire village where
he was brought up.

Typically, when Sutcliffe served in the army during the First World
War, he quickly rose from the ranks to become an officer. Later, following
Hobbs's example, he used some of the money he made from cricket to
start up as a sports outfitter while he was still playing. His powers of
efficient organisation ensured that the venture flourished and the image
of the successful business executive certainly suited him. His growing
prosperity enabled him in the mid-1930s to buy Woodlands, an impressive former mill-owner's house set in a seven-acre estate near Pudsey,
complete with orchards, stables, tennis courts and a cricket net. In
contrast to the south London suburban home that Hobbs owned, which
was a haven of quiet domesticity and a sanctuary from the pressures
of public acclaim, Woodlands was a glorious symbol of Sutcliffe's social
prestige. With its sweeping views over the Yorkshire countryside, it was
used for dinners, cocktail receptions, garden parties and local fetes.
Sutcliffe, it seems, revelled in every aspect of the social circuit, including
glamorous women attracted by his glossy, jet-black hair and purposeful,
masculine features that gave him the looks of a matinee idol. 'Never
get married until you've been to Australia because you will find that
the girls are absolutely magnificent,' he once told his son Billy, an outlook
that was confirmed by the England keeper and touring companion Les
Ames who remarked, 'Where there is a pretty lady, you will find Herbert.'

What made Sutcliffe's social progress so striking was the humbleness
of his origins. His father, a sawmill worker and publican, died from an
injury acquired playing amateur rugby when Sutcliffe was just four.
When he was eight, his mother died from tuberculosis, so Sutcliffe was
brought up by three aunts. He began his working life in a boot factory,
attaching soles to uppers, though his youthful talent for cricket soon
brought him to the attention of the authorities in Yorkshire, who
arranged for him to take on a bookkeeping job so he had more time
for the game.

Before the First World War, Sutcliffe had already distinguished himself
in the Bradford League. But his early privations help to explain his
granite toughness and the ferocity of his ambition. The hallmark of his

personality was his calm unflappability. He was, said Les Ames, 'ice cool in a crisis and quite unruffled in the face of the most hostile attacking bowling'. Nothing, it seemed, could ever rattle him, whether on or off the field. 'He is the serenest batsman I have known,' wrote the Somerset bowler Robertson-Glasgow, who added that if Sutcliffe was out, 'he appears to regard the event less as a human miscalculation than some temporary and reprehensible lapse of natural laws'. This supreme mental strength meant that Sutcliffe could always play every ball on its merits, as he revealed: 'If I am beaten all ends up and get away with it, I have forgotten about it as soon as the bowler starts his run for the next delivery.' The umpire Frank Chester wrote of Sutcliffe's unbreakable self-confidence, 'I sometimes chuckled at his imperious manner; he gave the impression that he was doing everyone a favour by taking over command of the crease.' His temperament allowed him not only to concentrate for long periods while batting but also gave him the ability to compartmentalise every aspect of his life. Bill Bowes described how Sutcliffe could return to the Yorkshire dressing room after scoring a century, dress methodically, then get out his papers to go through his accounts or write business letters. 'He would concentrate on this job as intently as he had concentrated on his batting, undisturbed by the shouts and cheers and the coming and going of the batsmen.'

In terms of technique, Sutcliffe had nothing like the stylish elegance of Hobbs, though he was a powerful hooker and had an effective drive. The writer Dudley Carew, who was one of *The Times* cricket correspondents during the interwar period, said of him: 'He is the dourest Yorkshireman of them all in his determination, power of concentration, and relish for a struggle against the odds. His style as a batsman has not the mastery of Hobbs, and a curious twist of the wrists as he plays forward, whilst it is as unmistakable a signature to an innings as Whistler's butterfly was to a painting, is not attractive in itself.'

Hobbs did not mind about the aesthetics. In Sutcliffe, he had found his greatest opening partner of them all. Together, they formed an association whose records last until this day. During a decade from 1923, they hit fifteen century stands together for England in Test matches and achieved an incredible average for their partnership of 87, still by far the highest despite the vast expansion in international cricket since their retirement. In all matches, they had no fewer than twenty-six century stands. So durable was their union in the face of all types of bowling that they gradually became an English institution, their very names synonymous with consistency and reliability. In their steadfastness, they appeared to epitomise the best of the national character: undemonstrative, loyal and diligent. Sutcliffe was almost the personification of the stiff upper lip, Hobbs of English reserve. Their association was all the stronger for mixing their contrasting qualities: northern grit blended with southern charm, rugged defence with elegant strokeplay, youthful vigour with massive experience.

Apart from their physical and mental gifts for batting, what also made their partnership such a success was their absolute trust in each other. This was most clearly manifested in their running between the wickets, where they showed both an uncanny judgement and faith in each other's decisions, as Les Ames remembered: 'Jack and Herbert would just play and run, sometimes when the ball had travelled no more than fifteen yards away from the wicket. They were not especially speedy as runners. Herbert only strolled. It would have been undignified for him to run as if he was trying to catch a train.'

Sutcliffe also displayed a heroic lack of ego in often playing the subordinate role to Hobbs, especially in their early years together. According to his estimate, Hobbs had about two-thirds of the strike when they first opened for England, but Sutcliffe said he derived nothing but pleasure from batting alongside Hobbs. 'I continued to learn from him all the time we were together. His ability was so great that he inspired confidence, just as the correctness of his run-calling inspired confidence,' said Sutcliffe in a 1934 interview with the *Yorkshire Evening Post*. In the same interview, Sutcliffe described Hobbs as 'a cricket marvel – a scientific wonder. When he went to the wicket he commanded the attention of everyone immediately because of his graceful stance. There he was, the complete craftsman, polished with a brilliance all his own. Each stroke he made was a masterpiece because his technique was complete and because everything – feet, body, shoulders and wrists – worked in harmony controlled by his alert brain. Of all the batsmen I have seen, Hobbs was the best because he could reveal his skill on any wicket.' In his turn, Hobbs valued the composure and resolution that Sutcliffe always brought to the crease, as well as running. 'Herbert seldom said no, he was a great runner, a great player. We had some happy times together. Right from the start we settled down and it was easy,' Hobbs told John Arlott in a BBC interview. In his 1935 autobiography, Hobbs focused on Sutcliffe's rock steadiness. 'He was a good judge of the game, and many a time we had a word together as to the line to adopt against particular bowlers. On one occasion, after a bowler had sent down an exceptionally deadly over and had beaten me twice, Herbert walked along to me and said, "Stick it, Jack, he can't keep that up." That's where Herbert was so great; if he was beaten, he would go on playing his natural game.'

Sutcliffe's first sight of Hobbs in action was during the war, when, while on leave from his regiment, he saw him a few times playing in the Bradford League for Idle. They had opened once together in the 1922 season for C.I. Thornton's XI at Scarborough, and in three matches during the 1923 season, twice for the Players against the Gents and the other time for England against the Rest in a Test trial. Against a fine attack that included George Macaulay and the Leicestershire all-rounder George Geary, they put on 86 for the first wicket, making a deep impression on *Wisden*: 'The wicket had become quite nasty, the ball popping up in the most disconcerting fashion. But Hobbs and Sutcliffe played superbly and overcame all difficulties. The greatness of what they did was hardly recognised until the other batsmen were seen against the same bowling.' Hobbs was first out, for 43, and Sutcliffe went on to 65, but no one else in the England team passed 26. It was this performance that convinced the selectors, once more chaired by Leveson Gower, that England might finally have discovered the right partner for Hobbs now that Wilfred Rhodes's batting had declined so drastically. In England's fifteen Tests since the war, ten other openers apart from Hobbs had been tried, and none had been successful. Indeed two of them, Alf Dipper of Gloucestershire and Wally Hardinge of Kent, were never picked for England again after their single appearances. The selection of Hobbs and Sutcliffe for the first Test of 1924 against South Africa at Edgbaston was cemented by another pair of solid starts in the trial for England against the Rest in May, as well as their own excellent form at the beginning of the summer. Shortly before the Test, Hobbs hit 203 not out against Nottinghamshire at Trent Bridge, the seventh double century of his career. His innings, which included a 6 and nineteen 4s, was described by the *Daily Express* as 'exceptionally attractive because of his cutting and driving. In these days, when so many leading batsmen devote their attention largely to scoring on the leg-side, Hobbs's display proved a sheer delight.' The double hundred also prompted the *Cricketer* to speculate that W.G. Grace's record of 126 centuries could soon be within Hobbs's grasp. 'The Old Man's figures are certain to be surpassed some day and it may well be that Hobbs will be the first player to gain the distinction, seeing that he has not yet completed his 42nd year and that his powers are unimpaired.'

The South African tourists of 1924, led by Herbie Taylor, were a poor side, lacking experience in their batting or penetration in their bowling. The glory days of the googly quartet were long in the past. Nevertheless, on that early June morning in Birmingham, there was the usual buzz of expectation that greeted the start of a series. The sky was grey; the pitch looked damp. Herbie Taylor won the toss and decided to field, hoping his bowlers could exploit the conditions. As he prepared to bat, Sutcliffe inevitably felt some nerves on his debut. But Hobbs, twelve years his senior, was a reassuring presence, as Sutcliffe later recalled: 'I was desperately anxious to do well, and I know that as we walked out to the middle that day, Jack chatted about one or two things. Then, just as we were separating to go to our ends, he said, "Play your own game, Herbert." That was all – nothing more than "Play your own game, Herbert" – but the quiet way in which the advice was given suggested to me that he was satisfied that my own game would be good enough for the occasion. That was all I wanted. My confidence was strengthened enormously by it and also by the comfortable and certain way that Hobbs took his stance to face the South Africans' opening attack. There, I felt, was a man in complete command of himself as well as the situation that we were facing. He was perhaps a little sterner in his outlook than in other matches in which I had played with him – there was the demand of Test cricket telling its tale – but he was, when all was said and done, just as free and easy, a rare source of inspiration and strength, I can say, to the youngster at the other end.'

For all the emotional support Hobbs gave, he nearly inflicted a disastrous blow on Sutcliffe in very first over of the match, bowled by George Parker. The inclusion of Parker, an eager but wayward fast bowler, was an indicator of the South Africans' weakness, for he had played just one first-class game and only weeks earlier had been plying his trade in the Bradford League. His initial deliveries were unthreatening. Then he sent down one on the leg stump which Hobbs, with characteristic ease, stroked to mid-on and called Sutcliffe through for a single. But he had underestimated the speed of the fielder, Mick

Commaille, who was also an international footballer for South Africa. As Commaille raced towards the ball, Hobbs suddenly realised that the run was not possible. He frantically sent back Sutcliffe, now almost halfway down the wicket. The throw came in with Sutcliffe still well out of his ground, but the ball missed the stumps by a few inches, and Parker the bowler was not backing up. It was the narrowest of escapes. Yet Sutcliffe, true to his nature, was completely unperturbed. He carried on batting and running as if nothing had happened. Soon, with the pitch becoming ever easier, he and Hobbs were flaying the South Africa bowling to all parts of the ground. Nor was their running inhibited by their early mishap, as Plum Warner reported for the *Cricketer*: 'Hobbs and Sutcliffe over and over again played the ball just in front of them and were off for a run.' In just over two hours, they put on 136 together, before Sutcliffe was out for 64. Soon afterwards, Hobbs fell for 76. Astonishingly, this had been his first Test innings in England for twelve years, the previous one having taken place during the Triangular Tourament when Sutcliffe was still a teenager.

The great alliance had begun in resounding fashion. Tiger Smith, the veteran Warwickshire keeper, saw every ball of the Edgbaston Test, and later wrote that after their early mistake, 'there were no misunderstandings and they became the best opening pair that I've seen. Hobbs and Rhodes were just as good at stealing singles but Herbert was a better player than Wilfred, so that clinched it in my book.' Another Warwickshire player who saw the game was Bob Wyatt, who had just started his first-class career. 'They would run almost as they hit the ball after playing it deliberately for a single. This made the field move in close to try and stop their singles, whereupon it became easier for them to crack the ball to the boundary. It was the perfect partnership. There can have been no greater pair of opening batsmen in the history of cricket than these two.' Their stand of 136 paved the way for a big England total of 439, only for South Africa to suffer a humiliating debacle. In barely an hour's batting, they were bowled out for just 30, the second lowest score in Test history and the lowest ever in England. The damage was done by the two England fast-medium bowlers from Sussex: Maurice Tate, making his debut, and Arthur Gilligan, the cheery new Test captain who finished with the unbelievable figures of 6 for 7. Though South Africa showed much more mettle in the second innings, their total of 390 was not enough to prevent an innings defeat.

They were just as badly beaten at Lord's in the second Test, when their first innings of 273 proved wholly inadequate once Hobbs and Sutcliffe began England's response. Having reached 28 without loss at the end of the first day, they began the second immediately on the offensive, quickly building a formidable stand with their combination of attacking strokes and quick singles. The difference in their styles was apparent to the *Daily Mirror*'s reporter: 'Sutcliffe was making practically all his runs by cuts and leg glances but Hobbs, playing beautifully, hit the ball where it ought to go every time and made his runs in all directions.' South Africa soon wilted under the onslaught, recorded the *Mirror*. 'All sorts of bowling changes were made before lunch, but all were futile.' As *Wisden* put it, 'Very seldom in a Test match has bowling been knocked about so mercilessly.' In two and a half hours of the morning session, Hobbs and Sutcliffe put on exactly 200, both of them reaching centuries before lunch. Hobbs later wrote of the pleasure that their stand gave him. 'We both felt in tip-top mood: we took all the risks in our stride and yet we never seemed to be in danger. How thoroughly we enjoyed our run-stealing that dove-grey, midsummer morning!'

The partnership was finally broken on 268, when Sutcliffe was bowled by Parker for 122. It was by far England's highest first-wicket stand against South Africa, beating the 221 that Hobbs and Rhodes had put on at Cape Town in 1909/10. But Hobbs was not finished. In tandem with Frank Woolley, he continued to plunder the South African attack. On 165, he reached the highest Test score made at Lord's, previously held jointly by Warren Bardsley and Arthur Shrewsbury. On 188, he passed his previous Test best. Having reached his first international double century, he looked certain to break the long-standing record for the highest Test score made in England, which had been set by the Australian captain Billy Murdoch with 211 at the Oval in 1884. But Hobbs, who took little interest in records and increasingly felt burdened by them as the 1920s wore on, had no idea he was so close to the landmark when he reached 211. 'Had I been aware of that record, I might have made a special effort for the required single, but players do not ponder over these figures when they are at the wicket,' he wrote. Instead of hitting the necessary run, he tamely drove the ball in the air to cover, where a relieved Herbie Taylor accepted the catch. The shot was borne largely of exhaustion, the combination of middle age and the lingering effects of his major operation having undermined his stamina. 'Never have I seen a batsman quite so weary as Hobbs was at the end of his innings,' wrote Laurance Woodhouse in the *Cricketer*. 'When one remembers, however, that he ran 89 of his own singles, some 30 to 40 of Sutcliffe's and a good few of Woolley's, one sees that he ran a mile or two during his innings.' Woolley himself went on to a century, the first time that the top three in the England order had all scored hundreds and an achievement not equalled until the Brisbane Ashes Test of 2009/10 when Alastair Cook, Andrew Strauss and Jonathan Trott all reached three figures. In an innings of tumbling records at Edgbaston, perhaps the most remarkable statistic of all was England's final total of 531 for 2 declared, the only time in Test history that more than 500 runs have been scored in a single day.

England's dominance continued in the third Test at Leeds where they beat South Africa by eight wickets. Hobbs and Sutcliffe contributed to England's match-winning first innings total with another successful opening stand, this one worth 70 before Hobbs was out for 31. Surprisingly, though, they had another near disaster early in their innings when Hobbs hit ball to cover, began to run, changed his mind and returned to his crease. But Sutcliffe had just kept sprinting down the wicket, with the result that they both ended up at the batsman's end. Again they were saved by poor South African fielding. Instead of taking his time, Hubert 'Nummy' Deane at cover flung the ball wildly towards the bowler, but his throw was so misdirected that it sped over the boundary. 'Hobbs ought to have been run out and could have blamed no one but himself had that been his fate,' said the *Yorkshire Evening Post*. When England took the field, Hobbs himself showed that he had lost little of his athleticism at cover, running out Commaile for just 4 to precipitate another South African collapse.

His excellent batting continued outside the Test arena in July, when he made 118 for the Players against the Gents at Lord's, though his innings, lasting four hours and twenty minutes, came in for some criticism because of its perceived caution. 'The innings was not typical of the man . . . Hobbs has never scored more slowly in his life,' complained the *Cricketer*. But the *Daily News* correspondent found this moan ridiculous because it took no account of his age or health or unique talent. 'At its best, his batting is as fluently pure as a Mozart melody, the most serenely beautiful thing in cricket. When he gives his second best we are apt to feel, I suppose, that we have been cheated out of our rights. We are also apt to forget that Hobbs is now over forty years of age. English bowlers still regard him as the most difficult batsman in the world to get out. But his health is not robust and one, who knows him well, tells me that after making 50 runs he is, in these days, a weary Titan.'

Soon after this hundred for the Players, Leveson Gower announced the England team for the fourth Test to start at Old Trafford on 26 July. Hobbs's name was not included. For the first time since his debut in 1907, Hobbs had been dropped. It seemed on the surface an extra-ordinary development, one that should have been completely unthink-able given Hobbs's record. The fact was that Hobbs had not been left out on any grounds of form or discipline or executive whim, but because he had turned down a place on the forthcoming MCC tour of Australia and the selectors, understandably, wanted to give more Test experience to those who were likely to travel. Equally understandably, Hobbs felt hurt at his exclusion, 'That was a bit hard on me, I thought, seeing that I had helped to win the rubber against South Africa.'

Hobbs had hesitated over accepting invitations to tour because of his devotion to his family and, to a lesser extent, his chronic seasickness. Since 1921, further obstacles had been added through the creation of his business and the lack of robustness in health, the reasons he had declined to tour South Africa with the MCC in 1922/3. At first Hobbs seemed just as determined to reject the invitation to Australia in 1924/5, particularly because of the strict rule against professionals bringing their wives on any trip, the condition that had prevented Sydney Barnes from joining the 1920/21 tour. This explanation was not given in public and, when making the initial announcement of Hobbs's rejection, the MCC merely said that 'he had been too unwell to accept'. The official line was taken up by the press. Hobbs declined the invitation, said the *Westminster Gazette,* 'it being understood that his health would not be able to stand the strain of the tour'. But then the episode became much more complex. At the end of July, Hobbs was approached by the Honourable Lionel Tennyson, the swashbuckling, sometimes intemperate, captain of Hampshire who was leading a private tour to South Africa that winter sponsored by Solomon 'Solly' Joel, the Anglo-South African financier and business tycoon. Hobbs was attracted by the idea, not only because the trip to South Africa was much shorter than that to

Australia but, far more importantly, because Joel offered to pay all
Ada's expenses so she could accompany him. While Hobbs was considering this offer, Leveson Gower, always alive to any gossip on the cricket
circuit, heard about it and immediately told Lord Harris, the Treasurer
of the MCC and one of the key figures in the Lord's establishment.
Harris sensed the chance of an opening. It is a tribute to Hobbs's
reputation that the MCC was so determined to secure him in the Test
side, even bending its own rules and the size of the squad for his sake.

The saga now continued into August, after the fourth Test at Old
Trafford had ended in a dismal washout. So heavy was the Manchester
rain that Andy Sandham, who had temporarily replaced Hobbs in the
England XI, did not even get the opportunity to bat. But Harris had
other matters on his mind. He approached Hobbs and asked him directly
if the news about Joel's offer was true.

'Yes, the privilege of going with my wife having been granted, I find
it possible to go to South Africa and that is why I cannot accept the
invitation for Australia,' Hobbs replied without any obfuscation. Harris
was not to be dissuaded. He asked Hobbs whether he might change
his mind if the MCC allowed him to bring Ada, though Harris stressed
that the MCC, unlike Joel, could not meet her expenses. Hobbs promised
to think about it and they agreed to meet again soon. But then, as he
contemplated his position, a new concern arose in Hobbs's mind, one
that reflected his sense of decency towards his fellow professionals. As
he told Harris at their next negotiation, 'I cannot go if it involves turning
somebody else out of the MCC team.' Harris suggested that one of the
MCC players be transferred to Tennyson's South African party. That
didn't seem fair to Hobbs. 'An Australian tour and a South African tour
are very different. There is nothing like an Australian tour – nothing
in all cricket,' he said. Harris, who was an experienced politician as well
as a cricket administrator and had served in two Tory governments,
now came up with the solution: Hobbs should go simply as an extra
member of the MCC party. Finally Hobbs agreed, though, typically, he
insisted that he should not be better remunerated than any other player.
The terms, it should be said, were fairly generous. Each MCC player
was to receive a basic tour fee of £400 and in addition there were
personal expenses of one pound ten shillings a week during the voyage
and two pounds a week in Australia. The sea passage, railway fares,
taxis, accommodation and laundry bills were all to be met by the MCC,

a far greater level of support than professionals received from their clubs at home when they were expected to meet their travelling and hotel costs. On another point of honour, Hobbs wanted it to be known publicly that he would be paying for Ada's trip. 'Any additional expense incurred by the request made by Hobbs will be defrayed out of his own pocket,' the *Daily News* reported, adding, 'In spite of the terrors of the Bay of Biscay, even more antagonistic than Gregory, it is understood that Mrs Hobbs is very keen on making the trip.'

Lord Harris had proved a supple, persevering negotiator behind the scenes but in public he tried to maintain the fiction that the MCC had made no departure from its traditional stance about professionals' wives. Rather absurdly, he claimed that Hobbs's change of mind was entirely the result of new medical advice 'that he could undertake the trip safely'. Even more disingenuously, he denied that the MCC had 'departed from its invariable practice of not finding passages for players' wives'. The issue had never been about the costs but rather the right to bring spouses on tour, something that has remained a source of contention to this day. Few in the cricket world cared about theoretical consistency. Most were just relieved that Hobbs would be where he belonged, with England in Australia. At the news of his acceptance, the *Cricketer* summed up the mood: 'No national side would be complete without the famous Surrey batsman and the moral effect of his presence will be tremendous. Hobbs is still one of the greatest batsmen in the world, as well as one of the finest cover-points.' Apart from indicating his central importance to England's cause, the negotiations provided two other lessons about Hobbs's character. The first was that, for all his diffidence, he was no pushover. His innate courtesy was not a form of meekness. He named his terms and compelled the MCC to accept them. Though some within the MCC were displeased at this effrontery from a professional, he had enhanced the respect, even awe, in which he was held. There could be no dispute that he was the commanding figure of English cricket. Second, he had displayed the strength of his devotion to Ada, whose happiness was even more important to him than his England place. But his determination to bring his wife with him to Australia meant a few practical difficulties, for their four children, aged between ten and seventeen, would need to be looked after for the whole winter. Happily the problem was solved when Jack's second youngest sister, also called Ada but known in the family as 'Beau', agreed to move into the Clapham home. Beau was so good at running the place that even after the tour she stayed on for a while as the family housekeeper, her culinary skills treasured by Jack. 'Beau originally went to Jack's house to look after the children but I must admit that she was a terrific cook. She did some fantastic cooking,' says Margaret Witt. Appropriately enough, Beau later married an executive from the Fray Bentos pie company.

Having agreed to tour, Hobbs was restored to his rightful place at the head of England's batting order for the fifth Test against South Africa at the Oval. The match was a rain-ruined draw, in which he made 30 in his only innings and, during a typically lively performance in the field, ran out one of the South African openers. England had hardly been troubled in their canter to a 3–0 victory. The team knew that a much sterner trial awaited them in Australia. Aside from the wrangle over his tour place, it was a highly satisfactory season for Hobbs, who scored 2,094 runs at 58.16 in all first-class games. His batting continued to evolve into its more sedate, dependable style without the flashes of his youth, as *Wisden* noted: 'Less audacious than in his younger days, he never inspired greater confidence. Something was lost in spectacular effect, but his more guarded method paid him exceeding well. Very rarely did he risk his invaluable wicket by trying to turn a straight ball to leg before he got the pace of the ground.' The *Cricketer* agreed with that verdict: 'If he is not the daring and brilliant attacker of the bowling he is probably sounder, for taking less risks the bowlers find his wicket more difficult to get.' In the same magazine, Raymond Robertson-Glasgow argued that, far from sliding into decline, Hobbs had advanced the art of batsmanship since the war: 'Modern Hobbs is a greater player than old Hobbs. Style in batting has undergone a complete reversal in the last fifty years. Forward play was once considered the main principle of successful batting, with back play as a subsidiary arm to fall back on in difficulties. Today back and pad play build up the ramparts. Forward play consolidates these ramparts and counter-attacks when the enemy are weary of vain assault.'

Soon after the end of the season, Hobbs wrote to his former Surrey colleague Ernie Hayes, now the coach at Leicestershire, about England's prospects against Australia: 'I think we shall turn out to be a good team and I consider we have an even chance of winning the rubber.' On paper, Hobbs's optimism seemed justified. In Australia, according to the *Daily Mail*'s correspondent in Sydney, 'The team is regarded here as the most formidable to visit the Commonwealth for many years.' England had a strong batting line-up, led by Hobbs and Sutcliffe, while the bowling looked like a reasonable blend of pace and spin. In particular, Maurice Tate was an outstanding prospect with his accuracy, stamina and zip of the pitch. Yet there was a cloud hanging over the England captain Arthur Gilligan, who was meant to be leading the new ball attack alongside Tate. During the summer he had been badly hit on the heart while batting during the Gents v Players match at the Oval in July, and he never recovered his full speed again. Moreover, his genial manner was outweighed by his lack of tactical nous and hard Test experience. His handling of the England attack against South Africa was severely criticised in print by one of his own players, Cecil Parkin, who was effectively banned from playing for England ever again but remained a source of simmering controversy throughout the winter. Many in the press and public felt that Hobbs's own county captain Percy Fender would have been a better leader, but his eagerness to challenge convention meant that he had fallen badly out of favour with the establishment. 'We don't do that sort of thing here,' Lord Harris had coldly told him after Fender had led out his whole Surrey team through a single gate onto the field at Lord's.

It is a rich irony that, in political terms, Gilligan was a far greater subversive than Fender. Behind the smile and the bonhomie, he was a supporter of the British Fascists, an extremist movement founded in 1923 by Rotha Lintorn-Orman, the alcoholic, paranoid daughter of an Essex army major. Inspired by the rise of Mussolini in Italy, she organised the group on quasi-military lines with the stated purpose of defending law and order in the event of a Bolshevik revolution in Britain. Her outfit was far less influential than Sir Oswald Mosley's British Union of Fascists of the 1930s, but, in the volatile political atmosphere after the war, with industrial discontent widespread and the traditional party structure in flux, MI5 was sufficiently concerned to put its leading members under surveillance. According to the historian Andrew Moore of the University of Western Sydney, the Australian secret service was informed by the authorities in London of Gilligan's political leanings, though there is no hard evidence that Gilligan actually used the tour to promulgate the fascist creed. Yet he was hardly reticent about his views. On his return from Australia, he wrote an article for the bulletin of the British Fascists entitled *The Spirit of Fascism and Cricket Tours,* in which he tried to draw a link between nationalistic solidarity and team unity on the cricket field.

None of this was known to the public in Australia, where Gilligan was hugely popular for his sportsmanslike good humour in the face of adversity. Contrary to Hobbs's prediction, England lost the series, but they did not play nearly as badly as the margin of 4–1 suggested. With a little more luck, shrewder captaincy, fewer injuries and better catching, they might have competed on equal terms; the *Sydney Sun News* estimated that England put down at least twenty-one chances in the series. A good all-rounder, such as Percy Fender, would also have helped, since England's tail proved far more fallible than Australia's. But, amidst this failure, there were two shining lights: the bowling of Tate and the opening partnership of Hobbs and Sutcliffe. With his beautifully smooth action, his whole-hearted effort, and his uncanny ability to make the ball lift off rock-hard surfaces, Tate was a revelation on his first tour, taking thirty-eight wickets in the five Tests, which is still a record for an English bowler in Australia. Hobbs and Sutcliffe were just as commanding. Between them, they hit seven individual centuries and enjoyed four opening stands of over 100. Thanks to their 'magnificent batting', said the *Cricketer*, 'one feels the prestige of English cricket is re-established'. Sutcliffe, continued the magazine, had 'immortalised himself', and 'there is no higher compliment than to say that he is the fitting partner of the great Hobbs, who seems as good as ever'.

After all the fraught negotiations over his request to bring Ada, Hobbs undoubtedly benefited from her presence on the tour. More relaxed than ever before, he fully justified his stance to the selectors. In later years, he claimed he always felt reassured by having her near. 'I would like to pay a special tribute to my wife. A man plays a much better game if he knows his wife is watching. If he strikes a bad patch, her consolation makes all the difference in the world,' he told *Everybody's Journal* in 1954. Ada herself, who was no wallflower, felt gratified by her contribution to his success, as she explained in a 1928 interview: 'My husband's career as a cricketer comes before everything else to me and I am proud enough to think that in a small measure I have helped him. Often when he is playing he looks towards the place I am sitting; he knows that I am watching him and though I am very proud of him, still I am his severest critic.' On the voyage out to Australia, she supported him in one very direct way. Never a heavy drinker, Hobbs had become even more abstemious after his operation in 1921. But he still took the occasional glass of wine or liqueur, and Ada felt that this habit had contributed to the indifferent health he had suffered in recent years, marked by bouts of fatigue, migraines or stomach upsets. While on board the ship, Ada suggested that he cut out drinking altogether. 'I believe he thought I was "fussing" a little, but evidently he came to the conclusion that his health made it worth the trial, and since then he has not touched alcohol in any shape or form. It is long since he was as well as he was in Australia,' she said in an interview on their return to England in the spring of 1925. As in prohibition America, this was the era when the anti-alcohol movement was at its peak in Australia. Due to its influence, most states had imposed severe restrictions on licensing hours, with pubs and hotel bars forced to close at six o'clock. The Australian temperance movement wanted to go even further, and saw Jack Hobbs as an ideal figure to promote its cause. 'When they got to know in Australia that Jack was a total abstainer we had requests from temperance societies for him to speak at meetings,' recalled Ada, who said that Jack wanted nothing to do with such evangelism. 'He is not a temperance advocate in that sense. Total abstinence suits his health at present and has evidently had no bad effects on his cricket, and he is content to leave it at that.'

Almost as soon as he arrived in Australia, Hobbs felt in excellent form. With a little overdone lyricism, he later explained his sense of deepening confidence on the tour: 'My bat was to me still a thing of magic. It still blossomed. But the blossoming was golden now. I reached the highest pinnacle of my maturity.'

Australian Test cricket in the 1920s was conducted in a completely different atmosphere to that in England. The Tests were timeless, compared to the English three-day affairs. The overs were of eight balls rather than six. The grounds were larger, the sun more intense. Above all, the pitches, largely made of Bulli or Merri Creek soil, were far more hard and smooth than anything in England. Just before the start of the series, the former Queensland batsman Robert Macdonald wrote in the *Cricketer* this description of Australian wickets: 'They are of a highly bituminous nature and possess the special properties of setting extremely hard and great cohesion. In preparation for a Test match, the wicket is flooded the day before and then caught very early next morning when it is in a putty-like condition by the heavy roller. In the course of a few hours it becomes in the Australian sunshine as hard and true as a billiard table. The pace of it is tremendous but it wears so well that at the end of a six day Test match you could re-chalk the creases and start another match on it. The grass is practically rolled into the face of the wicket and this tends, in conjunction with the extraordinary cohesion of the soil, to hold the wicket indefinitely together.' If conditions were damp, however, these surfaces become deadly, as the former Australian captain Monty Noble warned of the Melbourne pitch: 'After rain, and particularly if it is exposed to a hot sun, it cakes on top, leaving it soft underneath, and the ball, after striking the pitch, makes pace, gets up very quickly and breaks tremendously. It is a perfect terror under such conditions – the worst I have ever played.' Because of all these factors, international matches in Australia were almost as much tests of endurance as of skill. Yet Hobbs, reinvigorated by his abstemious regime and his new batting partner, easily rose to the challenge. In the first major state match of the tour, against South Australia at the Adelaide Oval, they put on 89 on a rain-affected wicket, Hobbs making 50 and, according to Noble, proving that 'he had lost none of the consummate skill that endeared him to Australian sportsmen years ago. He gave a perfect exhibition of wet-wicket batsmanship, again and again receiving the plaudits of the crowd on his skilful defensive play as well as his beautiful timing, his forceful punishment of anything over-tossed and his clever pulling of short-length ones.'

Hobbs and Sutcliffe did even better when the first Test began at Sydney on 19 December 1924. There was great excitement in the city at the opening match of the series, more than 33,000 people cramming into the ground for the first day. Australia, led by Herbie Collins, won the toss and made 450 on a typically perfect wicket. Once they were all out, Hobbs and Sutcliffe had an hour to bat at the end of the second day. Hobbs took the first over, against Charlie Kelleway, whose medium-paced away swing was precisely the kind of bowling that often caused him difficulty. He managed to survive but then Sutcliffe, who felt that Hobbs had struggled, came down the wicket and told him, 'Best to leave the new ball alone, Jack.' Given the difference in their age and experience, such a statement could have looked impertinent, but Hobbs was only too impressed by Sutcliffe's assertiveness. 'I knew we'd found the right opener for England,' he later said when recalling the incident. The pair easily made it to stumps, having put on 72 without loss, and they carried on in the same serene manner on the third day. Neither the

movement of Kelleway nor the bounding pace of Gregory posed much
threat to them. Then Collins brought on the leg-spinner Arthur Mailey,
who had been working on a new type of well-disguised googly that he
hoped would confuse the English batsmen. Mailey bowled a few deliveries to Hobbs, then prepared to unleash his secret weapon. As the ball
left his hand, Hobbs from the other end called out, 'Googly, Arthur,'
and pulled it straight to the boundary. Years later, Mailey was asked if
Hobbs's dismissive attitude towards this new delivery had annoyed him.
'No, you could never get annoyed with Jack Hobbs. He was such a nice
chap and always full of humour, although this never upset his concentration as he was a great competitor.' But the battle between Mailey and
Hobbs was not as one-sided as this incident might suggest. Mailey
admitted that in 1924/5 he found Hobbs 'even more difficult to handle'
than in 1920/21 'because he had the tenacious Herby Sutcliffe for a
partner'. Yet Mailey also believed that Hobbs did not always read the
googly and could also be deceived by minor variations in flight and the
line of delivery. Four times in his first five innings of the series Hobbs
fell to Mailey, though he admitted that Hobbs continued to score heavily
because his 'superb footwork could get him out of trouble if he was
unable to distinguish the wrong 'un from the leg-break'.

After dealing authoritatively with Australia's attack on the morning
of the third day at Sydney, Hobbs and Sutcliffe were still together at
lunch on 151, Hobbs 93 not out, Sutcliffe 55 not out. The Yorkshireman
fell soon after the interval for 59 but Hobbs continued inexorably
towards his seventh century against Australia, beating Victor Trumper's
record of six in Ashes tests and prompting a fervent reception from the
big crowd. 'He is undoubtedly the master batsman. His supreme confidence, his artistry, his quickness of perception, his intuition, his ability
to change from his first intent and then make the perfect stroke, clearly
mark him as a champion,' said the *Melbourne Argus*. The sense of relief
at reaching the landmark, however, seemed to undermine Hobbs's
concentration and suddenly he began to scratch around badly. All his
grace and fluency disappeared, replaced by awkward hesitation, as Noble
wrote in his account of the series: 'He was no longer the great Hobbs
we had known and admired so long but simply a shadow of himself.
He lost his skilful work and there was no certainty in his timing. He
poked around and made 15 more by very indifferent strokes, then pushed
one into Kelleway's hands off Gregory.' Once Hobbs had gone for 115,

England collapsed badly to 298 and, with Australia piling up another big total, Gilligan's team was set a mammoth 605 to win. Hobbs and Sutcliffe gave England another excellent start, putting on 110 before Hobbs, on 57, misread a flighted delivery from Mailey and popped it up to silly point. It was the first time in Test cricket that an opening pair had twice made a century stand in each innings and Sutcliffe went on to his first Ashes hundred. But their efforts were in vain. England lost by 193 runs.

In the second Test at Melbourne, beginning on New Year's Day 1925, Hobbs and Sutcliffe again had to open England's innings under tremendous pressure. On a typical Melbourne wicket, the glossy black turf shining under the fierce sun, Australia had made a shaky start on the first morning when they lost three wickets for 47, one of them to a run-out by Hobbs. But then, in front of a crowd of more than 50,000, which was a record for a Test, they had dramatically recovered to reach 300 for 4 at the end of the first day. On the second, they kept up the butchery of England's bowling as they built a total of exactly 600, again a new record in Test cricket. Beginning on the third morning, Hobbs and Sutcliffe had an immense task in front of them if they were to give England even a glimmer of hope. Yet they were completely undaunted. As the overs ticked by, they drained the energy from the Australians with their rock-solid defence, quick singles and swift dispatch of the bad ball. Even Mailey, after beating the bat a few times in the first session, was reduced to powerlessness by the afternoon, as was the fearsome Jack Gregory. 'If he can tame Jack, we might be there for a considerable time,' Hobbs had told Sutcliffe at the start of the innings, knowing how good the wicket was. His hopes were well founded. Having gone into lunch on 70 without loss, they were still together at tea with the total on 187. Their play, wrote Noble, was 'flawless and when we say that, what greater tribute can we pay to ability, tenacity, resourcefulness and indomitable pluck? It was English cricket at its best.' After tea, when he had been batting 195 minutes, Hobbs reached his century. As the batsmen crossed for the hundredth run, Sutcliffe stopped Hobbs for an instant in the middle of the wicket to congratulate him. Half an hour later, Sutcliffe reached his own century. 'We defied every change in the bowling. Sometimes we were defending, sometimes in aggression, but always careful and confident,' said Sutcliffe. By the close on Saturday evening, they had reached 283 without loss, almost halfway to matching

Australia's total. Neither of them had given a chance all day. The cricket correspondent of the *Australian* was almost overwhelmed by the achievement: 'Never have I seen sounder, safer batting. Hobbs and Sutcliffe are not of the belligerent kind, preferring to make their runs in a more delicate manner, but as to their skill and touch there can be no two opinions.' The former Oxford blue Philip Le Couteur, commenting for the *Cricketer,* felt that Hobbs and Sutcliffe had given him 'the finest cricket I have seen', but he was quick to see the difference in Hobbs's style compared to pre-war days. 'We had again seen the old Hobbs with the mastery of many shots but the old Hobbs with a difference; for the safe shots for one used to be equally safe shots for four and the many shots used to be very many.'

Sunday was a rest day, a welcome break for the dog-tired Australians. While he relaxed at his hotel, Sutcliffe contemplated Monday morning's play, when he and Hobbs would have the chance to break the Test record for an opening partnership, the 323 set by Hobbs and Rhodes at the same ground thirteen years earlier. His ambition was fuelled by a telegram he had received from Rhodes himself, congratulating him and Hobbs on their batting and wishing them good luck for Monday. At their hotel, the Australian side was also thinking about the record, and wondering how on earth they were going to dismiss either batsman. Collins and his men talked long into the night about ways to wrest back the initiative, as Arthur Mailey later recalled: 'We sat in the Windsor Hotel until two in the morning evolving attacking schemes, drawing field placings, thinking of all manner of distractions such as loose bowling sleeves à la Ramadhin,* bowlers wearing red caps designed with cricket balls and even our captain Collins, a man with a rich appreciation of the manly old game, lowered his ideals to such a state that he suggested in all seriousness an ordinary, under-arm "grubber". This goes to show how desperate one becomes in such hopeless circumstances.'

On the Monday morning the MCG was again packed, the spectators well aware that records and the match were in the balance. Before the start of play, Sutcliffe tried to persuade Hobbs to join him for some batting practice, largely so their eyes could adjust to the harsh light. Hobbs breezily turned down the suggestion and remained in the dressing

---

* The great West Indian spinner of the 1950s, Sonny Ramadhin, always bowled with his sleeves rolled down.

room while Sutcliffe had a net. Then they walked out to the middle to resume their colossal stand, Hobbs on 157, Sutcliffe on 123. The opening over was to be bowled by Mailey, operating with a light wind that helped his drift. Hobbs took strike as a wave of expectation ran through the crowd. The first ball was a full toss. Not wanting to overreach himself, he played it calmly down the pitch. Mailey turned and came in again. Never renowned for his accuracy, he sent down what appeared to be another full toss. Hobbs moved inside the line and, in an assured move-ment that he had repeated thousands of times in his career, he tried to place the ball wide of mid-on. But at the last moment the ball dipped in its flight, missed his bat and struck the leg stump. Hobbs was out second ball without adding a run. A deep sense of anti-climax descended on the England dressing room. The Australian team were ecstatic. Mailey said that his 'brain had been bursting with the brilliant ideas' on how to fox Hobbs, but then the ball had just 'slipped out of my hand and lo! Jack was cleaned bowled by a common full toss.' Hobbs himself said that he had misread the length and 'made a yorker of it'. Strudwick, watching in the pavilion, felt that Jack's failure to acclimatise himself to the morning sun was to blame. 'Hobbs seemed to play as if he did not see it. Somehow or other it got under his bat and bowled him. In Australia it is very difficult to see for the first two or three overs, for there is a nasty glare to which your eyes become accustomed after time. It would be wise to have a few balls in the nets before going in to bat.' This was exactly what Sutcliffe had feared. Hobbs had said, 'I'll be all right, Herbert,' when Sutcliffe had urged him to practise a little. 'But he wasn't all right,' wrote Sutcliffe with a note of disapproval and regret. In fact, Hobbs felt that his partner never entirely forgave him for allowing the attempt on the world record to slip so casually away. His belief was not entirely wrong. 'Often, since then, I have wished that he had gone out with me just for five minutes' work before the day's play started,' Sutcliffe once said.

England's innings subsided badly after Hobbs's dismissal. Despite Sutcliffe's heroic 176, the side was all out for 479. Australia, with a bigger lead than had looked possible at the start of the fourth day, exploited their advantage sufficiently to win by 81 runs, though not before Sutcliffe had hit his second century of the match and his third in succession. For all the glorious exploits of Tate, Hobbs and Sutcliffe, England had now sustained seven consecutive defeats in Australia since the war and

any hopes of regaining the Ashes now looked foolish. Gilligan might
have been a fine diplomat as leader, but his own bowling had badly
lacked penetration and as a captain he had been outmanoeuvred by
Herbie Collins. Frank Woolley, never a harsh judge, was one of several
who thought that Gilligan was too soft, too naive for the job.

Amidst this failure, Gilligan's harshest, most vocal critic, Cecil Parkin,
decided to re-enter the fray. Parkin had already finished his Test career
in the summer with an attack on Gilligan. Now he renewed his condemnation, sparking a high octane public row that would drag in Hobbs
and produce one of the most notorious utterances in English cricket
history. Shortly before the third Test, Parkin wrote an article in the
Weekly Dispatch in which he argued that Gilligan should never have
been chosen for the Ashes tour and that Hobbs would have made a
much better captain. Having experienced Hobbs's leadership against
the Gents, Parkin declared him to be 'the finest captain I have ever
played under', but he recognised that this idea was not feasible since
'such an unprecedented thing as a professional leading England would
not be tolerated for a moment'. So instead Parkin proposed that Percy
Chapman should take over 'under the supervision of Hobbs'. The *Weekly
Dispatch* knew the article was dynamite and gave it this headline on
the front page: 'Parkin's Drastic Suggestion for Friday's Test Team –
Hobbs as England's Super Captain'. Once more Parkin had touched a
raw nerve in the cricket establishment where the concept of amateur
captaincy was regarded as sacrosanct. At the Yorkshire County Cricket
Club's annual dinner a few days later, Lord Hawke gave full, scornful
voice to the indignation of the traditionalists. 'For a man who calls
himself a cricketer to write an attack on the England cricket captain
and at the same time to say that the best cricketer he ever played under
was Hobbs is beneath contempt.' Then Hawke uttered the lines which
soon became infamous and for which he will always be remembered.
'Pray God, no professional will ever captain England. I love and admire
them all, but we have always had an amateur skipper and when the day
comes when we shall have no more amateurs captaining England it will
be a thousand pities.'

Twenty years earlier, Hawke's outburst might have struck a chord
with a significant number of cricket followers, weaned on the ethos of
amateur superiority in the 'Golden Age'. But the world had changed
since then. Lord Hawke now looked outdated, patronising, even idiotic

in the new democratic age where Labour sat in government and women had the vote. The elite's fixation with social origins had badly undermined the army during the war and now seemed to be doing the same to English cricket. Moreover, Hawke's denigration of professionals sounded highly offensive to a British public that deeply admired men of stature and integrity like Hobbs, Sutcliffe, Woolley and Tate.

In the wake of his ill-received speech, the hostility towards Hawke was widespread. Sales of his recently published autobiography slumped and plans for another edition were scrapped. Resentment was felt by working-class cricket supporters, reflected by the popular, Labour-backing *Daily Herald*, which stated that if, 'as many cricketers think, Hobbs is the man to captain England, then surely snobbish ideas about distinctions between amateur and professional should not be allowed to handicap English cricket'. Within the cricket world itself, there was little vocal support for Hawke. Out in Australia, the England professionals mounted what the press called a 'moderate and dignified' protest at Hawke, claiming that he had been 'disparaging' towards them. At home, Harry Lee, the Middlesex stalwart, spoke for most of his colleagues when he said, 'I doubt if there is any cricketer, amateur or professional, who would not gladly have served under Hobbs.' Even Lord Foster, the Governor-General of Australia, who, as a Tory politician, old Etonian and former amateur first-class cricketer himself, might have been expected to take a pro-Hawke line, did the very opposite, publicly announcing during the tour, 'I would never hesitate to play under the captaincy of a man like Jack Hobbs.'

One of the few to speak up on Hawke's behalf was Plum Warner, a staunch, if sometimes slippery, defender of amateur supremacy. Having denounced Parkin as 'the first cricketing Bolshevist' who was 'bent on creating class warfare', he then asserted, in the face of all evidence, that the article with its suggestion 'that Hobbs should captain England or that Chapman should captain England under Hobbs's direction' had 'caused great annoyance to all true cricketers'. The responsibility of leadership, he claimed, was 'better shouldered by an amateur than a professional', not least because the amateurs were far more capable of performing the social duties off the field, 'especially on a tour abroad', a barely disguised sneer at the working-class backgrounds of most professionals. But Warner, struggling to mount a coherent defence, was forced to admit that Hawke had been 'somewhat hasty' in his remarks.

Meanwhile Hawke himself, shaken by the outcry, feebly tried to lessen the damage, only to incriminate himself again. 'Bless my soul! I never meant to hurt anyone's feelings, especially the professionals,' he told the press, before he asked, 'Why, how could anyone possibly allow a professional to be captain over an amateur? No, no, no. To have a professional captaining a team with even one amateur in it! Ha, ha, ha.'

The irony is that Hobbs was never interested in the England captaincy. He led the Players, and occasionally Surrey, out of his sense of duty, but leadership was never a role that suited him. Percy Fender, so gifted in man-management, found that Herbert Strudwick had a far sharper tactical mind than Hobbs. 'It may have been because he [Hobbs] was so unassuming a man. He would give his view if it was sought but that was as far as it went. It got to the point that when I had to leave the field for a meeting or something, I would say to Jack, "All right if Struddy takes over?" and Jack would say, "Yes please" and everyone was happy,' Fender told his biographer Richard Streeton.

Batting was always Hobbs's prime interest, and he was still doing it superbly. In the third Test at Adelaide, England yet again had to bat in response to a big Australian total, the tail having stayed with Jack Ryder to see him through to a double hundred and the total to 489. With England beset by injuries, Hobbs had to do a little bowling, sending down three tidy overs for 11. He also kept up his high standard of fielding in the fierce South Australian sun. There was just one hour left at the end of the second day, so Gilligan tried an experiment of sending in two night-watchmen to open. But the plan ended in failure as England reached the close on 18 for 2. The next day was full of high tension. Hobbs, who had come in at number five, was joined by Sutcliffe when England were 69 for 4, and again they looked in a different class to the other batsmen. When they had put on 90, Sutcliffe fell, but Hobbs carried on to make his third century of the series. 'He did not take any risks in forcing the ball to the on-side or cutting it behind the wicket but rather contented himself with playing "safe" most of the time. Yet it was the correct game to play in the circumstances and one could only marvel at his infinite capacity for suppressing himself and playing wholly for his side when the occasion demanded it,' wrote Monty Noble. Yet, even with Hobbs's 119, England trailed far behind Australia. Another massive defeat looked certain, especially when Australia were 211 for 3 at the close of the fourth day, 335 ahead with seven wickets in hand and the England attack incapacitated by injuries.

Then fate intervened in the form of rain the next morning. After the start had been delayed, Australia were caught on a classic sticky pitch and lost their last seven wickets for just 35 runs to the spin of Frank Woolley and the Yorkshire all-rounder Roy Kilner. England's target was 375, seemingly unobtainable on the still damp wicket. 'We knew that our task was a heavy one and that our responsibility was doubled on this gluepot,' said Sutcliffe. But Hobbs and Sutcliffe were supreme practitioners in such conditions. For over after over, they played skilfully, either leaving the ball or playing a dead bat. The longer they batted, the more the wicket began to ease. Hobbs, said Sutcliffe, 'displayed his great genius in combating spin bowling' in what was 'a masterly exhibition'. It did not last. With England's total on 63 and his own score on 27, Hobbs tried to pull the medium-pace off-spin of Arthur Richardson and was caught at square leg. 'How bitterly disappointed I was! I feared the effect on the rest of the side,' Sutcliffe recalled. His pessimism was misplaced. For the first time in the series, the middle and lower order fought hard. At the start of the seventh morning, the Test could not have been more finely balanced. England needed 27 to win with two wickets left. 'The crowd was tremendously excited and a lot of ladies in the grandstand were nearly hysterical. My wife encountered some Englishwomen whose anxiety showed itself as acutely as if there was a war on,' wrote Hobbs.

The not out batsmen were the pocket-sized Kent leg-spinner Alf Freeman and the captain Arthur Gilligan. Just before Gilligan left the pavilion, Hobbs said to him, 'If you get these runs, we shall win the rubber.' But it was not to be. After batting 110 minutes for 30 runs, a heroically restrained display that was out of keeping with his usual aggressive style, Gilligan mistimed a drive and was caught at mid-on. Moments later, Freeman edged Mailey to the keeper. Australia had won the series and retained the Ashes.

Hobbs's belief that Australia were not nearly as invincible as the scoreline suggested was proved in the next Test at Melbourne, where Gilligan won the toss for the first time and batted. Once more, Hobbs and Sutcliffe laid a solid foundation. The wicket had some juice in it on the first morning, which meant that they had to play cautiously to deal with the bounce and movement, especially from Gregory. But they weathered the storm to reach lunch on 70 without loss. In the afternoon, with the wicket now perfect, they could play in a more attacking vein,

and Hobbs brought up their fourth century stand of the series when
he cut Mailey to the boundary. 'I felt free of my usual responsibility
now that the fate of the tournament was settled,' he wrote. Yet, having
coped so assuredly with the front-line bowlers, Hobbs then fell to the
less challenging medium pace of Jack Ryder. With his score 66, Hobbs
played forward to leg-glance an inswinger from Ryder, but he missed
and momentarily overbalanced. In a flash, Bert Oldfield had taken the
ball down the leg-side and whipped off the bails, with Hobbs's back
foot just a fraction over the line. Oldfield later said that it was 'unquestionably my greatest stumping. So sure was Hobbs in his footwork,
generally so correct, that chances from him were rare and in most cases
somewhat difficult.'

Fortunately for England, the start was not squandered. Their total
of 548 proved too much for Australia, who were comprehensively beaten
by an innings, Tate and Kilner sharing most of the wickets. One crucial
moment in Australia's first innings occurred when Warren Bardsley,
such a dominant figure since the Edwardian age, was run out by Hobbs,
who had created a trap through his cunning routine of pretending to
be slouching in the field, as Noble described. 'Up to this time, Hobbs
had been fielding quite indifferently – suggesting to me a deep-laid plot.
He had failed to reach one or two that normally should have been easy
for him to stop; then suddenly, he dashed in and, picking up with one
hand, threw the wicket down before Bardsley, who had made the call,
could get back. Truly, it is never safe to trifle with an astute and
resourceful fieldsman, and Bardsley certainly should have known better.'

England had restored some pride with their big win at Melbourne,
but they ended the tour on a low note in the fifth Test at Sydney, crushed
by 307 runs. For once Hobbs and Sutcliffe failed in both innings, the
masterful keeping of Oldfield accounting for Hobbs on each occasion.
His dismissal in England's first innings caused a sensation at the packed
Sydney cricket ground. On the morning of the second day, after Australia
had been bowled out for 295, Hobbs faced the opening over from
Gregory. He negotiated the first five deliveries successfully without
scoring; the sixth, speared down the leg-side, seemed to offer an easy
opportunity to open his account. 'I came as near to executing the Ranji
glide as possible. "That's off the mark with four," I said to myself, quite
pleased. Alas, wicketkeeper Bert Oldfield made a flying leap to bring
off a miracle catch. I was out for a blob! "Sorry to do it on you like

that, Jack," remarked the wicketkeeper,' recalled Hobbs in the last ever article he wrote. Oldfield himself left this description of his brilliant move: 'Seeing that the ball was pitched on the leg-side, I anticipated its course by covering a greater distance and as soon as I heard the snick I stretched out my arms full length while in my stride, probably four or five yards wide of the wicket and brought off a catch which certainly thrilled me and brought the spectators as a man to their feet.' One of those spectators was the young Jack Fingleton, who called it 'the greatest wicketkeeping catch' he had ever seen. In the second innings, Hobbs had made only 13 when he was again the victim of Oldfield's gloves, this time to a stumping off the debutant leg-spinner Clarrie Grimmett, who ripped apart England with a match-winning 6 for 37.

Hobbs's failures in the last Test could not detract from his phenom-enal achievement in Australia. On a losing side, under the continual, claustrophobic strain of responding to big totals, he had created a matchless opening partnership with Sutcliffe and cemented his reputa-tion as the world's greatest batsman. Over the five Tests, he made 573 runs at an average of 63.66. If the England middle order had made even half the runs that he and Sutcliffe had, then the Ashes would have been won. At the conclusion of the tour, Monty Noble wrote that Hobbs had proved himself 'one of the most remarkable batsmen of all time'. He was, continued the former Australian captain, 'a player of great ability and mighty achievements, under all conditions, on all wickets and against players from anywhere and everywhere. In our day he has established himself as a batsman on a plane higher than that occupied by any of his contemporaries.' The *Cricketer* had no hesitation in endorsing that opinion: 'In a word, he is indisputably our greatest living cricketer, a batsman pre-eminent in any age and unique in his own generation.' But as Hobbs arrived home from Australia, he knew that there would be further fields to conquer.

13

'They Are Even Naming Babies After Him'

Cricket enjoyed a surge in popularity during the 1920s. Contrary to the forecasts of the pessimists who had warned that it would never recover from the First World War and the end of the Golden Age, the game was actually in better health than it had ever been. Inevitably, in a sport so addicted to nostalgia, there were grumbles from some quarters about cricket's supposed decline. Defensive batsmanship, over-prepared pitches, excessive run-scoring, and falling standards of bowling were among the targets for complaint. But, whatever the justification for such laments, the reality was that the British public was following cricket more keenly than ever before. Attendances were significantly higher than before the war, especially at the major grounds. At the biggest county, Yorkshire, the annual number of paying spectators rose from 112,603 in 1919 to 326,239 in 1925. Similarly at Lord's, the numbers going through the turnstiles increased from 270,950 in 1922 to 404,428 in 1926. Membership was also on the increase, up at the Oval from 2,860 in 1920 to 4,900 in 1927, and at Headingley from 2,100 to 7,600 over the same period. More were playing the game, too. Detailed research by Jack Williams of Liverpool John Moores University has shown that the number of teams playing in the Bolton area rose from 77 in 1919 to 165 in 1926, while in Birmingham the estimated number of sides, excluding workplace XIs, went up from around 200 in 1922 to about 300 at the end of the decade. Altogether, it seems probably that at least 200,000 people were participating in some form of the game every week in this period. Interest in Test cricket also reached new heights, fuelled partly by the major expansion in the popular press and the arrival of the first extended cinema newsreels. Increasing affluence and the introduction of more paid holidays helped to drive the boom. Cricket in this era was truly the national English sport, embraced by all classes and regions of the country. Just as the leagues thrived in the north, so there were few rural villages in the south that did not have their own side.

The advance in cricket's popularity improved the earnings and status of professionals, who made on average about £300 a year in the interwar years, double the pay of skilled workers. It could be, however, a precarious way to make a living because of the risk of injury or loss of form, since at many clubs players were paid match fees rather than an annual salary. Harry Lee of Middlesex thought that payment by matches was 'a cruel system' that meant any cricketer who was dropped 'often had nothing to fall back on but charity'. It was precisely to deal with the caprice of misfortune that several counties introduced minimum income guarantees to provide their capped professionals a degree of security. According to Ric Sissons, author of the groundbreaking study *The Players*, the sums varied. At impoverished Hampshire, the annual guarantee was only £200, whereas at Lancashire it was £325 and at Surrey £400. The Oval Committee could easily afford its enlightened stance; the accounts for 1930 show that the club had reserves of £43,000. But the leading professionals could earn much more than the minimum guarantee, thanks to bonuses and talent money. Some of the top players, like Patsy Hendren of Middlesex, were paid over £500 by their clubs, exclusive of outside earnings. Books, newspaper columns, endorsements, and sponsorships all brought in more money.

Senior Test cricketers were huge stars in the 1920s, achieving a level of celebrity that only W.G. Grace had previously attained. The radio and the press made them household names. Their faces were well known to the public from newspaper photographs, newsreels and cigarette cards, the craze for which was at its peak in the interwar years, not least because smoking was almost a universal habit among men. In fact, some traditionalists felt that the elevation of professionals had gone too far and longed for a return to the days when they were kept in their place. In his 1926 book *A Searchlight on English Cricket*, E.H.D. Sewell was full of almost parodical invective about the changing face of cricket's hierarchy. Professional cricket's 'fees and emoluments have advanced out of all proportion, either to the increased cost of living or to its own standard of play', with the result that 'there is a suspicion of pampering'. With mounting disgust, Sewell reported that 'players of today can and do afford to buy motorcars'. The 'spoilt darlings' were a far less sturdy bunch than the cricketers of the last century who 'jogged along very well without masseurs and without 100 per cent added to their talent money and were never heard to ask for a glass of sherry after lunch, which an international demanded on a certain occasion last season!' Like jazz, cocktail parties, motorcars and noisy hotels, the presumption of the modern, overpaid professional was regarded by Sewell as a symptom of the breakdown in the social order, and he detected the menacing hand of political revolution behind the change. 'This condition of affairs is, of course, largely part and parcel of the modern Bolshevistic attitude. The danger of the professionals coming into power in first-class cricket may be much closer than GHQ* knows, or would care to admit if it did know.'

The biggest cricket star of them all, Jack Hobbs, could hardly be described as either a power-seeker or a 'spoilt darling'. He was the embodiment of what the public held to be the best of the English character: straightforward, reserved, loyal and humorous, his self-effacement all the more impressive because of the extent of the public's adulation. 'Success never spoilt him in the least. He was always the same – modest, kind and appreciative of others. His gentle manner endeared him to people,' Plum Warner once said. 'Modest, quiet, rarely advancing an opinion unless asked, and then giving a shrewd, impartial one, he is as admirable in personal relations as he is on the cricket field,' wrote Leveson Gower in 1925. A striking description of Hobbs's fame at this time was produced in a *Daily News* portrait, which illustrated both the intensity of the hero worship and Hobbs's unassuming response to it: 'The scene is a Fleet Street tea shop. Office boys and businessmen, clerks and typists are drinking tea or munching buns with that placid four o'clock feeling that even Fleet Street cannot resist. Suddenly a broad-shouldered man walks in with a friend. His step is light and springy – as though he walked on turf. His face is tanned with recent sunshine. He brings with him an atmosphere of greensward and open air. Modestly, he tries to slip unobserved to a place at one of the tables – but the attempt is in vain. The tea shop at once becomes a place transformed. A hundred eyes – curious, appreciative, adoring – are turned on the modest newcomer. The office boys forsake their buns; the tea

---

* General Headquarters, by which Sewell presumably meant Lord's.

cools in the cups. Voices in low but thrilling tones chatter animatedly
and heads are nodded vigorously in the stranger's direction. Newspaper
sellers peer in through the glass panels of the door the better to see
him in the very act of drinking. There is a general feeling that the world
this afternoon is palpitating with interest and excitement. The miracle
is explained when I add that the modest man who had come in for a
cup of tea was the national hero, Jack Hobbs.'

As he rose to become a national icon in the mid-1920s, Hobbs never
lost that streak of bashfulness that he had possessed since childhood.
'You may not think it, but my husband is a very shy man,' Ada once
said. This is why he so preferred quiet domesticity to the glamorous
social whirl of the roaring twenties that, with his stardom, he could
have easily enjoyed if he had wanted. It was not that Hobbs was frugal
or self-denying about the comforts of life. He had never forgotten how
much he 'detested' the poverty of his Cambridge childhood or how
much he 'envied' the owners the 'big houses'. Cricket had enabled him
to escape that world, bringing him self-respect and financial security.
Hobbs was not remotely ostentatious, but nor did he undervalue his
earning capacity or the trappings of success. In early 1924, he signed a
five-year contract with Surrey that gave him a minimum guarantee per
year of £440, but bonuses, talent money, tour fees and appearance
money considerably boosted that income. In the 1920s, an England
cricketer was paid £40 for each Ashes Test and £27 for each South
African one, so a full Australian summer would bring in another £200.
It has been estimated that his direct earnings from cricket were around
£15 a week or £780 a year, this at a time when the maximum wage for
top footballers, even internationals, was just £8 a week during the season
and £6 in the summer.

Hobbs also had other sources of income. One was his shop, which
continued to do well throughout the twenties. Another was his endorse-
ment of a wide range of products, including Quaker Oats, Waterman
fountain pens, Barry's tailored suits and Berkeley's armchairs, the last
an advertising campaign that he supported alongside the actress Gladys
Cooper and the opera singer Dame Clara Butt. His upright, honest
image, allied to his sporting prowess, made him an ideal sponsor, as
this promotion of Alkia Saltrates shows: 'First-class cricket demands
both mental and physical fitness and I know of nothing else so wonderfully effective as Alkia Saltrates. A small pinch of it taken in one's tea

each morning keeps the whole body toned up.' Even the tobacco companies, which were annually spending £30 million a year on advertising
by the mid-1920s, recruited Hobbs to lend the gloss of health and
serenity to their products. 'Pinnace Quality Navy Cut' and 'Sarony Silk
Cut Virginia' were two of the brands he endorsed. 'A cigarette so fine
and satisfying at only half-a-crown for fifty passes all understanding.
To say that I am delighted with Saronys puts things very mildly. I feel
it would be impossible to improve on their flavour,' ran his copy for
one campaign.

Through the appeal of his name, Hobbs also made money in the
1920s from books and occasional articles, though all his material was
ghostwritten for him. He was too inhibited by his limited education
and his deferential nature to have much confidence in his own writing.
Even composing letters in response to the sackloads of fan mail, a task
he performed with typical diligence and courtesy, was difficult for him.
Moreover, he was not much of a reader, as he once confessed: 'What
with sports news, gossip, the wireless and my correspondence, no time
is left for books.' His chief ghost in the 1920s was the Lanacastrian Jack
Ingham, who worked for many years as a journalist on the *Star* and
also had a spell as the press agent to the show-business impresario
Bernard Delfont. It was Ingham who wrote Hobbs's first autobiography,
My Cricket Memories, published in 1924 by William Heinemann and,
due to its candour and readable style, probably the best of all the books
produced under Hobbs's name. In a generous review, the *Manchester
Guardian* praised its 'unquenchable enthusiasm for the game', and said
that it had 'a freedom from false modesty and a very human directness
that disarms criticism'. Hobbs's other literary venture was more unusual,
demonstrating that celebrity ghosted novels are not confined to the
modern age. In the mid-1920s, two works of fiction were produced for
Hobbs by the prolific Essex-born writer Sydney Horler, who turned out
an astonishing 157 thrillers under his own name between 1925 and his
death in 1954. Horler was heavily influenced by Edgar Wallace but lacked
the American's class, and his formulaic output, dominated by stereo-
typed characters, is little read today. Both his books for Hobbs were
less savage than his normal pulp fiction but no more convincing. One,
Between the Wickets, was essentially a clichéd schoolboy yarn, with
cricket used to celebrate uplifting moral values. The other, *The Test
Match Surprise*, was the tale of a romance between an Oxford and

England cricketer, heir to a baronetcy, and the daughter of an Australian cricketer. 'It is a curious relic; a frightful load of rubbish with just a trifle of the real stuff concealed in it,' Ronald Mason told *The Times* in 1978.

Including his books, sports business and advertising, it is likely that Hobbs was making about £1500 a year in the mid-twenties, this at a time when the average salary of a GP was £1000 a year. He was the fulfilment of Neville Cardus's rather wistful remark that the cricketer 'has become of bourgeois profession'. In a further indicator of his upward journey from his impoverished roots, he and the family moved in 1928 from Englewood Road to a much larger house at 39 Atkins Road, an attractive 1820s Italianate villa designed by the nineteenth-century master builder Thomas Cubitt. Secluded from the road by high trees, it provided the ideal refuge for Hobbs, as well as demonstrating that he could now afford a 'big house' of the type that had caused him such envy in his youth. Hobbs was also able to send his children to private school, the two older boys to Alleyn's in Dulwich, south London. According to the son of former classmate Edgar Lister, Jack Junior had one experience that graphically displayed the allure of his father's eminence. Every pupil was required to keep a journal, in which were recorded their marks for schoolwork, and this had to be signed each week by one of their parents. One morning Jack Junior took his journal 'out from his desk and found that some enterprising person had got busy with a pair of scissors and cut out every one of his father's signatures. The culprit would, of course, have had no difficulty in finding a ready market for the famous Jack Hobbs's autographs. They never discovered who did it. Young Hobbs got no sympathy from his form master. "You were a fool, Hobbs, weren't you?" he said. "Why on earth didn't you get your mother to sign?"'

All three boys loved cricket but only Leonard, the second son, showed any special talent. Indeed, he was a superb all-round sportsman who played football to a high standard, became a Surrey county champion at sprinting and was considered for the British athletic team at the 1932 Los Angeles Olympics. He also had a trial with Surrey in 1930 and even played alongside his father in one practice match but he was not quite good enough to make the step up to first-class cricket.

Jack never put the slightest pressure on any of his sons to take up sport, though he was gratified when Jack Junior followed him into his

Fleet Street outfitters' business, eventually taking over its management. 'I pity them sometimes. So much is expected of them simply because they are my sons,' he said in 1925. Gentle, uxorious and averse to confrontation, Hobbs could never have been a stern patriarchal figure in his own household. Instead, he created a benign atmosphere, as the *Express* correspondent Arthur David reported in mid-1925: 'The home life of Jack Hobbs is particularly pleasant; the affection and camaraderie that exist between him and his charming wife is very real. The fact that Mrs Hobbs accompanied her husband on the recent MCC tour to Australia made a vast difference to his spirits and therefore to his play.' Ada herself put it well: 'If we may judge from the time he spends in it and his ever-readiness to return to it, I think I can claim that my husband is happy in his home life.' She added that one of his favourite recreations at home was to turn on their player piano or pianola. This long obsolete instrument, which was at the peak of its popularity in the mid-1920s, looked like an ordinary piano but used an internal mechanical device to play music from a roll of perforated paper. 'Jack is passionately fond of music, though he can play no musical instrument,' she said. Hobbs himself wrote that when he was in London, 'it pleases me most to spend the evening at my own home, varied by a short stroll and winding up the wireless and a little music, in which I take great delight.'

All Hobbs's affluence and fame was predicated on his stature as the greatest cricketer in the world. Over the first two decades of his first-class career, through his style, his sheer weight of runs, and his longevity, he had elevated himself from a mere player into an English institution. The journalist Alfred Gardiner, reflecting in a 1926 essay that Hobbs was as famous as Charlie Chaplin, Lloyd George and Bernard Shaw, wrote that 'no picture of the life of our time, set down in terms of personalities who command the public attention, would be complete without him'. Through his never-ending stream of centuries for Surrey and England, he had truly earned the soubriquet of The Master. No longer the buccaneer, his style may have subtly altered since the war but the change only enhanced the pervasive sense of his grandeur and dominance. In the national consciousness, his very name conjured up images of towering achievement, of records broken and bowlers left powerless. Neville Cardus wrote of his golden maturity, 'As his years increased – and he was never powerful of muscle – he gradually slackened tempo and resisted temptation to show his virtuosity. He found a fresh vein, a rich one, by playing within himself. He ripened beautifully, became a classic in his own day, with power in reserve, experience changed to instinct.' Cardus was fond of telling a story that showed Hobbs's mesmerising brilliance in the post-war years. The young batsman Jack Iddon was playing one of his early games for Lancashire against Surrey and during the opening overs in the field, he was placed at mid-on while the Australian Ted Mcdonald bowled to Hobbs, whom Iddon had never previously seen bat. Suddenly Hobbs drove the ball to mid-on, where Iddon, barely moving a muscle, let it straight through his legs. His colleague Dick Tyldesley looked at him and said, 'What the ****, can't thee bend down?' Iddon replied that he had failed to stop the ball because he had been 'so hypnotised' by Hobbs's beautiful footwork, moving in and out of the crease to Mcdonald 'as though he were a cat playing with a dead mouse'. Despite his devotion to Lancashire, Cardus felt this explanation was 'entirely satisfactory'. Among John Arlott's many words of praise for his hero is this compelling passage, which captures the essence of Hobbs's style in the 1920s: 'Merely to see him lift or swing a bat at close quarters, to observe the flexing, tensing and relaxing of his grip on the handle was to perceive the profound sensitivity of his batting. To watch him play an innings was an impressive demonstration of his mastery: the capacity to play naturally and easily while the man at the other end struggled. To watch his running between the wickets and the unhesitating response of his partners was to appreciate his judgement.'

Hobbs's ascendancy throughout the 1920s made him part of the fabric of the Oval. Scoring his centuries for Surrey year after year, he almost seemed as integral to the famous old ground as the green gasometer and the red-brick pavilion. In his book *Batsman's Paradise*, Ronald Mason, born and bred a Surrey man, captured the sense of hero worship that Hobbs inspired at the club: 'From the moment when I became aware of it as an independent county, Jack Hobbs's name stood at the head of it, its supreme representative. Groping back in my memory, I cannot at all recall the first time I heard his name; he was *there*, in my consciousness, enthroned, before I ever had time or leisure to enquire why. In Surrey the name of Hobbs was paramount and sacred; from Vauxhall Bridge to Coldharbour, he was the undisputed king.'

It was an unpretentious kingdom, surrounded by municipal housing blocks, railway lines and red London bus routes, but that reflected Hobbs's unassuming character. Its ordinariness was why he felt so comfortable, certainly compared to the privileged exclusivity of Lord's. 'The Oval is my favourite ground. I love playing there; and strangely, though I have done very well there, I detest Lord's, and always have done,' he said in a 1925 interview. Apart from providing him with a reassuring home in cricket, the other great advantage of the Oval in the 1920s was the flatness of its pitches, which were the delight of batsmen and the despair of bowlers. The groundsman Bosser Martin, who was in charge from 1924 to 1940, regarded high scoring as a tribute to his craft, and he ensured the perfection of his wickets through copious quantities of marl and cow dung, applied to the turf with endless rolling. After the Second World War, when the pitches were relaid, it was found that Bosser Martin's marl extended as deeply as eighteen inches across the centre. The balance in favour of batting at the Oval was further assisted by the sparseness of grass on the huge outfield, which both roughed up the ball and helped it speed towards the boundary. The Surrey and England fast bowler Alf Gover described how difficult his job was in these harsh conditions. 'The Oval was like a dust bowl after the end of May . . . The ground was so hard that running up to bowl was akin to running on a hard tarmac road and soon one's legs began to ache and jar, necessitating a massage from the trainer at the lunch and tea intervals.'

Yet the fascinating point about Hobbs was that he was no flat-track bully. He was just as good on a poor wicket as he was on one of Bosser Martin's featherbeds. This is what, in the eyes of many of his contemporaries, made him unique. The Surrey cricketer and later acerbic writer E.M. Wellings argued that 'Jack Hobbs was the greatest batsman. He was the master of all types of pitch, his technique developed to overcome any difficulties. His superiority over Bradman stems from their difference in the wet.' The leg-spinner Ian Peebles, who bowled to both men, believed that while Bradman 'remains the greatest force of any cricket era', he had to 'yield first place as the complete master batsman to Jack Hobbs in his own. This is a sweeping claim, but all who knew Hobbs from his early days to his mid-forties were agreed that, the greater the difficulties with which he and his colleagues were confronted, the more marked his superiority.' That verdict was shared by the umpire Frank Chester, who umpired Test cricket throughout the interwar years: 'For all his greatness, Bradman had neither the technique nor the skill of Hobbs to succeed on a sticky wicket in favour of the bowlers.' Chester felt that Hobbs's secret in such conditions was that 'he had the keenest eye of any man I knew, which enabled him to play the ball later than anyone else. Frank Woolley has told me that he has bowled to Hobbs more than once on a sticky wicket and has beaten the bat – or so he thought – but in the last fraction of a second, with a twist of the magic blade, Hobbs sent the ball speeding to the boundary.'

Plum Warner once said of Hobbs that 'to hear him talk, you'd think he had never made a run in his life'. This was an exaggeration. Hobbs was well aware of his abilities. He just hated to boast about them. But he could be revealingly honest at times. On one occasion in 1922, he was playing for Surrey against Hampshire, and at his Southampton hotel he fell into a conversation with a cricket fan by the name of Evelyn Carmichael. Away from the public stage, Hobbs was always much more relaxed in the private company of genuine cricket followers and when Carmichael asked him why he was such an excellent batsman Hobbs's answer could hardly have been more candid: 'I think my success lies largely in my belief that, whatever ball is sent to me, I can beat it with my bat.' It was this innate self-confidence that gave him such a superb temperament for the big occasion. He was rarely inhibited by nerves, not even in Ashes Tests. 'I am not upset by big cricket. Crowds I don't fear. A crisis in the game does not shake me,' he said in a 1925 interview with the *Evening News*. But he admitted that he was 'very sensitive to criticism and perhaps when it is averse I take it too much to heart', showing that he cared more about his reputation than is sometimes claimed. The same pride was reflected in his habit of keeping books full of newspaper cuttings about his batsmanship. 'I used to keep the accounts of my fifties, but I only keep the hundreds now.'

Hobbs was famously generous to autograph hunters, especially enthusiastic boys, and never displayed any hint of arrogance or rudeness towards the cricket public. The one time he could become exasperated, however, was when he was preparing to bat and was focusing his concentration for the battle ahead. At such moments, he found any interruptions intolerable. The artist W. Smithson Broadhead once swept into the Oval dressing room between innings with the intention of arranging a sitting for a commissioned portrait. Hobbs curtly told him, 'I can't be bothered with that now.' Smithson Broadhead left, deeply offended, but Hobbs later explained, 'There's a time for all things and it was time for cricket just then.'

Hobbs had been an avid practiser in his youth, one of the reasons he developed such a sound technique, but as he grew older he played far less in the nets, feeling that he had enough innings out in the middle to keep himself in form. 'Today I don't like net practice. Best to keep away from the nets when you are getting so much actual play. Fred Boyington, our scorer, is forever telling us that Arthur Shrewsbury was often in the nets. The last time I took Fred's advice about practice at the nets before going in I was out for 5!' Hobbs said in a 1925 interview. As a schoolboy member of Surrey, Jim Swanton did have the chance, however, to see Hobbs batting in the nets once in 1921 and had this memory of seeing 'the great man at close quarters: black hair gleaming, always neat and tidy, twiddling the "Force" bat in hands encased in old brown-and-white leather gloves stuffed with horse-hair, quipping his bowlers and showing straight white teeth in a friendly grin'.

For someone so even-tempered and confident about his play, Hobbs was surprisingly superstitious, with a range of rituals that he observed in both the dressing room and the middle to bring him luck. 'I ground my bat within the crease at the end of every over; and I use one corner of the players' dressing room at the Oval for dressing – and I am always careful to put the right pad and the right boot on first.' He also had an irrational fear of the number 9, and disliked any score with that figure in it. In the Trent Bridge Test of 1930, he almost ran out the England captain Percy Chapman while trying to shift his innings from 39. In the context of Hobbs's superstition, George Bratley, a popular numerologist of the 1930s, claimed that he had been able to discern Hobbs's fate from a study of the mystical relationship between his name and certain digits. In a bizarre article in the *Daily Express* in 1934, Bratley announced the results of his analysis: 'Jack Hobbs was destined at birth to possess quiet ambition to be rewarded by honour and easy circumstances. At the same time he was threatened with a pessimistic nature and underhand methods. Among the careers indicated was agriculture. But, alas! judging by others of the same root number, poor Jack will either be hanged, fall out of an aeroplane or be murdered in Cannes,' predictions that could hardly have strengthened the credibility of this occult creed.

Aside from his superstitions, Hobbs at the crease had several quirks that came to be familiar to cricket followers throughout the world, from the twirl of his bat before each delivery to a regular tug at his collar. A keen watcher of her husband throughout the 1920s, Ada said she could always pick him out instantly at the crease, sometimes with a little prick of jealousy. 'He has a trick of lifting his cap every few minutes. Also he used to blow his nose so often that I had to tease him out of it. There was another lady who spotted his little habit and sent him a gay handkerchief with the request that he should use it. He flourished it about all day. I was watching him and I knew all about the handkerchief. The girl was delighted and I ragged my husband again.'

Perhaps the richest description of Hobbs's mannerisms while batting came from the pen of the fervent Surrey follower Ronald Mason: 'He never while I watched wore the Surrey cap at all; most often he chose the handsome MCC touring cap with the silver George and Dragon, less regularly the England blue with the lions.' In the pre-1914 days, said Mason, the cap was 'staidly set' on his head, but in the twenties it 'was cocked more often towards one eye; as his innings lengthened it would get pushed farther and farther back on his head. As he faced the bowler his left toe, symptomatic of his restless, active, attacking temper, would turn provocatively upwards; this was not pure swagger or bravado, but part of the fluidity of his movements towards the ball.' Between deliveries, Hobbs 'would let his weight go back on his heels and give his bat his famous twiddle, a gesture random and instinctive enough but appropriated by him as a trademark which, when met in other players, contrives to recall him alone; and he favoured copious pitch prodding'. There was one other familiar gesture, said Mason, that remained 'curiously his own – in the middle of a long innings he would whip his cap off and wipe the sweat from his forehead with the forearm of the same hand, all in one movement, before setting his cap back, a little farther to the crown of his head, twiddling his bat, cocking his left toe and returning wirily to the slaughter'.

Far less idiosyncratic was the trait he shared with most batsmen: the desire to get off the mark as soon as possible. 'I always like to make my first run quickly,' he said in 1930, and he usually did so with a dab into the off-side or a push off his legs. In a career that embraced 1,315 innings over twenty-nine years, Hobbs was out for a duck just forty-two times, and he avoided ever making a pair. Wally Hammond was once told by Hobbs that 'a pair was the only thing that worried him and, towards the end of his career, was taking care to prevent it by being more and more careful over the first runs'. There were two bowlers who dismissed him for o three times, Ernie Robson of Somerset and Tom Wass of Nottinghamshire. Tellingly, they both bowled fast-medium away swing and leg-cutters, exposing the one vulnerability in Hobbs's technique. But Hobbs was a better, more consistent starter than many players. Research by Tony Shillinglaw, who has devoted much of his life to studying Don Bradman's technique, reveals that Hobbs was actually more reliable than Bradman at reaching double figures. Hobbs, famously, never had anything like Bradman's ruthlessness in piling up the runs once he had reached a century. Often, through fatigue or a wish to give other batsman a chance, he would throw his wicket away in such circumstances by hitting out recklessly. 'When I have made a hundred, I am not really anxious to add to my score,' he said in July 1925.

Centuries were the overwhelming theme of that season, as the country became transfixed by his quest to break the record held by W.G. Grace. At the start of the 1925 summer, Hobbs had scored 113 hundreds, well short of Grace's lifetime total of 126. It seemed highly unlikely that he would make the required thirteen more before September, given that he was now aged forty-two and had never made more than eleven hundreds in a single season. Moreover, in the past, Hobbs had tended to have a poor summer after a lengthy Australian tour because of the fatigue and the switch in cricketing environments. But this time it was completely different. His batting triumphs with Sutcliffe seemed to invigorate him. 'After my return from Australia, I was feeling remarkably fit. I was in phenomenal form and started scoring centuries right away,' he wrote. In only the second match of the season, against Gloucestershire at the Oval, he hit his first hundred in a big Surrey victory by an innings. The leading bowler in the Gloucestershire attack was Charlie Parker, probably the finest left-arm spin bowler in England during the mid-twenties but not one who troubled Hobbs. Another Gloucestershire bowler, Tom Goddard, recalled how Hobbs used to reduce Parker to misery. 'Charlie couldn't take it. Old Hobbo used to knock him over cover and then over mid-off and we'd say to Charlie, "Don't take any notice", but then another one would go over. Charlie would go to third man and Jack Hobbs would settle down with a grin all over his face and make another hundred.'

Hobbs followed up this innings of 104 with a century in the next game, at the Oval against Glamorgan, who had only been given first-class status in 1921. Hobbs was now the first man to score centuries against all seventeen counties in the championship. A third hundred in successive matches at the Oval came against Warwickshire, prompting the *Daily Mirror* to report, 'There is no stopping Jack Hobbs just now.' For the first time, the press began to speculate that W.G. Grace's record might be surpassed that season. 'The record of W.G. Grace is obviously in danger,' said the *Cricketer*. 'Hobbs returned from Australia in fine health and condition and with ordinary luck, a great season is in front of him.'

A change of venue did not halt the astonishing flood of runs. In Surrey's first away game of the season, at Leyton against Essex towards the end of May, he made 129 before he was stumped off by his old bête noire Johnny Douglas. The only minor setback to this innings was that he strained a muscle in his heel and had to withdraw from the next game. But he returned for the Bank Holiday match against Nottinghamshire at Trent Bridge, where he made 189 and, after reaching his century, hit out in his old swashbuckling style, scoring the last 89 in little more than an hour. There was brief hiatus for two quiet away games, then in mid-June the flow resumed with another century against Essex, this one at the Oval. In the process, Hobbs became the first batsman to reach 1,000 runs in the season. 'He now requires but seven centuries to equal Dr Grace's record of 126 and with more than half the season to go he would be a bold man who would dare say the Surrey player will not break a world's record this season,' declared the *Daily Mirror*. Even better followed in the next match, against Cambridge University at the Oval, with Hobbs scoring a century in each innings, only the second time he had achieved such a double in his first-class career. Hobbs's performance was no reflection of the weakness of the students. In fact, both Cambridge and Oxford in the 1920s had a higher standard than some of the weaker counties, a point proved in this game by Cambridge's six-wicket victory after being set 426 to win on the last day. The remarkable sequence continued in the next fixture, against Somerset at the Oval, where at least 15,000 spectators paid to watch him take 111 off the West Country attack in a big Surrey win. Straight after this match, Surrey travelled up to Edgbaston to take on Warwickshire, whose attack included Harry Howell, Freddie Calthorpe and Bob Wyatt, all of them good enough to bowl for England at various stages of their careers. Yet their quality meant nothing to Hobbs in his rampant mood, as he hit 215 in just three and a half hours, with two 6s and twenty-six 4s. At one point, on the

march to his 123rd century, he hit Bob Wyatt for 27 in two overs. The
Cricketer was almost overwhelmed with admiration: 'Hobbs was the only
player in the picture. Using the long handle with the greatest freedom,
he simply hit the bowling when and where he liked. The spectators
shouted with delight. "Fetch a Lewis gun," yelled one.' Hobbs himself
claimed that the explosion in big shots at Birmingham had only happened
by accident, because he was actually trying to get out after reaching three
figures. 'I lashed out and tried to end my innings after the hundred but
actually couldn't get out! I did my best to get out. I found myself knocking
up the second hundred,' he told the *Evening News*. The innings was his
fourth century in succession and he now looked like he might threaten
the record of C.B. Fry, who in 1901 hit six hundreds in consecutive first-
class innings. But, when Surrey went in again, he was out for 31 to Wyatt,
bringing the run to an end.

He did little with the bat in his next three first-class games, though
he led the Players to victory against the Gents at the Oval, helping to
win an exciting contest with a couple of shrewd declarations. He then
returned to century making in dramatic style with 140 against the Gents
at Lord's in mid-July, an innings described by *Wisden* as 'superb' and
'quite free of fault'. The sense of freedom that he derived from his
superlative form was shown in the audacious way he dealt with Gubby
Allen, who was genuinely quick. Allen bowled one short outside the
off-stump, which most batsmen would have tried to square cut. Instead,
Hobbs pulled it straight back down the ground. The next ball was of
full length. Rather than drive it, Hobbs executed a delicate late cut for
four. 'He was at his very best, playing all the bowling easily and gracefully, and making every sort of stroke,' said the *Cricketer*. In an audio
interview recorded in late August 1925, which was subsequently turned
into a commercial gramophone disc, Hobbs explained how he felt during
this astonishing purple patch. 'I was actually fitter and in better general
health than I had been for some time. The first three months of the
season were favoured with good cricketing weather. The wickets were
made for run getting. I was batting as well as ever I did and I got off
to a flying start. All things working together for good, the centuries
came with an ease that surprised myself. Even when the press began to
display a more than usually active interest at the approach of the record-
breaking century, I could honestly say that I faced each innings with
no more nervousness than at any other stage of my cricket career and

I was never troubled much in that way.' By 20 July, the goal seemed to be within his grasp as he hit yet another century, this one an innings of 105 against Kent at Blackheath. 'The famous cricketer is now within one of W.G. Grace's record of hundreds,' reported the *Daily Express*, as the media cranked up the excitement. Interestingly, in contradiction of the pretence that Hobbs was some sort of selfless paragon of sportsmanship, Hobbs did not walk at the end of this innings when he appeared to have edged Woolley to Arthur Day at slip. Having remained at the crease, he was given out by the umpire.

The summer of 1925 was a time of epochal developments in Britain and abroad. Turmoil reigned in the coal industry, with a nationwide strike only averted by massive government subsidies to keep up miners' wages. Winston Churchill, the Chancellor of the Exchequer, returned sterling to the Gold Standard, a move that the Cambridge economist J. M. Keynes* warned would ultimately sink the country into depression. Abroad, the Swiss town of Locarno hosted crucial negotiations over the post-war settlement of Europe's frontiers and the future of the German republic. In Italy, Mussolini announced his assumption of dictatorial powers. The summer also saw the publication of *The Great Gatsby* by F. Scott Fitzgerald, perhaps the most perfect novel in the English language, and *Mein Kampf*, by Adolf Hitler, certainly the most sinister political manifesto written in the twentieth century. Yet in England the public's imagination was gripped by the exploits of a shy, middle-aged cricketer with a beaky nose. Interest in his attempt on the record reached frenzied new levels, spilling out from the sports sections and on to the front pages. Hordes of photographers followed Hobbs everywhere. Vast crowds gathered for his every appearance. People came to see, not cricket, but Hobbs. In late July, just after his Kent century, Hobbs had tried to sound nonchalant about this national obsession: 'Perhaps in the old days, I was nervy, temperamental. But I now have no nerves in regards to hundreds,' words that appeared to tempt fate. One aspect of the drama that puzzled him was how the press and public

---

* Keynes, born in Cambridge in 1883, was almost an exact contemporary of Hobbs. In his highly original book, *Golden Ages at the Fenner's Margin*, Adrian Wykes propounds the idea the Keynes' economic theories were heavily influenced by his youthful devotion to watching cricket in Cambridge during the late-Victorian age. An invented, but all too believable, line from Virginia Woolf, 'Look how much fuss is made of that funny little boring man Hobbs,' is typical of the book's style.

had focused on the milestone of equalling W.G. Grace's rather than beating it. 'To me the 127th century was – and is – the more important,' he said in his audio interview. But that was not the prevailing view in the high summer of 1925. Parity with the Grand Old Man was what counted. Most of the country seemed to be willing him towards that goal, and, as the fevered expectations mounted, Hobbs came under remorseless pressure. 'I felt that every eye in England was focused on me, and I began to get harassed,' he recalled. Until then, no cricketer had been subjected to anything like this intense scrutiny; in Grace's era, there were no mass circulation papers, no cinema newsreels, no radio bulletins, no reporters looking for 'a quote', no prying photographers. Now Hobbs experienced the pack in full cry. When he travelled down to the south coast for the next game against Sussex at Brighton, he was accompanied by a large caravan from the media, as well as a cinematographer from the company New Era Films which, with his agreement, was making a documentary about his life. As soon as he arrived in his hotel room on the eve of the match, he received a call from a journalist in London asking him how he felt about his 'big day tomorrow'. Hobbs had to explain that there was nothing inevitable about making a century. 'It's not as easy as all that,' he said testily before hanging up. Soon afterwards, he had another call, this one from a photographer asking if he would pose for some pictures the next morning in his swimming costume on the Brighton beach. Even in the face of Hobbs's objections, the photographer pressed on. 'You can get up early, Mr Hobbs, before anyone's about and you needn't go in the water.' Hobbs declined the offer. The next day the disappointment of the press and public was almost palpable as Hobbs was dismissed by Maurice Tate for 1, though Surrey went on to an innings victory.

This was the beginning of a dramatic change in form after the glories of the first three months of the season. Through a mixture of fatigue and pressure, Hobbs lost his touch. His timing deserted him, his stroke-play became awkward. Even when he made a start, he did not capitalise in his customary manner. Against Kent at home he made 22, then 52 and 38 at Gloucester. At the beginning of August came the big match against Nottinghamshire, which drew a crowd of over 31,000 when Surrey batted on the second day. So great was the multitude to see Hobbs that the ground authorities, having closed the gates after lunch, struggled to maintain order. According to the *Daily Chronicle*: 'directly

Hobbs commenced Surrey's innings signs of restiveness were apparent. The longer Hobbs remained at the wicket the more intense became the excitement and gradually the crowd swept down the barrier of the few police around the ground and encroached to such an extent that the boundaries were in several places shortened by at least 50 yards.' In the crush, the two captains had to appeal to the crowd not to gather in front of the sightscreens and more police had to be drafted in 'to push back the hordes who were invading almost to the playing area of the ground'. The vast throng's wishes were not to be gratified. Hopes rose when Hobbs passed 50 against an attack that included Harold Larwood and Fred Barratt, two of the fastest bowlers in England. But then, on 54, he was lbw to Barratt. His dismissal instantly cast a pall of gloom over the packed ground. So great was the disappointment that, according to *The Times*, 'his admirers played him the subtle compliment of letting him return to the pavilion with 54 to his credit almost unapplauded. Hobbs is like Madamoiselle Lenglen* in that not only can he fill a ground but he can also empty it. After Hobbs was out the crowd streamed away.'

After this innings, newspaper placards all over London read 'Hobbs Fails Again', a rather harsh interpretation of a half-century but one that reflected the relentless focus on the century record. The media's attitude only weighed Hobbs down with more anxiety. 'Their belief that I had only to go to the wickets to get a century and the procla- mation of my "failure" whenever I got fewer than a hundred runs were getting me into a state that was not likely to do me or my side any good,' he said near the end of the season. Hobbs had a genuine failure in the second innings when he was caught off Larwood for 1. The next game against Middlesex followed the same pattern, with Hobbs out for 49 in the first innings in front of an eager crowd of 22,000, his dismissal prompting a headmasterly rebuke from *The Times*: 'Now nobody wishes to be hard on Hobbs. But it must be pointed out to him that this is the seventh consecutive occasion on which he has permitted himself to be dismissed for a score of less than three figures. In the ring seats, we are already beginning to suggest that the Old Man would have done the trick a week or more

---

* The flamboyant French tennis star Suzanne Lenglen. Nicknamed 'The Divine One', she was the first female sporting celebrity.

ago.' Hobbs could only make 4 not out in the second innings against Middlesex before rain fell. Rain also ruined the next fixture against Leicestershire, when Surrey only had eighty minutes to bat, though this was still enough time for Hobbs to be dismissed for just 31. After this further setback, Hobbs, normally so placid, gave vent to his feelings of stress and frustration through an article in *Westminster Gazette*. Referring to his innings of 49 against Middlesex, he said that it was 'scarcely deserving the stigma "failure". I little thought that in making twelve centuries this season I was shaping a rod for my own back.' He then confessed to feeling weary at the whole circus he had to endure. 'The coming end of a busy county season, on top of a trying Australian tour, finds me just a little tired of cricket.'

The nation was almost as fretful and exhausted as Hobbs by the time Surrey went down to Taunton for the match against Somerset that began on Saturday 15 August. Already feeling tense, Hobbs was disturbed to find on his arrival at his hotel on Friday that he been allocated room 39, which he saw as doubly unlucky, for it not only contained the number 9 but also represented, in his superstitious mind, three times thirteen. Hobbs confided in Andy Sandham, who was sympathetic rather than judgemental, and insisted that they swap rooms. In another attempt to entice good fortune, Hobbs brought down to Taunton a four-leaf clover which had been sent to him by a lady member of Surrey CCC. Throughout the forthcoming match, he had carried this charm in the pocket of his flannels.

The next morning Somerset, led by Jack 'Farmer' White, won the toss and batted first on a firm wicket in bright sunshine. But they could not take advantage of the favourable conditions and were bowled out for 167 before tea. Now it was Surrey's turn. Hobbs said that in the field he had 'felt fairly normal' but, on hearing the bell for the start of Surrey's innings, his nerves suddenly worsened. His tension was obvious to the Somerset fielders as he reached the middle. 'What did Hobbs look like at the start of this innings? I can tell you very well. Great player though he was, he was obviously very anxious,' recalled Raymond Robertson-Glasgow in a later BBC interview.

Hobbs's nervousness betrayed itself in the very first over, as he hit one of Robertson-Glasgow's straight into the cover's hands. Groans went up from the from the crowd, only to turn into a cheers of relief as the spectators saw the umpire's signal of no-ball. Hobbs himself had started to walk off to the pavilion when the catch was taken, but he later revealed that this was 'just my joke' because he heard the umpire's call early and knew he had not been dismissed. This was a rare moment of levity, however, in a tough battle. Soon afterwards, with his score on just 7, Hobbs popped up another catch, this time from a legitimate delivery from Robertson-Glasgow, only for the mid-on fielder Jack MacBryan to miss it by moving too slowly. 'I do not know what happened with mid-on. He was what you might call basking in vigilant content,' said Robertson-Glasgow. Hobbs continued to struggle for the rest of the afternoon. On 14, he gave a difficult chance to the wicketkeeper off Jim Bridges. On 30, he survived a loud appeal for lbw. Twice before the close he was almost run-out. When he had scored 87, he played the ball to mid-on and called his partner Donald Knight for run. Then he realised that the single was too risky and tried to send back Knight who by now was already halfway down the wicket. In the confusion, both Surrey batsmen had ended up in the middle as the throw came in towards the wicketkeeper. Showing remarkable selflessness and quick-thinking, Knight resumed his run, passed Hobbs and carried on towards the keeper's end, knowing that he was certain to be out. This act of chivalrous self-sacrifice was in itself a tribute to the esteem in which Hobbs was held by Knight and his teammates. Not all other opening batsmen in cricket history have inspired such altruism among their colleagues. With Hobbs having added only 3 more to his total, he was almost run out again, when he played a ball towards short leg, where Randall Johnson picked up and threw at the bowler's end as Hobbs went for a single. The ball just missed the stumps. If it had hit them, Hobbs would have gone. It was his last run of the day. Somehow he had survived. He was now 91 not out, just 9 short of the cherished milestone.

While Hobbs spent the remainder of the weekend in his Taunton hotel room apart from a brief foray to church on Sunday morning, the press worked itself into a fever in the build-up to Monday. 'Good luck, Hobbs! Nine runs to make and a great record to equal. Surely seldom in the history of the game have nine runs been awaited with such keen interest by friend and foe alike,' said an editorial in the *Daily Mirror*, summing up the mood of the nation. 'Everywhere there was an electric atmosphere of which I had had a foretaste on Sunday when the trains disgorged an army of photographers and visitors

from London and elsewhere,' recalled Hobbs. Indeed, the Great
Western Railway put on a special early morning excursion train on
Monday, with a return fare of thirteen shillings and sixpence for the
round trip from Paddington to Taunton. The influx from outside
Somerset brought the crowd up to over 10,000. 'The route to the
ground was an amazing sight of people and vehicles,' recalled Andy
Sandham. Play could not actually start until 11.25 because of the
delays in allowing spectators into the ground, with the queue outside
stretching for more than half a mile.

Waiting in the dressing room, Hobbs was a fidgety, silent figure. 'All
the talk of the whole cricket world was, "Will he get them?" How he
did it in such an atmosphere I do not know – the poor fellow was
worried to death,' recalled Herbert Strudwick. Hobbs later confessed
that he had only once experienced a similar bout of nerves, and that
was during the fifth Test at Sydney in 1921, when, as he limped out to
bat after tearing his thigh muscle, he was given such a tremendous
ovation by the Sydney crowd that his knees 'were positively shaking'.

Once Hobbs was out in the middle, he felt a little calmer. But Somerset
still made him fight for every run. Just before the resumption, a reporter
came up to Robertson-Glasgow and suggested that he give Hobbs the
runs. 'Oh for heaven's sake, let Jack do it,' the journalist said to him.
'We had no intention of letting Jack do it,' recalled Robertson-Glasgow.
But they could not stop him either. With the Surrey vice-captain Douglas
Jardine as his partner, Hobbs crept towards the target. There was a
significant release of tension when Robertson-Glasgow bowled a long-
hop which Hobbs pulled to the square leg boundary to move to 98.
Despite the shot, Hobbs was apparently unsatisfied with his bat and
had another one brought out. The interruption did not distract him.
He scored another single to reach 99. Despite its excitement, the crowd
was almost as silent as a church congregation with the moment of
destiny so near. Then, shortly before noon, Hobbs pushed Bridges wide
of short leg for the vital run. Immediately, the whole county ground
erupted in prolonged cheering. The roar of the applause, reported H.J.
Henley for the *Daily Mail*, could be heard 'at the railway station a good
half-mile away and the porters and the people waiting for their trains,
realising what the mighty shout meant, applauded, although they had
not been so lucky as to see the runs made. On the ground itself, nearly
all those present leapt to their feat, some waving hats, some waving

handkerchiefs. And Hobbs, who had for once seemed desperately nervous, lifted his cap time after time and waved his bat with the air of a boy who felt himself free from trouble at last.'

The scenes of mass enthusiasm meant that the game could not be resumed for several moments. Hobbs shook hands with the umpires and other players, then Percy Fender, with a characteristically unconventional gesture, came out to the middle with a celebratory goblet of ginger ale, which the centurion raised to the crowd amidst more loud cheering. At the same time in London, a large crowd had gathered outside Hobbs's shop in Fleet Street, and there was more pandemonium when the news came through by cable that the precious 9 runs had been made. The same was true in the West End, where the bureau of information at the Selfridge's department store had kept the public informed of Hobbs's progress towards the landmark. Further east, in the resort of Margate on the Kent coast, Ada received the telegram that Jack had arranged for the Taunton groundsman, Harry Fernie, to send to her, emblazoned with the single sentence, 'Got it at last, Jack.' Inevitably, she too was besieged by the press. 'I am of course highly elated with my husband's success,' she said, before explaining why she had to be in Margate rather than Taunton. 'I had promised the children we should have a holiday together as I have been away so much with my husband and I could not disappoint them.' But, she added, 'the children are also overjoyed at their father's success.' Hobbs could hardly contain his glee in his interview after he was out for 101. With his usual courtesy, he praised the 'splendid crowd' at Taunton and the whole-hearted effort by the Somerset team, who 'gave nothing away in the field and bowled like fiends until the last ball'. After describing his century as a 'pretty useful one', he confessed, 'I am very happy at equalling the Grand Old Man's record and I feel my well-wishers are happy with me.' He also expressed his gratitude to his club and its supporters, saying that his only regret was that he had not reached the milestone in front of his home crowd. 'The Oval people have always been kind to me. Equalling and breaking records, playing good cricket for the team, is about the only way I can repay the kindness.'

In the warm afterglow of his triumph, Hobbs was deluged with tributes. On Monday morning alone, more than 200 telegrams arrived in the Surrey dressing room at Taunton. The press was full of adulation.

'Jack Hobbs climbs to the pedestal of cricket beside the immortal W.G.', proclaimed the *Daily Mirror* on its front page. In its editorial, *The Times* stated that 'in the field and off it, he is a great cricketer and sportsman in the highest sense'. The *Daily Mail* told its readers that 'not only is Hobbs a batsman whose perfection of style and graceful posture have been a delight to the eye from the beginning of his public career, but he is so modest and even-tempered and he so obviously plays the game in the true spirit of the game that his reward is peculiarly fitting'. From the cricket world, his England skipper Arthur Gilligan called him 'the most genuine sportsman of his age', and leading Australia Test players, including Herbie Collins and Bert Oldfield, cabled their congratulations. That night a celebratory banquet was held in a Taunton hotel, attended by both the Somerset and the Surrey teams.

The torrent of praise was given another surge when Hobbs beat W.G. Grace by scoring his 127th century in Surrey's easy win by ten wickets. This time there were no nerves, no chances. Released from the incubus of the record, Hobbs played in uninhibited style. 'Never could the Somerset bowlers find the edge of his bat. With faultless precision he made the middle of it find the ball every time,' reported Colonel Philip Trevor in the *Daily Telegraph*. With this second hundred, Hobbs not only became cricket's greatest century maker but he also set up a new record for the most centuries in a single season, this being his fourteenth. In contrast to the Monday, there was a much smaller crowd at Taunton to witness the second round of drama. Nevertheless, Hobbs was led by the Somerset team to the top tier of the pavilion to receive yet more cheers from the spectators at the ground.

Across the wider British public, the reaction to Hobbs was unparalleled in its exuberance, as shown by this passage in the *New York Times*: 'Any American in London or elsewhere in England yesterday and today instantly realised that something had turned the country topsy-turvy. Barbers, bus conductors, financiers, shopkeepers, policemen, stenographers, tripping to and from work, dignified lawyers and vociferous street vendors – all had a topic in common which made them kin for the moment. Tonight there are newspaper cartoons showing Jack Hobbs leaning on his cricket bat and the dumb adoration of Julius Caesar, Mahomet and Napoleon and other lesser lights. Jokes have been hastily interpolated into the reigning London theatrical success about Jack Hobbs. Matters such as international politics and imminent coal strikes must wait their turn in line. Today is Hobbs's day. They are even naming babies after him all over Britain.'

Because of the unique mental and physical strain he had been under, Hobbs was rested for Surrey's next game, against Glamorgan at Cardiff, much to the annoyance of the Welsh authorities who missed out on the chance of a bumper crowd. Instead, he took a break with some friends in Dorset before returning to London at the end of the week. He was utterly fatigued by the time he arrived at Paddington and, with unaccustomed tetchiness, refused to pose for any photographs or give any comment to reporters at the station. Having shaken off the press, he made it home to Clapham, only to find that he could 'scarcely open the front door because of the mass of postal material behind it', as he put it. Among the letters was one from King George V praising his 'remarkable success', as well as a less solemn message from the Navy, Army and Air Forces Institute in Kennington, telling him that 'the Oval gasometer, which has witnessed so many of your achievements, sends affectionate greetings and heartiest congratulations'. After his brief rest, Hobbs returned to the fray against Yorkshire and was given a heartfelt ovation by his Surrey fans, though in a rain-ruined contest he could only make 19. But he was not finished yet with his record-breaking. For the Players against the Gents at the Scarborough festival, he hit 266 not out, the best score of his career to date and the highest innings ever made in the series. 'He was extraordinarily alive and alert during the whole of his display,' reported the *Cricketer*. His sixteenth and final century of the season came in the last match, for the Rest against Yorkshire, the champion county, at the Oval, where his 104 led *The Times* to comment that 'he played as if happily unconscious of intervals, centuries and aggregates'. Altogether, in the season that would always be associated with his name, he made 3,024 runs at 70.32, putting him top of the national averages for the first time. *Wisden's* verdict was unequivocal: 'Hobbs will go down to posterity as one of the greatest figures in cricket history. A masterly batsman under all conditions, possessed of exceptional grace of style, remarkable in the variety of his strokes, ready to run any risk for his side and a superb field, he has been at once the wonder and delight of all cricketers of his generation.'

Yet for such a private, shy man, there was one heavy price to pay for his phenomenal success in the summer of 1925. He was forced to dwell in the limelight, performing tasks that his self-conscious nature made a trial. In late August, he gave his first talk on the BBC about his career and beating W.G. Grace's record. Though his presentation was scripted, he later said, 'It was one of the most terrifying ordeals that I had ever faced up to then, far outweighing any Test match.' He had no need to be so anxious, as he delivered the broadcast perfectly well and his script was interesting, ranging from anecdotes about the Taunton century, like that of the four-leaf clover, to some memories of W.G. Grace. He also had to speak at a number of formal dinners, including one hosted at the Savoy Hotel by Lord Dalmeny, his first Surrey captain, another at the London Press Club, and a third at the Cambridge Guildhall organised by the Cambridge Cricket Association. This last function was the most pleasant, since he had always retained a deep affection for his birthplace. 'If this old town of Cambridge takes pride in her sons, her sons are no less proud of her,' he said to loud applause, going on to point out that of the three cricketers who had made one hundred centuries, 'two of them were born on the banks of the Cam'. At the dinner, the association presented him with a silver cigarette box and an illuminated address, and also announced that a pavilion would be erected in Hobbs's honour on Parker's Piece as 'a perpetual reminder to everybody not only as to how cricket should be played but also the perseverance, integrity and *esprit de corps* through which a man might rise from Cambridge to the highest possible heights of first-class cricket'.

There were some requests for public appearances at which Hobbs drew the line. One was an offer from the impresario of the London Coliseum, Sir Oswald Stoll, to go on stage in a show that would provide a demonstration of stroke making. Despite the astronomical proposed pay of £250 per week, Hobbs turned it down, explaining that to 'appear as a variety turn would be to belittle the great game of cricket' and that he might end up 'making a fool of myself'. He also rejected a film offer, as well as a request from the Balham Liberal Association to stand as their parliamentary candidate. Having told the Liberals that he was flattered by the idea of becoming an MP, he could not accept the invitation because he wanted to carry on as a professional cricketer and, more importantly, 'I could not make a speech to save my life. Of course I have had to get up now and again and say "thank you". And a precious fool I have felt on those occasions.' There was also the matter of his

Hobbs going out to bat with Andy Sandham, his prolific Surrey partner in the post-war era.

Jack Hobbs and Herbert Sutcliffe, the greatest opening partnership in Test history. 'The complete craftsman, polished with a brilliance of his own,' was Sutcliffe's description of Hobbs.

Hobbs on his way to a century against Australia at Lord's, 1926. Bert Oldfield is the
wicketkeeper and Jack Gregory is at slip

Hobbs becomes the first professional to lead out England during a home Test, Old Trafford 1926

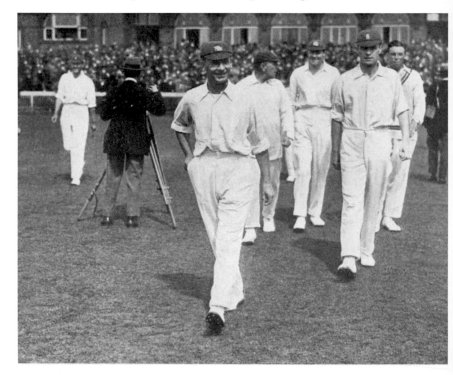

Hobbs drives through mid-on during his crucial, Ashes-winning partnership with Sutcliffe on a spiteful wicket in the Oval Test of 1926 .

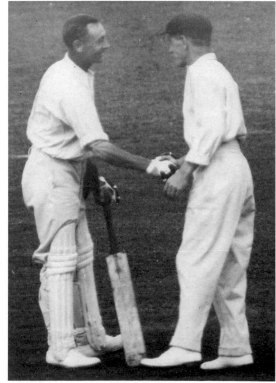

Hobbs is congratulated by the Australian captain Herbie Collins on his historic century during this match. 'The finest piece of batting I have ever seen,' said Collins later.

Jack's wife Ada on the beach at Margate in 1925, with their son Jack junior behind the makeshift wicket

Jack with his beloved Ada in April 1929. 'It was miserable when we were parted,' she said.

Jack and Ada teaching the rudiments of cricket to their youngest two children in the back garden of their Clapham home. Vera is about to bowl to the determined Ivor.

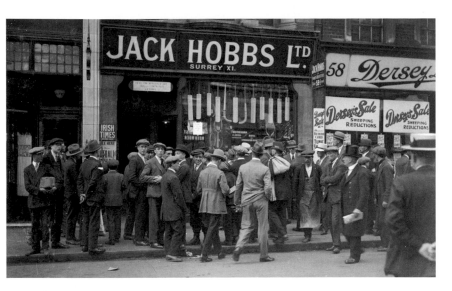

A crowd gathers outside Hobbs's Fleet Street shop to hear news of another big score in the summer of 1925

Hobbs pictured in 1922, choosing the willow from which his bat is to be made. 'As a general rule, narrow-grained wood is best for driving power and a broad grain for durability,' he said.

Hobbs gives his autograph to a delighted young admirer. Despite all his phenomenal achievements, he never lost his boyish enthusiasm for the game.

Hobbs sets off on the run that brought him his final century against Australia, Melbourne 1929. To this day he remains the oldest man to have scored a Test hundred.

The Master in action on the county circuit, pulling to leg on his way to a century against Derbyshire at the Oval, 1924

A rare moment of vulnerability: Hobbs is bowled by the young Nottinghamshire left-arm medium pacer Dennis Bland, September 1929

A pensive Jack Hobbs driving into Lord's for his final Test at the ground, June 1930

Ted a'Beckett dives to catch Hobbs during the Leeds Test of 1930. An explosive controversy erupted when Hobbs refused to accept the word of the fielder and had to be given out by the square leg umpire.

The end of an era: the Australian team give Hobbs three cheers at the start of his final Test innings at the Oval, 1930. The gesture 'brought a lump into the throat' confessed Bert Oldfield.

Hobbs in his retirement, coaching the next generation

Hobbs at the ceremony to mark the opening of the gates erected in his honour at the Oval, 1934

(*Below*) Hobbs shakes hands with a police officer on his arrival at Buckingham Palace to receive his knighthood, 1953. He was the first professional cricketer to be accorded such an honour. (*Right*) Hobbs pictured in his Fleet Street shop on his 70th birthday. The easy smile and fluid wrist movement had still not deserted him.

fluid political convictions. 'I am afraid it is a sign of weakness but I have actually voted both Liberal and Conservative.'

In his speech at the London Press Club dinner, Hobbs had looked forward to the visit of the Australian team in 1926. For the first time since the war, he said, England had an 'even' chance of winning the Ashes, and if the wickets were soft, 'the odds should rather be on England'. Whatever happened, the cricket world knew that the performance of Hobbs would be crucial to the outcome of the series. As *Wisden* put it: 'The great occasion is at hand and we look to him to "speak to the enemy at the gate". It would be a glorious climax to a historic career were he, by his batting, to play the outstanding part in so-long delayed a triumph of England over Australia.' They were to be prophetic words.

14

'The Greatest Piece of Batting I Have Ever Seen'

The cricket season of 1926 opened against a backdrop of industrial crisis. As the players walked out for their first county championship matches at the beginning of May, frantic negotiations were underway in London between the Conservative government and the Trades Union Congress to avert the looming General Strike. The threat of such action had been intensifying for months, as a result of proposed wage cuts in the coal industry and the pledge by the labour movement to show solidarity with the miners. With the government refusing to give any assurances on pay, the talks broke down and, at midnight on 3 May, the only General Strike in British history began. According to the TUC, more than two million people walked out; the government's own Ministry of Labour estimated that at least 1.5 million workers participated. The railways, trams, buses and docks came to a complete halt. A host of other industries were affected, from steel to construction, electricity to chemicals. Action by the printers meant that no newspapers appeared at the start of the strike. Yet contrary to the government's worst fears, there was no mood of panic or revolution in the country. In that typically British way, which was later to be manifested in the Blitz, the public tried to hold on to a semblance of normal life. Essential supplies of food were maintained by the armed forces and a large group of volunteers, and there was surprisingly little violence on the streets, even at picket lines, the government's task again helped by volunteers who acted as special constables to keep order.

The attitude of stoicism was reflected in the world of cricket, where every attempt was made to continue as usual. 'The counties should carry on their programmes as well as circumstances permit although, owing to transport difficulties, some matches may have to be reduced to two days or even abandoned,' read the MCC instruction to the counties. Prime Minister Stanley Baldwin, a conciliatory rather than ideological Tory, strongly supported the drive to keep the game going because he felt it was 'a means of promoting good feeling between all sport-loving classes'. Baldwin himself was a keen cricket enthusiast, as was his wife Lucy. Predictably, the Lord's establishment strongly supported the voluntary initiatives to lessen the impact of the General Strike. A few counties were weakened because of the large number of amateurs who volunteered to serve as drivers or policemen. Douglas Jardine, the Surrey vice-captain, was amongst those offering his services. One of the more surprising sights of those tumultuous days was that of Plum Warner, then Chairman of the Selectors, standing outside Scotland Yard in his uniform as a special constable. At Oxford and Cambridge, so many students volunteered that three of their matches had to be cancelled. But the disruption to the game was surprisingly limited. There were a few late starts because of the transport difficulties, crowds fell significantly at some grounds, and Plum Warner's *Cricketer* could not appear because of the printers' walkout. The visiting Australian team experienced some inconvenience when, during their match against Essex, the lorry carrying their cricket gear was held up by pickets. Yet, as in the wider country, predictions of chaos proved misplaced. By the second week, it was obvious that the government had the upper hand. On 12 May the TUC called off the strike, leaving the coal miners to carry on their battle alone. The unions' climb-down was widely hailed as a triumph not just for Baldwin, but also for the British public, which was said to have demonstrated its preference for social harmony over strife. Some even claimed that cricket had played its part in the creation of this atmosphere. 'Can you imagine a cricketer becoming a Lenin?' asked Plum Warner. In the same vein, Sir Theodore Cook, editor of the *Field,* argued that the values of 'sportsmanship and fair play' were 'respected by nearly everyone in our community from the highest to the lowest'.

As the events of the previous summer had graphically shown, Jack Hobbs was held to be the embodiment of those sporting virtues. If the strikers of 1926, in all their disillusion and confrontation, represented a troubled aspect of England, then Hobbs represented another, more comforting side. Where the General Strike brought division, Hobbs promoted unity. Adored by all classes, his deferential outlook was the antithesis of class war. With Europe increasingly menaced by extremist ideology and Soviet totalitarianism, the more militant unions carried a taint of alien subversion about them, whereas no man could have been more English than Jack Hobbs. His quiet, modest character was quint-essentially English, as was the game he loved. All his career he had been a loyal servant of his club and country. The fantastic riches of the cinema and theatre could not entice him away, even at the age of forty-three, from the job he still cherished. But he was reaping the rewards for his steadfast service in other ways.

Early in 1926 the Surrey Committee agreed that he should be given a third benefit, an unprecedented honour for any professional in the game, even though the circumstances of his 1914 benefit had been unusual because of the war. In a further gesture of recognition, the committee gave £100 to start off the fund, and also guaranteed £1,000 from the gate receipts, instead of the normal £750. Inevitably, given the public's admiration for Hobbs, the guarantee was not needed. Altogether, his 1926 benefit raised £2,670, which helped him in the family's move to the larger house in Atkins Road in 1928. At Test level he was given another high accolade, one that would have been unthinkable when he first started in the Edwardian age. It was a reflection of how far the status of professionals had advanced since then that he and Wilfred Rhodes, now aged forty-eight, were asked to serve on the England selection committee chaired by Plum Warner. The other two selectors were Arthur Gilligan, still captain of Sussex but no longer in contention as a Test player, and Percy Perrin, the fine Essex amateur batsman who made his living as a property developer. A shy, self-contained individual, Perrin has often been described as the best batsman never to have played for England, his poor fielding the reason for his exclusion. The idea behind co-opting Hobbs and Rhodes was to provide a seasoned perspec-tive from both the south and the north of England, though some felt that a professional would be reluctant to pass judgement on a colleague. Frank Woolley, for instance, believed that paid players should be 'excused the duty of having to vote on their brother professionals'. In contrast, Hobbs saw the elevation as an 'important compliment' to himself and Rhodes, while Warner felt that they did a valuable job. 'They were in closest touch with cricket and brought a long experience to our task'.

Of Hobbs's qualities as a selector, Warner said that he 'possesses a sense of proportion and brings a judicial mind to bear when discussing the qualifications of any individual cricketer'.

The other member of the selection panel was the new England captain Arthur Carr, the skipper of Nottinghamshire. A free-scoring batsman, aggressive captain and hard drinker, he was a dramatic contrast to his more emollient predecessor Gilligan. His charisma had always attracted both controversy and admirers. When he was at school at Sherborne, one of his fellow pupils Alec Waugh, the brother of Evelyn, fell madly in love with him, and subsequently wrote of his romantic yearnings in his semi-autobiographical novel, *The Loom of Youth*. The hero of the book, Lovelace Major, was a thinly veiled portrait of Carr: 'Haughty, self-conscious, with sleepy-looking but watchful eyes, he towered over his contemporaries by the splendour of his athletic achievements and the strength of his all-mastering personality.' At Nottinghamshire, Carr carefully nurtured his young fast bowlers Harold Larwood and Bill Voce, and in the field adopted belligerent tactics that exploited their pace and bounce. Carr's pugnacity was widely seen as exactly what England required in 1926 to win back the Ashes. The *Cricketer* claimed that his appointment 'seems to have met with unanimous approval. His reputation as a leader ranks deservedly high.' The magazine also felt that his offensive batting methods were 'ideal' for Test matches in England, which, unlike those in Australia, were still restricted to just three days. Though he did not push his objections, Hobbs was one of the few who had his doubts about Carr, partly because he always felt that his own county captain Fender was by far the best man to lead England. Hobbs also believed that Carr was a weaker man than his bullish image suggested, once suggesting that 'he let the cares of leadership affect him unduly'. For his part, Carr had a more ambivalent attitude towards Hobbs than most other cricketers. While he recognised Hobbs's greatness as a batsman, he never rated the Surrey man's cricketing judgement and even questioned his courage against pace. Moreover, they were polar opposites in character: the brash, well-oiled squire versus the quiet, teetotal artisan. The nascent friction between them was to grow during the series and would ultimately result in lasting bitterness once Carr's captaincy had slid towards disaster.

The Australians of 1926, led by Herbie Collins, were a less formidable side than Warwick Armstrong's of 1921, though they still had great

players like all-rounder Jack Gregory, the leg-spinners Mailey and
Grimmett, and batsmen like Warren Bardsley, Bill Woodfull and Charlie
Macartney, known as the 'Governor-General' for his dominating style.
Previewing the series in the *Cricketer's* spring annual, Hobbs wrote
that he viewed 'our cricket future with confidence. In fact, we seem to
be on the crest of a wave of optimism.' He felt that England's bowlers
would prove more effective than Australia's in the home conditions
and he also highlighted some of the emerging talent in the counties,
especially George Macaulay of Yorkshire and Harold Larwood, who,
he said, 'has a big future. His right-arm fast-medium-bowling is faster
than it looks.' Hobbs's own form in the run-up to the first Test at Trent
Bridge, without approaching the splendour of the previous summer's
early months, was solid enough in the dampness that prevailed. In
addition to a century against Gloucestershire at the Oval, he made
several other fifties, including 85 in the Test trial for England against
the Rest at Lord's, though he came in for some criticism for the slowness of this innings from Charlie Kelleway, the former Australian
batsman, now acting as a reporter for the *Daily Express*. 'His display
was simply not worthy of England's greatest batsman. It was a plumb
wicket and the bowling did not deserve the respect he gave it.' The
question of Hobbs's caution would become an issue again later in the
Test series. Once the Ashes opener arrived in early June, he had little
chance to prove himself against the Australian attack, since the match
was almost a complete washout, heavy downpours falling in Nottingham
on all three days. Only fifty minutes' play was possible on the first day,
during which Hobbs and Sutcliffe put on 32 without loss before they
were driven back to the pavilion by the rain. According to Monty Noble,
the famous pair 'batted with ease and confidence and showed all their
old understanding between the wickets'. There was no chance of
resuming play after that, the ground coming to resemble 'Lake
Windermere', in the words of Arthur Gilligan. On the third day some
ducks belonging to the groundsman could be seen paddling on what
was usually the middle.

In contrast to this sodden affair, Hobbs enjoyed one of the most
scintillating performances of the season when Surrey hosted Oxford
University shortly before the second Test. In bright sunshine on a flat
pitch against a weak undergraduate attack, he scored 261 and put on
428 for the first wicket with Andy Sandham in just five hours. Their

stand still remains the opening partnership record for Surrey and was only broken when Sandham, taking pity on the exhausted students, deliberately gave his wicket away to Errol Holmes, the Oxford captain who was also on the Surrey staff.

Three days after this enjoyable rout, Hobbs had to face the much more demanding opposition of the Australians at Lord's. England's bowling had been strengthened by the addition of Harold Larwood, for whom Hobbs had made a strong case at the selection committee even though the young Nottinghamshire paceman had only limited first-class experience. What had won over Hobbs was his disquieting experience in the Surrey game against Nottinghamshire earlier in the season when Larwood had bowled him out cheaply in each innings. 'You're here because you're fast enough,' said Hobbs in a paternal manner when Larwood turned up on the eve of the Test. But Larwood and the rest of the England attack were blunted by an excellent Lord's wicket when Australia batted first, a big century from Warren Bardsley helping them to reach 383. Hobbs and Sutcliffe started England's reply at 12.20 p.m. on the second day and immediately demonstrated their class as they stroked their way to 77 without loss at lunch. After just two hours, they had put on 150 in confident style. 'In my humble opinion, Hobbs is still the greatest batsman in England. If not the brilliant player that he was some years ago, he has a remarkable temperament for a big match,' wrote Plum Warner. Yet as Hobbs came near to his century, he became increasingly cautious. The flashing strokes disappeared; the Australian bowlers tied him down; the 33,000-strong crowd grew restless. As he crept through the 90s, Hobbs seemed to be playing for himself rather than the team, an offence of which he had never been accused before. Sutcliffe fell for 82 when the score had reached 182, but the arrival of Frank Woolley did not galvanise Hobbs. It was true that Arthur Richardson and Jack Ryder were bowling defensively to well-set fields but in the past he would have tried to seize the initiative. Now he plodded along towards his century, labouring over every run. Eventually he was out for 119, but his tenth hundred against Australia was received with nothing like the praise that had greeted the previous nine. Typical was the comment of Monty Noble: 'Hobbs must have been seeing the ball as big as a hayrick and it really seemed that getting his century was uppermost in his mind. Only Hobbs himself can say but to us who were watching it seemed

that for that period the interests of his side were a secondary consideration.' Charlie Macartney went even further, arguing that Hobbs's
self-absorption undermined England's chances in the match. In his
memoirs, the Australian wrote that Hobbs 'took an interminable time
from 90 to 100. This waste of time on the second day went a long way
towards robbing England of a win as the pace should have been forced
to enable Carr to close his innings earlier.' Even normally supportive
voices were critical. 'Hobbs held himself back in such strange fashion
that he took an hour to raise his score from 90 to 100. Admittedly the
leg-theory bowling was very accurate and the fielding keen, yet it is
difficult to think that, whatever the nature of the attack on a good
wicket, Hobbs could not have pushed along more vigorously,' said
Wisden, while Arthur Gilligan remarked that Hobbs had been through
'an exceptionally slow period' on his way to his hundred.

A year before, almost every hundred had been a cause of rapture for
the press and public. Now a century against Australia at Lord's, a supreme
achievement for any England player, led to a chorus of disapproval. As
Hobbs learnt, the public mood could be fickle, yet he believed that much
of the condemnation was unfair, since England were still not in a position
of safety when he was batting. 'Richardson bowled leg-theory and I really
did not see why I should oblige him by taking risks. Also Ryder bowled
wide of the off-stump to keep me from making runs. The critics took
the attitude that I ought to have taken risks. A characteristic British trait,
is it not, that in order to be fair to others, we cause our own to suffer!'
he wrote with some asperity in his 1931 book *Playing for England*. The
truth, as Hobbs further pointed out, was that three-day Tests on the
excellent wickets of the 1920s made it hard for either side to achieve a
result. Eventually England declared with their score on 475, and Australia
easily batted out the rest of the final day. This time Carr came under
attack, 'blamed for providing the Australians with a valuable afternoon's
batting', to quote Hobbs.

It was at the beginning of the third Test at Headingley that Carr's
captaincy really imploded. After just two matches, he was feeling under
severe pressure in the role, compounded by the fact that he had not yet
batted in the series. So great was his stress that he told the selectors
that he did not think he was worth his place in the side. Reassuring
Carr of the committee's faith in him, Warner was on his most oleaginous
form. 'You are the best captain we have had for ages and you are worth

a hundred runs an innings,' he wrote in a letter. 'We all have the very greatest confidence in you and I wouldn't be without you for anything. Don't worry for a minute, I beg of you, please. A captain like you is worth many, many runs. Love from yours affectionately, Plum.' As events would prove, insincerity was perhaps the strongest quality of that missive.

Having retained his job, Carr then had his confidence broken by a series of appalling blunders on the morning of the crucial Leeds Test. The first occurred over selection. Following heavy overnight rain at Leeds, the selectors called up Charlie Parker, the Gloucestershire slow left-armer, because they expected a sticky wicket. Those instincts seemed to be confirmed when Carr, Hobbs, Warner and Gilligan went out to inspect the pitch before the toss, though Carr was annoyed that Rhodes, the selector who knew Headingley better that anyone else, was not present because he was playing for Yorkshire at Northampton. After much prodding, discussion and some advice from the groundsman, Carr decided that he would put Australia in to bat if he won the toss. Hobbs later admitted that, as one of the selectors, he gave the decision his 'full approval'. Yet, having decided the wicket would be ideal for Parker, the selectors left him out, instead giving the final place to the Leicestershire all-rounder George Geary. It was a bizarre move, and one that made a mockery not only of Parker's last-minute call-up to the squad but also of Carr's inclination to field first. Plum Warner, slippery as ever, claimed that Carr was wholly responsible: 'he had exactly the side he wished', wrote Warner, though Carr himself denied that he had a free hand. 'I was constantly being advised to do this and that.' With more honesty, Hobbs accepted his share of the blame. 'We thought that George Geary, with his running-away ball, would be as dangerous as a left-hander. Also Geary was a better bat and very fine at slip-fielding,' he later wrote, reflecting perhaps some of his own dislike of fast-medium away movement, whereas he rarely struggled against Parker.

Having rushed from Gloucestershire to Leeds overnight, Parker was shattered by the news. 'Real tears came to his face – big, strong, cheery fellow as he is – when the decision was made known to him,' recalled Patsy Hendren. In later years, Parker turned to violence; he once grabbed Warner by the lapels outside a lift at the Grand Hotel in Bristol and called him a 'bastard' before letting him go. Parker certainly had grounds for fury at the injustice he suffered. He was the third highest wicket-taker in the history of first-class cricket, yet only won a solitary England cap. It might all have been different if he had played at Headingley. Bob Wyatt, a future England captain, summed up the selection fiasco. 'If the pitch justified sending in Australia to bat, it certainly justified including Charlie Parker in the side. It is hard to imagine how such a thing could happen.'

Carr duly won the toss and elected to field. When Warren Bardsley, who was captaining Australia in the absence of Collins due to illness, returned to the pavilion and explained to his team that they would be batting, Charlie Macartney remarked, 'Well, I'm glad you won the toss.' The Governor-General, certain that the pitch was 'a batsman's paradise', was incredulous when he was told that Carr had sent in Australia. Yet even then, the quixotic move might have paid off. With the very first ball of the match, Maurice Tate dismissed Bardsley. Then, off the fifth ball, he induced Macartney to edge the ball towards second slip, the position occupied by none other than Arthur Carr. Normally a brilliant close fielder, Carr put down the catch. Hobbs wrote that it was 'a difficult chance' but he was being generous. In fact, the ball went at waist height to Carr's left and he easily got both hands to it. He knew he should have held it. Macartney capitalised on the mistake in the most glorious manner, smashing the England attack all round Headingley in one of the most captivating exhibitions of batting ever witnessed in Ashes cricket. 'I didn't know where to bowl at him; he was irresistible,' confessed Tate. He scored a century before lunch, only the second man to do so in Tests after Victor Trumper, and each of his thunderous blows increased Carr's agony. 'I think I spent the most dreadful luncheon interval in all my experience of cricket. Every blessed thing had gone wrong for me . . . To add to my miseries, P.F. Warner sat at the table a few places away with a face like nothing on earth.' Macartney eventually went for 151, but Australia piled up 494 with further centuries from Bill Woodfull and Arthur Richardson. Hobbs and Sutcliffe gave England a reasonable start in response as they put on 59 for the first wicket, but neither of them progressed to fifty, and the middle order, including Carr, failed miserably. Only a gusty 76 from George Macaulay at number ten prevented a massive lead for Australia, but England were still all out for 294 and had to follow-on.

Shortly before lunch on the third day, Hobbs and Sutcliffe walked out with a match to save. The wicket was starting to crumble and the Australian leg-spin pair of Grimmett and Mailey could hardly have been more threatening on such a surface. But throughout the afternoon, England's openers handled the Australian attack with consummate skill. According to Macartney, they were 'great not only in technique but in temperament' and their partnership 'was of the highest class on a worn wicket against clever and determined bowling'. In his analysis of their stand, Arthur Gilligan made the interesting point that Hobbs and Sutcliffe complemented each other in their styles, for, in his maturity, the Surrey master tended to favour the leg-side, while Sutcliffe scored more towards the off. 'It is impossible for any opposition to keep on changing the set of the field every time a stroke for an odd number is made. It is not generally recognised that, owing to this characteristic of the batting of these two, their partnership almost amounts to that of a right-hander and a left-hander together. When they get set it certainly has that effect on the fielding side.' After tea, Hobbs and Sutcliffe took England to safety. Having reached 77, Hobbs became the heaviest run-scorer in the Anglo–Australian Tests, beating the record of 2,660 runs held by Clem Hill. It looked a certainty that he would make yet another Ashes century when, on 88, he chopped Grimmett into his stumps. His disappointment was alleviated, however, by the knowledge that he and Sutcliffe, with their partnership of 156, had helped to keep the series all-square.

For the next Test at Old Trafford, England made three changes to the XI. Chapman, Geary and Macaulay were dropped. In came Ernest Tyldesley, the tough Lancashire batsman, Fred Root, the inswing, leg-theory specialist from Worcestershire, and Greville Stevens, the young, Middlesex, leg-spinning all-rounder. Significantly, apart from Carr, Stevens was the only amateur in the side, a far cry from the early Edwardian era when the England batting line-up was dominated by the likes of MacLaren, Fry, Jackson, Ranji and Jessop. The miserable weather and Carr's misfortune continued in this match. On the opening Saturday, 24 July, only ten balls were possible. Then on the rest day, the England captain went down with an attack of tonsillitis. On the Monday he had a raging temperature and was unable to speak. It was obvious that he could not take the field. England would have to find an alternative leader. Warner immediately went into conference with Perrin and Gilligan. Initially, according to Warner's account in *Cricket Between Two*

Wars, they decided to offer the job to Strudwick, who was the most senior member of the team in terms of age and was regarded as tactically astute. Strudwick declined the offer, as Warner had predicted he would. A few moments later, Warner walked into the England dressing room and told the rest of the team of Carr's illness. Turning directly to Hobbs, he said, 'Jack, we've talked things over and we would like you to lead the side.' Hobbs's response was typical of the man, 'You are doing me a great honour but Mr Stevens is in the eleven.' Hobbs was so immersed in the tradition of amateur leadership that still, despite all his experience stretching back two decades, he felt he should defer to a neophyte playing his first Ashes Test.

'Yes, we know. We would like you to take it on, all the same.'

'I'll do my best,' he replied.

Hobbs later admitted that he felt a profound sense of pride at becoming the first professional to lead England onto the cricket field in a home Test.* 'It is splendid to have captained England,' he wrote. Despite his temporary promotion, he continued to believe, right up to his retirement, that amateurs should generally be in charge in Test cricket, 'chiefly because of its social side and because of the natural dislike of professionals to boss their own fellows'. He also emphasised, however, that any amateur captain had to be fully worth his place in the side as a cricketer.

Even if he was second choice, the award of the England captaincy was a personal tribute to Hobbs's standing in the game, as well as a reflection of the lessening prejudice against professionals. The old barriers were coming down, not just in captaincy and selection committee, but even physically within pavilions. The Lord's Test of 1926 was the first time that all the England team had shared one dressing room, an innovation that Hobbs welcomed because it 'gave us a better chance to discuss tactics'. Because of the enormous respect in which he was held, Hobbs's temporary leadership was universally accepted by his England colleagues. He had already gained considerable experience of captaincy since the war, both as an occasional deputy to Fender at Surrey and as a regular skipper of the Players against the Gents since 1922. Although Hobbs was too diffident to be a natural leader, most

---

* The Nottinghamshire professionals Alfred Shaw and Arthur Shrewsbury had led England on two Australian tours in the 1880s.

cricket followers believed he was perfectly competent at the helm. His test colleague Patsy Hendren argued that Hobbs 'certainly should have captained England often', and added: 'I venture to state that there is no amateur player of my time who would not have been perfectly happy to have played in an England side captained by professional Jack Hobbs.' But there were some dissenters from that view. The ferociously reactionary E.H.D. Sewell wrote that Hobbs's captaincy of the Players in the 1925 season had been full of 'grotesque mistakes', such as setting the wrong field for the pace bowlers and putting on the left-arm spinner too late in one innings. Hobbs had, he continued, 'strained cricket intelligence' with the batting order he used in the Lord's match of 1925. But Sewell was a highly jaundiced observer, for he fully agreed with Lord Hawke's notorious outburst against the idea of professional leadership. Claiming that Lord Hawke had been subjected to 'a vicious propaganda campaign', Sewell warned that it would be a 'retrograde and damaging step', as well as 'an extraordinarily sad match for English cricket', if her XI were to be 'captained by a professional'.

The moment dreaded by Hawke and Sewell came on Monday 26 July when Hobbs, with his habitual warm smile on his face, led out England to loud acclaim. According to the *Daily Mirror,* the announcement that he would take over from Carr 'created a sensation among the crowd at Manchester'. Sadly for England supporters, he could work no tactical miracle on a soft, placid pitch against the strong Australian batting in the first two sessions, as Woodfull and Macartney again posted centuries. But later in the day and on the third morning, Hobbs's bowlers fought back, and Australia collapsed from 252 for 2 to 335 all out, Fred Root taking 4 for 84 in a marathon contribution of fifty-two overs. Hobbs's handling of England won general approval from the selectors and the players. 'He proved himself a good leader and his side worked very happily together under him,' wrote Warner, a view endorsed by Fred Root. 'Jack was a grand skipper. Although I knew he did not favour my theory, his great knowledge of the game was brought into operation to get the best possible results.' Even the Australians felt the same way, as reflected in the words of Bert Oldfield. 'It was no surprise to any of us that Hobbs proved an excellent leader,' though Arthur Mailey, in usual witty style, was struck by the transient nature of Hobbs's role. 'Although Jack did have the honour of captaining England, he felt at the time like the best man who was asked to become a bigamist because the groom failed to appear.' The groom, in fact, was in the pavilion watching the play unfold. A brooding, melancholic figure, reduced to silence by his illness, Carr claimed not to have been impressed by what he saw of Hobbs's leadership. 'Captaincy was never one of his strong suits. I have seen him in charge of a side several times and, if I may say so, I thought he was a rotten captain. But then, I am afraid most pros are not much good at the job,' said Carr later, bitterness apparent in every sentence.

Like the previous three Tests, the match at Old Trafford ended in stalemate after England easily batted out the rest of the day. Hobbs led the way with a solid innings of 74, prompting Monty Noble to praise his 'pluck, resource and judgement', as well as his 'rock-like defence'. After this fourth successive draw, there was now widespread recognition among cricket administrators that three days were insufficient for an Ashes Test. On 28 July the Imperial Cricket Conference, chaired by Lord Harris, agreed that the final match at the Oval should be without a time limit. 'A fight to the finish,' proclaimed the *Daily Mirror*, warning with comic exaggeration that the decider might degenerate into a 'war of attrition. Jack Hobbs and Sutcliffe, for instance, could keep the enemy at bay for many days.' The news of the timeless nature of the Test, however, paled beside the controversy that exploded over the England captaincy. Ahead of the vital Oval contest, the selectors knew that they had a heavy responsibility, for national prestige, as well as the Ashes, were at stake. It was fourteen years since Australia had been beaten in a series by England, who had won just one of the nineteen Ashes Tests since the war. Well aware of this burden, Carr arrived at the committee meeting on 8 August expecting to discuss the team he would lead at the Oval. 'I very soon sensed that something was not quite right where I was concerned, and it was not very long before I found out what it was. I was sacked,' he recalled. Warner, who said he found the business 'distasteful', told Carr that neither his health nor his form were good enough to keep him in the England team. In a subsequent public statement, Warner claimed that Carr himself, because of his tonsillitis, had 'generously offered to resign', his 'unselfish action' accepted by the selectors 'with the greatest possible regret'. But this was nonsense. Carr was instructed to stand down and, in a move that only damaged him further with the selectors, gave his version of events to the press. 'I am perfectly fit,' he said. 'I am exceedingly disappointed to be omitted from the side. It is not a question of ill-health. I have been dropped because of my form.' According to a later account that Carr gave in his memoirs, based on what he had been told about the meeting, Gilligan and Rhodes wanted to keep him as captain, but Warner, Perrin and Hobbs outvoted them so he had to go. The man they chose to replace him was Percy Chapman, who was in good batting form that summer, had an optimistic nature, but lacked experience; he was not even captain of Kent in 1926. The sacking of Carr generated a huge row in the press, particularly because there were such doubts about Chapman's suitability for the role. The fractious mood was well caught by the *Daily Express*, which regretted English cricket's continuing obsession with amateur leadership: 'There is a want of candour somewhere. Assuming a change is desirable, the public also wishes to know why Mr Chapman was chosen over Rhodes and Hobbs?' On a personal level, the decision changed for ever the lives of both Chapman and Carr, who said he was left 'broken-hearted'. In later life, as his disillusion worsened, he even expressed regret that he had devoted so much of his time to cricket.

Hobbs, normally sympathetic to fellow cricketers, had no time for Carr's self-pitying attitude. As he showed in his vote, he did not think much of him as an England captain and he found the hysteria over the sacking ridiculous. 'I really can't understand why all the fuss is made when a captain is superseded. There was nothing like such a to-do when they left out Frank Woolley and lots of others who were ordinary members of the eleven,' he wrote in *Playing for England*. His antipathy to Carr was demonstrated in an incident at the Oval during a game between Surrey and Notts, when Maurice Allom felled Carr with a short delivery. 'Come on, get up, Arthur, take the bouncer like a man,' said Fender, a remark which so infuriated Carr that he lashed out wildly at the bowling until he was caught soon afterwards. As he left the middle, Hobbs ran over to Fender and shouted with delight, 'Well done, skipper, you certainly talked him out.' For his part, Carr nursed his grievance against Hobbs and occasionally let his resentment show. In addition to calling Hobbs 'a rotten captain', he made the sulphurous accusation that Hobbs was scared of the Nottinghamshire pace bowlers. Having claimed that Hobbs in his later years 'never came to play for Surrey at Trent Bridge', Carr wrote: 'It was quite openly and freely said that he did not relish having to face Larwood and Voce.' Carr then asserted that the

real reason was because there were no sightscreens on the ground, so
he used this explanation for another barb at Hobbs. 'The absence of
screens never worried me. But some players are fussy about them.' It
was a deeply unjust charge. Hobbs played regularly at Trent Bridge
throughout his late forties, even facing Larwood there in 1931 at the age
of forty-eight. In the summer of 1928, when he was forty-five, he took
a century off the Notts attack led by Larwood, who, unlike Carr, was
always full of admiration for Hobbs. 'He was the classical stylist, a
polished performer who played on all types of wickets with an easy
artistry,' said Larwood.

The Nottinghamshire pace bowler, after missing the previous two
Tests, was brought back into the side for the Oval Test. But there was
one far more extraordinary and romantic comeback than this. The
Yorkshire veteran Wilfred Rhodes was persuaded by his fellow selectors
to return to Test cricket, having not played for England since 1921. In
fact, they had urged Rhodes to play in the early summer Test trial but
he had rejected the suggestion, saying that they needed a younger man.
But with Parker out of favour and Roy Kilner having proved ineffective,
the selectors were certain that Rhodes was the experienced spinner
they needed. 'You are still the best left-handed slow bowler in England,'
said Warner at the meeting, to which Gilligan added, 'And you make
runs for Yorkshire.' Rhodes monosyllabically replied, 'I can get a few.'
Hobbs then chipped in, 'And your fielding is all right.' A wry smile
appeared on the veteran's lips, 'The further I run, the slower I get.'
After the meeting, Rhodes began to have regrets that he had accepted
the invitation. 'A man's nerves do not improve with age, and I was
getting on for fifty.' He was to let no one down once the match was
underway. The other major change was the replacement of the veteran
Herbert Strudwick by George Brown of Hampshire, who was a less
accomplished keeper but a better batsman. As it turned out, Brown, a
giant of a man who could tear apart a pack of cards with his bare
hands, was injured in a county game just before the Test and Strudwick
had to be recalled.

The importance of the Oval Test meant that public interest was
intense. 'It is no exaggeration to say that no game in this country has
ever been more eagerly looked forward to,' wrote Warner in the *Cricketer*.
There was continual speculation in the press about the quality of the
pitch, the strength of the teams, the effect of the captaincy change, and

the potential size of the crowds. Outside the Oval on the night of Friday 13 August, a queue began to form of England supporters desperate to get into the ground for the start of next morning's play. The *Manchester Guardian* sent a reporter to speak to the line of fans, who included 'muffled lads from Camberwell', several 'young gentlemen', 'a burnt-cork banjoman', some 'shy greenhorns', a few couples, and a blind man accompanied by his wife and baby daughter. The blind man explained that his wife helped him by providing a running commentary and that, as a Surrey supporter, 'whenever I can, I come along to see Jack Hobbs and his pals at their little tricks'. Indeed, what struck the *Guardian* reporter was the universal hope invested in Hobbs. 'He is the uncrowned king of Kennington and it is believed here that he will conquer not only the tough problem of the Australians but even the problem of the English weather.'

Yet all the hype about vast multitudes and the problems of getting a ticket proved counter-productive. On the first day of the Test, Saturday 14, only 16,000 spectators turned up, barely half the Oval's capacity. Those that did attend had an exciting day, if a disappointing one from England's point of view. Percy Chapman did his first duty successfully: he won the toss and elected to bat in fine weather. The crowd's early nerves were settled a little by another solid start from Hobbs and Sutcliffe, whose partnership had not failed in any completed innings of the series. Once more they looked comfortable against both pace and spin as they cruised past 50. Among those watching the Test was the young John Arlott, who had travelled up from Hampshire for the day, equipped with sandwiches and the tuppence admission charge for boys. In his autobiography, *Basingstoke Boy*, Arlott recalled the contrast between the two men: 'Only when one looked at Sutcliffe, painstakingly precise, was it possible to understand that Hobbs was doing it all with the untroubled, easy air of a man pottering in his garden. Unquestionably, Sutcliffe was a great batsman, fine in temperament and technique, but this unremarkable man at the other end was all but disappointing in making it all so simple; he pushed or stroked or flicked the ball away and had 37 of the 53 in under an hour.' Then something inexplicable happened. Arthur Mailey, looking for more flight, sent down a high full toss. Hobbs could have hit the ball almost anywhere but he decided to place it wide of mid-on. Somehow, as he executed the shot, he lost the ball in the darkness of the pavilion, missed it and heard the deadly rattle of the stumps behind him. Mailey burst out laughing, and Hobbs, initially dumbfounded, responded with an ironic laugh himself before he started the walk back to the pavilion. 'What a turn-up for the books,' said the ecstatic Australian Tommy Andrews, fielding at silly point, as he was passed by Hobbs, who had never heard the expression before but he understood only too well its meaning. 'Fancy missing a thing like that,' Hobbs muttered to himself. England's innings faltered badly after this shocking dismissal, too many of the batsmen playing bold shots before they had gauged the pace of the wicket. Only the ever reliable Sutcliffe reached 50 as England were bowled out for 280, Mailey taking 6 for 138 in his last Test. It looked as if the home side had squandered a golden opportunity in excellent batting conditions. The wicket, wrote Hobbs in a *News of the World* article, was 'plumb', as 'good a wicket as I have ever played upon'. Yet on that first evening Australia were equally brittle, finishing on 60 for 4.

On the second day, Monday 16, England were well on top when Australia slid to 122 for 6 but then Jack Gregory, with a typically bellig-erent innings of 71, led a recovery to 302. The lead was 22, far more than England might have hoped earlier in the day. The game was now in the balance. Everything depended on Hobbs and Sutcliffe, who had one hour to survive before the close. Plum Warner confessed that he could 'hardly bear to watch the cricket'. His fellow selector Arthur Gilligan wrote that 'a failure by either of England's first pair, but espe-cially on the part of Hobbs, would have meant an Australian victory'. What made the situation all the more pressurised for Hobbs was that, after a hot day in the field, he was suffering from one of his painful migraines. But neither he nor Sutcliffe showed any sign of the nervous apprehension that gripped the spectators, the atmosphere made all the more fraught by the distant rumble of thunder. Instead, the pair went about their business in their usual calm, authoritative manner. Gregory and Grimmett were dealt with easily and then, when Mailey came on, Hobbs took six from his first over and seven from the next, alleviating some of the anxieties of the 31,000 strong crowd. 'These two batsmen are even greater, if possible, in temperament than in skill,' recorded Warner. At stumps, England were 49 without loss, having wiped out the deficit. The great throng left the Oval at the end of the second day in a more confident mood than they had been an hour earlier.

After changing, Hobbs returned home to Clapham. Tired by his labours, he slept peacefully that night until two o'clock, when he was suddenly awoken by a violent storm that filled the night sky with claps of angry thunder and jagged flashes of lightning. Hearing the sound of the torrential rain on his roof, Hobbs felt a sense of foreboding about the next morning and could sleep only fitfully. In his hotel room, Sutcliffe too had a disturbed night. 'I was always fortunate to sleep soundly, but on this particular occasion I was awakened by the loud peals of thunder. My thoughts immediately turned to the Oval wicket, and I wondered if fortune had once again ruined our chances of victory.' Meanwhile at the Oval, two policemen who were on duty protecting the middle had to run for shelter when the heavens opened. Soon the pitch was drenched, for in England until the late 1970s, Test wickets had to be uncovered once play had begun, though both ends could be protected. The rain kept on falling through the night, covering the outfield with a vast sheet of water which glistened intermittently when a bolt of lightning pierced the air. Finally the weather relented in the early morning but the damage had been done.

After Hobbs had risen, he looked out on his garden and could see how damp the ground was. He knew the Oval must have been soaked. Following his breakfast, he left the house at ten o'clock and walked to a nearby tram-stop, from where he took a three-halfpenny ride to the ground.* The weather in south London was now clammy, the sun trying to break through the grey clouds. On his arrival at the Oval, Hobbs signed a few autographs, walked through the gates and went up to the England dressing room, from where he could look out on the middle. Due to all the dampness, the colour of the pitch seemed to have changed from straw to almost black. Even more disconcertingly, steam was rising from the turf as the warm temperature drew up the moisture. He knew that batting could become a nightmare against the Australian spinners if the sun broke through and beat

* Some of the details here are taken from Ralph Barker's 1964 book, *Ten Greatest Innings*, for which Hobbs gave a lengthy interview to the author. The meeting with Sir Jack, said Barker, was 'one of the great moments of my life'. Hobbs himself had a long ghostwritten article in the *News of the World* on 22 August about the 1926 Oval Test. In contrast, his accounts of the match in his two 1930s autobiographies are rather perfunctory.

down on the pitch. When he went out to have a chat with Bosser Martin, his darkest fears were confirmed. 'It's drying quicker than I thought,' said Martin. Yet neither Hobbs nor Sutcliffe allowed this gloomy reality to affect their remarkable determination and self-control. Towards the public and their colleagues that morning, they gave no hint of anxiety or defeatism. The Labour MP Harold Laski once wrote that Hobbs was 'the representative Englishman' of his era because, amongst his many virtues, he had a 'stolid calm in a difficult position', the quality that had so often served the nation in times of crisis. Exactly the same could have been said of Sutcliffe. The umpire Frank Chester was amazed to see the pair's composure when he called on the England dressing room just before the teams were due out. Chester, having seen the state of the wicket, expected 'to find a very worried eleven. But Hobbs and Sutcliffe might have been preparing for a festival match. Hobbs sat quietly, contentedly, puffing at his pipe, while the ever-immaculate Sutcliffe was casually brushing his sleek black hair; they were divorced from the tension of the crowd outside.'

With the surface water having drained away, there was no reason to delay the start. Chapman ordered the heavy roller to try to deaden the pitch. Collins, now restored as Australian captain after his illness, ordered sawdust for his bowlers' footholds. Everything was prepared for the key stage of the battle. Just before eleven o'clock, the umpires Chester and Harding 'Sailor' Young walked out, followed by the Australian team brimming with confidence. Finally, to loud but nervous applause from the 28,500 spectators, came the England pair, Sutcliffe hatless, Hobbs in his three lions England cap. The sky was still overcast, but it was obvious that the clouds would soon part. Clarrie Grimmett bowled the first over to Hobbs, a maiden full of leg-breaks that turned appreciably if not rapidly. At the other end, Charlie Macartney, bowling orthodox slow left-arm, also opened with a testing maiden that took several divots where the spinning ball cut into the turf.

At the end of that second over, Hobbs and Sutcliffe met while they were patting down the pitch with their bats. 'Pity about the rain,' said Hobbs. 'It's rather cooked our chances.' Sutcliffe nodded in agreement. Moments later, Hobbs repeated the same comment to umpire Young, who replied, 'Yes, it's bad luck.' Privately, Hobbs thought England would be lucky to make another 80 runs. Still, even in adversity, he showed no inclination to surrender. In the next few overs from Grimmett and Macartney, he mixed cool defence with judicious attacking strokes, while Sutcliffe concentrated entirely on keeping out the ball. After forty minutes, England had added 26 runs, all of them from Hobbs's bat. But soon conditions began to worsen. The sun was now coming out, with the result that the drying wicket was bound to become much more spiteful. At the Vauxhall end, Collins took off Macartney and replaced him with Arthur Richardson, who bowled highly accurate off-breaks at medium pace. Collins was certain that Richardson's brisk turn, delivered to a packed close field, would be unplayable. Watching from the other end, Sutcliffe sensed the tightening of the screw against England, as he later recalled in a passage about facing this attack. 'It was a vile, sticky wicket from the start, but when the hot sun started to bake the ground just before noon, it was one of the worst glue-pots I have ever experienced, and it continued to be so throughout the day. To play on such a brute of a wicket calls for the utmost courage, patience and above all skill. The ball responded to the least spin applied by the bowler, turning viciously, quickly and popping most disconcertingly. It was essential for Hobbs and myself to concentrate deeply on every movement of the bowler in his run-up to the wicket and especially on his grip of the ball and final finger spin.'

A hush descended on the crowd as Richardson came in to bowl. An England wicket seemed inevitable. Sure enough, his first ball lifted and turned prodigiously. But it also dropped short. Hobbs, his weight already on the back foot as usual, was on to it in a flash and pulled it over the heads of the three short legs to the boundary for four. The shot brought up his half-century. A few deliveries later, Richardson dragged the ball down again with the same result. Hobbs and Sutcliffe, against all the odds, appeared momentarily to be weathering the storm. The crowd's fragile confidence was given a further boost when the pair crossed for the run that brought up yet another one hundred partnership, an incredible achievement in the circumstances. But few felt it could last, especially when Richardson, having switched to bowl round the wicket, found his length and settled into a groove. By now, with the sun high in the sky, the ball was turning extravagantly and Collins brought up two more close catchers on the leg-side for the imminent edge or gloved stroke. Watching the action at close quarters, Frank Chester felt it was 'the worst sticky I have seen. I did not give England

a chance.' Yet somehow, Hobbs managed to avoid his downfall, either
by dropping the ball dead in front of the fielders or by allowing it to
hit his body. His method was well described by the author Ralph Barker,
based on a detailed interview he once conducted with Hobbs about
the Oval Test. 'He stood well clear of his wicket, his bat planted nearly
a foot outside the leg stump, giving himself plenty of room to play the
ball pitching on middle-and-leg straight down the wicket. The moment
Richardson released the ball he judged its length and direction and
then moved quickly into position to play it. Some eye-witnesses aver
that he actually *ran*, ran into position, not down the wicket, but across
when Richardson sought to counter his tactics by bowling at or outside
the off-stump.' Richardson and Hobbs were locked in a mesmerising
contest. For over after over, the off-spinner wove his web. At one stage,
he sent down eight successive maidens to the Surrey batsmen, a tribute
to his remarkable accuracy but, no matter what he tried, he still could
not entrap Hobbs.

By this stage, Collins was becoming a little worried at Australia's
inability to make the breakthrough, knowing that the longer England
batted, the more the wicket would lose its venom. So he brought on
Arthur Mailey at the pavilion end, a slightly risky move because Mailey
could be expensive. In his first over, Sutcliffe took a quick single which
brought Hobbs on strike. 'Now then, Arthur, play the game, no more
full tosses,' he called out. 'All right, Jack,' replied Mailey, who was planning something much more lethal. His first ball was a perfectly pitched
leg-break that turned past Hobbs's bat and just missed the off-stump.
The second was even better, a googly that landed on the line off-
stump and straightened enough to hit Hobbs right in front of middle.
Sutcliffe, standing at the bowler's end, felt Hobbs was plumb lbw, as
did Frank Chester, who recalled, 'I was ready to put up my finger' for
'it would have been one of easiest lbw decisions I had ever made'. To
the amazement of Chester, Sutcliffe and Hobbs, none of the Australians
appealed. Neville Cardus once complained that Mailey's appeal was 'a
somewhat apologetic whimper', but this time there was not even
a whimper, only silence. Nor was there any noise from Oldfield, who was
not normally distinguished by his reticence. The chief explanation
was that the bowler and keeper were convinced that the googly had
pitched outside the off and under the lbw law that existed before 1935,
no batsmen could be dismissed by a ball that did not land directly in

line with the stumps. Mailey added his own, more poignant reason, which demonstrated his frustration with Hobbs and Sutcliffe. 'All I recollect is that I thought I had appealed too much during that match and was a bit tired of hearing my own voice crying in the wilderness.' Yet it was still peculiar that neither of them even bothered to ask the question. Oldfield soon sensed that they had been foolish, as Chester's account recorded. 'He said to me a little later, "That second ball from Arthur to Jack pitched outside the off-stump, didn't it?" Before I could answer he turned away, but I think he realised they had blundered in not appealing.' Frank Chester further revealed that Hobbs knew how lucky he had been. 'He asked what had happened. When I told him he was plumb in front, he half smiled.'

The escape was symbolic of Australia's misfortune and ineffectiveness. Gradually, with the wicket becoming easier, they began to lose confidence, while Hobbs and Sutcliffe grew in authority. Mailey was forced out of the attack after taking some punishment, and Hobbs now even broke free of Richardson's bonds by driving him through mid-on for 4, his shot greeted by a resounding cheer from the crowd. The writer John Marchant, who was one of the spectators that day, described the mood of almost hysterical relief after that boundary: 'It was as though St George had slain the dragon, or David had done all that was necessary to Goliath, or the siege of Verdun had been lifted.' The dramatic, agonising duel between Richardson and Hobbs became the subject of a vigorous debate in the aftermath of the match, particularly over claims that Hobbs, with all his feline cleverness, had engaged in a gigantic game of bluff against Australia by making Richardson look harder than he really was. The aim of this supposed tactic was to prevent Collins putting on other, more penetrative bowlers at the Vauxhall end while the pitch was at its worse. The theory was largely the work of Monty Noble, who was reporting for the *Evening Standard* and wrote that, 'Richardson was kept on for far too long, bowling round the wicket at leg stump but Hobbs was responsible, for with consummate artistry he contrived to give the impression that he was in difficulties.' This theme was taken up by several other writers, becoming almost part of conventional wisdom about the Test. But there was no basis to it. In reality, Hobbs needed every ounce of skill to deal with Richardson: 'The ball came through so awkwardly that I just couldn't get it away.' This was confirmed by Sutcliffe, who explained, 'I can truthfully say that bluff was completely foreign to Hobbs's ideas.' Indeed, Hobbs was rather annoyed at Noble's suggestion, which he felt diminished the skill he had shown in combating the off-spinner. In *My Book of Cricket and Cricketers*, published in 1927, Patsy Hendren recounted this conversation he overhead between Hobbs and a Surrey member on the morning after the great partnership:

'Another honour this morning, Jack.'

'That so? What is it?'

'Monty Noble writes today that you were only kidding Collins when you weren't scoring yesterday. Says you were playing England in by pretending Richardson was difficult. All the time you were playing for time, to give the wicket a chance to improve.'

'Well, he's wrong. Richardson was bowling well. I'd have scored if I could.'

As Hobbs revealed in a 1930 radio interview, he was actually trying to do the very opposite of what Noble believed. 'The wicket was really bad before lunch but I did my best to make the Australians think it was not very difficult.'

Another myth was that Hobbs shielded Sutcliffe from Richardson but this was even more absurd. The only reason Hobbs faced a lot of Richardson during his initial spell was simply because he could take neither a risk nor a single. The thought of nursing Sutcliffe never entered his head. 'He was far too good a player to need it,' Hobbs said. Others, including Neville Cardus, made the argument that Richardson would have been more effective if he had bowled over the wicket instead of round and changed his line to outside the off, but again there is no evidence to support this. He bowled his first two overs to Hobbs from over, and they were his most expensive. Moreover, such a line of attack would have largely removed the chance of lbw from the equation. The Surrey bowler E.M. Wellings, later a perceptive cricket writer, felt that the criticism of Richardson's methods was misplaced. 'In those conditions, Richardson's tactics and field place were precisely what George Macaulay employed. And Macaulay went through sides on stickies as quickly as any left-handed spinner.' Wellings further pointed out that a similar approach was used by all the leading English off-spinners of subsequent generations, including Tom Goddard, Jim Laker and Fred Titmus. The real problem for the Australians, said Wellings, was that Hobbs was the 'complete master. He played Richardson as surely as he played the other spinners on that spiteful turf.' Richardson himself told his biographer, Les Hill,* that 'in his own opinion, his captain Collins was correct in allowing him to continue bowling as he did throughout the innings,' but he 'could not succeed against the superlative batting technique of Hobbs and Sutcliffe'.

At lunch England had reached 161 for no wicket, with Hobbs on 97 and Sutcliffe on 53. While the Australians disconsolately trooped back to the pavilion, the two batsmen remained for a few moments out in the middle to flatten the wicket with the backs of their bats, like butchers pounding a particularly tough slab of meat. 'Well played, Herbert,' said Hobbs. 'Well played, Jack,' replied the Yorkshireman. Those two lines were a classic example of English understatement. Behind the restraint, they were brimming with admiration for each other. Sutcliffe was 'magnificent', wrote Hobbs soon after the match. 'The Yorkshire batsman has one of the finest Test temperaments I have known. He is a great-hearted battler.' For his part, Sutcliffe praised his partner's 'super scientific defence, coupled with the ability to take advantage of any scoreable ball and at the same time to execute the stroke with the ability and skills of a master.' After the interval, during which both teams had lunch in the pavilion with the Prince of Wales, Collins brought on Gregory for the first time. It was a move that several critics felt should have been made much earlier, but it made no difference to the serenity of Hobbs and Sutcliffe. Hobbs moved to 99 and then prepared to face Gregory again. The great Australian came in with his distinctive, bounding run. With a leap and a rapid swing of his arm, he sent down a good-length ball on the off-side. Wellings described the next moment, which captured the essence of the famous pair's running between the wickets, as well as Hobbs's instinctive sensitivity towards the ball: 'He played the ball from Jack Gregory with such delicacy that for a few strides Hobbs and the ball seemed to be moving together. In fact, the ball slanted towards Andrews, one of Australia's finest fielders, who was at very short cover. Andrews never managed a shy at either wicket. Sutcliffe was on the move as Hobbs played the stroke and by the time Andrews reached the slowly trickling ball he was sliding his bat safely across the batting crease.

* Les Hill, *Eighty Not Out: The Story of Arthur Richardson* (1968). Unpublished typescript.

Andrews had to turn and throw at the far wicket, and Hobbs had ample time to trot home without ever breaking into a sprint.' A stupendous roar went up from the crowd, as if all the pent-up emotion of the last three hours had suddenly been released. 'When he reached home safely at the end of that utterly impertinent run, he was waving his bat in the air. Then he waved his cap. Then, as the riot continued, he waved his bat and cap at once,' wrote John Marchant. The *Daily Express* called it 'the most wonderful tribute ever made to any cricketer'. The spectators, the paper went on, were 'no longer partisans of England or Australia. They were Jack Hobbs partisans, every man, woman and child in the closely packed crowd. They rose and cheered for, it seemed, minutes on end, hats, sticks, newspapers and scorecards waving. The Australian fieldsmen joined in the cheering and hand-clapping. H.L. Collins, a smile on his usually solemn face, shook hands with Hobbs. Someone in the crowd called for "Three cheers for Jack!" and as the roars broke out afresh, Hobbs took off his cap and waved it in thanks. There was far more in the demonstration than mere cheers for a three-figure innings. It was the crowd's salute to a great cricketer – a message of respect and affection.'

Almost immediately after this moving scene, Hobbs was bowled by Gregory for exactly 100, the ball flicking the off-bail. For a moment the crowd was stunned into silence, as he began the walk back to the pavilion. Then there followed another prolonged bout of cheering in recognition of Hobbs's achievement, which had put England in a commanding position, 150 ahead with nine wickets still left and the wicket certain to crumble once it had fully dried out. Given the circumstances, from the importance of the match to the quality of the pitch, Hobbs's innings was hailed as the finest of his long Test career. It was a performance that defined his monumental greatness. The essence of his heroic character and supreme technique were distilled in those 100 runs. 'I have seen him play many more spectacular innings than this one, but for soundness no performance of his could beat this latest hundred,' wrote Charlie Kelleway. With generous sportsmanship, Collins described it as 'the finest piece of batting I have ever seen.' After umpiring Test cricket over four decades, Frank Chester felt that it was 'the greatest century I have ever watched. Only a genius could have hoped for survival for even a short time. Hobbs not only survived; he actually mastered the attack, which kept the ball popping and turning like a mad thing . . . It was a great pity that a full-length film was not made of that Oval innings. Cricket students would have marvelled at it and it would have enriched the curriculum at all our coaching schools. Hobbs was so very easily the first cricketer of his generation.' Within the England camp, Arthur Gilligan spoke for all the selectors when he said, 'This must be regarded everywhere as one of the greatest innings Hobbs ever played and therefore, naturally, one of the greatest in the history of cricket.'

With 161 to his name, Sutcliffe fell in the last over of the day but by then England, on 375 for 6, were almost impregnable. Hobbs was thrilled when he arrived home and the family shared in his pleasure. 'Even my dog seemed to have a special welcome for me,' he recorded. Later that evening, he went out for dinner in the Trocadero restaurant in Shaftesbury Avenue, the establishment owned by the J. Lyons conglomerate. With its baroque architecture, concert hall, grill room and lavish menu at reasonable prices, the Trocadero was seen as the epitome of populist fine dining and entertainment in the interwar years, just the sort of place for a respectable, middle-class gentleman to celebrate. While he was there, Hobbs was struck at how the Test match seemed to be the only topic of conversation. 'No one there or elsewhere for that matter seemed to have anything to think about but the day's cricket – and tomorrow!' Throughout the duration of the match, the excitement in the capital had been building, fuelled partly by newspaper placards, partly by information bureaux like the one in Selfridges. Outside the offices of the *Morning Post* at the Aldwych, a large scoreboard had been erected to provide instant updates. When Hobbs had been approaching his century in the early afternoon, a huge crowd had gathered in the street, and when he hit the single, the roar had been almost as loud as that at the Oval. Later that evening, Hobbs, still ecstatic, went to the cinema, where he was amused to see a silent newsreel of the great opening partnership. 'I cannot remember being as exhilarated as I was that night,' he recalled.

The euphoria continued the following morning at the Oval, as the England tail built up a formidable lead of 414, then, on the badly worn wicket, their bowlers demolished Australia. Every one of the selectors' decisions was rewarded: Harold Larwood ripped through top order, taking three of the first five wickets; Wilfred Rhodes fully justified his recall with a superb spell of accurate, menacing spin that ensnared four of the Australians; and even Percy Chapman, derided for his inexperience, marshalled the side well, though Rhodes joked that England's success in the field was because Chapman 'did what me and Jack told him'. There may have been some truth in this. At the start, Hobbs urged Chapman to move George Geary into the slips and bring Rhodes up to gully. The very next ball, Bill Woodfull edged the ball straight to Geary, leaving Australia 1 for 1. It was a grim procession after that and Australia collapsed to 125 all out, with England the victors by 289 runs.

The moment the last wicket fell just after six o'clock, when Geary bowled Mailey, there was pandemonium. A human floodtide washed across the Oval as the players raced to the pavilion. Hobbs, who had been at cover, got cut off from the rest of the England team and had to be protected by the police while he struggled to make it off the field. 'I have never seen a crowd rush so determinedly before or since. They were swarming everywhere, making joyful if irrational noises. There they were, jammed in a solid mass, pressing against the pavilion railings and stretching right back to the lately abandoned pitch,' said the Yorkshire writer A.A. Thomson. Among those in the pavilion were the Prime Minister Stanley Baldwin and most of his Tory cabinet. The mood of the country was very different to the one that had prevailed more than three months before on the eve of the General Strike. Now, in place of discord, there was national rejoicing. Champagne flowed in both dressing rooms, and the two captains, their arms linked and glasses upraised, posed for photographs while the throng outside kept up the wild applause and shouts. Hobbs left this description of the delirious scene: 'A huge black mass, cheering, yelling, waving their hats, packed the space in front of the pavilion, and demanded each of us in turn. We hung back. Murmurs behind us: "go on". And at last we went forward on to the balcony: we stared down upon a vast sea of faces. Curious, is it not, that although I gazed as through a mist at the wonderful spectacle I picked out my wife among all those thousands and tens of thousands!' As Hobbs stood there on the balcony, Collins came alongside him, and, in a mock show of anger, shook his fist and growled, 'We've got you to thank for this,' before breaking into a smile. The crowd would not depart, but Hobbs and Ada managed to slip away through a side entrance to the ground, where Andy Kempton was waiting for them with his car. So Hobbs left 'one of the most magnificent scenes I have ever taken part in'. The scene would never have happened without him.

15

'A Triumphant March'

By way of celebrating England's Ashes triumph, Hobbs kept up his excellent form during the rest of the 1926 season. Just three days after the Oval victory, he and Sutcliffe found themselves on opposite sides in the county championship as Surrey took on Yorkshire at the Oval. In a hard-fought draw, both made centuries.

A far more expansive innings by Hobbs followed at the end of August when he played at Lord's against Middlesex. In an astonishing display lasting almost seven hours, Hobbs carried his bat for 316 not out, by far the biggest score of his career and the record individual score on the ground until Graham Gooch beat it in 1990 with 333 versus India. In all he hit forty-one 4s, most of them on the leg-side. What made this performance all the more remarkable was the quality of the Middlesex attack. Four of them, Jack Durston, Nigel Haig, Greville Stevens and Gubby Allen, all bowled for England during their first-class careers, Allen with considerable success. The other intriguing aspect was that, according to the Middlesex professional Harry Lee, Hobbs tried to abide by his usual practice of throwing his wicket away once he had made a century, but he blazed away so successfully that, almost inadvertently, he reached the triple hundred mark. In his memoirs, Lee gave this description of the innings: 'He scored his first century with orthodox brilliance. Then he began slashing and carving, and as no one could oblige him with a chance to return to the cool pavilion, he soon found himself with 150. You could almost see what went on in his mind. "Well," he said to himself, "we've got so far. Two hundred's a nice round figure. Why not make it 200?" So he played correctly for the other 50, punishing bad balls as they deserved, but no longer the slashing buccaneer of the previous period. When his 200 went up, he began slashing again, almost scientifically, but taking every possible risk. The 250 appeared. Again the unfortunate fielders could read his thoughts: "Come to think of it, I've never scored three hundred at Lord's. It's a beautiful day. Everyone seems very kind and helpful. I must see what I can do." When the inevitable 300 went up, someone said to him, "Why don't you stay and beat the record, Jack?"' That record for Lord's had been set at 315 the previous summer by Percy Holmes, Sutcliffe's Yorkshire partner. Once Hobbs had passed the landmark, Percy Fender declared and Surrey had an easy innings victory. Altogether it was another wonderful season for Hobbs, in which, despite his onerous England responsibilities, he scored ten centuries and topped the national averages at 77.60 from 2,949 runs. 'He is, by universal consent, the most accomplished run-getter among professionals that the game has ever known,' said the Cricketer.

After the glories of 1926, the following season was something of an anti-climax. Hobbs started the summer in majestic style, making a century in each innings against Hampshire at the Oval, but at the end of May he became ill with a nasty skin infection contracted from food poisoning. Inevitably, his poor health led to murmurs that he had started to show his age, though Hobbs tried to reassure the public: 'It is nothing serious, but enough to make a man feel uncomfortable. There is no cause for alarm.' After an absence of five weeks, Hobbs returned to first-class cricket at the beginning of July when he turned out for the Players against the Gents at the Oval. A solid innings of 43 signalled that he had almost recovered, and in his next game, he confirmed his return to fitness with 121 against Kent at Blackheath. It was the 142nd century of his career and his hundredth for Surrey, a feat never achieved by any batsman before. It was 'a magnificent effort', said the Daily Mail. 'Not a single county has escaped the scoring skill of the master batsman, for he has registered centuries against them all.'

But this landmark was followed by a heavy blow. The MCC had chosen the teams for the annual Lord's match between the Gents and the Players before Hobbs made his century at Blackheath and, to his vexation, he found himself left out of the Players' side. Given his lengthy absence due to illness, it might have been an exaggeration to say he had been dropped yet that was the way it was seen by Hobbs. Usually so reluctant to engage in any public confrontation, he now fully aired his grievance against the MCC. 'The Gentlemen v Players match at Lord's is one in which it is form and worthiness that count. They are trying to push me out, I suppose they want to get rid of me. That is the only explanation I can see. They think I'm too old. "Only another year in any case," they say.' This slightly histrionic outburst showed the pride and sensitivity that lay below his serene exterior, with a touch of insecurity about his advancing age now an added ingredient. Conscious that he might sound self-indulgent, Hobbs then claimed, 'It's not that I mind so much. I suppose it will give me a rest. It is my family who will feel it.' In response to Hobbs's attack, the MCC remained silent, but the attitude of the club's Secretary William Findlay could be gauged from this item in the Daily Express: 'When a newspaper report of a statement by Hobbs was placed before him, he threw it aside with a contemptuous gesture.' It was a remarkable change from the mood in the cricket establishment of less than a year earlier, when Hobbs was the unalloyed hero.

His determination to prove the MCC wrong resulted in a burst of heavy scoring in late July and early August, including a big century for Surrey against the New Zealand touring side, who had not yet attained Test status. The innings, said the Daily Express, 'was another brilliant display' in which he 'hit splendidly to leg'. An even more exhilarating performance came at home against Nottinghamshire, whose attack was torn apart with a century before lunch. Scoring at more than a run a minute, Hobbs made a mockery of Carr's insinuation that he was scared of pace bowling. 'Everything else in the day's play was dwarfed by the really brilliant batting of Hobbs, who, perhaps, had never been seen to greater advantage. He scored freely against all the bowling brought against him, making runs in all directions and never offering a chance,' said the Cricketer. Soon after this, however, Hobbs suffered another setback when he tore a thigh muscle while taking a quick single with Sutcliffe during a Test trial game at the Oval. The injury was not nearly as serious as that of 1921 but he was still forced to miss the next two matches. He returned to the side in formidable fashion at the Oval on 20 August, making 150 against the mighty Yorkshire attack led by Rhodes, Kilner and Macaulay. Although he was slightly handicapped by his damaged muscle, Hobbs had been particularly keen to do well in this game because it was a benefit match for that most loyal and unassuming of Oval servants, Andy Sandham. 'We had some great times together. He was full of dry humour and we must have run more short singles than I did with Wilfred and Herbert put together. He had a lovely off drive and his late cut was worth walking miles to see, and he was always a very good friend,' said Hobbs in a BBC interview. Unfortunately for Sandham, the match was badly affected by rain and turned into a dull draw. The *Cricketer* described the 'sad sight' of the beneficiary standing under his umbrella as the 'rain lashed down, as melancholy an object as a farmer watching his cut sheaves swimming round the field'. At the end of the season, Hobbs showed there were no hard feelings with the MCC by turning out for the Players against the Gents at the Scarborough. In the festival atmosphere, he made his seventh century of the summer and the 146th of his career, the innings full 'of off drives and leg hits, together with a number of cleverly placed twos and singles,' according to *Wisden*. Despite his absences through injury and illness, it had been a successful, if not dazzling, season for Hobbs, with his average reaching 52.64 from 1,641 runs.

Cricket remained as popular as ever in 1927, the game fortified by the national exultation over the Ashes triumph. That year the Board of Control, English Test cricket's governing body, was able to redistribute £18,000 to the counties from the £60,000 profit made on the previous summer's Tests. As a result of this largesse, allied to continuing good crowds, most counties remained financially viable. But the cricket authorities feared that the game was not as healthy as it superficially appeared. Dark clouds were perceived to be looming on the horizon. There was, said many analysts, a surfeit of cricket, which encouraged too many draws, too many rain-affected games, and too little concern for maintaining public interest. One of the absurd features of the jam-packed county programme was that matches usually stopped at 4.30 p.m. on the third day in order to allow the teams more time for their journeys to their next fixtures. 'There can be no point in this. Modern travel is nowhere more comfortable than in this country, and there is no excuse for these early stoppages. What would the theatre public do if some of the leading actors decided that they would like to dine at home twice a week and put the piece on at 4 p.m.?' argued the *Cricketer*.

But by far the greatest concern in the late 1920s was the dominance of bat over ball, due largely to over-prepared pitches, better protective equipment and the evolution of batting techniques to embrace the use of pads as a second line of defence, a tactic fiercely denounced by *Wisden's* editor C. Stewart Caine as 'an outrage' and 'against the spirit of the game'. Hobbs himself was an assured practitioner of the negative art of pad play, as even his greatest admirer John Arlott admitted: 'His judgement of the pitch of the ball and his feeling for the position of the stumps were such that he could work to inches in padding up and his standing was such that he was unlikely to be given a bad decision.' While batting grew in its ascendancy, so bowling was increasingly nullified by dead wickets and partial laws. With their efforts so unrewarded, many bowlers turned to negative forms of attack, such as inswingers delivered to packed leg-side fields, which did nothing for entertainment. The imbalance between batting and bowling left the veteran Warwickshire keeper Tiger Smith disillusioned towards the end of his career: 'There were too many high-scoring matches on featherbeds and too many mediocre players worried about their averages.' Hobbs might have benefited from this environment, but he too felt uneasy about the prevalence of high scores. 'I blame the super wickets we play on now. They give the bowler no help. They are fast without being lively. On sporting wickets batsmen would be more induced to have a go. Nowadays we can sit back and wait in confidence for the runs to come,' he told a BBC interviewer. To reinvigorate bowling, Hobbs suggested in a 1926 article in the *Cricketer* a number of reforms, including smaller, more uniform boundaries, a new ball for the fielding side after 150 runs had been scored rather than the current threshold of 200 runs, and a reduction in the ball's size, though he opposed calls for wider, higher stumps or narrower bats. The MCC, which, for all its attachment to traditionalism, shared the widespread belief that something had to be done, was already working on plans for change. At the start of the 1927 season, the law was amended to shrink the ball's circumference, bringing the maximum down from 9.25 inches to 9, and the minimum from 9 to 8.81 inches.* Less in keeping with Hobbs's view was the decision taken by the MCC in 1931 to raise the height of the stumps from twenty-seven to twenty-eight inches, and the width from eight to nine inches. It was only after Hobbs retired that the MCC, in 1935, made the most far-reaching change when the lbw law was extended to cover balls that pitched outside the off but would have hit the stumps, thereby eliminating the worst excesses of pad play.

* The rather tortured, pre-metrication wording was actually 'eight and thirteen-sixteenths of an inch'.

The reduction in the ball's size appeared to make little difference to the bat's superiority. Scores in 1927 had been somewhat restricted by the poor weather, but the gloriously dry conditions of 1928 were made for batting. There were thirty-seven totals of more than 500, seventy-two games produced an aggregate of more than 1,000 runs and five players passed 3,000 runs. Now aged forty-five, Hobbs shared in this run feast, his appetite unsated by the passage of the years. In Surrey's very first game of the season, he scored a century against the MCC, and three more followed before the end of May, including another one at Trent Bridge, which again demolished Carr's sneers about his alleged weakness against raw pace. This century, the 150th of his career, led the *Daily Mirror* to report, 'Although from time to time one hears the voice of the pessimist declaring that Jack Hobbs is past it, he is still getting runs with the greatest facility.' But his body did occasionally show signs of vulnerability. In early June he again pulled a leg muscle, this time chasing a ball to the boundary. His recovery proved slow and he was out for six weeks, which meant that he missed the opening Test of the summer. The West Indies were the visitors that season, playing their very first Test series. Despite their novice status, their arrival was eagerly awaited by the English public because, in those times of featherbed wickets and negative tactics, their side contained three genuinely quick bowlers: Learie Constantine, Herman Griffith and George Francis. Moreover, they had fluent strokemakers in openers Clifford Roach and George Challenor and a popular skipper in Karl Nunes, who was also their wicketkeeper. For all his qualities, the position of Nunes, by coincidence a contemporary of Arthur Gilligan's at Dulwich College, reinforced the patronising contemporary belief in senior cricket circles that black Caribbean players were unsuited for the leadership role, an attitude that lasted right up until 1960 when Frank Worrell became the West Indies' first non-white captain.

The previous West Indian tourists of 1923 had done well, winning twelve of their first-class matches and making a strong case for the islands to be given promotion. But full Test cricket came as an abrupt shock to Nunes' team in 1928. Their catching was atrocious, their batting frail. Even their pace bowling, which had seemed to promise so much, disappointed, though Constantine remained a favourite with the crowds. Their first ever Test, held at Lord's in late June, was lost by an innings against an England side that was significantly changed from the Oval

Test of 1926. Douglas Jardine made his Test debut, Wally Hammond played his first Test in England and Charlie Hallows of Lancashire, then in the middle of a golden patch of form having passed a thousand runs in May, replaced the injured Hobbs. With a score of just 26, Hallows did not do enough to justify his retention in the England team for the second Test at Old Trafford. By then, Hobbs had fully recovered and had resumed his century habit with yet another hundred, this one at Northampton.

When the West Indies won the toss and batted first on a soft wicket at Manchester, Hobbs immediately showed that, even in his mid-forties, he could still be wonderfully athletic. He was fielding at mid-off when Roach drove to his left-hand side. He moved across swiftly and, with a single flowing action, picked up the ball and hurled it straight into the gloves of the keeper, Harry Elliott, who ran out the despairing Challenor by yards. The West Indies struggled to 206 all out, and then Hobbs and Sutcliffe resumed their Test partnership for the first time since the 1926 Oval Test. There was a minor controversy in the opening overs when Constantine, bowling with great fire, sent down several bouncers to the batsmen, causing a protest about intimidatory bowling. 'Hobbs complained that I was bumping them and said he did not mean to be knocked about,' recalled Constantine. The West Indian all-rounder added sardonically that, for all the 'sharp comments', his leg-side deliveries kept disappearing towards the boundary. Hobbs overcame the storm, and, with an air of inevitability, he and Sutcliffe put on another century stand before he was caught at long-on for 53 going for a big hit. In its report, *Wisden* rebuked Hobbs for dancing down the pitch and throwing his wicket away when he 'looked to be in great form'. But his dismissal did nothing to impede England's progress towards another big innings victory.

There was no criticism of Hobbs after the third Test at the Oval. He and Sutcliffe opened with yet another century partnership, their eleventh for England, as they took advantage of some inaccurate pace bowling. After Sutcliffe was dismissed with the score on 155, Hobbs carried on relentlessly, despite some signs of fatigue. As so often in his later years, he was strongest on the leg-side, but he also placed the ball with his customary certainty. Eventually, with England in a commanding position, he was caught at short leg off Francis for 159, his fourteenth century in Test cricket. Learie Constantine had heard a lot about Hobbs over

the years and now saw that reality lived up to the accounts: 'I opened
the bowling against Hobbs several times and really saw something of
his style. Up he would come as the ball left my hand, shift his right
foot to the middle of the wicket, his left shoulder guiding his bat; then
he would follow with his famous single or perhaps a lovely late cut, or
a leg glance played just as accurately as a billiard player will do. Always
that ease and economy of movement that marks the really great batsman;
the ball glides away to the boundary as if of its own volition but always
out of the reach of the fielders, no matter how carefully they may try
to forestall it. Serene temperament, unruffled judgement, a master's
execution. I suppose he will not play much more cricket now, but his
name will live for ever.' Thanks to Hobbs's century, England built up
another big total that enabled them to win for the third time in a row
by an innings.

It was an embarrassing series defeat for the West Indians, and Hobbs
was not impressed. Speaking of their temperament, he wrote that 'they
were very high up in the air one minute, very down in the mouth the
next. They were just big boys . . . I am afraid we did not treat them too
seriously,' he wrote. In fact, by the end of his career, Hobbs felt that international cricket had been demeaned by the decision of the Imperial Cricket
Conference to grant Test status to the West Indies, New Zealand and India.
'There are only two really top-class cricketing countries – England and
Australia,' he wrote in *Wisden* in 1935. 'The honour of wearing the England
cap with the three silver lions on it has, I am afraid, become rather cheap
since its inception. These caps should only be awarded to cricketers who
have appeared in England against Australia Tests.'

Hobbs kept up his majestic form right until the end of the 1928
summer. In his last eight matches of the season he hit four centuries,
including 119 against the West Indies for Leveson Gower's XI at the
Scarborough Festival and 150 for the Rest against Lancashire, the
champion county, in the last match of the season. Of this final innings,
Wisden reported, 'Completely at ease against the frequently changed
attack, Hobbs was particularly severe upon Macdonald, whom he often
hooked to the boundary and hit high over the slips, while his driving
and cutting all through reached a very high level.' Overall that season,
he hit 2,542 runs at 82, with twelve centuries, finishing just behind Douglas
Jardine in the national batting averages. The *Cricketer* gave this analysis
of his style in a golden summer for batting: 'Hobbs has never had a

better season; he is still without a superior when runs are really needed. His proportion of single runs in big innings is greater than when he was so essentially a strokeplayer but his wonderful judgement in running and his power of rising to the occasion at a critical junction make him prima facie still the finest match-winning batsman in the country today.'

England were to tour Australia that winter and Hobbs was a certainty for selection if he were willing to make his fifth Ashes trip. Indeed, to many, the idea of an MCC team in Australia without Hobbs was unthinkable. Not since the winter of 1903/4 had there been such a side, a fact that in itself was a tribute to his longevity. As Monty Noble put it, 'Some cricketers linger too long on the stage. The hero of yesterday walks, scantily clothed, in the threadbare garments of "has been". Not so Hobbs. He is as necessary to England as salt is to a boiled egg.' The problem was that he would reach the age of forty-six in the middle of an Ashes series which, with timeless Tests under a baking sun, would put brutal physical and mental strains on him. 'We must recognise that the probability of my appearance in another Test is slender,' he had said soon after the Oval victory of 1926. Yet by the early summer of 1928, he had firmly made up his mind to go to Australia if invited.

This fixity of purpose was in stark contrast to most of his previous Ashes tours, when he had hesitated because of his concerns about his separation from his beloved Ada and the demands of running his business. But those two difficulties had disappeared by 1928/9. His son Jack Junior and Doug Brown could manage the Fleet Street shop smoothly in his absence, while the precedent he had set in 1924/5 meant that there was no question about leaving his wife in England. His determination to bring Ada was not universally welcomed, especially because he was the only professional to be granted such a privilege. 'The Australians have invited our men as cricketers and not family men,' Minnie Hendren, the wife of Patsy, said tartly, to which Ada replied, 'Of course it would not do if all our wives went; we might not agree. Do I think wives are in the way when their husbands are playing cricket? Well, some wives, perhaps.' Hobbs never had any doubts about insisting on Ada's presence: 'It cost me a lot of money, but it was well worth it.'

Apart from the marital issue, there were two other reasons why Hobbs did not demonstrate his usual hesitation about the trip. The first was that he was keen to renew many of the friendships he had made over the years in Australia. Though shy in the public arena, Hobbs was an affable man among cricket people he trusted, while his good-natured personality and classless appeal made him almost as popular in the famously hospitable continent as he was in England. 'Things have changed a lot in Australia. The motorcar has opened up the country,' he said in an interview shortly before leaving. 'I knew no one when I went out twenty-one years ago. Now I have lots of good friends in Australia. That makes a lot of difference.' The other change that lifted Hobbs's spirits was the improvement in the size and quality of the ocean liners, something that he believed would lessen his misery from seasickness. The ship due to carry the MCC team was the SS *Otranto*, a 20,000-ton vessel built in 1925 in Barrow and capable of carrying 1,700 passengers. 'With modern big ships you don't feel the sea much unless you get in real rough weather and I'm looking forward to my voyage with the *Otranto* with much less fear than I did twenty-one years ago.'

As in the 1926 Ashes series, Hobbs was co-opted onto the selection committee for the 1928/9 tour. Given England's fine recent record, the panel, which was chaired by Lord Harris, did not have too difficult a task. Chapman, captain throughout the West Indies series and still a national hero, was the obvious choice as leader. The batting, headed by Hobbs, Sutcliffe, Hendren and Hammond, looked exceptionally strong, though there was a minor row over the exclusion of Frank Woolley in favour of the Hampshire veteran Phil Mead. The selectors' reasoning was that in timeless Tests, Woolley's attractive but fallible style would contribute less than Mead's solidity. On the bowling front, Larwood, Tate and Geary provided an excellent pace attack, though the spin department seemed weaker. Alf Freeman, the Kent leg-spinner, had been unimpressive on the previous Ashes tour, and Jack 'Farmer' White, the left-arm amateur from Somerset, had played just two Tests seven years earlier. In a BBC radio broadcast shortly before the side left, Hobbs told listeners, 'We have a good strong side and with every man producing his form as it is known in England, we may have a fifty-fifty chance. We are going out to do our best; I know you will credit us with that.' On the day before he left, Hobbs performed one private deed which again illustrated the compassion and decency of the man, as his close friend Andy Kempton recounted: 'I was with Jack Hobbs in his car some miles away from the Oval. He had a hundred duties to perform and every second was valuable when suddenly he exclaimed, "We'll have to go back!"

'"Why? What's wrong?" I asked

'He did not reply but drove hard, with set teeth, and had many narrow escapes before he brought the car up with a jerk in front of Bobby Abel's shop at Kennington. When he got back into the car, he explained, "I couldn't go away without saying goodbye to old Bob. He might not be here when I return." I wonder how many people who are supposed to be cricket enthusiasts trouble to think of Robert Abel, once England's number one batsman."*

Some of the MCC party left England on 15 September, receiving an enthusiastic send-off from a crowd of over 2,000 people at Victoria station. Hobbs and eleven other players were detained in England by the final match of the season, Lancashire against the Rest, and they travelled by train to Toulon where they met the *Otranto* when the ship docked after its journey through the Bay of Biscay and the Straits of Gibraltar. The five-week voyage to Australia was largely uneventful, the good spirit in the England team obvious to other passengers. The optimistic mood continued on arrival at Fremantle, where Percy Chapman engaged in the kind of banter with one dockworker that made him so popular in Australia.

'Have you brought the Ashes with you?' asked the docker.

'Yes I have, and I will show them to you on the way back,' replied Chapman.

'I'll have a quid with you on that.'†

'I'll take it and collect it on the way home.'

England looked a powerful unit in the opening state games, scoring heavily and remaining undefeated. Hobbs found his touch quickly, as did Douglas Jardine, whose classical orthodox defence would become one of England's mainstays in the series. Some of the ferocious determination that Jardine showed at the crease was undoubtedly driven by his antipathy towards the Australians. When he scored a battling century against New South Wales, his four-hour innings was accompanied by non-stop barracking from the crowd.

'They don't seem to like you very much here, Mr Jardine', said Patsy Hendren.

'It's fucking mutual,' replied Jardine.

The seeds of the hostility that would result in the Bodyline conflict

---

* In fact Abel, who suffered blindness in his old age, lived until 1936.

† The Australian dollar did not replace the pound sterling until 1966.

had already been sown. Though he had no Ashes experience, Jardine already had a natural air of authority, which led to his inclusion in the tour party's selection committee alongside Chapman, Hobbs, White, and Ernest Tyldesley. For the first Test, starting at Brisbane on 30 November, the committee agreed to play just three specialist bowlers, Tate, Larwood and White, with Hammond's medium-pace as back-up. It was a risky strategy that made it essential that the batsmen built a big total. The burden on the bowlers was not quite as great as in 1924/5, since Australia had decided to employ six-ball overs in this series rather than the usual eight. Nevertheless, the heat and the hard wickets were always a daunting challenge.

The series opener was the first ever Test held in Brisbane, and during the summer the MCC had expressed some concern about standards at the city's Exhibition Ground, which was owned by the Queensland's Royal National Agricultural Society.* Indeed, the playwright Ben Travers, who was travelling with the England party, felt that much of the city, with its dusty streets and wooden buildings, 'looked as if it had been transported from a Hollywood Western'. The England hotel could hardly be described as modern, he wrote, for he remembered 'sitting with some of the team on the hotel's antiquated and ramshackle wooden veranda, politely enduring George Geary's efforts to entertain us on his ukulele'. The facilities at the hotel were so limited that on the morning of the Test, said Travers, 'I had to share a bath with Percy Chapman.' Once he reached the cricket ground, Travers was disappointed to find that its amenities were rather 'behind the times', certainly compared to the accommodation of Sydney and Melbourne. His bathing partner Chapman won the toss and elected to bat under the hot sun in front of 20,000 spectators. Travers, sitting in a stand above the players' dressing room, had a vivid recollection of the first Test delivery sent down in Brisbane: 'Hobbs took guard and Jack Gregory began his splendid giant-stride run. Before he had gone two paces a great roaring thunderclap of encouragement burst from all round the ring. The ball sped well outside the off-stump and Hobbs watched it with an air of respectful contemplation. He was the coolest – perhaps the only cool – man on the ground.' Off the third ball, Hobbs demonstrated that self-assurance by hooking a bouncer for four. It was a shot that set the tone for yet

* In 1931 the Queensland Cricket Association moved down the road to the Gabba.

another fine opening stand before Sutcliffe was caught at fine leg for 38 when the score was 86. But Percy Fender, who was reporting on the series for the *Star*, felt that the two batsmen were not quite as comfortable as they had been in their previous Ashes series. 'They had not run between the wickets anything like as well as we are used to seeing them do. There were several misunderstandings in the period.' Even worse confusion followed after lunch, when Hobbs, on 49, fatally hesitated over going for a third run from a square cut executed by England's number three Phil Mead. The fielder who chased and threw an accurate return to Oldfield was a twenty-year-old called Don Bradman, making his Test debut but already a well-known name in Australian cricket. As the *Daily Mirror* reported, 'Bradman, true to his reputation as a fine outfielder, made a beautiful return and Hobbs was helpless, well out of his crease, when the wicket was broken.' Amazingly, it was the first time Hobbs had been run-out in seventy-six Test innings. What impressed Travers was Hobbs's lack of recrimination or self-pity, a reflection of his Kiplingesque gift for 'treating those two imposters, triumph and disaster, just the same.' Not long after his innings was over, Hobbs came up to see his wife in the stand. 'Hobbs possessed a marvellously even temperament. I never saw or heard him incensed or contentious,' wrote Travers who was amused to see Hobbs make a joke of his dismissal. 'His wife was sitting near me and when he had been run out for 49 he came up to see her. He said, "It was all my fault. I started late. I ought to have taken a taxi."'

Thankfully for England, Hobbs's dismissal did not precipitate a collapse. A big century from Hendren, plus fifties from Chapman and Larwood, ensured a total of 521. During Australia's long spell in the field, Gregory broke down with cartilage trouble in one knee, a problem that had plagued him for several years. Having retired to the pavilion, he was told by the Australian team doctor that he would never play cricket again. Between the innings, he went to give his opponents the news, as Patsy Hendren recalled. 'He came into our dressing room looking the picture of misery. "Boys, I'm finished," he said. "Never again shall I bowl any of you out." And as he bade us farewell, the tears streamed down his face.' Hobbs was deeply affected by the departure of his old adversary. 'It was a tragic conclusion to the career of a magnificent cricketer,' he wrote.

Battered and exhausted, Australia wilted before the onslaught of

Harold Larwood, who ripped apart the batting order with 6 for 32. Hobbs said later that this was the fastest he ever saw Larwood bowl, his pace even more quick than in any of his incendiary performances in the Bodyline series. To widespread surprise, Chapman did not enforce the follow-on despite England's lead of 399 but instead he batted again, a decision with which Hobbs agreed. 'We might have had a big second innings score made against us and then found ourselves batting on a crumbling wicket.' Hobbs went cheaply, lbw to Grimmett, but England batted well enough to set Australia a gargantuan 742 to win. For a second time, they collapsed miserably, all out for just 66, leaving England the winners by 675 runs. Ominously, Jack White's left-arm did much of the damage as he returned the remarkable figures of 4 for 7. To this day, England's victory remains the largest winning margin by runs alone in the history of Test cricket.

The second Test at Sydney was one of fluctuating fortunes for Hobbs. Early on the first day, when Australia batted after winning the toss, he was embroiled in a highly controversial incident over the dismissal of Alan Kippax, whose stumps were dislodged while he attempted to sweep a leg-side delivery from Geary. But Kippax was convinced that he was not out, claiming that the ball had rebounded from the pads of the England wicketkeeper George Duckworth. He stood his ground, and the umpire at the bowler's end, George Hele, gave him 'not out' before signalling 'over'. But Hobbs was equally certain Kippax had been legitimately dismissed. Before the new over began, he led a chorus of England appeals to the square leg umpire, Dave Elder, and grew so furious that he launched a personal attack on Kippax. 'Alan, you're no sportsman standing there when you know you're out,' he said, harsh language from such a mild individual. Much to the astonishment of Kippax and a large section of the crowd, Elder put up his finger. Back in the Australian dressing room, several of the players felt that Elder should have had no jurisdiction in the matter from his position at square leg and they wanted their captain, Jack Ryder, to go out to the middle to challenge his decision. Ryder wisely refused and Kippax was forced to leave the crease as booing echoed round the ground. Duckworth, suspected of sharp practice, was a particular target for the crowd's hostility. But there was also some annoyance towards Hobbs, especially from the Australian team. According to Ashley Mallett, Grimmett's official biographer, 'Clarrie didn't like what he saw of that incident in Sydney, and he was none too pleased with Hobbs's behaviour.' It was not the first time on the tour that Hobbs's sportsmanship had been questioned. In the state match against Queensland in late November, Hobbs had been batting against the fast-medium pace of Pud Thurlow when he was struck on his body by a big off-cutter. The ball then started to roll back down the pitch, with Hobbs well out of his crease. Thurlow moved forward to pick it up, only to find Hobbs kicking the ball away. As the Reuter's report stated, 'Much adverse criticism is being voiced over the Hobbs incident. Some maintain that his action was tantamount to obstructing the field.' Such rows do not mean that Hobbs's renowned attachment to fair play was a myth, only that, through the sepia lens of nostalgia, the extent of his chivalry has often been exaggerated. Hobbs was, after all, a competitive professional. In the case of the Kippax affair, he did what he thought was right, since, as he wrote in his tour diary, 'I saw the whole incident perfectly clearly and there was not the slightest doubt that Kippax was bowled off his pads.' He admitted, though, that 'things were quite unpleasant for a time', and in the evening he apologised to Kippax for the intemperate language he had used. The apology was accepted.

Yet the next day, the mood in the ground was transformed. After Australia were all out for 253, Hobbs and Sutcliffe, batting more cautiously than usual, put on 51 for the first wicket before Sutcliffe fell. Hobbs then reached 36 not out by the mid-afternoon when rain began to fall on the SCG. Once the dark clouds had passed, the interruption provided an opportunity for a moving display of affection towards Hobbs by the Australian public. All the bad feelings of the previous day were forgotten, replaced by a surge of warm gratitude. Never before or since has any cricketer been shown such fondness by his opponents' followers. The catalyst for all this affection was Hobbs's birthday, which fell in the middle of the Sydney Test. A shilling fund, known as 'Bobs for Hobbs', had been started by the *Sydney Sun* newspaper to organise a birthday gift for the great batsman and during the break the presentation was conducted in front of the pavilion by the former Australian captain Monty Noble. The crowd that witnessed this unique event was by far the largest ever seen at a cricket match up to that point, with 58,446 people packed into the ground. Such was the compression of the multitude that even the spectators on the famous Sydney Hill had to stand all day. At the ceremony, Hobbs was given a gold-mounted wallet containing forty-six sovereigns, one to mark each year of his life, and a boomerang mounted with a gold shield, on which was the inscription: 'To John Berry Hobbs on his 46th birthday, from friends and admirers in New South Wales'. There followed a short speech by Noble and a heartfelt, if nervous, reply from Hobbs, the words of both men relayed across Australia in a live radio broadcast. Then the whole ground, almost in unison, started to sing 'For he's a jolly good fellow', accompanied by a brass band. But the crowd was far from finished in demonstrating its appreciation. Through their incessant cheering and shouting, the spectators made clear they wanted to get a closer view of the hero of the hour. So Noble took Hobbs by the arm and led him on a tour right round the outfield. 'Cheer upon cheer rang out with a fusillade of hand-clapping and hands were stretched over the fence to shake hands . . . One man jumped over the fence to offer his greetings, and farther round a youngster ran on to the field with a bat, which was readily autographed. The wonderful feature of the demonstration was its spontaneity. It was a triumphant march which will live in the memory of all those present on a great occasion,' wrote Noble. Fender was equally touched by the extraordinary scene: 'Each section of the crowd seemed to vie with the immediately preceding section to give Jack a bigger cheer. This eventually culminated in an enormous roar from the grandstand at the end of the tour, and the band again struck up "Jolly good fellow" as he returned to the pavilion gate. Here he was met by a crowd of enthusiastic members who picked him up and carried him shoulder-high into the dressing room.' Patsy Hendren, who had been watching with his colleagues, believed the episode was 'the most wonderful tribute paid to a cricketer I have ever seen – and the tribute was paid to a man who can best be described as the wonder batsman of cricket'. Harold Larwood also said it was 'the most warm-hearted applause I've ever heard', though he added that Hobbs 'was clearly embarrassed'. Hobbs himself later admitted that he was 'conscious of blushing all over at the reception these lovable people gave me,' but he did his best to express his thanks. In an interview with the *Sydney Sun,* he said, 'I never dreamed that people would do such a thing for a visiting cricketer. I cannot imagine it happening in any other part of the world. I will buy a portable wireless set with the money subscribed and have the boomerang placed upon it.'

Hobb's concentration was understandably affected once play resumed that afternoon. Having added just 4 runs, he was caught by Oldfield off Grimmett for 40. Once again, however, England's middle-order batting was far too strong for the Australian attack. The total of 636, which included 251 from Hammond, set a new Test record and England went on to win by eight wickets. During this Test, the former Australian batsman Charlie Macartney had written that Hobbs's batting appeared to be in decline, 'his ability was never in doubt, but there is a lack of that power in his strokes that marked his exhibitions of former years.' That verdict seemed to be confirmed in the third Test, when England opened their innings late on the second afternoon after Australia were all out for 397. Hobbs had the pleasure of passing 3,000 runs in Ashes cricket but when he had made just 20 he was caught behind trying to cut the accurate, fast-medium pace of Ted a'Beckett. 'Jack Hobbs has yet to find his form in the present series,' said the *Daily Mirror* mournfully. *The Times* was even more critical: 'Hobbs was out to a poor stroke when England went in and he is clearly nothing like the Hobbs of four years ago.' Another Hammond double century saw England gain a narrow lead, but then Australia responded well to make 351, Bradman the top-scorer with his first Ashes hundred. Hobbs noted in his diary, 'Bradman is the youngest player who has ever scored a century in a Test match between England and Australia, beating Clem Hill by a few months. There was a great scene when he completed it.' Many more such scenes would follow over the next nineteen years. Thanks to Bradman's effort, Australia had closed the fifth day on 347 for 8, meaning that England were certain to be facing a tough target on a worn pitch, however quickly the tailenders were dismissed the following morning.

What was difficult seemed to have become almost insurmountable during the night when heavy rain fell, for there was no more demanding wicket in the world than a Melbourne sticky. In his hotel bed that night, Percy Fender was disturbed to hear the rainfall: 'Listening to it, while in bed, was like listening to nails being driven into England's coffin. I had seen and played on Australian wet wickets.' The rain was still falling the next morning, which meant that the start of play was delayed until 12.30, just half an hour before lunch. The last two Australians were quickly dismissed, leaving England with a target of 332 and the English opening pair managed to negotiate their way to the interval. But no one at the ground gave England a chance. Once the sun came out in the afternoon, the wicket would be all but unplayable. Indeed, in the ten minutes that Hobbs and Sutcliffe had batted, bits of turf were already coming off the top.

As he walked into lunch, Douglas Jardine ran into Hugh Trumble, the former Australian off-spinner who had become Secretary of the Melbourne club on his retirement from playing. No one knew the MCG wicket better. 'He speculated that we should make between 50 and 70 runs – a total of 100, he said, on such a wicket, would be a wonderful batting feat, little short of a miracle.' The playwright Ben Travers was in the Melbourne pavilion, attending a lunch hosted by the Victorian Cricket Association. 'They were all very genial in their undisguised elation and jocular in their sympathy towards me, representing England.' At one stage, a senior police officer came into the dining hall to ask the Association's Assistant Secretary how many constables would be needed on duty the next day. 'The next day? The Assistant Secretary laughed and told the officer that he did not know much about cricket,' wrote Travers. Hobbs, realistic if not down-hearted, was of the same view. According to Travers, he came into the England dressing room at lunch and said, 'Well, there it is, I'm afraid it will be all over by tea-time.'

That gloomy prognosis appeared to have been confirmed soon after lunch when Hobbs, on only 3, received a sharply rising ball from a'Beckett and edged it to Hunter 'Stork' Hendry at slip. It was a straightforward chance but Hendry put it down. At the time, few would have envisaged how costly the miss would be, for the wicket was rapidly deteriorating as the sun beat down on it. Furthermore, the Australian attack possessed variety in speed and type of turn. With Mailey having retired, Clarrie Grimmett was now the finest leg-spinner in the world, and he was supported by the accurate slow off-spin of Don Blackie, who had taken 6 for 94 in the first innings, and the quicker off-breaks of Ron Oxenham, as well as the seamers of a'Beckett, Ryder and Hendry. It was a combination that should have been deadly in the conditions. 'The wicket behaved as badly as it could,' reported Fender. 'About three balls in five hopped head or shoulder high, some turning as well, and all stopping almost visibly as they hit the ground. The batsmen were hit all over the body from the pads to the shoulders, and in two or three cases even on the neck and the head – all from good or nearly good length balls.' Hendren almost shuddered. 'What the bowlers were doing with the ball in the early part of the innings may be imagined when I mentioned that Oldfield had twenty byes chalked up against him in no time. The ball rose to such a height that he hadn't a chance of stopping it – yet so worked up were some of the spectators that they thought Oldfield should have got to these balls. And they told him so. Actually he would have needed a step ladder to reach them.' The scent of England's impending defeat brought huge numbers rushing to the ground throughout the afternoon, more than 20,000 passing through the turn-stiles after lunch. At its 70,000 peak, the crowd easily surpassed the record set at the SCG only a few weeks earlier. Looking at the vast influx, one Australian in the press box turned to Fender and said, 'You didn't know we had fox-hunting in Australia, did you?'

'No, why?'

'Look at them hurrying to be at the death.'

Sutcliffe later said that the wicket was even worse than that of the Oval in 1926, yet he and Hobbs showed the same astonishing skill, bravery and concentration in dealing with the attack. 'We were bruised on almost every part of our body, preferring to be hit by the lifting ball rather than risk playing defensively and giving a simple catch to the close-in field who clustered round within a couple of yards of the bat,' wrote the Yorkshireman. Blackie, potentially the most dangerous of the bowlers on the drying turf, initially came over the wicket but his spin was so great that the ball broke more than a yard; in classic off-spinner's style, therefore, he decided to attack around the wicket to a nest of close leg-side fielders. It was a draining ordeal for the batsmen. At one stage, a ball to Hobbs popped so violently that it hit his head and knocked off his cap, which almost fell on his stumps. But just as in 1926, the two England openers managed to survive through over after over, knowing all the time that the pitch would eventually become easier. With his intuitive understanding of technique, Fender gave this fascinating insight into their methods: 'First and foremost they did not play a single ball at which they were not bound to play. When they did put, or try to put, the bat to the ball in defence, it was always a 'dead' bat. Except the pull shot, which was the only forcing stroke either batsman permitted himself, every other was made with the bat loosely held, and when the ball hit the middle of the bat it merely dropped dead in front of the batsman so close that silly point and short leg could not reach it, creep in as they would. Never a sign of a drive nor of a forward stroke. It was always right back on the wicket, or just a back stroke where they stood.' For all the masterly courage and judgement of Hobbs and Sutcliffe, many Australians felt that their bowlers failed to exploit the conditions, just as they had in 1926. Even with the quality of these openers, they argued,

England's task should have been impossible. 'We were presented with a gun and we did not know how to use it,' wrote Arthur Mailey. In particular, Blackie and Oxenham were said to have persistently bowled too short, allowing Hobbs and Sutcliffe to remain on the back foot. As Monty Noble put it, 'The policy should have been to force them to play forward and hit at the ball. Blackie did not exploit his slow ball, which would have been a tempting delivery in view of the state of the pitch. Foolishly he crossed to bowl round the leg stump and going away, just as Arthur Richardson had done at the Oval in 1926.'

After the tea interval, with the Australians increasingly demoralised and the century partnership approaching, Hobbs made a dramatic move. He signalled to the England dressing room that he wanted to change his bat, but it was really just a ruse to pass a message on to the captain. Douglas Jardine, who had been watching with his usual hawk-like astuteness, explained what happened: 'Why I cannot tell but I had a hunch that he had something to impart so instead of letting the twelfth man (that gallant tyke Maurice Leyland) take the bats out, I took them myself. Hobbs cut short my whispered congratulations with the remark, "I want you to come in next." For an awful moment I thought he meant he had been hurt or had pulled a muscle. But no; he said that there was just an outside chance if we could last the day, without losing too many wickets, we might get the runs on a good wicket the next day, and pull a lost match out of the furnace.' Hobbs knew that Jardine had the best defensive technique in England's middle order, so in the circumstances, he should be promoted from his usual number six position. Not for the first time, Chapman bowed to Hobbs's wise judgement once he had received the message and ordered Jardine to pad up. Later Hobbs defended his unorthodox method of contacting his skipper. 'I simply had to get the message through somehow and I could think of no other way.' Soon afterwards, he and Sutcliffe passed the hundred mark, only for Hobbs to fall lbw to Blackie when he was just one run short of his half century and the total was on 105. England still faced a demanding job, but the heroism of the Surrey master had made it immeasurably easier. What he had done, wrote Fender, 'was worth many hundreds for his side'. Sutcliffe paid this tribute to his partner: 'Never in the history of cricket has there been a Test match batsman of the class of Hobbs or one more trustworthy in a crisis.' Apart from his contribution with the bat, Hobbs was absolutely right in urging that Jardine be sent in at number three, for England did not lose another wicket until the score reached 199, by which time victory had becoming a realistic prospect.

Eventually, with Sutcliffe making 135, Chapman's team won by three wickets, a margin that sounded much narrower than it really was, for England were within just 14 runs of their target when their fourth batsman was out. A late flurry of dismissals flattered Australia but the result was never in doubt in the final stages. When Geary hit the winning four, he screamed with the delight, 'Dammit, we've done them.' Back in the pavilion, Ben Travers found himself standing between Chapman and Hobbs. 'We all flung our arms around each other.' England's lead in the series was unassailable. The Ashes had been retained.

There were only two regrettable notes struck in the wake of England's triumph, one private, one public. First of all, in the England dressing room, Wally Hammond was vexed to learn that a wealthy English enthusiast had promised Hobbs and Sutcliffe a hundred pounds each for their batting in the second innings. Always inclined to moroseness, Hammond moaned that his own phenomenal batting in the series had been ignored. 'I'm not going to make any more bloody hundreds,' he said bitterly. The other, more public, development was one that briefly shook the cricket world when Hobbs appeared to signal the sudden end of his Test career. Shortly before the end of the game, Hobbs had told the *Daily News*, 'If England win this match, I think I may have played my last Test. It is time I made way for somebody else.' The statement reflected Hobbs's generosity of spirit, in that he genuinely believed that, with the Ashes safe, England should consider giving other, younger players a chance. But he was not a free agent on the question. The composition of the Test side lay with the selectors, who were determined to win as many matches as possible and had no intention of letting Hobbs go, especially not after his performance in Melbourne. So on 7 January, two days after the Test victory, he issued a clarification. 'The report of his immediate retirement from Test matches is incorrect. He is ready and willing to play in the two remaining Test matches if his services are required. After this tour, however, he intends to confine himself to county cricket. "There is too much mental and physical strain in Test matches," he said,' ran the news item in the *Daily Express*.

England were grateful for his retention in the side for the fourth Test at Adelaide. Batting on the first morning, he and Sutcliffe yet again showed their stature by hitting 143 for the first wicket. 'Both played with the utmost confidence and ease, and never once looked like getting out until Hobbs, attempting a square cut, was caught at slip off Hendry,' reported the *Daily Mirror*. His score was 74, made in 164 minutes, but England for once failed to capitalise on their good start and were all out for 334. The rest of the match was a thrilling affair, in which the initiative constantly switched sides until the tense final morning when Australia needed just 41 to win with three wickets left. Crucially, one of those wickets was that of Don Bradman, who had made a chanceless, authoritative 58. Then Oldfield pushed the ball to Hobbs's right hand at cover and called Bradman through for a single. The result could have been predicted, as Hendren recounted. 'Jack pounced on the ball and though the return was not a typical one, George Duckworth performed a wonderful feat of acrobatics and managed to break the wicket before Bradman got home. That clever bit of fielding turned the game in our favour.' Amid scenes of high tension, England won by 12 runs, Jack White the bowling saviour with an astonishing display of stamina that brought him eight wickets from 64.5 overs.

White was England's captain in the final Test at Melbourne in early March, when Chapman stood down through a mixture of poor health and poor form. Sutcliffe also dropped out as a result of injury, so Jardine was designated as Hobbs's opener. It was the first time in eight years that Hobbs had gone in first for England without Sutcliffe at his side and the Yorkshireman said he was 'bitterly disappointed' at not being able to play, especially given that the match was certain to be Hobbs's last in Australia, perhaps even in Test cricket. The change, however, did not seem to affect Hobbs. Against some tight seam bowling on a lively first morning wicket, he displayed all his old assurance and technical application, guiding England to lunch without the loss of any wicket. After the interval and the fall of Jardine, he played more expansively, 'full of sparkle and old time form', wrote Noble. In the press box, Fender delighted in seeing his Surrey colleague at his strokemaking best: 'He was always sound and the master not only of the bowling but of himself in every way and he played with the utmost ease and freedom. He was never really pressing for runs but he took full advantage of anything approaching the loose while he showed his old ability to force runs here and there, as and when he wanted them without taking the faintest shadow of a risk.' At 4.40 p.m., having given one chance when he was on 77, Hobbs took the single that brought him to his twelfth century against Australia and his fifth at Melbourne.

Once more the Australian spectators greeted him as one of their own, giving him a thunderous reception. Shortly before the close he was out for 142, lbw to Jack Ryder but he appeared to have put England in an immensely strong position. 'His display, after twenty-one years in Test cricket, was masterly in the extreme. His timing was as perfect as ever and his placing to leg and leg glances beautifully executed,' said the *Daily Mail*. That night Hobbs at his hotel was given another illustration of the respect in which he was held in Australia. When he and Ada went down to dinner in the restaurant of the Windsor, the orchestra immediately struck up 'See the Conquering Hero Comes', followed by 'For He's a Jolly Good Fellow'. More than 400 other guests simultaneously stood up and sang the chorus, Hobbs acknowledging their enthusiasm with a typically modest smile and bow.

In the aftermath of his hundred Hobbs told the press, 'I feel extremely gratified at making a century in what may be likely to be my last Test. Some time ago I doubted whether I was justified in accepting the invitation to play in these Tests. I thought the time had arrived to make way for a younger man. This innings, however, has largely dispelled my doubts on the question.' Unfortunately for Hobbs, his performance was not enough to secure the victory that might have brought a whitewash for England. Despite making 519 in their first innings, Jack White's team went down to a five-wicket defeat on the eighth day of the match. But this loss could hardly detract from the phenomenal success of the trip nor Hobbs's own achievement. He had scored over 1,000 first-class runs and averaged 50.11 in the Tests. 'It has been a great tour,' he said when the MCC party arrived back at Victoria to an ecstatic welcome from the public. One paper even suggested that he should be given a knighthood. 'He has wound up his amazing Test match career in a wonderful fashion, and a royal tribute to that career would be the most popular form of celebrating our spectacular recovery of the Ashes. If it is objected that Hobbs is a "professional", what of the similar honours that have been showered on actors, actresses and at least one comedian* who are also professional entertainers,' argued a leader page article in the *Star*.

There was one big mistake in that editorial: Hobbs had yet to wind up his Test career.

---

* Presumably a reference to Sir Harry Lauder, the Scottish music hall star, knighted in 1919.

16

'So He Fell, This Prince Among Batsmen'

The former England captain Arthur Gilligan once reflected in a BBC interview on how mischievousness was central to Hobbs's character. 'When that same pro is a god-fearing, clean-living, family-loving man, smokes little and drinks hardly ever, well you may feel the others might find him a bit heavy-going, but not Jack, oh no. His sense of humour saved him from that.' This humour, said Gilligan, was most clearly manifested in Hobbs's love of 'simple, harmless jokes that hurt no one and left Jack slapping his thigh with delight'. Indeed, Hobbs's enthusiasm for practical jokes was notorious throughout the cricket world, and it meant that he was never, to his relief, treated with the kind of sycophantic or anxious reverence that his deeds might have inspired. As Harry Lee put it, 'To go on piling up runs without relaxing to laugh – that would have made cricket unendurable for him.'

One of Hobbs's favourite japes was to sit in the pavilion when his side was batting and fool the incoming batsman, who might be waiting anxiously in the corner of the dressing room or just dozing, into believing that a wicket had fallen through a sudden cry of 'He's out!' Having not been following the play, the victim would then grab his gloves and bat, rush out on to the field, only to see that his two team-mates were still standing in the middle, utterly unaware of the frantic scene that Hobbs had just created. The pavilion at Lord's was especially well adapted to this prank, because of its maze of dark corridors and the poor view from the players' dressing room. During one Gents v Players match at Lord's, Jack Newman was slowly putting on his pads when he heard Hobbs yell, 'That's done him. Come on, Jack, you're in.' In a panic, Newman finished putting on his gear and ran out into the sunshine, only to find himself a solitary, embarrassed figure on the edge of the outfield. No wicket had fallen. Newman sullenly returned to the dressing room, gave Hobbs a stare and sat down on the bench. Soon Hobbs was at it again. 'He's out. In you go, Jack!' Newman refused to move, only to be greeted a few moments later by the appearance of the dismissed batsman asking him. 'What the hell do you think you're doing?' Hobbs also used the wheeze at the Oval, though on one occasion the Surrey players got their revenge on him. A night-watchman had gone in overnight and was batting well, while Hobbs, who was due in next, was sleeping on a massage table in another room. His Surrey teammates sneaked in and very quietly tied the laces of his boots together as he remained asleep. Then they shouted in unison, 'He's out!' Hobbs immediately tried to jump to his feet, only to fall flat on his face.

His old Surrey colleague Razor Smith said that 'fooling others was the great hobby of Jack Hobbs; nor did he care who he fooled. The greater the pal, the better the joke.' Hobbs would hide bails and balls to fox the umpires, or issue a sudden warning of 'mind your heads', accompanied by a ducking action, as he pretended that a dangerously misdirected throw was sailing in from the deep. His humour could also infuriate bowlers. He loved to rouse the ire of the hot-tempered George Macaulay by constantly dodging in and out of his crease as if he were about to run. Similarly, Maurice Allom remembered this incident from a match between Surrey and the South Africans in 1929: 'Denys Morkel, the South African fast-medium bowler, was trying to get Jack to play him to his strong cover field. He bowled him one well wide off the off-stump. Jack moved lightly across and with a twist of the wrists drove him all along the ground through square leg for four. Morkel looked astonished, as well he might be. He tried again. The next ball was further outside the off-stump. Exactly the same thing happened. Morkel persevered. The third ball was aimed at second slip. Hobbs stood still. The umpire signalled a wide. Jack roared with laughter.' Hobbs's impishness was also reflected in the way he treated Joe Small, one of the black players in the West Indian team of 1928, though his behaviour would hardly be regarded as appropriate today. 'He had a smile that was all over his face at once. Small was uncommonly ticklish; he simply couldn't bear to be touched. If you tickled him in the ribs he jumped a mile – no, not quite a mile – in the air. I seldom missed an opportunity of making him do it.'

He was just as big a joker away from the cricket arena. John Arlott once described him as a 'wonderful pocket-picker. He would give you back all your possessions when you left him.

"'Is this your fountain pen?" he'd say.

"'Good heavens, yes. Where did that come from?"

"'It was on the table." Then he would produce your wallet and your diary and you'd realise that he'd gently picked your pocket while lunch was going on.'

During an away game to Essex, when the Surrey team were staying in a Southend hotel, Razor Smith witnessed how Hobbs's foolery could even lead to minor damage. 'We were resting in the lounge. One of our side wandered up to a high gallery surrounding the lounge on which flowers and plants were displayed in pots and vases. Jack rose and, standing under the edge of the gallery, invited his pal to drop an aspidistra in a pot, at the same time shaping his hands for the catch. The other player accepted the challenge and dropped the pot – only to see Jack walk away. The manager took a deal of convincing that it was an accident.'

Hobbs's close friend Andy Kempton was once appalled to see Hobbs commit what seemed an act of spiteful vandalism, only to discover the motive a few months later. In 1927 Kempton was sitting in the professionals' dressing room with Hobbs at the Oval when Fred Boyington, the long-serving Surrey scorer who had recently retired, came past. 'Jack Hobbs snatched the soft felt hat from the old man's head and, after kicking it up to the ceiling, jumped on it, the spikes in his cricket boots wrecking the poor chap's headgear. I walked out of the room and, for the first time in my life, ignored some words that Jack spoke to me, as the incident left a nasty taste in my mouth.' Later that year, Boyington died and Kempton attended his funeral. 'When it was over his widow, whom I have known for many years, spoke of Jack Hobbs as the greatest friend her late husband ever had, mentioning, among other things, the fact that whenever Fred's hats were the slightest bit shabby, Jack insisted upon providing new ones. And then I understood.'

For all the boyish silliness of most of his pranks, there was sometimes a harsher edge to them, particularly when they were directed at amateurs. Hobbs was generally a traditionalist when it came to respecting cricket's hierarchy, but he could not resist the chance to poke occasional fun at those who enjoyed positions of superiority over the professionals. Percy

Fender told this story which showed how Hobbs could use sly humour both to mock the airs of some of the amateurs and to make a point about the poor quality of the professionals' accommodation. One morning in 1932, shortly after Jardine had taken over the Surrey captaincy from Fender, the two men were sitting in one of the amateurs' rooms at the top of the Oval pavilion when Hobbs rang up from the players' quarters below 'on the old-fashioned intercom – you know the kind of thing that you had to blow into and then put to your ear – which was typical of what you'd expect to find in the servants' hall and I suppose it fitted the image of the Players' pokey little dressing room in the basement'. According to Fender's account, Hobbs said to Jardine, 'Skipper, we've got an argument going on down here. It's about the proper extent of the follow-through for the off-drive. Would you come down and settle it for us?' So the two amateurs went downstairs to the professionals' room, which, said Fender, 'really was a bit of a rabbit hutch'. Fender's tale continues: '"Now then, Skipper," Jack said, handing him a bat, "you've got that model off-drive they taught you at Winchester; would you mind showing us your follow-through?" Douglas had originally jibbed a bit at the whole suggestion but was intrigued and the reference to his Winchester upbringing didn't hurt Jack's case a bit. Anyway, he swung the bat through and Jack and all the boys said, "Oh no, Skipper, that's nothing like your full follow-through." So Douglas had another go and – wham – he knocked out the overhead light. We both beat a hasty retreat with various irreverent remarks round our ears about "not being room to swing a bat – let alone a cat"'.

The amateur Middlesex all-rounder Walter Robins, who combined a high opinion of himself with a certain touchiness, was another victim of Hobbs's antics. During the second Test against Australia at Lord's in 1930, Robins had received requests from three of his county colleagues, Nigel Haig, Jack Durston and Jack Hearne, to pick up new England caps for each of them. All of the trio had played for England against Australia in the early 1920s, but since then their dark blue caps with the crested silver lions had become rather faded. Robins did as asked, discreetly went to the box of new caps in the corner of the England dressing room, picked out three of them and put them in his own bag. But when his attention was elsewhere, Hobbs took all the remaining stock from the box and dumped it in Robins' bag. Then Hobbs arranged for Leveson Gower, his club President and the Chairman of Selectors,

to be summoned to the England dressing room to be told of the disappearance of the new, much treasured, England caps. Perplexed and
red-faced, Leveson Gower demanded an explanation for what appeared
to be an act of blatant theft. Somehow, the name of Robins was insinu-
ated into the proceedings. When the Middlesex all-rounder, with a
mixture of defiance and guilt, refused to open his bag, he became the
obvious culprit. Eventually, he consented, and out-spilled the entire
consignment. Leveson Gower was outraged; Robins embarrassed.
Neither of them saw the funny side when Hobbs, worried that his joke
was getting out of hand, owned up as the man responsible.

In his paean to Hobbs, Gilligan said 'perhaps one of his most valuable
and endearing qualities is his simplicity'. That was not the way the
England captain Percy Chapman felt after Hobbs played one of his
audacious tricks. With his rascally eye, Hobbs noticed that during lunch
intervals at Test matches Chapman was in the clandestine habit of
putting a little gin in an empty ginger beer bottle, which he then hid
somewhere in the dressing room or in his bag so that he could have a
stiff drink at the tea interval. On one occasion, Hobbs found the bottle,
replaced the gin with water, and then put it back in its hiding place.
When the tea interval arrived, Chapman rushed to the bottle, took one
mouthful and spat out the contents over the floor, uttering the words,
'That bastard Jack Hobbs.' Hobbs later recalled fondly, 'He got it right
straight away, dear old Percy.' But there was a tragic side to the story.
That minor indulgence during Test matches was the first sign that
Chapman had a dangerous weakness for alcohol. It was a susceptibility
that would hasten his premature exit from the game and turn him from
a much-loved, extrovert personality into a shuffling, incoherent embarrassment. In his long, inebriated twilight, marked by falls and rows and
ill health, he was a man to be avoided rather than cherished. Even giving
him a lift from Lord's risked having the car's interior covered in vomit.
Undoubtedly the events of 1930, when Chapman felt brutally rejected
by the cricket establishment, played a part in his descent, just as after
1926 Arthur Carr never entirely recovered from his rejection, though
he resorted to bitterness rather than the bottle. In both cases, the role
of the mild-mannered, deferential Hobbs was central.

Hobbs and Chapman had returned from the Australian tour as heroes
but they barely featured in the 1929 Test series against South Africa.
Remarkably for an incumbent skipper, Chapman did not play for

England in any of the five Tests. Having been away on holiday with his wife in New Zealand and Canada for the first half of the summer, he then sustained a bad injury on his return and missed the rest of the season. Injury and ill health were the main explanations for Hobbs's absence, though he was also assailed by concern about the mental strain of continuing to play Test cricket. For Surrey, when his fitness allowed him to play, he was again in excellent form, the tone for his batting set by 154 against Hampshire at the Oval in the opening match of the season. But, from mid-May, he missed five successive matches with a damaged knee and a chill. Then, soon after his return at the start of June, he wrecked his shoulder while trying to make a catch at cover during the Test trial at Lord's, which meant another lay-off for seven matches. Ironically, the batsman who hit the ball to him was his own county captain Percy Fender, who was captaining the Rest and was on the verge of a romantic, if brief, recall to the England side. Hobbs had recovered by the first week in July and came back in prolific style, hitting 150 against Kent and 204 against Somerset at the Oval, the latter an innings described by the *Daily Express* as 'an effortless display'. The *Cricketer* felt that Hobbs's form was 'remarkable even for the Surrey champion. Evidently his skill is as pronounced as ever.'

Despite his high scoring for Surrey, Hobbs refused invitations to play in the third and fourth Tests against South Africa in July. 'He did not feel justified in accepting. His health has not been too robust this season, and although he is well enough for ordinary matches, he does not feel equal to the strain of a Test game,' reported the *Sunday Pictorial*. Judging by such reports, it seemed as if Hobbs's Test career had finally come to an end, something that Trevor Wignall, the *Daily Express*'s chief sports commentator, felt was a deep cause of regret. 'Apparently he has finally made up his mind never again to figure in international cricket, but it is to be doubted even today whether there is a batsman in the world who is his superior. Test cricket seems to be lacking in something essential when he is not playing.' Wignall voiced the hope that Hobbs might still change his mind, as did the *Daily Mirror*: 'The present Tests have been like *Hamlet* without the Prince in the absence of the Surrey crack. Our Jack is too modest in standing down so long. His scores for Surrey have proved that.' As well as regret, Hobbs was also subjected to the personal criticism that he preferred to pile-up runs on the county circuit rather than serve his country. Always sensitive, he strongly rejected the charge, pointing out that the problem with his fitness lay in fielding, not batting. 'The fact was that I was fit to bat and Surrey could hide or nurse me in the field; moreover, I could go careful on myself, so that Surrey were willing to play me with all my disadvantage. To play for England, however, is a very different matter; one cannot there be a passenger in the field.' Further centuries in August, allied to an improvement in his fielding, enabled Hobbs to meet the desire of the cricket public by declaring himself fit for the fifth Test at the Oval. His inclusion was all the more necessary, for the two men tried as partners for Sutcliffe, Ted Bowley of Sussex and Tom Killick of Middlesex, had both failed. Once more, as had happened continuously since 1926, there was speculation that Hobbs was about to play his last match for England. 'This will probably be his last Test. He decided to play in deference to the generally expressed wish that he should make his last appearance for England on the ground where he first found renown,' said the *Daily Express*, under a headline which read, 'Today's farewell at the Oval'. The paper further pronounced with some certainty that 'as his form at the moment is as good as ever, it is likely he will make his exit with another century'. The prediction was too optimistic. In a rain-affected match, Hobbs only made 10 in the first innings, though in the second he hit a graceful, rapid 52 that helped England to a comfortable draw. *The Times* report on his second innings mixed chastisement for giving away his wicket with praise for his 'brilliancy', during which 'it was almost impossible to place the field for him'. Sutcliffe more than made up for Hobbs's failure to reach three figures; he scored a century in each innings for the second time in Test cricket.

Despite all the talk of exits in 1929, there was little sign of any decline in Hobbs's batting powers at first-class level, as he topped the national averages with 2,263 runs at 66.55, with ten centuries. 'When fit to play Hobbs was as superb as ever, though, as a rule, more deliberate and contenting himself with many singles that of yore would have been fours,' said the *Cricketer*. Bill Bowes, the Yorkshire fast bowler who made his first-class debut in 1929, quickly discovered how far Hobbs had retained his superlative talent. 'The first time I bowled at him, he went down on one knee and hit me past the left-hand of square leg. The ball pitched seven or eight inches outside the off-stump. My jaw dropped and George Macaulay at mid-on shouted reprovingly, "It's no good you peepin' – he'll do it three times an over when his eye's in."'

Hobbs's capability in his late forties was also experienced by another young bowler, the Middlesex leg-spinner Ian Peebles: 'A beautifully orthodox batsman, his judgement of length was impeccable and his reading of the bowler's intentions was seemingly infallible. By now, however, he did not chase bowlers to destruction but played the spinners from the crease, showing the full face of an impeccably straight bat. Thus although I got the impression he had spotted the wrong 'un as soon as I started to run up, it was not alarming but rather an intensely interesting experience to bowl at him, and always something of an occasion.' Nor had his fielding appeared to betray his advancing years, as Frank Woolley recalled: 'Jack's fielding in the last ten years of his career was even more wonderful than his batting. I question if ever before anyone has retained quickness of foot and hand movement, not to mention that of eye, so late in life to the amazing extent that Jack did. When well over the forty mark he was even more agile than many young men under twenty-five.' As elsewhere, however, the embittered critic Arthur Carr used Hobbs's fielding as another stick with which to beat him, making the bizarre complaint that Hobbs had never bothered to train himself to be ambidextrous at cover. 'Jack was such a supreme cricketer that such an accomplishment should not have been beyond him and think how useful it would have been.'

But Hobbs could not go on for ever. At the start of the 1930 season, he was aged forty-seven and his fitness, if not his skill, was not longer reliable. As *Wisden* pointed out in the 1930 annual, Hobbs had missed forty of Surrey's 108 championship games over the previous four summers due to various indispositions. For years, Hobbs had been publicly talking, at least in theory, about his imminent retirement. Every series since 1926 had ended with warnings that Hobbs had supposedly played his last Test. On the other hand, cricket's greatest prize, the Ashes, was at stake in 1930 and few cricketers could resist its allure. Just as importantly, the partnership of Hobbs and Sutcliffe, synonymous with England's recent Ashes glory, was still seen as essential to success and no alternative opening batsman had emerged in the late 1920s. If Hobbs's international career really was soon to come to an end, there could be no grander arena in which to say farewell than a series against the old enemy.

The significance of Hobbs to the outcome of the Ashes was reflected in a humorous moment when, soon after their arrival in London, the

Australians were introduced on stage to the audience during a variety show at the Coliseum Theatre. As part of the welcome, the famous cartoonist Tom Webster gave them a wire-haired terrier as a mascot, handing the dog over with the warning, 'He has instructions to bite anybody who gets Jack Hobbs out in the first over.' Hobbs, who was in the auditorium at the Coliseum, recalled that the team, led by Bill Woodfull, was given a 'tremendous reception', which reflected how much excitement there was over the forthcoming series. 'It is difficult to recall a season in which the cricket public have looked forward so eagerly as is the case this year,' wrote Plum Warner in the *Cricketer*.

As the Tests approached, England's followers were confident of maintaining the recent run of victories. Part of this buoyant mood rested on the perceived weakness of the Australian side's bowling, which was heavily reliant on Grimmett and contained no other Test stars. 'Batting strong, fielding brilliant, with bowling an unknown quantity. I see no reason why we should lose the Ashes,' was Hobbs's balanced verdict. Several Australian commentators were much more negative: 'They might easily be a colossal failure. I don't see how they can be a tremendous success,' wrote Charlie Macartney. What none of the analysis could have foreseen, however, was the almost freakish dominance of Don Bradman, who was to rewrite numerous records in the series, sink the England team into bewildered helplessness and establish himself as by far the greatest batsman in world cricket. During the MCC trip of 1928/9 England had seen his talent at first hand, but he had seemed then just another fine Australian player rather than a superhuman genius. This lack of any feeling of awe was reflected in the assessment that Hobbs made at the end of the MCC tour in March 1929: 'Don Bradman is very good indeed; he has the strokes and he also has the asset of confidence. If he comes to England next year, as no doubt he will, I am sure he will be popular with the crowd.' In another forecast, made in January 1930, Hobbs compared Bradman with himself in his youth. 'Bradman reminds me of my own early days. He is a cheeky bat, who does not always realise the dangers as we older players do. I used to go for the bowling all out and play some brilliant knocks when I did not know enough to be afraid of certain strokes. Bradman is like that.' As with the rest of the cricket world, Hobbs's admiration would change to stupefaction as the summer unfolded.

In the spring of 1930, Hobbs had settled all the doubts as to whether he would play in the Tests if invited. Returning from a golfing holiday with Strudwick in Cornwall at the end of March, he gave an interview to the journalist and novelist James Lansdale Hodson,* then working for the *Daily News*. When Hodson asked him about the upcoming series, he said, 'I've no option but to play if asked.' Hodson was certain that Hobbs was ready for the task ahead, as he noted with his literary touch, 'Bronzed with the golf at St Ives, his brown eyes bright and clear, his lithe strong hands gripping yours with the firmness of a cricket bat, he looks admirably fit for the practice that starts in three weeks' time.' But Hobbs warned of the exhausting pressure that Test cricket imposed on England players at home. 'It keys you up tremendously – far more than a Test abroad. You are as an actor on his first night – only your audience, seen and unseen, is infinitely greater.' Such stress did nothing to alleviate the migraines that always plagued Hobbs. But here he was at the age of forty-seven, ready to throw himself into the fray once more.

There was no doubt that, having declared his availability, Hobbs would be chosen for England, particularly as he immediately found his form at the start of the season. In the very first match of the season, against Glamorgan at the Oval, he made a century in each innings for the fifth time in his career. 'Hobbs the incomparable! Once again the idol of Surrey cricket has shown that age cannot dim his brilliance,' declared the *Daily Chronicle*. 'Hobbs is certain to open for England again in the forthcoming Tests. The Australians admit that Hobbs is a "nightmare" to them, and while early proof of his form may be appreciated, it will not be altogether welcome.'

Hobbs kept up his run-scoring in the next few weeks. In ten matches before the first Test in mid-June, Hobbs scored seven half centuries, including a fine 80 for England in the Test trial against the Rest at Lord's, though this innings ended in controversial circumstances, when he was caught low down at slip by Kumar Duleepsinhji, a nephew of Ranji's, off the medium-pace of Stan Worthington, the Derbyshire all-rounder. Again belying the myth of his unalloyed gallantry, Hobbs refused to accept the word of Duleepshinhji that the ball had been cleanly caught. Instead he stood his ground and the Rest had to appeal to the umpire, who gave him out. An even bigger row over a similar incident would soon follow in the Test series.

---

* His greatest novel, *For King and Country*, was an epic about the First World War. It was later turned into a successful film with Dirk Bogarde.

For the first time in England the 1930 Tests were scheduled over four days, to avoid the glut of draws that had marked the 1926 series. Once more Hobbs and Rhodes were co-opted onto the England selection committee, which was chaired by Leveson Gower, with Jack White and the former Middlesex captain Frank Mann the other members. Their job became increasingly difficult as England wilted under the onslaught of Bradman's bat. Yet the first Test at Trent Bridge seemed to offer the hope of ultimate victory in the series over Woodfull's side. Restored to the captaincy, Percy Chapman elected to bat after winning the toss. There was some moisture in the wicket on the first morning, but Hobbs and Sutcliffe gave England their customary solid start against lively bowling from Tim Wall and Alan Fairfax, putting on 58 before the Yorkshireman fell. The rest of the batting order struggled after that, except for Hobbs who lasted almost the whole day until he was seventh out for 78, caught in the slips off Stan McCabe. Plum Warner wrote that Hobbs showed 'his usual skill and judgement, and England would have been in a sorry plight but for him', while the Daily Mirror was even more effusive. 'Of Hobbs's batting, it is impossible to speak too highly. From the start he was quite happy, never attempting scoring feats but playing every ball absolutely on its merits. He scored from the loose ones and occasionally picked bumping balls from Wall almost from his eyebrows. Grimmett had no terrors for him, although he played him watchfully and carefully. It was just Jack saving England again.' Even with Hobbs's contribution, the score of 270 looked inadequate until Australia subsided to 144, giving England a lead of 126.

In his second innings Hobbs capitalised on this advantage with a captivating return to his old, more aggressive style during a stand of 125 with Sutcliffe. His first real mistake occurred only when, on 74, he advanced down the wicket to Grimmett, misjudged the flight and was stumped by Oldfield. Fender described the innings as 'one of the most brilliant' he had ever seen from Hobbs. 'He gave the bowlers no rest and though he did not take any real risks, he introduced an ingenuity and versatility into his batting which soon had Woodfull and his bowlers at their wits' end. No one could keep him quiet and whenever he found runs difficult to get in the orthodox way, he would step in front of his off-stump and sweep the ball from outside that stump to the leg boundary with precision and confidence.' In the same vein, the Daily Express reported that 'the autumn of his cricketing life has not yet been reached, and anyone who did not know him or who was a trifle short-sighted would have said today that he was a sprightly youth, with his best years before him.' The paper further argued that Hobbs 'must not be permitted' to retired prematurely, claiming that 'in many respects, Hobbs is England'. Don Bradman was another who was impressed. 'I only saw him when he was past his prime but he was the best-equipped batsman of all – in the technical sense, English or Australian. I could detect no flaw in his attack or defence. His footwork was always correct, stroke-production sound.'

Hobbs was the top scorer in England's second innings of 335, a total that set Australia a daunting 429 to win. Woodfull's team mounted a heroic challenge, aided by an ominous 131 from Bradman, and at one stage, when Stan McCabe was cutting loose, it looked as if the target might just be reached. Then came the final day's extraordinary turning point. England had been forced to field a substitute, Sydney Copley, after Sutcliffe's thumb had been split by a short ball from Wall in the second innings. A member of the Trent Bridge ground staff, Copley had never played first-class cricket but he had a good reputation as an outfielder. 'On my arrival that morning the tannoy system was calling my name to report to the secretary's office,' Copley remembered years later. 'On arriving there I met the captain Percy Chapman and Jack Hobbs. I was asked how I would like to substitute for England. I was thrilled to do so, of course. I had done a lot of twefth-man duty for the Nottinghamshire XI so I was not too nervous, just a little. Hobbs put me at my ease with a few kind words.' Copley was fielding at mid-on when Stan McCabe, on 49, smashed the ball to his right. It was a ferocious drive, not far off the turf but Copley ran forward and dived full-length to make the catch one-handed. 'I seized the ball and turned a somersault, still clinging to the ball,' he said. A dangerous partnership was broken. Australia's last hopes vanished as England went on to win by 93 runs. Sadly for Copley, the rest of his game did not match the quality of his fielding. He made only one first-class appearance before emigrating to the Isle of Man, where he became a groundsman and coach.

At this stage of the season, Hobbs seemed to have the full measure of the Australian bowling, his authority reinforced by an innings of 146 for Surrey against the Australians straight after the first Test. 'He has done enough to prove that he is still absolutely indispensable for England's best eleven,' said the *Cricketer*. The problem was with Sutcliffe, whose injured hand meant that he was unfit for the second Test at Lord's. The obvious choice for the selectors would have been to bring in Hobbs's own Surrey partner Andy Sandham, who not only made 176 against Essex in the week that the Lord's team was chosen, but had also demonstrated his temperament in April when he made 325 for England against the West Indies in Jamaica, the first triple century in Test cricket. Indeed, Sandham was called up to the England squad but, at the last minute, his claims were ignored. Instead, the selectors decided to move Frank Woolley up the order to open with Hobbs, despite the fact that Woolley had failed dismally in both innings at Trent Bridge. The change badly unsettled Hobbs. His sureness deserted him, his running was uncertain. From his vantage point behind the wicket, Oldfield felt that Hobbs was 'strangely affected by having a new partner', while Peebles wrote that, 'Hobbs was always the senior partner accustomed to make the going and dictate policy. It was clear that Woolley would pursue his own line from sheer force of habit and was not, in the nature of things, capable of playing second fiddle to anyone, however great.' Hobbs's unease saw him dismissed for just 1 in the first innings and 19 in the second, as England slumped to a seven-wicket defeat after Australia scored 729 for 6, still their highest ever Ashes score. Don Bradman, with 254, was said by Neville Cardus to have committed a 'cool, deliberate murder' of the England bowling.

Hobbs was so disconcerted by his performance in the second Test that he actually told the selectors he felt he should stand down. What had particularly disturbed him was the nature of his dismissal in the second innings, when he was bowled around his legs by a Grimmett half volley. The selectors, however, would hear none of it, and insisted that he play in the third Test at Headingley. Despite the restoration of his partnership with Sutcliffe, whose split thumb had healed, Hobbs's woes continued, as did those of England. On the first day at Headingly, Bradman slaughtered the bowling attack to score 309 runs, a record that will probably never be beaten. 'He was too good; he spoilt the game. He got too many runs. He was mechanical. He was the greatest run-machine of all time. I do not think we want to see another one quite like him,' Hobbs once said. Eventually, on the second day, Bradman was out for 334, made off only 448 balls. England, beginning their first innings shortly before lunch, faced a colossal Australian total of 566 but Hobbs and Sutcliffe managed to negotiate their way to 53 with few alarms. Then, with his score on 29, Hobbs was out in a sensational manner. He pushed a leg-break from Grimmett defensively but uppishly to the leg-side, where Ted a'Beckett was fielding at silly-mid on. With electric reactions, a'Beckett dived forward, rolled over and came to a kneeling position with a smile on his face and the ball in his hands. The Australians came over to congratulate him. Hobbs refused to budge, uncertain as to whether the ball had bounced before a'Beckett caught it. 'If I had been sure I was out I would not have stayed a moment. I would rather be in the pavilion if I knew I was out,' he wrote in his 1931 book *Playing For England*. According to his account, he turned to Bert Oldfield and asked, 'Did he catch it, Bertie?' to which Oldfield apparently replied, 'No.' This led Hobbs to remark, 'If Oldfield had said I was out everything would have been different.' Yet Hobbs's approach was not nearly as high-minded as it might superficially have sounded. Effectively, he was arguing that Oldfield's word was to be trusted but not a'Beckett's. Such an approach ran counter to all the best traditions of chivalry in cricket, where the honesty of a fielder who had made a borderline catch was meant to be accepted. In a sense, it was the exact reverse of the Kippax incident of eighteen months earlier. Most of the Australian players were indignant that Hobbs had not walked and vociferously appealed to Tom Oates, the umpire at the bowler's end. He said he was unsighted and so referred the decision to his colleague at square leg, Bill Bestwick, who gave Hobbs out after a long delay that only heightened the feverish mood of the crowd. The *Sydney Sun* reported, 'Eventually Hobbs walked out, looking disturbed. From the press box, behind a'Beckett, one thing was definitely clear and that was that the square leg umpire must have seen what had happened. In addition, there was a spontaneous appeal from all the players.'

Such testimony rather undermined Hobbs's claim that Oldfield disagreed with a'Beckett, as did the admission of Sir Edwin Stockton, the Chairman of Lancashire County Cricket Club and former Tory MP, who said that he was 'in a fairly good position and it was a clean catch'. This was confirmed by subsequent photos, which showed beyond dispute that the ball had carried to a'Beckett. Later that day, according to Don Bradman's authorised biographer Roland Perry, 'Hobbs went to the Australian dressing room to explain his hesitation at the wicket and met with a barrage of unnecessary abuse from Vic Richardson, who told the Englishman to check the scoreboard.'

In the face of a superb spell from Grimmett amid some lengthy interruptions for rain, England were unable to avoid the follow-on, and the opening pair went out at the start of the second innings on a heavily overcast final afternoon. Soon Hobbs was enveloped in more controversy when he appealed against the light once Grimmett came on at the pavilion end. Given that England were fighting for a draw, it was a perfectly understandable move, but it went down badly with the fans who felt that conditions were playable. The umpires did not agree and took the teams off. As Hobbs and Sutcliffe walked back to the pavilion, they were greeted by the unprecedented sound of loud booing from their own supporters. Hobbs was infuriated by the whole episode, calling the condemnation of his action 'deplorable' since the critics had no idea what it was like to face Grimmett, with his 'low trajectory' bowling against the backdrop of a 'big shadowy stand' with storm clouds above. 'It is so very easy to see from the pavilion seats,' he said later with heavy sarcasm.

Soon the light improved, forcing England to return to the middle. Hobbs's misery continued a few overs later, when he hit Grimmett towards mid-off and called Sutcliffe through for what appeared to be another of their classic quick singles. But they had not reckoned on the speed of Don Bradman, who ran out Hobbs with a direct hit on the stumps at the bowler's end. It was the first time in their long partnership that there had ever been a run-out. Reporting for the *Sydney Sun*, Arthur Mailey thought that Hobbs may have been the victim of the kind of deception he had so often practised against his opponents. Earlier in the over, wrote Mailey, 'Sutcliffe played a ball to Bradman, who lazily threw it back to the bowler, giving Hobbs and Sutcliffe the impression that an easy run could be obtained. Next ball, Grimmett sent down a similar delivery, and Hobbs played it to Bradman who, unseen, had sneaked five yards closer. Picking it up like lightning, he threw Hobbs's wicket down. Hobbs never looked at the umpire, being yards out of his crease, but walked to the pavilion with bowed head.' Hobbs had made just 13, his fourth failure in a row. There was a poignant symbolism about the dismissal, the sense not just off of Hobbs's increasing fallibility, but also of the baton of greatness passing from one generation to another.

England held on easily for a draw at Headingley, the last afternoon shortened by more poor weather. But Hobbs was despondent at his lack of runs and exhausted by the hysteria that Test cricket now generated. His wife Ada felt that his selectorial duties were interfering with his batting. 'He has worried himself a great deal over the selection of the England teams. His work as a selector has meant much inconvenience for him and I am certain all this has done Jack's play no good,' she said. Again, on the eve of the fourth Test at Old Trafford, he offered to stand down for a younger man. This time certain commentators, such as the *Daily Mirror's* sports editor P.J. Moss, supported his view and called on the selectors to bring in a new opening pair. 'We have relied too much on the old brigade; the day of the old Surrey–Yorkshire partnership is surely past. Hobbs says he is tired, and that one match a week would be enough for him,' wrote Moss. In contrast, Trevor Wignall of the *Daily Express*, Hobbs's stoutest defender in the press, was outraged at the calls for his hero's omission. 'This saddens me. The selectors can do what they like about Woolley, Hammond, Hendren, White, Allen and Robins, but Hobbs – oh no, he cannot be dropped.' That was how the other selectors felt and Hobbs, against his better judgement, stayed in the XI for Manchester. 'I'm too old. I'm forty-seven. Forty used to be the age when cricketers finished with first-class matches. But I've no option if I'm asked,' he told the *Daily News*.

In contrast to the pattern of the previous two Tests, England's bowling attack at Manchester managed to contain the Australians. Their total was only 345, though many felt the Australians should have been out for much less after they had slumped to 243 for 7 and Bradman had made just 14, a victim of Ian Peebles's clever leg-spin. After his recent failures, Hobbs was determined to do nothing rash at the start of England's reply. He opened in restrained style, only to find that his movements were further restricted by a vicious break back from Tim Wall that thudded into his groin and left him in agony. He limped on courageously until he and Sutcliffe had put on 108, their eleventh century partnership against Australia. Then, on 31, he tried to cut a short delivery from Wall and only succeeded in edging it to Oldfield. His had been a brave innings of stout defence spread over two hours but it had no effect on the outcome, as heavy rain on the third and fourth days prevented England from even completing their first innings. The two teams would now go to the final Test at the Oval with the series all square. As in 1926, since the outcome was still undecided, the match would played to a finish.

Whatever the result, Hobbs made it clear that, if he were picked, this would definitely be his last appearance in Test cricket. The speculation about his international future had dragged on for years and he was determined to bring it to an end. 'There will be no more after the Oval game. I'm getting on, you know,' he told the press. The feeling of relief that the end was in sight seemed to revive Hobbs after all his recent travails against Australia. Soon after the fourth Test, Hobbs scored 106 against Sussex at Hastings, a 'faultless' performance, according to the *Cricketer*. This innings meant that Hobbs had scored a century home and away against every county during his career. It was also his 125th hundred for Surrey, his 152nd in England and his 174th in all first-class cricket. His score left him just fifteen short of W.G. Grace's career aggregate of 54,896 first-class runs, and he looked almost certain to break the record in Surrey's second innings at Hastings when he was struck down with painful neuritis in his shoulder. So, on his doctor's orders, he had to sit out the match in a deckchair under the August sun, puffing on his pipe with Ada on one side and his bespectacled daughter Vera on the other, both of them having come down to the south coast for a break. Hobbs had sufficiently recovered to play in the next game, a friendly against Middlesex at the Oval, during which he scored 40 and passed the record set by W.G. Grace. Hobbs often liked to adopt a pose of insouciance towards statistics, but, as he showed in the draining summer of 1925, they could matter to him. 'I hope this year – or next – to pass W.G.'s record,' he said at the start of the season. On 8 August 1930 he did so, prompting the *Daily Express* to state in an editorial, 'This is the occasion to thank him for all he has done for the national game, not only by his prowess at the wicket and in the field but through the influence of his sterling, modest and most sportsman-like personality.' The *Star* paid tribute to his 'magnificent achievement' and urged him 'to go on play for as many years as he himself feels sufficiently fit to stand the strain'.

Praise for Hobbs's aggregate was eclipsed, however, by the feverish excitement over the selection of the team for the deciding Oval Test. As soon as the Old Trafford match was over, sensational rumours began to circulate that Percy Chapman was about to be sacked from the captaincy. The symmetry with the 1926 series was striking. Once again a dynamic but flawed leader, with an aggressive batting style and a fondness for drink, had presided over a series that hung in the balance, only to find himself the target of selectorial discontent as the final match approached. Most of the press and public thought that the talk about the threat to Chapman's leadership was nonsense. 'I cannot credit even now that anything like the suicidal policy of dropping Chapman has been contemplated,' wrote Trevor Wignall, the *Express's* influential pundit. Yet the reality was that the Leveson Gower's selection committee, including Hobbs, had indeed lost faith in Chapman. There were several reasons for this. One was that his batting was felt to be too inconsistent, too cavalier for a timeless Test. It was true he had scored a century in the second innings at Lord's by blazing away heroically, but the match had been all but lost by then. There was also a feeling that he had lost his tactical awareness in the field. At Manchester, his field placings and bowling changes were heavily criticised. Typical was Fender's complaint that Chapman had handled Peebles badly and been 'slow on the uptake' over the setting of the slip cordon. In the *Cricketer* Plum Warner, always a barometer of establishment opinion, argued that Chapman 'is not the tactician he was' and had given away 70 runs in the field with his poor deployment of his men. But another, more personal factor was at work, hidden from public view. This was the mounting disapproval within official circles towards Chapman's enthusiasm for alcohol, which some felt was undermining his leadership ability and setting a poor example. There were whispers that at Old Trafford he had not been entirely sober every session, and a few eyebrows were raised at his eagerness to attend the after-dinner parties jointly hosted by the cartoonist Tom Webster and the playwright Ben Travers in their Manchester hotel. The selectors, said Travers, 'didn't think that Percy Chapman was conducting himself as an England captain should'.

The imminence of Hobbs's international retirement added a further ingredient to the cocktail of intrigue about Chapman's position. In the days before the Oval Test, a flurry of reports appeared, claiming that the selectors planned to give the captaincy to Hobbs as a gesture of appreciation at the end of his wonderful Test career. The idea had actually been first mooted in late June in the *Star*, the evening paper of the *News Chronicle* group, which had commented on a proposal from several journalists and retired players in Australia that the elevation of Hobbs to the leadership in the final Test 'would be graceful tribute to the prince of Test batsmen'. Little attention was paid to this item until 7 August, the eve of the selectors' crucial meeting to pick the team for the Oval, when the *News Chronicle* appeared. Under a banner headline that read

'Will Hobbs Replace Chapman?' the *Chronicle* reported that 'rumours were current yesterday of sensational changes in our next Test team, involving even the captaincy. Cricket gossips in London were discussing the matter with much head-wagging . . . One interesting suggestion heard last night was that, if there is to be a change of captaincy, it would be a graceful compliment to Jack Hobbs if he were invited to lead England in the last Test match in which he is likely to play.' In an editorial in the same edition, the *Chronicle* gave its full backing to the change. 'If, as is rumoured, Chapman is to be left out of the Oval match, there will, we are sure, be general agreement with the suggestion that the captaincy should be offered to Hobbs. No better occasion could be chosen for setting the precedent of deliberately selecting a professional cricketer to captain an English side . . . He has done more for English cricket than any other man of his time, professional or amateur. His knowledge of the game and his experience in the field are unsurpassed, and there is no cricketer in the world better liked by his colleagues or whose judgement carries more respect.'

A few days later, before the team had been announced, the *Chronicle* was keeping up the drumbeat for Hobbs. 'The choice of Hobbs, should it be made, would be an immensely popular one.' The *Chronicle*'s coverage was not mere over-excited guesswork, but showed signs that it was partly based on inside information. One possible conclusion is that Hobbs himself, always a more complex, subtle man than his image of simplicity suggested, was feeding snippets to the paper. He was, after all, far closer to the *Chronicle* publications than to any other newspaper. He regularly wrote exclusive articles for them. Excerpts from his 1928/9 tour diary were published in their papers. His devoted chief ghostwriter, the burly Lancastrian Jack Ingham, was on the group's staff and Hobbs joined the company as a columnist when he retired from Test cricket. The flaw in this argument is that Hobbs never wanted the captaincy of either England or Surrey, so he had little reason to give his backing to a newspaper campaign for his promotion. What is more likely to have happened is that Hobbs, through his closeness to Ingham and his sense of obligation to the *Chronicle* group, privately explained the thinking of the selectors and this was then turned into sensationalist reports with added journalistic conjecture. But Hobbs would not have kept feeding the *News Chronicle* and *Star* if he had objected to their coverage. His willingness to do so may have had three motivations. First of all, he wanted to heighten the pressure for Chapman to be sacked on grounds of both his batting and his capacity for leadership. Hobbs was no prig, but as a teetotaller he cannot have been impressed by Chapman's incipient alcoholism. Second, his innate sense of mischief must have relished all the swirling gossip; his pleasure in sowing confusion and annoyance lay behind much of his practical joking. The third was simple delight in acclaim. Hobbs was renowned for his modesty, but the insecurities from his upbringing meant that he liked to be accorded the respect he deserved. He kept scrapbooks filled with press cuttings about his achievements and, as he admitted, he was 'highly sensitive' to criticism. In such a context, it would have been hard for him to resist feeling gratified at the stream of plaudits about his stature.

The selectors met on 8 August 1930 and the England team was formally revealed four days later, the delay caused by the need to check on the availability of the new captain. The *News Chronicle* had been proved only half right. Chapman was indeed dropped. His replacement, however, was not Hobbs but the Warwickshire skipper Bob Wyatt. Remote, tough, a solid batsman and useful bowler, Wyatt had nothing like Chapman's charisma or popularity, yet the selectors believed he was the man to instil more discipline into the England side, though he may not have been their first choice. According to the *News Chronicle*'s report of the meeting on 8 August, the decision to sack Chapman was not unanimous. White and Rhodes were said to favour his retention, while Hobbs, Mann and Leveson Gower wanted 'fresh blood'. Leveson Gower subsequently denied that he had used his casting vote in favour of change, claiming that there had been no vote at all at the meeting but there was no doubt that the selectors were divided. The *Chronicle* reported that, having reached this decision, the committee then offered the captaincy to Hobbs who turned it down because of his ingrained modesty and dislike of responsibility. Such a move is certainly conceivable, since Leveson Gower, Surrey's President, was a strong admirer of Hobbs. Rhodes and White also thought of him highly through their long experience of serving with him for England. In confirmation of this report, it is perhaps telling that on the county circuit, there was a widespread belief that Hobbs had been offered the job and rejected it. Bill Bowes, in his readable autobiography *Express Deliveries*, recorded that Herbert Sutcliffe was 'deeply disappointed' with Hobbs's decision. 'For the sake of the professional cricketer, he should have accepted,'

Sutcliffe told Bowes, a view that contradicted the *Chronicle*'s assertion
that 'Hobbs refused for reasons which will certainly not diminish the
affectionate regard in which the greatest cricketer of the day is held.' It
was, apparently, only after Hobbs's rejection that the committee turned
to Wyatt. Though he found the whole controversy overblown, Hobbs
in later years said he came to regret what the committee had done to
Chapman. 'As I look back, I think we made a mistake in leaving him
out,' he wrote in his 1935 autobiography. 'He was a very popular captain;
he knew his men and he also knew the Australians. The sole idea of
the Selection Committee was to strengthen the England batting.'

   The dramatic news of Chapman's sacking caused a storm. The former
captain and selector Arthur Gilligan spoke for many when he described
the move as 'one of the biggest cricket blunders ever made. It is a
national calamity – even more, it is nothing short of a crime.' *The Times*
said that 'you would have thought the entire country was in support
of the previous captain'. Such was the level of outrage that Wyatt received
a telegram with the message, 'If you play at the Oval, pistols await you.'
There was wild talk of a mass demonstration outside the ground and
protests inside.

   As it turned out, much of the uproar was media froth. Wyatt was
given a warm reception when he went out to toss with Woodfull on
the first morning, without a single voice of dissent from the near-
capacity crowd of 30,000. He called correctly and elected to bat in bright
sunshine on what looked to be a perfect wicket. Hobbs and Sutcliffe
started smoothly, and then the Surrey master began to play with more
freedom, displaying the cuts, drives and pulls that had barely been seen
since the first Test at Nottingham. A deft hook for four from a bouncer
by Tim Wall brought him to 47 in 115 minutes, with the England score
on 68. When Wall pitched short again with next delivery, Hobbs went
for another hook, only this time the ball was faster. To the agony of the
crowd, he miscued it to short leg, where Kippax held a simple catch.
'Twenty years ago the ball would have been at the boundary, but at
forty-seven you do not see the ball as quickly as you do at twenty-seven,'
said the *Cricketer* rather cruelly. After Hobbs's dismissal, England slipped
to 197 for 5, only to be rescued by a defiant stand of 170 between
Sutcliffe and Wyatt, who received another fervent round of applause
when he went out to bat. But England's total of 405 looked woefully
inadequate once Bradman got going. He hit his third double century

of the series, taking his aggregate to 974, still easily a record for Test cricket. 'A run-getting machine,' was how Hobbs described him. 'Bradman never hit the ball in the air. He had an exceptionally accurate sense of timing. He had marvellous sight. The pace he got into his hits on the leg-side was astounding.' Helped by some dire wicket keeping by Duckworth, Australia reached 695 towards the end of the fourth day. England, 290 runs behind, now had forty-five minutes to survive until the close.

Fearing that Hobbs might be affected by the emotion of the occasion, allied to exhaustion from nearly two days spent in the field, Wyatt offered to send in another batsman alongside Sutcliffe that evening. Ian Peebles, who witnessed the scene in the dressing room, wrote that 'the Master was adamant. This was his last appearance for England and he was determined to open the innings, a desire which Bob granted without further argument and so it was.' Wyatt confirmed this in his memoirs. 'I asked Hobbs himself what he would like to do. He was absolutely definite. He would like to open the England innings in his accustomed way.' So, for the last time, Hobbs and Sutcliffe went out to bat together. The light was beginning to fade as evening clouds gathered above the famous old gasometer. A mood of pathos hung in the air. The yearning of the spectators for Hobbs to save England once more was mixed with the melancholic recognition that the end of an era had arrived. Then, out of the darkness of the Victorian pavilion which had witnessed so many of his triumphs, Hobbs emerged wearing his dark blue England cap, accompanied by the raven-haired, hatless Sutcliffe. A sudden, heart-rending roar went up from every part of the ground, the ovation lasting until the pair reached the middle. Then, as the cheering diminished, Bill Woodfull performed an unprecedented act. Having gathered his team round the wicket, he led them in a chorus for three cheers for Hobbs. The salute for the old warrior could hardly have been more affecting. 'It certainly brought a lump into the throats of our players,' recalled Oldfield. Visibly moved by the gesture, Hobbs took off his cap to acknowledge the applause, which had now been taken up once more by the crowd. He wanted to shake Woodfull by the hand, but, typically, his self-conscious nature prevented him from doing so, for, as he put it, 'I was afraid lest the onlookers behind the ropes would think I was "playing up", so I drew back.' But he had been profoundly touched by the incident. 'I shall never forget it as long as I live. It went right to my heart. It still goes to my heart whenever I think of it.'

The opponents might have been united in chivalry, but they now had to proceed with the game. England desperately needed another of those immense partnerships in which Hobbs and Sutcliffe had special-ised for so long. It was not to be. Hobbs, the batsman with the iron-clad Test temperament, was for once edgy. He was almost out when he stopped a ball dead in front of him and started to run. The bowler Tim Wall hurtled down the wicket, kicked the ball at the stumps and just missed them, with Hobbs stranded well out of his crease. Then in the next over, with his score on just 9, Hobbs had to face the medium-pace of Alan Fairfax, not a bowler who would have given him much trouble in the past. Fairfax came in and sent down an inswinger on his off-stump. Hobbs shaped to pull but only succeeded in bottom-edging the ball into his wicket. He had been bowled for single figures, a bitter anti-climax. 'He paused sadly for a moment, then walked quietly back to the pavilion and out of Test-match cricket. He took with him much of England's hope of recovery in the current match, and a quarter of a century of glorious memories,' wrote Peebles. *The Times* left this moving description of his exit: 'So he fell, this prince among batsmen, and departed from the scene he had dominated for twenty years. It was a saddened man who walked into the pavilion. Emotion, it was obvious, had seized him. He dropped his glove as he went and stooped, like a man in a dream, to pick it up. The Oval spectators, disappointed as they were, cheered affectionately. The little wicket gate swung – Hobbs passed through and disappeared for ever from the Test-match scene.'

Stopped by a reporter inside the pavilion, Hobbs made a brief comment: 'Well, that is the end. I wish I could have made some runs. England needs them so badly.' He then retreated into the sanctuary of the England dressing room, and was commiserated by the other players, for whom he had only a disappointed smile. Watching his departure in the encircling gloom had been Ada, so full of pride for her beloved husband. 'The most dreadful moment of my life! That was how I felt when Jack was out in the second innings of the Oval Test match. He felt so fit; he was so anxious to do well,' she said soon afterwards. 'I knew it was a terrible disappointment to Jack when he chopped that ball into his wicket before he reached double figures – a ball that might just as easily have gone in a hundred different directions. I believe many of his friends in the stands were as moved as I was. All were most sympathetic.' Even Bradman, famous for his ruthlessness, shared in this sense of regret. 'I felt sorry when the old Master pulled a ball from Alan Fairfax into his wicket for 9. I wanted to see him make a good score in his final appearance,' he wrote.

The sense of dejection worsened the next day as England plunged to an innings defeat, all out for 251. The national game had lost both its greatest player and the Ashes. But Percy Fender, while admitting to 'an empty feeling' over the events at the Oval, tried to raise spirits by reminding the public of Hobbs's achievements: 'None of us can stage our exit in exactly the manner we would choose and Jack has had a wonderful career in Test as well as in all other cricket. Quite apart from the runs he has made, The Master has something equally if not more valuable to his credit, and that is the respect, almost the veneration, in which his name is held, not only by those who have played with and against him. The most perfect batsman of his generation, perhaps of all generations, he has charmed and thrilled thousands with his genius, and added to the glamour of his name and deed by the delightful nature of his personality and bearing. Jack was a Power, but remained a Man, and his name represents the high-water mark in cricket and the very best in the character of an Englishman.'

17

'It Was Too Much For Jack'

Hobbs experienced a profound sense of disappointment after his farewell at the Oval. His batting against Australia, apart from the Nottingham Test, had been mediocre, with his average falling to 33.44, and for the only time in his career he went through a full Ashes series without scoring a century. A week after the end of the series, he expressed his feelings in a BBC interview conducted by the former South African all-rounder Aubrey Faulkner:* 'I really started off this season not wanting to play. But I was persuaded to start again – and I am disappointed I did not do better. I was ever so keen on justifying my inclusion.' With a refreshing lack of false humility, he also admitted that his pride would be dented by his retirement from Test cricket. 'It's not comforting to feel I will no longer be a power in the land. I have found personal success very gratifying. I think it's going to be hard for me to drop out of it all.' Yet this regret was mingled with relief that he would no longer have to endure the strain of Test cricket, which he had found increasingly tiring in his late forties. Furthermore, he was touched by the expressions of public goodwill that followed his exit, reflected in accolades from former cricketers and in his huge postbag. 'I want to say how deeply I appreciate the many tributes which have been paid to me. I have received scores and scores of letters and they are still being delivered as a write,' he said in the *Star*.

Yet it would be wrong to exaggerate the depth of the public grief over his departure from the Test arena. The attention given to Hobbs

---

* Tragically, less than a fortnight after this broadcast, Faulkner committed suicide. He had been plagued by depression for years. Hobbs said that the news of his death came as a deep shock, for he had been 'very cheery' during their interview.

in August 1930 was nothing like that in 1925, the year of the challenge on Grace's record, or even in 1926, when he and Sutcliffe helped to wrest back the Ashes. The series loss and Hobbs's ordinary form militated against another vast display of public affection. This was graphically illustrated when the *Daily Herald* decided, during the Oval Test, to set up a testimonial fund for Hobbs 'as a tribute to our greatest player'. To ensure the widest possible participation, the paper fixed the minimum contribution at just sixpence. 'Nobody should be shy of sending a single sixpence if it is all they can afford,' said the paper, whose scheme had been inspired by the hugely successful shilling fund established as a testimonial for W.G. Grace in 1895 when the Grand Old Man was forty-seven, exactly the same age as Hobbs on his Test retirement. Grace's testimonial, which had been jointly led by the *Daily Telegraph* and the MCC, raised a phenomenal £9,073 but the *Herald* hoped easily to eclipse that sum with its sixpenny fund for Hobbs. 'There is not the smallest reason why it should close with a total of 1,000,000 sixpences. If every reader of the *Daily Herald* sends one sixpence only, it will very much exceed this total,' said its editorial. One million sixpences translated into £25,000, almost ten times what Hobbs had received in his 1926 Surrey benefit. Yet the *Herald* was confident the target could be achieved, and over the next month it kept up a barrage of publicity for the cause. There were continual reports about the money rolling into the paper's Fleet Street office. The sixpenny fund was said to have caught the imagination of the British public, with donations coming from every walk of life. 'Cabinet Ministers, racing men, sombre politicians and football enthusiasts have jumped at the idea,' proclaimed the paper. The Labour Prime Minister Ramsay MacDonald, Charlie Chaplin, and the tea merchant Sir Thomas Lipton were all reported to be backing the fund. Herbert Sutcliffe, Prince Ranjitsinhji, Maurice Tate and Bob Wyatt were among the leading figures from the cricket world to lend their support. 'Hobbs has done more for the greatest of English games than any other individual player. He is worthy of national appreciation and I hope the fund will be a great success,' said Wyatt. But the increasingly desperate hype could not hide the reality that the sixpenny testimonial was a flop. Far from raising tens of thousands of pounds, the fund brought in only £500, just 2 per cent of the original target. Even this modest total overstated the public's contribution, for around £250 came from the *Herald* itself, and another £52 was given by the popular sports paper, *Sporting Life*. In late September the *Daily Herald* rather sheepishly handed over the £500 cheque to Hobbs, the figures having been rounded up by the paper's management to prevent further embarrassment. With typical courtesy, Hobbs expressed his gratitude. 'It is a wonderful thing to have done, and I appreciate it very much,' he said. Privately, he told the *Herald*'s reporter that 'the money will be invested in gilt-edged securities', another indicator of how far Hobbs had risen; gilt-edged securities had certainly never been discussed round the bare kitchen table of 4 Rivar Place in the 1890s. But Hobbs was well aware of how badly the testimonial had fallen below expectations, and struck a defensive note when he explained, 'Under the circumstances of the fund being launched at the wane of the season, the result is very pleasing.' It was true that the timing had contributed to its failure, coming at the very moment when the Ashes defeat and Hobbs's decline were felt most keenly. But there were two more political factors that doomed the *Herald*'s initiative from the start. One was the harsh economic climate. Following the Wall Street crash of 1929, Britain had been gripped by severe depression and rising unemployment, so there was little sense of personal prosperity in the country. The second, more specific problem lay with the *Herald* itself, whose good intentions towards Hobbs were undermined by its radical political stance. The paper was not just left-wing in its opinions, but it was also intricately involved with the labour movement as the official organ of the TUC. This meant that, despite its high circulation among the working class, it only had a limited appeal to the more affluent sections of the cricketing public, precisely the people who would have been the biggest donors to the Hobbs fund. In particular, the conservative-minded cricket establishment wanted to maintain its distance from a trade union paper that had backed the General Strike and opposed Britain's entry into the First World War. When Leveson Gower was asked by the *Herald* to back the testimonial, he could hardly have been more lukewarm: 'I hope the fund will be very successful. I shall bring it to the attention of the MCC.' The MCC did nothing. Like Hobbs's own final Test, the sixpenny fund slid from high hopes into frustrated anti-climax.

A happier fundraising experience for Hobbs occurred in mid-September, when he brought a team of top cricketers, including Test stars like Herbert Sutcliffe, Maurice Leyland and Patsy Hendren, to his native Cambridge to play in a charity match that marked the opening of the Jack Hobbs pavilion on Parker's Piece. Given the quality of Hobbs's side, it was no surprise that a crowd of over 10,000 spectators gathered on the Piece to see the game and they were rewarded by the sight of Hobbs scoring a century against a Cambridge Cricket Association XI. As well as celebrating the inauguration of the red-brick pavilion,* which was erected through a public subscription, the event also raised money for the worthy cause of Addenbrooke's hospital in Cambridge, Hobbs himself starting the collection with a donation of a hundred pounds given in crisp ten-pound notes. It was Hobbs's last game of an uneven season, his difficulties in the Test series counterbalanced by his high scoring in other cricket. In all first-class matches he made 2,103 runs at an average of 51.29, with four centuries, leading *Wisden* to remark that the wonder 'is not that he should have failed to equal some of his great seasons but that at the age of forty-seven he should retain his form to so large a degree'. Still in love with the craft of batting, Hobbs had no thoughts of retirement, telling Surrey in September that he would be available the following season. Being a professional cricketer was an occupation he cherished, and no alternative career had the same appeal to him. 'Several attractive coaching jobs have been put to me, but I don't fancy the idea very much,' he told Faulkner in his BBC interview.

In keeping with his continuing enthusiasm for the game, that winter he toured India and Ceylon with a private team organised by the Maharajah Kumar of Vizianagaram, the wealthy aristocrat, politician and cricketer known as 'Vizzy' who had been educated at Haileybury and later became captain of the Indian Test side in the mid-1930s. Originally the MCC had intended to send a party but that visit was cancelled due to civil disturbances against British rule, so the Maharajah decided to fill the void, in the process giving himself an enhanced reputation as a leader in Indian cricket. Accompanied by Ada and Herbert Sutcliffe, Hobbs revelled in the trip, which was far more relaxing

---

* In September 2010, a special match and exhibition, organised by the Cambridge Time Traveller Group and presided over by the Mayor of Cambridge, was held on Parker's Piece to celebrate the eightieth anniversary of the pavilion, part of which has been turned into a Thai restaurant.

that his previous Test tours. Nor was there any doubt about his popularity. 'Everywhere we went Sutcliffe and I were garlanded with flowers and players and spectators were genuinely disappointed if we did not make big scores,' he told the *Sunday Despatch*. He went big-game hunting for the first time in his life, enjoyed the hospitality of Sir Stanley Jackson, the former England captain who was now Governor of Bengal, and saw many of the renowned sights of the continent, including the ancient city of Jaipur and the temple of the Taj Mahal. 'Its grandeur fairly takes your breath away,' he wrote.

Compared to Tests and the county championship, the cricket was not too competitive, though much later in Hobbs's life, when he was in his seventies, the status of these matches gave rise to an enormous controversy over the number of centuries that he had scored in his career. Several statisticians wanted retrospectively to include two of the hundreds he made on the tour in his career record, though Hobbs himself was opposed to such revisionism. Both of the contested games were in Ceylon, and Hobbs specifically told John Arlott, when they were discussing his record, 'Don't include those. They were exhibition matches. Vizzy wanted to list our hundreds on the walls of his pavilion. We knew we'd got to score hundreds – so did the bowling side. They were not first-class in any sense.' Crucially, *Wisden* agreed and, despite a lingering debate, has never recognised this pair of centuries. A more immediate problem arose over Hobbs's strong Christian faith. Many of the games had been scheduled to include Sunday play, something that ran counter to Hobbs's Sabbatarian principles. 'I have never played Sunday cricket and never shall,' he wrote in 1935. 'My early religious atmosphere brought me up to respect Sunday, to remember the Sabbath day and keep it holy, to make it a day of rest for mind, body and spirit.' While there was widespread disappointment in India about his decision, he attracted vocal support from religious organisations in Britain. The Lord's Day Observance Society sent him a cablegram which read: 'Bravo Jack. You have made many scores in your time but never a better one than on New Year's Sunday when you made a great moral score in favour of the quiet British Sabbath.' Similarly a meeting of the Welsh Presbyterian Church passed a resolution declaring that 'we rejoice in Mr Jack Hobbs's stand for the sanctity of the Sabbath in refusing to play on that day'. This was the only time Hobbs's Christianity caused any conflict with his profession. Mostly his faith was unobtrusive, a facet of his private sphere.

Indeed, Hobbs said in India, 'I do not want to impose my opinions on other people.' As his Surrey teammate Alf Gover put it, 'Jack was a religious man, although he did not wear his faith on his sleeve. Whenever we played away at weekends he would slip away quietly on the Sunday morning to the nearest church accompanied by his old pal Herbert Strudwick. The rest of us would nip to the nearest golf course, but we always respected Jack for his convictions.' In fact, he so disliked any suggestion of ostentatiousness about his faith that he refused to read the lesson at a sportsmen's church service in 1925. 'I would rather face the Australian bowling for three weeks than read a lesson in church,' he said. It was a tribute to the enormous respect for Hobbs in India that the Maharajah neither complained about Hobbs's stand nor put him under any pressure to change his mind, despite the inconvenience. Instead, he rearranged some of the three-day matches so that they lasted through from Saturday to Tuesday, with a rest day on Sunday. 'I owe him a tremendous lot for his kindness,' said Hobbs.

Hobbs and Ada arrived back in England in February 1931, refreshed after their long break. His appearance was striking to his ghost and *Star* writer Jack Ingham: 'I cannot ever remember having seen him look fitter. He is burnt Lido brown and there is a sparkle in his eyes that bodes ill for the bowlers in the coming summer.' Free of injury and the pressure of Test calls, Hobbs fulfilled these expectations of success. Throughout the 1931 season, he was in impressive form, belying the reality that he had reached the age of forty-eight. In the second week of May, he gave a sign of what was to come with an innings of 128 against Somerset at the Oval, during which he put on 231 for the first wicket with Sandham. It was the 150th century opening partnership of his career, 'a figure quite unparalleled', said the *Cricketer*. He did almost as well with Sutcliffe in early June, when they put on 203 for the first wicket against the Gentlemen at the Oval, Hobbs making his fourth century of the summer. By now, Hobbs's reliance on back-foot play, leg-side strokes and short singles was more pronounced than ever, but he was still a formidable opponent for any bowling attack. When Hobbs became the first batsman of the season to pass 1,000 runs, P.J. Moss wrote in the *Daily Mirror*: 'English first-class cricket will be very much poorer when you do stop playing. I would now suggest you take a protégé under your wing and coach him to be as good a batsman and a fieldsman as you.'

Hobbs's scoring was so consistent that, towards the end of July, there was speculation that he was about to be recalled to the England side to play in the second Test against the New Zealanders, who, according to the *Daily Telegraph*, 'have expressed the wish that Hobbs should play against them'. But Hobbs strongly denied such rumours: 'I have not heard a word. I can hardly think it is true. I should naturally be proud if such a request had been made, but I am afraid I could not accept it. I must make way for others. I have had a good spell,' he told the press. In fact, far from seeking a quixotic return to the Test arena, Hobbs continually spoke throughout the 1931 season of the proximity of his retirement. 'It would be stupid to pretend that I am still at my best,' he said in one interview, while in another he complained, 'I take twice as long over the job as I used to. I get very tired, too, and I can't see the ball so well when I am tired.' To his friend the Reverend F.S. Girdlestone, a Midlands vicar and cricket enthusiast, he wrote on 5 June, 'I am afraid my fast scoring and brilliant days are over, but I feel thankful that I am to carry on and score runs at my age. Days in the field completely tire me out and I think I ought to give up at the end of the season. I feel I ought to get out while the going is good.' But Hobbs showed little determination to act on such language, especially when he was playing so superbly. Towards the end of August, he hit his eighth century of the season when he carried his bat for 123 not out against Yorkshire at the Oval, the attack led by Bowes, Macaulay and Hedley Verity. 'He's a cracker, this chap,' Macaulay said at one moment after Hobbs had executed one of his classic pulls.

The festival matches at the end of the season produced another burst of heavy scoring in league with Sutcliffe. For the Players at Scarborough, they put on 227, followed by a stand of 243 for Leveson Gower's XI versus the New Zealanders, the 26th and final century partnership of their glorious association. 'He is the greatest of living cricketers and I think there is no one to touch him. To bat with Jack Hobbs is an inspiration,' Sutcliffe said. Indeed, he admired Hobbs so much that he gave the name William Henry Hobbs to his eldest son Billy, who in the 1950s became an unsuccessful Yorkshire captain. Hobbs's own score in that 1931 game against the New Zealanders was 153, his highest innings of the season. 'His grace, his supreme footwork and his own command were there all the time,' said the *Daily Mail*.

The century, his tenth of the season and the 185th of his career, was a glorious high note on which to end the summer. In all first-class games in 1931 Hobbs hit 2,418 runs at an average of 56.23. 'Had he wished, his form would have made him good enough for England yet again. If the runs did not come by the old measures, the new strokes furnished remarkable exhibitions of clever placing,' said the *Cricketer*. Such was Hobbs's reputation that at the end of the season, the *Illustrated London News*, not normally a gossip monger, carried this report: 'As we go to press, we learn that John Berry Hobbs, the famous England batsman, is to be knighted. It is this sort of recognition that will give status to cricket.' The report was premature by more than two decades.

In February 1932 there was a significant departure at the Oval. It was not that of Hobbs from the Surrey team but that of Percy Fender from the captaincy. Almost since the First World War, his leadership had been a fixture at Surrey and, like many others, Hobbs was sorry to see him go. 'He was the best captain I played under. He was quick and clever and he thought out more batsman than any other captain I have ever known,' said Hobbs. The great difficulty that Fender had always laboured under was the weakness of his attack on the perfect Oval pitches, which is why he was so resourceful and innovative. The Surrey committee, however, decided that, after almost twenty years without winning the county championship, it was time for a change and replaced him with the vice-captain Douglas Jardine. Apart from Surrey's own interests, it has been suggested that an ulterior motive lay behind the move, in that the MCC had lined-up Jardine as the likely captain for the tour of Australia that winter, and wanted to give him more leadership experience. The Surrey historian Gordon Ross certainly took that view. But there are two serious flaws in such an argument. First, Jardine had already been appointed England captain for the series against New Zealand in 1931, when Fender was still in charge of Surrey. Second, in February 1932, it was by no means certain that Jardine would be the Ashes leader that winter, since other figures like Bob Wyatt and Percy Chapman remained contenders. When, later in the summer, Jardine was indeed formally appointed the MCC skipper, his old Winchester cricket master Rockley Wilson prophetically warned, 'He might well win us the Ashes but he might lose us a dominion.'

Fender, always a sanguine individual, showed no resentment about the change and said he was keen to play under Jardine, whom he admired as a tactician. In fact, Hobbs was more regretful, telling the press, 'I would have liked to finish my association with Surrey under my old skipper.' But he carried on nonetheless, and continued to defy his age with remarkably consistent scoring. In his very first innings of the summer he made 84 against Worcestershire at the Oval, his innings 'reminiscent of his best' according to the *Daily Mirror*. Though he was forced to miss seven championship matches due to fatigue, a torn thigh muscle and knee trouble, his batting never slumped. Altogether, he scored 1,764 runs in first-class games at an average of 56.90, with five centuries. Against Essex at the Oval in June, he was largely responsible for Surrey's nine-wicket victory when he hit 113 in the first innings and 119 not out in an exciting run-chase on the final afternoon, 'a display of high-class batting that could not have been surpassed,' said *Wisden*. It was the sixth time he had scored a century in each innings, yet another record. His other hundreds included 123 at Taunton, the ground that had such happy memories for him, and 111 against Middlesex at Lord's, putting on 203 with Sandham in just 150 minutes. Probably his greatest performance of 1932 was against the Gents at Lord's in July, when he carried his bat for 161 not out. His innings, which lasted five hours and ensured a draw for the Players, was his sixteenth in the Gents v Players series and beat the record of W.G. Grace. His success seemed to invigorate him and, unlike in previous years, he did not indulge in a running commentary about his imminent retirement. His five-year contract with Surrey, signed in 1927, was due to expire at the end of 1932 but in July he announced that he did not yet plan to retire. 'I certainly hope to play a few times for Surrey next summer. I feel as fit now as I have been for some years.' His contentedness was reflected in his batting style. 'Much of his old freedom in scoring had returned and he compiled his runs in fine fashion, often able to make beautifully timed boundaries in lieu of the snicks on which he relied in 1931,' said the *Cricketer*. Hobbs himself told the Reverend Girdlestone that the 'warmer weather' of 1932 had 'made a big difference' and 'helped me to get into better form'.

Yet all this sunny optimism in English cricket was deceptive. The brutal encounter of the Bodyline series was looming on the horizon, threatening to tear the game apart. A precursor of the storm that lay ahead occurred towards the end of August during the championship match at the Oval between Surrey and Yorkshire, when Hobbs, much to his outrage, was subjected to a barrage of short-pitched deliveries by Bill Bowes. Late on Saturday afternoon, in front of a large crowd, Hobbs was batting serenely and was well past his half-century, as Bowes recalled, 'Seeing very little of the stumps, because Jack always had his legs well in front of them, but seeing a lot of a very broad bat which seemed to get wider as the day wore on, I bowled an occasional bouncer. Some were majestically hit for four; some, as intended, had an element of surprise, even for Jack.' After one of these bumpers, Hobbs came down to the pitch and patted the turf near the bowler's end, signalling his disapproval of Bowes' methods. At the sight of this gesture, George Macaulay came running over to Bowes and told him, 'Tha's got him rattled. Go on – gie him another.' Bowes did exactly that, and dug the ball in so short that it flew over Hobbs's head, sparking loud abuse from the crowd and demands that he be taken off. This time Hobbs walked right past the stumps at the bowler's end, remonstrated with some of the Yorkshire players and then patted the ground in the middle of Bowes' run-up. 'Not to be outdone, I bowled another bouncer, but Jack had had enough of the farce. He stayed where he was, and we carried on with the game.'

Bowes thought that was the end of the matter, but he had not reckoned on the uproar in the press. Typical was the comment in the *Daily Express* about Hobbs's ordeal: 'Ball after ball whizzed about his head with extreme unpleasantness.' But by far the most strident condemnation came from Plum Warner in the *Morning Post* in which he wrote: 'Bowes bowled with five men on the on-side and sent down several very short-pitched balls which repeatedly bounced head high and more. Now that is not bowling; indeed it is not cricket and if all fast bowlers were to adopt his methods, the MCC would be compelled to step in and penalise the bowler who bowled less than halfway up the pitch.' What made this passage so important was not just that Warner was regarded as the voice of the establishment but also that he had been appointed the manager for Jardine's tour. His words would soon come back to haunt him once England's tactics in Australia became clear. The irony was that, after all the controversy at the Oval on Saturday, Hobbs was out for 90 on Monday to a well-pitched-up away swinger, always the most effective delivery against him.

Hobbs had been central to the first display of Bodyline bowling in England, and he was also to have a role in the fraught series as a journalist, having been sent out to Australia with Jack Ingham to cover the

tour for the *News Chronicle* and the *Star*. The evolution of the tactic
of fast short bowling to a packed leg-side field lay in the continuing
dominance of the bat in the early 1930s, thanks to featherbed pitches,
pad-play and the narrowness of the lbw law, all of which rendered so
much bowling ineffectual. More specifically, the method was devised
as a means of reducing the unique threat of Don Bradman, whose blitz
in the summer of 1930 had so traumatised the England side. Jardine
was convinced that Bradman had a weakness against the short ball,
and in Harold Larwood, he believed he had a bowler with the pace and
accuracy to exploit this chink in his armour. With his clipped voice,
multicoloured cap, and aloof manner, Jardine might have seemed to
the Australian public like the classic stereotype of the condescending
British aristocrat, but in truth, he was more of a rebel than an
establishment figure. His iron-willed ruthlessness led him to treat the
traditional spirit of cricket with mocking disdain. He sent a shudder
through the MCC's ruling elite with his cold determination. 'I wish
never to see him again. His outlook and mentality are all wrong,' said
Warner towards the end of the tour. His closest allies on the tour were
not his fellow amateurs but the two fast bowlers from Nottinghamshire,
Larwood and Bill Voce, 'a pair of swollen-headed, gutless, uneducated
miners', in the view of Gubby Allen. Nor was Jardine remotely conventional in other aspects of his life. Anti-monarchist and hostile to
Christianity, he developed interests in the supernatural, Hinduism and
reincarnation. This unorthodoxy, allied to his ingrained, almost patho-
logical, hatred of Australians, provoked the most tempestuous series
in Test history, in which England's recapture of the Ashes was over-
shadowed by accusations of bad sportsmanship, dangerous injuries to
key Australian players, an atmosphere of vengeance in the crowds and
political turmoil even up to the level of Downing Street. The ill-feeling
that Jardine's methods engendered was perfectly encapsulated in Bill
Woodfull's famous statement when Plum Warner came to visit him in
the Australian dressing room at Adelaide after he had been hit over the
heart by a ball from Larwood: 'I don't want to see you, Mr Warner.
There are two sides out there; one of them is trying to play cricket; the
other is not.'

Smooth, diplomatic, an expert at oiling the wheels of the Lord's
machinery, Warner was out of his depth in dealing with hardened,
stubborn men like Larwood and Jardine. Moreover, he was hopelessly

compromised by his *Morning Post* article about Bowes' attack against Hobbs. The Australian public knew exactly what he thought of fast leg-theory, for, as Bert Oldfield revealed, the stir caused by the Oval incident 'was heard all around the world'. Yet Warner refused to act when Bodyline was practised by his own side. 'I believe history will find me guiltless,' he once wrote, but such words were just wishful thinking. To a lesser extent, Hobbs was also badly compromised by his position as England's leading press commentator on the series. His stature as the England's greatest cricketer gave him unrivalled authority, but he refused to use it either to condemn Jardine's methods or to let the British public really know what was happening in the Tests. Instead, he largely mixed anodyne descriptions of the play with criticism of the Australian crowd and press. No one reading his reports from England would have had any idea of the true nature of the intimidatory bowling and field placings. Gilbert Mant, Reuter's cricket correspondent, described Hobbs as 'a lovely fellow traveller, modest, unassuming, and good natured' but admitted that his bland reports for the *Chronicle* and the *Star*, written by Ingham, 'said nothing one way or the other'.

Hobbs's potential influence was all the greater because none of the English national dailies had sent out their own specialist cricket reporters. The only other full-time English journalist on the tour was Bruce Harris of the *Evening Standard*, but he was hardly a reliable observer, partly because his real interest was tennis rather than cricket, and partly because he was an unthinking cheerleader for Jardine, portraying the entire series as a battle between noble Englishmen and Australian squealers. The journalist originally booked to go out for the *Standard* was Jim Swanton, who would have provided much more incisive, less jaundiced coverage, but sadly his paper's management lost faith in him when he failed to reach a public telephone to file his copy after Percy Holmes and Herbert Sutcliffe set a new world-record opening partnership of 555 at Leyton against Essex in June 1932. If he could not deliver a report from East London, thought his bosses, how on earth could he get one through from the other side of the world? Swanton might have been an epic social climber and an infelicitous writer, but he was a man of integrity. If he had gone to Australia, English attitudes might have been different. He might also have helped Hobbs lose his painful inhibitions about criticising Jardine's tactics. As Swanton later wrote in one of his autobiographies, 'I have recently reread the Hobbs cables and confirmed my memory that so long as the tour was in progress, though regretting the outcry, he refrained from condemning the cause.'

There were several reasons for this reticence. One was Hobbs's diffi-dent, shy nature that loathed confrontation. Another was his severe lack of any journalistic experience. In 1931, he had reported on one Test against New Zealand for the *Daily Mail*, but covering an Ashes series in Australia was in a different league, even with Ingham at his side. 'At first, I was, I must confess, rather nervous of the ordeal,' he wrote later. A third was his understandable reluctance to criticise those who had, until recently, been his England teammates. Above all, Jardine was Hobbs's own county captain so, given his deferential respect for cricket's hierarchy, he was hardly like to launch a fusillade against the England skipper. But none of this helped him be a courageous or objective analyst of the disaster that unfolded. To give just a couple of example of the kind of insipid, uninformative material he produced, here is a tribute to Jardine after England had won the Ashes through victory in the fourth Test at Brisbane. 'He has done everything possible, though "up against it" the whole time. And though "up against it" may seem a cloak, perhaps it is wisest to leave it at that,' he wrote, adding, rather absurdly, 'I am here to criticise, and meaning to do it, I could find no fault.' Equally weak was his attempt to blame the Australian media for the outcry over Bodyline: 'I cannot see what good purpose Australian journalists think they are serving in dishing up this backstairs gossip. It is doing cricket no good, but merely hampering the efforts of those who are trying to arrive at a peaceful solution.' What, in reality, was doing cricket no good were Jardine's methods and the failure of the British press and administrators to challenge them. And why should there have been any need for 'a peaceful solution' if England had been playing fairly? So loved in Australia, Hobbs's reputation was a little diminished by his writings. The maverick journalist Frank Browne said that Hobbs's cables 'provided additional evidence in support of a belief . . . that the English have two sets of rules: one for themselves and one for the other people'.

The rich irony of Hobbs's journalism in Australia was that one of his reports did actually provoke a minor row, though the subject was not the one that really mattered, fast leg-theory, but the far more trivial question of Sutcliffe's scoring rate. Commenting on Sutcliffe's innings in the first Test at Sydney, Hobbs had written that the Yorkshireman 'failed to show a proper appreciation of the situation, pottering along at a very slow rate'. All too predictably Lord Hawke, when he read these words, launched another of his public attacks on his long-standing enemy. At a meeting of the Yorkshire club in Leeds in January 1933, Hawke said, with scant respect for the concept of press freedom, 'We deplore his cable about Sutcliffe. Such ungenerous criticism should be impossible.' Then for good measure, the Yorkshire President harked back to the Oval match of August 1932. 'We do not approve of Hobbs's attitude to Bowes,' he said regally. The legacy of the Bradford League was still being felt almost twenty years after Hobbs had signed for Idle. Exasperated by Hawke's continuing grudge, Hobbs responded, 'Almost every year he has a go. Surely Lord Hawke cannot seriously mean I should apologise to Yorkshire. Isn't his suggestion rather silly? I have come out here to comment, I hope fairly and accurately on the play.' He added that it was 'ridiculous' of Hawke to suggest that he was disparaging Sutcliffe, 'for everyone knows his value as a batsman'. Hobbs concluded, 'It appears that Lord Hawke must have forgotten that I was running short ones with Wilfred Rhodes thirteen years before Herbert appeared in Tests. As for the Bowes incident at the Oval, I am sorry there still should be persons who persist in grossly exaggerating it. But I am even more sorry that I should so often arouse the disapproval of the President of the Yorkshire County Cricket Club.' But Hawke was unrepentant, saying that he strongly objected to the very concept of player-writers. 'I still think Hobbs was wanting in tact,' he concluded. There was one, even more absurd spat involving Hobbs during the tour, which illustrated the hostility that the Australian cricket authorities felt towards anyone associated with the England party. In February 1933, as the MCC party suffered injuries and exhaustion, Hobbs and Warner were both drafted into the team to play in an upcountry game against Northern Districts at Newcastle. Usually the presence of Hobbs in any side would have been welcomed, but on this occasion there were protests from the Australian Board about England playing a weakened side. Warner replied that he 'could not believe that people did not want to see Jack Hobbs'. As it turned out, Hobbs made a nonsense of the complaint with a useful 44, described by the *Daily Mirror* as 'a delightful innings'.

The fall-out from the Bodyline tour continued when the MCC and its entourage returned home, the superficial mood of triumph matched by an acute uneasiness about the manner of victory. Warner's own magazine, the *Cricketer*, embodied this contradiction in its spring annual for 1933. On one hand, said the journal, 'no serious damage was done nor was any intended by the bowlers', and if there were injuries, 'it has been the batsman's own fault'. On the other, the *Cricketer* admitted that leg-theory would 'destroy cricket as a spectacle' if it continued. 'We certainly do not want it employed ad nauseam here.'

Back on English soil, Hobbs continued to indulge in the illusion that much of the uproar was the fault of the Australian media, as shown by this passage from a private letter to one of his friends. 'The press have a lot to answer for and half the trouble on the tour was the outcome of scores of its representatives who followed the team. They were on the lookout for "stories" all the time and half of them did not really understand the game.' But for the first time Hobbs also felt free to attack Bodyline publicly. In several articles he urged the MCC and the counties to crack down on its use and the deployment of packed leg-side fields. 'Cricket will be all the better for the passing of Bodyline. Apart from being very dangerous, it was never anything but against the spirit of the game,' he wrote in the *News Chronicle*. 'The whole thing is wrong,' he said in a column for the *Star*. Hobbs repeated his objections in his book about Jardine's tour, *The Fight for the Ashes*, which was published in June 1933 and was largely a rehash of his constrained match reports from Australia. But in the final section of the book, he launched a powerful condemnation of the tactic, calling it 'a most venomous thing', full of 'marked elements of danger' and designed 'to intimidate the batsmen'. Anyone 'facing a fast bowler who sends down leg-theory has to play strokes more in protection of his body than with the idea of defending his wicket or scoring runs,' he wrote.

Already disillusioned at the way the cricket world had ostracised him on his return from Australia, Harold Larwood was angered that the hero of his youth should join the chorus of disapproval. In a gramophone record he made after the tour, he pointed to the apparent double-standard whereby there was uproar over leg-theory but none over pad play, of which Hobbs, of course, was a prime exponent. 'Does Jack really think that an action which robs the bowler of a wicket to be fair cricket? I know it is not against the laws of cricket but neither

is my fast leg-theory . . . Actually it was pad play that was partly responsible for the leg-side attack. So if the latter's not cricket, those who use
their pads too much must shoulder at least some of the
blame for it.' The dig at Hobbs was very obvious. In fact, leg-theory
and pad play both ended up being drastically restricted in the 1930s by
changes in the law that banned intimidatory bowling and widened the
scope of lbw.

The Bodyline tour was one of the less uplifting episodes of Hobbs's
late career. His criticisms would have carried far more weight if he had
dared to voice them during the actual tour. Indeed, through the strength
of his moral influence, he might have effected a change in England's
approach. One of the tragedies of Bodyline is that it undermined appreciation for the quality of Jardine's side, which was exceptionally rich in
batting and bowling. It is possible that, with Larwood, Allen, Voce and
Verity all at their peak, the Ashes might have been won without the
resort to underhand methods.

After all the exhausting bitterness of the winter, Hobbs was relieved
to return to the batting crease as the 1933 season got underway. Even
at the age of fifty, there was little indication of a serious decline in his
powers. He missed the first few games of the summer with influenza,
but his return to the Surrey team in late May caused a sensation. Against
the touring West Indians, whose bowlers included the genuinely quick
Herman Griffith and Manny Martindale, Hobbs hit a massive 221 spread
over five hours without giving a chance, the 191st century of his career.
'The strokes, all round the wicket, flowed from his bat with characteristic
ease and grace. By accurate placing, not hitting the ball, Hobbs preserved
his energy judiciously and his innings was a sheer delight to watch.
Hobbs is still the master batsman,' wrote Charles Buchan in the *News
Chronicle*. 'Mr Hobbs, you are a great player,' said Martindale at the
end of the match.

The achievement of a double century at the age of fifty against an
international side provoked a sense of wonder in the English cricket
world, and the newspapers were deluged with yet more tributes and
profiles, such as this insightful interview conducted over tea in the Oval
pavilion with a reporter from *Daily Mail*. 'Yes, he felt stiff and sore and
he ached. With an "ooch", he stretched his legs full length and gave a
sigh of relief. Gradually he drew them up. "Ah, that's better," he said,
and his bronzed face broke into that Jack Hobbs smile as he added,

almost in a whisper, "I am not so young as I used to be. I never thought I could do it," he continued, "I always go to the wicket feeling I am not going to get runs and if I don't I am very disappointed. But when I make them I feel delighted with myself and the more I can score the happier I am. That was what I felt like when I found myself against the West Indies, and I wanted to go on batting for ever."' The *Mail* then asked about his future. 'Will I retire this season? Well, perhaps, but I cannot say yet. Maybe I will. I don't want to go on playing and rust at the wicket. Although I feel so stiff and had to be massaged when I came back to the pavilion, I enjoyed every minute of it.' Because of his age, Hobbs was allowed by the Surrey Committee to pick and choose his games, but when he appeared, the results were often striking. During a wonderful patch in mid-June, he hit 100 against Warwickshire, 85 against Essex, and 118 against Cambridge University in three successive innings. According to Trevor Wignall in the *Express*, who had watched him in action against Warwickshire, his fielding was showing little signs of decline. 'He is nearly as spry as ever, but his certainty in getting to the ball when it is hit anywhere in his direction is principally due to his remarkable powers of anticipation.' Two more centuries followed in July, against Kent and Somerset, taking his official career total to 195.

It is a paradox of Hobbs's late career that he should have always professed so little interest in statistics, yet so much of the public interest in his batting was dominated by the quest to set new records. That was never more true than from mid-1933, when the milestone of two hundred first-class centuries seemed to be attainable. It should be emphasised that the two made in Ceylon on the private tour in 1930/31 never featured in any discussion of this mission, which is another reason why they should not be retrospectively counted in his career total. If they had been included at the time, then Hobbs's whole approach to the record might have been different. As it was, Hobbs did not want too much emphasis put on the two hundred, in case he had to leave the public with unfulfilled expectations. After the Reverend Girdlestone had written to Hobbs to congratulate him on his Somerset century, he replied, 'Now! We must get all idea of the 200th coming this year out of our heads. If I can get two more this season, I shall be more than satisfied and it will help make up my mind to continue playing next year.' In fact, he made just one more in 1933, his 196th, in the fixture against Nottinghamshire at the beginning of August. Facing an attack that including the Bodyline practitioner Bill Voce, Hobbs delighted a 20,000-strong crowd with another masterly display on a day of sweltering heat. At one point his bat was hit out of his hands by a short ball from Voce, who was bowling with four short legs. The sight prompted a long outburst of barracking from the Surrey fans but, unlike Bowes the year before, Voce did not keep up the bouncer assault. The final moments of Hobbs's progress towards his century were well captured by the *Star*: 'The deep ring of spectators was a kaleidoscope of white and light colours and only in the dignified members' seats did men fear to sit in shirt sleeves boldly showing their braces . . . When he reached 94 the great crowd went absolutely silent, willing him to get his hundred. He called for water, but had hit a 2 and a 1 before a tray of refreshments was brought out for all hands. With a great pull for 4, Jack reached his 196th century. The crowd gave him a tremendous ovation – one of the finest of his career.' Soon after-wards, he wrote to Girdlestone, 'The last century gave me extreme pleasure, perhaps more than any other this season.' Stiffness, exhaustion and a pulled muscle meant that Hobbs only played three more matches in 1933, but it had been another fine season for him, as he finished third in the national averages with 1,105 runs at 61.38. 'Hobbs, when he appeared, was still supreme,' declared the *Cricketer*.

Hobbs's evergreen batting led, predictably, to a burst of press specula-tion that he might be included in the MCC team to India that winter, which was to be led by Douglas Jardine and would play the first ever Tests on the sub-continent. 'It would not cause any surprise in well-informed circles if Hobbs were invited to make the tour. He is very popular in India,' reported the *Daily Mirror*. The rumour was unfounded, though Hobbs did go out to India as a reporter for the *Star* and played in one exhibition game in Bombay, making 22 before he fell to a catch at the wicket, much to the disappointment of a large crowd which drained away once he was out.

While he was in India, he received a telegram from Leveson Gower, the President of Surrey, seeking his agreement to a richly deserved honour that would mark his thirty-year association with the club. In 1933 Surrey had decided to erect a high brick wall around the Oval to stop non-paying spectators, especially juveniles, sneaking into the ground. As part of this development, it was decided to install a major new entrance, complete with two columns and wrought-iron gates. The predicted cost of all the works was £4,500, with the estimate for the gates themselves coming in at around £1,000. As a tribute to Surrey's greatest cricketer, the committee agreed to name the entrance after Hobbs and to launch an appeal to club members to meet the £1,000 bill. But knowing how modest he was, the committee first had to secure his agreement to the scheme. So Leveson Gower sent him the cable about the proposal, which Hobbs was only too thrilled to accept. 'Certainly I agree to suggested appeal. The wonderful compliment gives me great pleasure,' Hobbs cabled back. It was almost thirty-one years since Hobbs had nervously got out at the Oval tube station in advance of his trial with Surrey, and he was deeply moved by the honour. 'When you come to think of all the great players that Surrey have had – men who added lustre to the amateur and professional history of Surrey cricket, it hardly seems possible that I should be singled out for this very great compliment,' he wrote in 1935. After gaining Hobbs's approval, the club moved with alacrity. The affection for Hobbs meant that there was no problem about raising the money, as the committee minutes noted: 'The idea of associating these gates with the name of Jack Hobbs received the enthusiastic approval of a large number of members who quickly subscribed the £1,000 asked for.' Work started at the beginning of February and by mid-April the wall and new entrance had been completed. The inscription in the elegant ironwork on the gates read: 'The Hobbs gates in honour of a great Surrey and England cricketer.' At the official opening ceremony, Leveson Gower turned to Hobbs and said, 'It is impossible for me to thank you adequately for the very great pleasure you and your wonderful skill have afforded many thousands of people.' In reply, Hobbs, characteristically, said he hoped that 'my colleagues will feel that this is a great tribute to them and the whole club'. Demonstrating that his mind was still focused on the two hundred milestone, he concluded, 'I have to score four more centuries, and if I do so I shall be pleased by the thought that it will be something to justify these gates.'

With a typical lack of sentimentality Sir Donald Bradman once said that Hobbs, because he was so 'desperately keen' to reach the landmark of two hundred centuries, 'played on after realising that he should give up.' But at the start of the 1934 season, Hobbs certainly did not feel that he was past it. He had kept fit by playing golf with Strudwick and had even taken up squash again after fifteen years. In the opening match of the season, against the MCC at Lord's, he made a half-century, followed by a fighting 62 in the second innings of a Surrey defeat by Glamorgan on a rare turning wicket at the Oval. Faced with the vicious off-breaks of Johnnie Clay, no other Surrey batsmen reached 20. 'There was a class about Hobbs's batting, and by this I mean that he possessed polish, grace, fluency and ease of movement to a greater degree than anyone else,' said Errol Holmes, the Oxford blue and successful businessman who had taken over the Surrey captaincy from Jardine. A stylish batsman and sympathetic leader, Holmes allowed Hobbs to choose his games in his quest for the double-hundred. 'I never "picked" him but used to ask him if he wanted to play and was delighted if he said he would like to.'

A description of Hobbs in action during that Glamorgan game was provided by the journalist Charles Dettmer, who, as a thirteen-year-old boy, was taken to the Oval by his father, a keen Surrey supporter. Before the start of play, Dettmer had the chance to see Hobbs in the nets. 'He was as graceful and lithe in his movements as a man half his age. Those few minutes in the nets presented not only a lesson in cricket; they presented a lesson in life. For Hobbs showed that he did not do things by halves. He wielded the willow in his hands just as definitely there as he did in his subsequent innings. It wasn't simply a case of going through the motions. Almost every shot and every stroke he knew were brought out for display.' Dettmer recalled Hobbs then walking out to bat with Sandham. 'Not for Hobbs the cavalier attitude. There was not the cockiness of a jaunty cap, no semblance of a swagger. Hobbs walked to the wicket as upright as a larch; his hat was middled squarely on his head and he carried his bat as a headmaster might carry a cane when about to deal with an offending schoolboy.' The young Dettmer marvelled at Hobbs's strokeplay. 'Even his defensive strokes carried more power than some of the puny attacking strokes we see today.' One particular shot stuck in Dettmer's memory when Hobbs cracked the ball back over the bowler's head. 'Ah! The execution of that stroke. He poised himself on the back foot, left foot forward and raised about 12 inches from the ground, with the bat raised vertically in line with his head. Then forward and down on the left foot, a flashing, circular movement of the bat – perhaps a little tweak of the wrists and away went the ball. That one stroke will remain as a memory of the man who put almost a poetic emphasis on batsmanship.'

Hobbs's confidence was reflected in a letter to Girdlestone, in which he declared himself to be in 'quite fair form', though he added, 'I am badly in need of centuries.' One of them came at the end of the month, when he agreed to play against Lancashire in George Duckworth's benefit match at Old Trafford. On a bitterly cold Manchester day, the damp wind freezing his elderly bones, he made 116, his innings inspiring this piece of lyricism from the pen of Neville Cardus: 'Hobbs batted four hours and he hit 48 singles. The innings was one of the Master's offerings for an Occasion. He went his way sure of every touch, masterfully but quietly. The ripeness of his cricket was autumnal and grand; the great wheel of his career had come full circle. He wanted to do honour to Duckworth and, like a great batsman, he was able to crown the match with a laurel which, because it was given to us modestly, was all the more beautiful.' In a BBC interview, Duckworth himself gave this moving account of Hobbs's contribution: 'He made a lot of it in singles, a good many short singles, just to keep himself warm running. But he made it and that was the point and the match went to three days. It is a memory that will stay as a tie between Jack and me all our lives. As the match ended, we all stood back and let Jack lead the way in. Quite slowly, he walked towards the pavilion and we all trooped along behind him. And as he got near the members, every one of them stood. Somebody started to sing "Auld Lang Syne". Somebody else joined in and then two or three more and it got louder and louder until everyone on the ground was singing it. It was too much for Jack. With his head down and one hand waving a bit vaguely, Jack ran through the members and went out of sight at Old Trafford for the last time. I believe he was crying.'

After this occasion, Hobbs's season rapidly went downhill. In line with his practice of choosing his games, he noticed in early June that the Brentwood wicket in Essex seemed to be yielding a colossal number of runs; Kent had scored no fewer than 803 for 4 declared at the end of May, with Bill Ashdown making a triple century, Les Ames a double, and Frank Woolley a single one. Surrey were due to play there at the start of June and Hobbs actually took the trouble to phone Ashdown to check what the wicket was like. 'Well, I suggest you look at the scores, Jack,' said Ashdown. So Hobbs decided to play. On his journey out to Brentwood by rail, he ran into Frank Woolley at Liverpool Street station. 'Eh, Jack, there's a century waiting for you there,' said Woolley cheerily. Reassured by all this testimony, Hobbs went out to bat on the first morning. The opening over was to be bowled by a tall, unknown amateur called Holcombe 'Hopper' Read,* who had played two games for Surrey in 1933 before being rejected and moving to Essex. He had only been called into this game because Morris Nichols, Essex's leading pace bowler, was at a Test trial. Hobbs calmly settled into his stance on this alleged batsman's paradise. The first ball whistled past his ears, almost knocked off his cap, flew over the wicketkeeper's head and smashed into the sightscreen with a resounding crack on the second bounce. The fourth ball raced off the edge of Hobbs's bat through the slips for four. The last ball of the over took out his off-stump. Read had been sitting accountancy exams for a whole week before this game, and recalled that when he took the field at Brentwood, 'I was absolutely pent up with energy, raring to go. It was a very fast pitch, and I was running slightly downhill, with a strong wind over my shoulder. I didn't knock Jack's cap off with my first ball, but he gave me a helluva look after it had lifted steeply. He wasn't used to such wild bowling.'

After this humiliation, Hobbs did not play in Surrey's next two games, but then he decided to try again against Sussex at Horsham. In its own way, the result was almost as embarrassing as the Brentwood fiasco. On paper, Hobbs looked to have played well despite Sussex's win, scoring 34 in the first innings and 79 in the second. But it was the manner of his run-making that so depressed him. His legs were tired, his stroke-making almost non-existent. *The Times* journalist Dudley Carew was among those watching this melancholic performance: 'It is doubtful whether anyone could recognise in Hobbs's batting on that day any kinship with one of the most perfect techniques that has ever been seen on a cricket field. Perhaps something of the old sureness, but not of quickness, of footwork, was there, and certainly every movement at the crease was the movement of a man who knew his job, but where before everything had been free and masterful, there was now an intolerable sense of strain and frustration. It was painful to watch Hobbs scratch for runs on that June afternoon – for the man was made for greatness and greatness that day was not in him.'

For years Hobbs had heavily favoured the leg-side, as he explained,

---

* So known because of the eccentric leap in his run-up. Holcombe Read (1910-2000) gave an interview to the author in 1991.

'People told me I was as good as ever, but I knew I wasn't. I knew I could no longer hit the ball on the off-side. It was practically closed to me. Growing age was the reason. I wasn't seeing the ball so quickly. It took longer to judge the length of a ball and the limbs did not act so promptly.' But now even his more limited leg-side repertoire was failing him. 'His eyesight and reactions were not quite so keen, while he used to tire quickly while batting,' said Errol Holmes of these sad, twilight weeks. Yet the passion for those three last centuries still burned within him. He refused to give up just yet, still hoping that the old magic might come back. 'He seemed to have his heart set on this with an intensity which was strange, in one so far removed from being an amasser of runs for their own sake,' wrote E.W. Swanton. But it was a forlorn task. In the middle of June, he turned out against Somerset at the Oval, batting down the order, but only made an awkward 15. Even worse, after misfielding a ball at cover, he was barracked by his own Surrey supporters, an experience that had never happened before. He was so disillusioned that he privately swore he would never play for Surrey again. His teammates at the Oval sensed he was finished but were reluctant to acknowledge the reality, as Alf Gover recalled, 'We all felt very sad and the corner of the dressing room which was traditionally the senior professional's was left empty for the rest of the season with the heir apparent, Andrew Sandham, waiting until the next season before moving in.' At the end of August, however, Hobbs went back on that vow by playing in a championship match at Cardiff, partly at the request of the Glamorgan authorities who felt his presence on the Bank Holiday would boost their dire finances. The result was another failure, as he fell lbw to Johnnie Clay, a sad end to a county career that had lasted almost three decades.

The end of his first-class career had almost arrived as well, and with it the last flickering hope of the 200 milestone. His penultimate game was against the 1934 Australian visitors at the Folkestone festival, and, perhaps inspired by a final contest with his greatest adversary, he fleetingly recaptured some of his old brilliance. 'The Australians had a taste of Jack Hobbs at his best at Folkestone yesterday,' reported the *Daily Mirror*. 'Though making only 38, Hobbs showed much of his old mastery and skill in strokeplay during a stay of an hour and 50 minutes.' The curtain fell for the last time in a match for the Players against the Gents at Folkestone, where he made 24 in the first innings, bowled by Allom, and only 18 in the second before he was caught off Hopper Read. It was ironic that the last two bowlers to dismiss him should have both played for Surrey during their careers. There was also intriguing symmetry in that Hobbs's maiden first-class game had been against the Gentlemen and his score had again been 18.

Hobbs knew that his career was over, but he did not formally announce his retirement until February 1933 when he wrote to Leveson Gower to explain his decision. 'I need hardly tell you that it is with very great regret that I ask you to accept my resignation as a playing member of the Surrey County Cricket Club. The happiest years of my life have been spent with the Surrey Club, but I feel I have had a long innings and that I should now make room for younger men. If you will allow me to thank the committee for the kindness and consideration I have always received at their hands. The honour they conferred upon me last year in placing the new gates at the Oval in my name touched me very deeply and I will only add that it makes it all the harder for me to come to the decision I have.'

In subsequent interviews, Hobbs said that it was 'a big break but it has been coming to me for a long time'. The failure to reach the cherished milestone still rankled, as he admitted. 'I can't help feeling I've let my friends down a bit. They expected me to get those two hundred centuries and I haven't got them. I wish I had, for their sakes. For that reason alone, I found it hard to come to a decision. I felt I'd like to go on but you know everybody has to finish some time. If I had stayed and gone after those two hundred centuries, I should have perhaps missed them. People might have said, "He ought to have retired last year." So I'm out, permanently as far as county cricket is concerned.' In a more personal letter to Percy Fender, Hobbs expressed his gratitude 'for the kind friend you have been to me ever since you started playing for Surrey and in particular during the years you were my skipper. It will always be my regret that I did not finish my career under you. We have indeed had many happy times together and nothing will take them from my memory.'

Though Hobbs had only played seven championship games in 1934 and had reached the age of fifty-two the previous December, the official news of his retirement reverberated through the cricket world, sadness at the announcement mixed with admiration for his deeds. In his tribute, the Kent leg-spinner Tich Freeman said, 'He was undoubtedly the best batsman I ever bowled against. Yet I would rather bowl against Hobbs than any batsman I know. He always made the game a battle of wits and one got real enjoyment out of it.' The taciturn Wilfred Rhodes was moved to a rare effusion, 'He was the best and most consistent batsman of my time. He was a joy to watch and a great judge of the game. He was a good companion on tour and one was happy to be associated with him.' From Australia, Monty Noble described him as 'one of the finest and most modest batsmen the world has ever produced'. Frank Woolley concentrated on his character, 'Everything about Jack Hobbs has been clean and above board.' Inevitably, the loyal but determined Ada felt her husband had made the wrong decision. 'I think it is a great pity he has given up. He is well worth watching even now. He might have played another year and gone for those three centuries.' But, unlike his wife, Hobbs had recognised that continuing to play into 1935, simply for the sake of a record, would have smacked of self-indulgence. He might have been able to arrange it, through university matches, festival games and appearances for the MCC, but he had too much respect for the game of cricket to demean it with such a narcissistic pantomime. The achievement itself would have been devalued if it had been contrived in this way. As the journalist Alfred Gardiner put it, 'His self-denying ordinance was typical of the man and his genius.'

In his reply to Hobbs's formal resignation, Leveson Gower wrote back, 'It is quite unnecessary to say that your decision to retire was received with very deep regret, not only because the county will be deprived of the services of the greatest batsman of his time – to say nothing of your fielding at cover-point – but also because your fine, modest example both on and off the field will be even more missed than your outstanding achievements with the bat.' Leveson Gower then explained that as a special tribute to Hobbs, the committee had decided to make him a life member of the club, 'the highest honour the committee can confer'. He was the first professional to be recognised in this way. The President concluded with this generous accolade for Hobbs's moral influence in English cricket, 'It is because of men like yourself that the profession to which you belong is held in such high esteem.'

Apart from the Surrey life membership, there was one other major farewell tribute arranged for Hobbs in 1935. This was a gala dinner in his honour, sponsored by the *News Chronicle* group and held at the Dorchester Hotel on 17 July. The tables of the opulent dining room that evening were filled with dignitaries and figures from Hobbs's career, including Plum Warner, Sir Stanley Jackson, Lord Rosebery, his first county captain* and Lord Moynihan, the surgeon who had saved his life in 1921. One paper said that four entire England XIs could have been assembled from the number of top-class cricketers who attended. It was a reflection of Hobbs's stature that even King George V sent a telegram of congratulations 'to that great cricketer'. Shortly before the dinner, Hobbs confessed to Girdlestone of his apprehension about being in the limelight, 'I know I ought to feel grateful, but I cannot say I am looking forward to the ordeal. I know you will be in full sympathy and I want you to be there to witness my discomfiture. I suppose I shall blunder through somehow.' As it turned out, buoyed by the display of affection from his friends and admirers, Hobbs performed with graceful aplomb. He was warm in his thanks, endearing in his recollections and modest about his record. Above all, he expressed his gratitude for the chances he had been given. 'If I could live my life over again, I assure you I would desire no other. It has been a wonderful life, full of delightful associations, varied experiences, happy memories, enriched by friendships formed at home and beyond the sea. Looking back, I have not one single regret having chosen professional cricket as my career.'

The cricket world felt exactly the same way.

---

* Lord Dalmeny had succeeded to the Rosebery title on the death of his father in 1929.

Epilogue

When Jack Hobbs was growing up in late-Victorian Cambridge, many professional cricketers faced a dismal retirement. Low pay, lack of pensions and chronic job insecurity meant they struggled to provide for their old age. Even benefits for the long-serving stalwarts were subject to the whims of weather and committees. In 1901, the year that Hobbs first played minor counties cricket, the famous Nottinghamshire fast bowler John Jackson died in a Liverpool workhouse as a pauper, his estate valued at fifteen pounds. Similarly the popular Surrey wicketkeeper Ted Pooley, having worked after his playing days on a building site, spent the last nine years of his life in a Lambeth workhouse before his death in 1907. 'It was the workhouse, sir, or the river,' he said to one writer who had been moved by his plight. But the vast improvement in the status of professionals, as well as the creation and expansion of the welfare state, meant that cricketers of the 1930s faced nothing like this penury. Those at the top, such as Hobbs, Woolley and Hendren, could be described as successful members of the upper middle-class, with substantial homes, cars, income and investments.

Hobbs's retirement in 1935 certainly did not involve the prospect of any financial constraints. He was now a man of means, the harsh early days of Rivar Place far behind him. He still had plenty of well-paid work through his journalism, though it must be said that his position in the press box owed more to the lustre of his name rather than the incisiveness of his ghostwritten prose. In his penultimate season of 1933, the *Star* gave him a weekly column on cricket. Initially, Jack Ingham acted as his ghostwriter but from 1935 the role was taken over by the sports journalist Jimmy Bolton. Together, they travelled out to Australia for the 1936/7 series, his last trip there for an Ashes series. Hobbs also had a quartet of lucrative books published under his name in the 1930s. Two of them were essentially just compilations of his press reports on the 1932/3 and 1934 Ashes series, but more interesting were his pair of autobiographies. The first, *Playing for England*, covered his entire Test career and was written by the versatile journalist, author and poet Thomas Moult, a close friend of Neville Cardus. The book had the occasional striking passage but was devoid of revelations and did not match the quality of Ingham's 1924 volume for Hobbs, *My Cricket Memories*. The weakest, however, was *My Life Story*, written by Bolton and published in 1935. Much of the text was just lifted from the previous two books, while key dramatic incidents, like the Bodyline series or the 1926 Oval Test, were dealt with in a perfunctory manner. To be fair, the problem for all Hobbs's ghosts was the essential decency of his character, which meant that he both hated to criticise others and shrank from anything he perceived as boasting. As Gordon Ross, the historian of Surrey, once put it, 'Rarely can you get him to talk about himself.' Unlike hard-nosed reporters whose lifeblood was controversy, Hobbs shied away from it, as shown by this comment in November 1936 about an umpiring dispute in the Ashes series: 'The press box is not a good position from which to judge a leg-before decision but I know that umpires are only human beings and are liable to make mistakes, although they are in the best position to see.' This was hardly the kind of material to set an editor's pulse racing. The other problem for his cricket writing was that, because the game came so naturally to him, he was not the most perceptive analyst of techniques. On one occasion the Essex amateur Leonard Crawley came off the field after witnessing another of Hobbs's superlative innings. 'I would love to ask him how he does it, but I know he wouldn't be able to tell me,' he said to a teammate.

Hobbs's earnings from his books and articles were augmented by the success of his Fleet Street shop, where he worked at least three days a week in his retirement if he did not have other commitments. All this maintained a comfortable life for his family, and throughout his later years he exuded an air of prosperity. 'He dressed quietly but fastidiously: dark grey suits; white shirts; a Surrey or England tie; well (self-) polished shoes,' wrote John Arlott. He liked driving and, over the years, owned a series of solid British saloons. No longer burdened by the demands of top-class cricket, he gave up his teetotalism and allowed himself to enjoy wine, champagne and the occasional liqueur, as well as cigars.

The same understated affluence was reflected in the new family home, for in 1933 the Hobbses moved further out of London from Atkins Road in Clapham to a detached 1920s house on Dunstall Road, Wimbledon, that classic suburban location. But Jack and Ada never took to their new place and two years later, they were on the move again, this time to an apartment in a modern art deco mansion block at Woodside, still in Wimbledon but very different to their previous homes. The house in Dunstall Road, however, was retained in the family and for several years the two youngest children, Ivor and Vera, continued to live there.

Part of the reason for this upheaval was that Ada was beginning to show the first signs of frailty, anxiety and dependence that would dog their later years together, and she was tired of the burden of running a large house. Moreover, their children had grown up and were pursuing their own lives. His eldest son Jack was now well established in the family shop, while Len, still a successful amateur athlete, had gone into the banking sector. Ivor, the third son, was starting out in the petroleum business, though he would later emigrate to southern Africa to farm in Rhodesia. By the end of the 1930s, much to his delight, all three of his sons were married. The youngest child Vera, less ambitious than her brothers, worked as a clerk. In 1941, she married a serviceman called Norman King, but it was to be a union that would bring much distress to her parents in the 1950s.

The one dark spot in the family saga during the pre-war period was the death of Jack's mother Florence in 1938. Despite the poverty she had experienced and the premature loss of her husband, she had lived to the age of eighty, witnessing the rise of her beloved son to international fame. 'A large circle of friends paid their last tributes to Mrs Florence Matilda Hobbs at the Mill Road Cemetery where she was laid to rest with her husband,' reported the *Cambridge Evening News*.

A brief outline of Hobbs's way of life in the mid-1930s was provided by a slightly condescending diary item in the *Daily Express*: 'He is a man of regular habits . . . regular but not puritanical. He likes a glass of champagne, or occasionally two. He also likes a good cigar, though I have more often seen him smoking a pipe. Like many pipe-smokers, he is a pleasant rather than an exciting companion . . . No cricketer living has done better out of the game that Jack Hobbs. I imagine that he could easily lay his hands on £5,000 at half an hour's notice.'

EPILOGUE   369

For all his wealth, Hobbs was not remotely acquisitive. Indeed, thanks to his Christian principles and his natural benevolence, he was an indefatigable supporter of charities throughout his life. He kept a separate charity fund in his accounts from which he made regular annual donations, and he also lent direct support by giving signed gifts or by making personal appearances. Hospitals, then largely voluntary institutions before the creation of the NHS in 1948, were one of his most favoured causes. Between 1910 and 1934 alone, Hobbs secured £15,100 for the Nelson and North Wimbledon hospitals by organising an annual charity match at a local cricket club, while he also raised funds for St Bart's Hospital in Fleet Street by auctioning autographed bats and other equipment. Among the wide-ranging other causes he backed were the Greater London Fund for the Blind, the Musician's Benevolent Fund, the Tonypandy Unemployed Club, the fund for the widow of the South African cricketer Jack Cameron, and an appeal for a new home for foundling boys in London. A classic instance of his generosity was recounted by an ordinary member of the public, Mr J. W. Chance, who explained that he once went into Hobbs's Fleet Street shop to buy a cricket bat. This was to be raffled as a part of a fund-raising drive for the repair of a church in Buckinghamshire. 'Having completed the purchase I asked Jack Hobbs whether he would do me the honour of autographing the bat. On learning the charitable nature of the request, he immediately agreed to do so and then asked me whether I would care to collect as well the signatures of the Surrey XI.' Mr Chance was only too delighted. Hobbs then gave him his own Oval pass so Chance could easily get to the Surrey players for their signatures. 'But that was not all. A few days later, I received a £1-note from Jack Hobbs to buy tickets for the raffle. I have subsequently heard from another Surrey cricketer that anything to do with the church always evoked his sympathy and support.'

Yet the view of Hobbs as a wonderful benefactor was not universally shared. Again, just as in the First World War, the negative opinion arose from within Hobbs's own family and the cause was the lack of support, it is claimed, for the widow of his younger brother Harry, who died in 1940. Mark Hobbs, Jack's great-nephew, has this intriguing memory of talking with his grandmother about her resentment. 'I was six when Jack Hobbs died. I was sitting at Dad's mum's house and there was the announcement in the *Cambridge Evening News* that he had died. Now my nan was not a critical person. She was nobody's fool. I said to her, "I see Jack Hobbs had died." She replied, "I asked that man for ten pounds when his brother died and he did not even lend it to me." She was talking about Harry's death. She had to keep up house and she had four children. It was very difficult. Yet Jack did not even allow her to borrow the money. My nan would always pay her debts. She never went into debt for anything. It must have been a huge weight on her shoulders to ask the man for ten pounds. He wouldn't give it or lend it. And she carried that right till he died. She didn't usually bear animosity but there was that one incident.' As so often in famous lives, private friction within a family can be at odds with the experience of the wider public.

Despite his retirement from first-class cricket, Hobbs kept up his fitness with his active involvement in several different sports. He enjoyed badminton, table tennis and billiards, and continued to have rounds of golf regularly, especially with his old Surrey friend Herbert Strudwick. Playing off a 12 handicap, he won a veterans' championship at the Malden Club in August 1936, following this up with an amateur handicap prize at the same club two years later. His healthy diet also kept him in good shape. For breakfast, as he explained in a 1935 *Daily Mail* interview, he liked to have porridge, followed by 'bacon and eggs, plenty of bread and butter or toast, tea or coffee and always generous quantities of raw fruit'. Lunch was usually a joint or grilled meat, with the evening meal comprising 'grilled or fried fish, or a cold joint and salad, or a roast joint with greens and potatoes', again with plenty of raw fruit. 'Mr Hobbs never takes cream, but uses butter freely,' reported the paper approvingly. Again, the legacy of a childhood without much fruit or meat is all too apparent.

Nor did his childhood passion for playing any kind of cricket leave him. When that other England opener Geoff Boycott retired, he never once picked up a bat again because he missed professional cricket so much and feared he would be overwhelmed with emotion at the reawakening of old memories. Hobbs was very different. He adored participating in almost any kind of match below first-class, including club and charity. Typically, in one of his first club games of 1935, for Merton, he almost scored a century. Later in the summer, he appeared again at Lord's for an ex-county cricketers XI against a team of actors. 'Hobbs, until he reached 50, batted in the broiling sun almost as carefully as if he were facing Yorkshire again with the championship depending on the result,' reported the *Star*. Even in this short innings, the predominance of his leg-side play, such a feature of his final years as a professional, was obvious. 'Most of Hobbs's runs were made by deflecting strokes to leg and quickly run singles.'

Remarkably, faith in Hobbs's retention of his batting ability was so powerful at the Oval that in July 1936, almost two years after he had played his last county game, he was actually asked to turn out for Surrey again in their championship match at home against Warwickshire, because four key players, Holmes, Gover, Brown and Laurie Fishlock, were taking part in the Gents v Players game at Lord's. Despite his continuing enthusiasm for playing, this was a step too far even for Hobbs at the age of fifty-three. 'He says he would prefer not to take up cricket in a big way again,' reported the *Daily Mirror*. But he remained on hand to give advice at the top level. Proving that trans-national trainers are nothing new in Test cricket, Hobbs gave some coaching at Lord's to the visiting Indians in the summer of 1936. He also made himself available for individual England cricketers, as was recalled by Harold Gimblett, the hugely talented Somerset opener who was plagued by introspection and depression throughout his life. Always highly strung, Gimblett was in despair when, in the same 1936 series, he was out early in the first innings of his Test debut to the inswing of Amir Singh. 'I put on my civvy clothes and started wandering round the ground. I was disconsolate and there was this horrible black cloud. Here I was playing for England and I'd made a hash of it. Suddenly I heard this voice, "Whoever's trodden on your foot, Harold?" It was Jack Hobbs, in the crowd, near the clock. "Oh Jack, did you see my performance?" He said I'd made 11 and that was better than some of them. And he went on, "You had your feet in the wrong place, that's all. Here, come and have a cup of tea." Scores of people recognised him. No one knew who I was. He chatted encouragingly over our cuppa. Then with his umbrella he explained the technique of playing inswing bowling.' Gimblett went out in the second innings and scored 67. He was convinced that Hobbs's advice 'made all the difference'. Sadly, because of mental illness, Gimblett never fulfilled his enormous promise as a cricketer.

Hobbs carried on with his happy combination of retailing, journalism, club cricket and family life until Britain was plunged into the cataclysm of the Second World War. In contrast to the First, Hobbs had no hesitation about enlisting for service. He joined the New Malden

Company of the Local Defence Volunteers or Home Guard, which was
soon nicknamed Dad's Army, Hobbs fitting exactly the classic profile
of the eager but elderly recruit. He was, he said with irony, 'a full blown
private', and in a radio broadcast to Australia in February 1941, he
explained his duties. 'They take up about two or three nights a week,
drilling and training. I spend one night on guard and two nights on
parade.' For all his own problematic experience in 1914, Hobbs was
proud that all three of his sons volunteered for the armed forces, though
it was the return of Len on leave after a tour of the Middle East that
landed Hobbs in trouble with the authorities. One night, Len, his wife
and their new baby came to visit Jack and Ada at their flat in Wimbledon.
While putting the baby to sleep in a cot, Ada accidently dislodged the
blackout curtain, immediately letting light out into the street. The
London Blitz was still continuing at this time and a police officer quickly
noticed the illegal illumination from the apartment block. The door
was knocked, names taken, apologies made, reprimands issued, as a
result of which Hobbs was hauled up in front of Wimbledon Magistrates'
Court for breaching Home Office regulations. In his defence, Hobbs
gave the tale of Len and the baby, but the judge was not swayed. 'We
will have to make the score a double figure,' said Mr E. Trim, the
Chairman of the Bench, as he fined Hobbs twenty shillings. Later in
the war, while serving in Italy, Len Hobbs found the grave of Hedley
Verity, the great Yorkshire spinner who had been mortally wounded in
July 1944, during the battle for Catania. As he told his father in a letter,
the grave was in a civilian cemetery without any inscription so he
arranged to have a name engraved on it.

Hobbs had an infinitely less traumatic war than those, like Len, who
were directly involved in the blood-soaked conflict. Nevertheless, these
were not easy years for him. Ada's health was poor. There was the
continual anxiety about the fate of his sons. His Fleet Street shop, for
so long a welcome source of income, became a heavy strain because he
had to run it almost single-handedly since Jack Junior was on active
service and the full-time manager Doug Brown had died in 1940. 'I'm
a manager and everything else. I have no staff and no stuff,' he joked.
Above Hobbs's shop was the London office of the Bristol newspaper
the *Western Daily Press* and one young clerk who worked there during
the late 1930s and the first year of the war was W.J. Stockbridge. He
looked after the petty cash, of which there was a continuous flow because

of the number of customers placing classified adverts, and sometimes he had to go to downstairs for change. 'Jack Hobbs's son ran the shop, was always kind and helped me out. On a couple of occasions the great man himself was there and I felt very proud when I had to approach him. Like his son, he joked with me about it and was very kind. If it was possible, I liked him even more after those instances,' he told the BBC history archive. Also in 1940 Hobbs sent a bat to a seven-year-old batsman who had scored 93 in a prep school match, a feat so astonishing that his headmaster had written to Hobbs about it. Along with the bat, Hobbs enclosed a letter, 'Dear Mr Cowdrey, I hear you are very keen on the game so I feel sure you will score many centuries in the years to come.'

For all his pleasure in helping youngsters like Colin Cowdrey, Hobbs was feeling his age and the burden of his shop. He poured out his feelings in a letter of April 1944 to Girdlestone, who had been complaining about being shifted from one parish to another. 'I have been pushed around too in another way. The manager of our business – joint partner too – died about four months after the war started and as we had already lost two assistants who had gone to the services I had to take over and devote my whole attention to the business. This left me with one original assistant and we managed very well, but he was taken fifteen months ago and my worries increased from that date. My wife helped me for six months and then Bert Thompson, who was head ground bowler when I first went to the Oval, called in one day and offered his services as he was tired of having nothing to do. I accepted and now two old men are running Jack Hobbs Ltd. There's quite a lot of business about but nothing is easy these days. I am sadly in need of fresh air and exercise and I fear I am looking – and feeling – a bit ancient.' Hobbs also explained that despite the German bombing raids, 'we have escaped damage at home although, like everybody else, we have had many near things'. Moreover, the shop windows 'were blown out at one stage'. He was also concerned about Ada, who had 'a bad turn two years back'. On top of all this, he and Ada had been through two more moves within Wimbledon, the first back to Dunstall Road and then on to Malcolm Road. Hobbs's strangely nomadic existence during this period, living at five different addresses over the space of eleven years, was reminiscent of the first years of his marriage when he moved rapidly from one rented house to another and it was in graphic contrast to the stability of Herbert Sutcliffe, who had firmly established his domain at Woodlands.

Hobbs could derive a little comfort from cricket, though this was severely restricted by both wartime and his own commitments. 'I've had just four games against school teams this year. I can still see the ball but I find it very difficult these days to get enough practice to get into form, because I have to stick to business,' he said in his Australian broadcast in 1941. As usual he was being too modest. During that summer, he regularly drove with Ada to Kimbolton, the independent school in Cambridgeshire, where he gave some coaching to the pupils on Wednesday afternoons. They became good friends with the headmaster, William Ingram, and one day in June, according to Hobbs's account 'he roped me in for the Fathers' XI against the School'. Rolling back the years, Hobbs scored a century, his last in any form of cricket. Though he continued to coach at Kimbolton into the late 1940s, his very last formal appearance as a player came in June 1945 in the final months of the war. As a favour to his old friend Andy Kempton, who was in charge of the Surrey youth teams but had to be absent on business, Hobbs agreed to captain the Surrey Colts against King's College School in Wimbledon. But he did not bat and fielded in the deep. Later that year he confirmed that he was finished with playing any form of cricket. The only sport he still pursued was golf, 'just a round occasionally and never mind your handicap. But not when it is cold. A book and a fire are more attractive to me then at my age.' On the cricket front, however, Hobbs had one pleasant piece of news towards the end of the war when he was elected to the Surrey Committee, the first professional to be so rewarded at the Oval. The next summer, 1946, he made his last appearance on a cricket field in any official capacity, acting as an umpire alongside Strudwick in a Surrey versus Old England match at the Oval.

By the end of the war, Hobbs was feeling his age more than ever, so he and Ada decided to change drastically their lives by moving to Hove on the south coast. 'Both my wife and self have been under the weather for the past few months, and we believe we shall enjoy better health by the seaside,' he told Girdlestone. 'We toyed with the idea several years back but decided the time was not ripe. Both of us have been working too hard and soon I hope to leave the business in other hands, travelling up two or three days a week.' With some abruptness, Hobbs then

turned down a request from Girdlestone to open a church fete. 'My
time is fully occupied with business and I feel I've had enough of it.'
In any case, said Hobbs, 'I always hated doing such things.' Because of
his age and the move to Hove, Hobbs turned down the chance to cover
the 1946/7 tour of Australia, the first trip he had missed in more than
forty years. But the change of scenery lifted his mood. 'We are now
settled in at Hove and we are quite happy. The change of air suits us
both and since I started playing golf again I have felt much fitter. I
think it would have been a mistake for me to go to Australia. The voyage
and train journeys and being continually on the move would have been
too much for me,' he told Girdlestone from his new home in Sunnyside
Mansions.

Then a new crisis blew up that cast a shadow over their lives, as Vera's
marriage descended into crisis because of her husband Norman's
infidelity and gambling debts, the problem made all the worse because
the young couple had two children. 'He's really a very odd fellow,' wrote
Hobbs in August 1948. 'Vera is very loyal and it is a great pity he does
not respond.' The pair separated for a while, Vera and the children
staying with Jack and Ada, but in January 1949 the worst seemed over.
'You will be pleased to hear that there is an improvement in this direction. Norman is home again and has assured me that he will try to
make a go of things. Anyhow, I settled a few of his debts and we are
hoping for the best,' said Hobbs. Those high expectations were dashed
a few months later. 'The young man now has a woman in tow and I'm
afraid there is no hope. Vera has despaired of him and wishes to be free
but the situation is difficult as Vera doesn't want to lose the children
and she dare not leave until she has sound proof.' At one point in this
drama, Hobbs felt rebuked by Girdlestone over his handling of the
mess, particularly his leniency towards his errant son-in-law. 'I expect
you mean that if I wasn't so soft, I would be better able to deal with
Vera's problem,' he wrote, showing some insight into his own gentle
character. The marriage was a wreck, yet Vera never formally divorced
and remained Mrs King until her death.

The turmoil did nothing for Ada's fragile health, both mental and
physical. His letters to Girdlestone are littered with references to her
decline from the beginning of 1950. 'I'm afraid my wife is beginning to
worry again but I hope it is only temporary,' he wrote in July 1950. A
year later, he told his friend, she had experienced 'another bad fall three

weeks ago. We had hoped she had got over this trouble but this time she shook herself up worse than ever. She has a broken nose and had to have a stitch put in at the point of her nose but she is not badly disfigured. There is a thickening at the bridge but it is quite straight still.' In January 1954, he reported that Ada, 'has slipped back a bit these last few months and we are waiting for better weather to get her on the right track again.' Six months later he described her as 'very poorly and shaky'. John Arlott, who became close to Hobbs after the war, admitted that 'she became eccentric with the years'. Her spirits were occasionally revived by the four trips they made to southern Africa to stay in a holiday retreat in Cape Town and to see their son Ivor in Rhodesia. Jack still suffered on the voyages: 'I'm no better a sailor but the ships are bigger than in those early days and I don't attempt to fight seasickness now,' he wrote. But Hobbs enjoyed the climate so much that he sometimes talked wistfully, if not realistically, about seeing out his last years in the region. It was on one journey in December 1954, travelling on the liner *Edinburgh Castle*, that he took part for the last time in any kind of cricket match when he appeared in a knockabout between the passengers and crew when the ship docked at Cape Town. He made a duck in both innings, but took seven wickets, not a bad performance for a seventy-one-year-old.

Back in England he was still involved in cricket during the 1950s through his journalism, now mainly with the *Sunday Express* rather than the *Star*, though Jimmy Bolton still acted as his ghost. More than ever, his reluctance to criticise reduced the sharpness of his copy. John Woodcock, the distinguished *Times* correspondent, remembers sitting near Hobbs in the press box while he was expressing to Bolton his strong disapproval of the technique of Peter Richardson, the Worcestershire and England left-hander. Yet when Bolton came to write the article, Hobbs said, 'No, we better leave all that out.' Unlike some other retired players, he never indulged in endless nostalgia about how standards had fallen since his day, though he did dislike the negative batting that blighted cricket in the 1950s and was concerned that the quality of Test cricket had been devalued. In addition, despite welcoming the improvement in the status of professionals, he regretted the rapid decline of the amateur, which he felt took some sparkle out of the game. 'There were more stars then; many good amateurs are lost now because of high costs and taxes.' The Caribbean writer C.L.R. James felt he was a shrewd watcher of the play. 'He sat quiet, saying little, speaking usually only when spoken to. But how he watched the game! He never took his eyes off it. I learnt much from him. In the press box he always wanted to tell you in his quiet voice what you wanted to know, what you had seen and not noticed. He himself missed nothing.' Jack Fingleton wrote that, just as in his playing career, he was a much-loved figure in the press box. 'It is a joy to see him, to greet him, and have a few words. Like his stroke-making, there is nothing uppish about Jack. He is everybody's friend and I think he appreciates that as much as his great string of records.'

In December 1952, Hobbs celebrated his seventieth birthday, an event that led to another flood of congratulations and accolades. 'Happy birthday Jack Hobbs,' said Denzil Bachelor in the *Picture Post*, paying his tribute to 'the most immaculate batsman of an age when whisky cost 3s 6d a bottle and England basked in Empire'. In the *Evening News*, Bill McGowran described him as the most famous of all Englishmen, apart from Winston Churchill. His name, said McGowran, 'chimes like a bell in the hearts of sportsmen the world over. It is more than a name. It is a national institution.' Charles Bray of the *Daily Herald* conducted an interview with him in which he described Hobbs 'as a very young seventy. There is no sign of a stoop. His slim erect figure moves with the same grace as it did in those glorious days of his cricketing prime. His eyes still have the twinkle and that world-famous smile quickly transforms his sharp-featured face.' Hobbs told Bray that what worried him most about his birthday was the arrival of the letters, cards and telegrams which, with his usual diligence, he would have to answer. But it was a pleasant burden. 'When you get to my age it is delightful to know you are not forgotten. They say the public has a very short memory. I have not found it so.'

Hobbs was the centre of even more celebratory attention the following summer, when it was announced that he was to be given a knighthood by Queen Elizabeth II in the Coronation Honours. He was the first professional to be awarded such a title, another recognition of his unique standing in the game. Yet according to John Arlott, Hobbs had severe doubts about accepting the honour and was only persuaded to do so by Sir Walter Monkton, the President of Surrey and Minister of Labour in Churchill's Conservative Cabinet. 'Jack Hobbs was a great man who never realised he was a great man. When he got the letter explaining that Churchill was pleased to offer him a knighthood, he was really distressed. So he went to Sir Walter Monckton and said, "Sir, I wonder if you could stop all this nonsense. It makes me blush." But Monckton concealed his mirth and convinced Jack that this was an honour not only to Jack but to all professional cricketers. He then accepted it with natural grace and he wore the knighthood with the dignity of a prince.' Soon afterwards, Hobbs wrote to his old partner Herbert Sutcliffe, 'I am easier in my mind now, for I realise that it is a compliment not only to myself but to cricket in general and the professional in particular.' Ever the uxorious husband, Hobbs further said he was 'charmed' that Ada would now be addressed as 'Lady Hobbs'. The public was gratified that he accepted, for the honour added to the buoyant mood of Britain after all the years of austerity in the difficult post-war era. 'Here it is – the Honours List that is different. No dreary catalogue of political favours but a sparkling list of familiar, respected and popular names, names like Jack Hobbs,' said the *Daily Mirror,* though the paper added, with some justification, 'Jack Hobbs, of course, should have been knighted nineteen years ago, when he retired from active cricket, and he is now seventy. Still, better late than never for this fine Englishman.'

A few months after the Coronation, Hobbs was honoured in a more personal way by John Arlott through the establishment of the Master's Club, a select group of friends and their guests who met for lunch at the Wellington Restaurant in Fleet Street, near his shop. With its traditional fare, the Wellington, run by an amiable Belgian called Emile Haon, was a favourite haunt of Jack's and he regularly ate and drank there. When Harold Larwood was about to emigrate with his family to Australia, Jack took him for lunch there on the eve of his voyage. Demonstrating that his days of abstention were long gone, Hobbs and Larwood worked their way through several bottles of champagne. 'I drank more glasses of champagne that I can remember. After lunch I didn't wake up till midnight and had the worst hangover the next morning that I ever had in my life,' recalled Larwood. John Arlott was Hobbs's most regular lunch companion and in September 1953, the arrangement was formalised through the creation of the Master's Club. Two other friends were present at that inaugural meeting, the BBC executive Kenneth Adam and the former Surrey fast bowler Alf Gover. It was such a convivial occasion that the Master's Club luncheons became cherished events in Hobbs's calendar, and over the years many of the legends of the game attended, ranging from Hobbs's old friends like Sutcliffe and Tate to current stars like Peter May and Colin Cowdrey. Politicians, writers, actors and businessmen were only too happy to accept invitations. The club, whose membership in the 1950s never exceeded twenty, evolved several rules. There were to be no speeches and only one toast, to The Master. On Hobbs's birthday, only those who had played Test cricket with him could attend, and the menu that day had to consist of his favourite meal: soup, roast beef and baked potatoes, apple pie and cream. One other tradition was for Alf Gover to recount, with embellishments added by each retelling, the story of how he once opened the innings for Surrey with Hobbs in a game at Northampton. This unique moment came when Surrey had to survive a brief spell at the end of the day and Hobbs decided to take in Gover as a night-watchman. Somehow Gover, much nursed by Hobbs, managed to survive. The next morning he continued his innings and he began to feel growing confidence until Hobbs came down the wicket.

'Alfred, would you do me a favour?'

'Of course, Jack.'

'Do you mind getting out now. There's a lot of good players waiting to come in.'

Gover obliged the next ball.

Arlott said of the Master's Club, which has survived to this day, that it derived 'its impetus from a spirit compounded of love of a game and pure adulation, nurtured through boyhood and grown full in manhood, of a man who played it supremely well'. An essay to mark the tenth anniversary of the club contains this description of Hobbs's manner if he felt compelled to address the luncheon, despite the unwritten rule against speeches: 'It is not certain to happen but sometimes, perhaps especially moved by the spirit of the gathering and the sight of old friends, the Master elects to stand and answer the toast. Diffidently, nervously, twirling an almost empty wineglass by the stem, he will let his eye wander round the table. Then gently, with delicate and devastating wit, Sir Jack Hobbs relates anecdote after anecdote as his gaze flickers, settles, flickers and settles again among the faces who were great with him.'

The former England leg-spinner Ian Peebles was a member of the club and, after his playing days were over, he went into business with a company selling German wines. Part of Peebles' responsibility was to organise lunches for clients to taste his products and, to enhance the appeal of these events, he often invited special guests, one of whom was Hobbs. 'Jack modestly disclaimed any extensive knowledge but was very fond of a glass of hock. When it was known he was coming to lunch there were broad hints from many vintners of his generation that they would like to come too, but accommodation was limited.' His presence was always a special occasion for the hosts, wrote Peebles: 'There was about him until the last months of his life a youthful air, enhanced by a lively sense of humour and, as a guest, he had but one failing – it was difficult to get him to talk about his own career, a subject everyone wanted to get him to talk about. But when he had a glass or two of hock and a cigar, which he dearly loved, we would slyly guide him on to his active days and the company would listen enthralled, putting in strategical questions when he threatened to turn to other subjects.'

Even into his late seventies, Hobbs continued to commute from Hove to work Mondays, Wednesdays and Fridays in his Fleet Street shop. 'My memory is of an old-fashioned shop, small and dark inside with a mahogany or French polished counter. One had the sense of a shop which was clean and not markedly prosperous – none of the modern fancy or flash fittings. There were bats hanging from nails behind the counter suspended with pieces of string. It was all very modest, homely, down-to-earth and very English in the post-war way of things,' says the Conservative MP Bill Cash, who bought a bat from Hobbs in his boyhood and was good enough to have a trial with Yorkshire in the early 1960s. Hobbs still wrote the occasional article, attended the Surrey Committee and played a round of golf, his handicap having risen to 16. But his last years were dominated by his care for Ada, who from the late 1950s was disabled. Because she was wheelchair-bound, they moved to a ground-floor flat in Palmeira Avenue in Hove. Terrified that she would have to go into a residential home, he did everything for her, as Arlott recalled, 'He bathed, dressed, undressed and nursed her; combed her hair and adjusted her hat to her liking.' It was an exhausting routine for a man who celebrated his eightieth birthday in December 1962, but his tenderness revealed his enduring adoration and love for the woman he always described as his 'inspiration'. The end came in March 1963, when she passed away after developing cancer.

Hobbs was filled with sorrow at this loss after fifty-six years of marriage, yet he was also relieved that Ada's struggle had come to a merciful close. In that summer of 1963, he spent much of his time watching Sussex play at the county ground in Hove, where Ted Dexter was a particular favourite of his. He made occasional trips to London and one to Hampshire for the christening of John Arlott's son Robert, for whom he was a godfather. But in the autumn his health began to fail. He lost weight and found that he no longer enjoyed his daily glasses of champagne. For the first time since its foundation, he had to miss a meeting of the Master's Club. Hobbs also had to give up his car, though the sale of his vehicle was a further illustration of Hobbs's essential decency, as recalled by the purchaser, Richard Burton of Purley: 'In a letter to Sir Jack I requested that, only if it was convenient, I would appreciate it if he would kindly endorse the cheque that I sent in payment for the car. In due course, the cheque was returned to me from my bank. On the back, obviously carefully but painfully inscribed, was that great gentleman's signature. I subsequently learned from a member of the Hobbs family that making this signature was indeed a great effort for Sir Jack and that it took him ten minutes of painful endeavour. It was, in fact, the last signature he ever wrote. Of course, if I had realised just how ill he was at the time, I certainly would not have made my request but this incident does explain how truly kind-hearted and ever anxious to please was Sir Jack.'

By December, it was clear that he was fading away. Old age had simply caught up with him. John Arlott visited Hobbs at this time with his son, and recalled that, though 'he could no longer speak', his eyes 'still twinkled with a smile of greeting that seemed like a blessing'. Confined to bed in his Hove flat, he had his daughter Vera constantly by his side. 'He is not suffering – just slipping very quietly and peacefully away,' she said on 16 December 1963. Five days later he died quietly in his sleep, mourned by a nation he had served so well. The end, said his son Jack, was 'very, very peaceful'. His epitaph lay not just in his epic achievements with the bat but also in the profound impact that his character had on the game. 'He was the greatest batsman in the world for most of the quarter of century when he was playing,' proclaimed his obituary in *The Times*. 'It was my proudest cricketing boast that I played in the Surrey side with him, for to me he was a great player and a great man,' wrote E.M. Wellings in the *Evening Standard*, sentiments that were echoed across the cricket world. 'He was a gentleman always, on and off the field,' said Sydney Barnes.

True to Jack's quiet, orderly nature, he had organised everything efficiently before he died. In his will, he left an estate of £19,445, with the shares in the shop going to Jack Junior, and the residue of his property given to Leonard and Ivor. He also set up a trust for Vera and her children, presumably so the wayward Norman would not be able to claim any part of the inheritance. After a private family service in Hove, he was buried alongside his beloved Ada in the north side of the town's cemetery.

To allow the wider public to pay their last tributes, a memorial service was held for Sir Jack at Southwark Cathedral on 20 February 1964. 'As a boy, he always regarded the Bible as a great guide to life and as a standard of values. He never wavered from them,' said the Provost of the cathedral, the Reverend E. Southcott. 'It is good that the Master of cricket should be honoured in the Master's House.' Almost all the great living figures of English cricket attended, including Len Hutton, Les Ames, Ken Barrington and Ted Dexter. Peter May read one of the lessons, the Reverend David Sheppard another, while the ushers included Alec Bedser and the present Surrey captain Mickey Stewart. In his address, the historian Harry Altham extolled Sir Jack's modesty, kindness and humour. 'He was honoured wherever the game is played.' The final hymn, so suitable for Hobbs's Christian devotion, was 'God be in my head, and in my understanding'. As the congregation filed out into the pale February sunshine, it was his dearest friend Herbert Strudwick who found the most appropriate, eloquent words of all: 'No finer man ever lived.'

Bibliography

Ackroyd, Peter, *London: The Biography* (2000)

Allen, David Rayvern, *Cricket on the Air* (1985)

——, *Arlott: The Authorised Biography* (1994)

——, *Jim: The Life of E.W. Swanton* (2005)

——, *Jack Hobbs and the Master's Club* (2009)

Ames, Les, *Close of Play* (1953)

Andrews, Bill, *The Hand that Bowled Bradman* (1973)

Arlott, John, *Cricket in the Counties* (1950)

——, *Jack Hobbs: Profile of 'The Master'* (1981)

——, *Basingstoke Boy* (1992)

Arlott, Timothy, *A Memoir* (1994)

Arthur, Max, *Lost Voices of the Edwardians* (2007)

Armstrong, Warwick, *The Art of Cricket* (1922)

Arnold, Peter and Peter Wynne-Thomas, *An Ashes Anthology* (1989)

Barker, Ralph, *Ten Great Innings* (1964)

Barker, Tony, *Cricket's Wartime Sanctuary* (2009)

Batchelor, Denzil, *Great Cricketers* (1970)

Birley, Derek, *The Willow Wand* (1979)

——, *A Social History of English Cricket* (1999)

Booth, Keith, *The Father of Modern Sport: The Life and Times of C.W. Alcock* (2002)

——, *Ernest Hayes: Brass in a Golden Age* (2008)

Bosanquet, Mrs Bernard, *Social Conditions in Provincial Towns* (1912)

Bowes, Bill, *Express Deliveries* (1949)

Bradman, Don, *Farewell to Cricket* (1930)

Brown, Freddie, *Cricket Musketeer* (1954)

Butcher, P.E., *Skill and Devotion: A Personal Reminiscence of the Famous*

No.2 Squadron (1971)

Carr, A.W., Cricket With the Lid Off (1937)

Carew, Dudley, To the Wicket (1946)

Charles, J.A., One Man's Cambridge: The Life and Times of J.H.V. Charles
    1887–1932 (2006)

Chester, Frank, How's That! (1956)

Cooksley, Peter, Royal Flying Corps Handbook (2000)

——, The Home Front (2006)

De La Noy, Michael, Bedford School: A History (1999)

Denham, Richard, In the Line of Fire (1998)

Douglas, Christopher, Douglas Jardine: Spartan Cricketer (1984)

Down, Michael, Archie: A Biography of A.C. MacLaren (1981)

Ducat, Andrew, Cricket (1933)

Duckworth, Leslie, From the Hearth (1951)

——, S.F. Barnes: Master Bowler (1967)

——, Holmes and Sutcliffe (1970)

Fender, P.G.F., The Turn of the Wheel (1929)

——, The Tests of 1930 (1930)

Ferguson, W.H., Mr Cricket (1957)

Fingleton, Jack, Fingleton on Cricket (1972)

——, The Immortal Victor Trumper (1978)

Florey, R.A., The General Strike of 1926 (1980)

Foot, David, Harold Gimblett: Tormented Genius of Cricket (1984)

——, Wally Hammond: The Reasons Why (1998)

Foster, Frank, Cricketing Memories (1930)

Frewin, Leslie (ed.), Cricket Bag (1965)

Frindall, Bill (ed.), The Wisden Book of Test Cricket (1979)

Frith, David, England versus Australia (1977)

——, The Golden Age of Cricket, 1890–1914 (1978)

——, Bodyline Autopsy (2002)

——, Frith on Cricket (2010)

Fry, C.B., Life Worth Living (1939)

Gardiner, Juliet, The Thirties: An Intimate History (2010)

Garnsey, George (compiler), Bradman's First Tour (1980)

Geddes, Margaret, Remembering Bradman (2002)

Gibson, Alan, The Cricket Captains of England (1979)

Gilligan, A.E.R., Collins's Men (1926)

Peter Glazebrook (ed.) Jesus: The Life of a Cambridge College (2007)

Gover, Alf, *The Long Run* (1991)

Gray, Arthur and Frederick Brittain, *A History of Jesus College* (1979)

Gregory, Adrian, *The Last Great War* (2008)

Haigh, Gideon, *The Big Ship* (2001)

Hamilton, Duncan, *Harold Larwood* (2009)

Hamilton, Peggy, *Three Years or the Duration* (1978)

Hattersley, Roy, *Borrowed Time* (2007)

Hendren, Patsy, *My Book of Cricket and Cricketers* (1927)

——, *Big Cricket* (1984)

Hill, Alan, *Hedley Verity: Portrait of a Cricketer* (1986)

——, *Les Ames* (1990)

——, *Herbert Sutcliffe* (1991)

Hill, Les, *The Arthur Richardson Story* (1968)

Hilton, Christopher, *Bradman and the Summer that Changed Cricket* (2009)

Hobbs, Jack, *Recovering the Ashes,* (1912)

——, *How to Make a Century* (1913)

——, *My Cricket Memories* (1924)

——, *Between the Wickets* (1926)

——, *Playing for England* (1931)

——, *The Fight for the Ashes* (1933)

——, *The Fight for the Ashes* (1934)

——, *My Life Story* (1935)

—— with Herbert Strudwick and Maurice Tate, *The Game of Cricket* (1926)

Holmes, Errol, *Flannelled Foolishness* (1957)

Howat, Gerald, *Walter Hammond* (1984)

——, *Plum Warner* (1987)

——, *Cricket's Second Golden Age* (1989)

Huggins, Mike, *The Victorians and Sport* (2004)

Jardine, Douglas, *Cricket* (1936)

Jebb, Eglantyne, *Cambridge: A Brief Study in Social Questions* (1906)

Jenkinson, Neil, *C.P. Mead: Hampshire's Greatest Run-maker* (1993)

John, Angela and Claire Eustance (eds.), *The Men's Share?* (1914)

Kay, John (ed.), *Cricket Heroes* (1959)

Kent, William, *Fifty Years a Cricket Watcher* (1946)

Kynaston, David, *Bobby Abel: Professional Batsman* (1982)

Larwood, Harold, *The Larwood Story* (1965)

Lee, Harry, *Forty Years of English Cricket* (1948)

Lemmon, David, *Tich Freeman and the Decline of the Leg-Break Bowler* (1982)

——, *Johnny Won't Hit Today* (1983)

——, *Percy Chapman* (1985)

——, *The Crisis of Captaincy* (1988)

——, *For the Love of the Game* (1993)

Leveson Gower, Sir Henry, *On and Off the Field* (1953)

Levine, Joshua, *Fighter Heroes of WW1* (2008)

Low, Robert, *W.G.* (1997)

Lyon, M.D. *Cricket* (1938)

Macartney, C.G, *My Cricketing Days* (1930)

MacLaren, A.C., *The Perfect Batsman* (1926)

Mallett, Ashley, *Scarlet: Clarrie Grimmett – Test Cricketer* (2008)

Major, John, *More than a Game: The Story of Cricket's Early Years* (2007)

Mant, Gilbert, *A Cuckoo in the Bodyline Nest* (1992)

Marchant, John, *The Greatest Test Match* (1953)

Marshall, Michael, *Gentlemen and Players* (1987)

Marwick, Arthur, *The Deluge* (1965)

Mason, Ronald, *Batsman's Paradise* (1955)

——, *Jack Hobbs* (1960)

——, *Warwick Armstrong's Australians* (1971)

Meredith, Anthony, *Summers in Winter* (1990)

Midwinter, Eric, *Darling Old Oval* (1995)

Mitchell, Ena, *Notes on the History of Parker's Piece, Cambridge* (1984)

Midwinter, Eric, *W.G. Grace: His Life and Times* (1981)

Mortimer, David, *The Oval: Test Match Cricket since 1880* (2005)

Moult, Thomas, *Bat and Ball* (1935)

Moyes, A.G., *A Century of Cricketers* (1950)

Mulley, Clare, *The Woman who Saved the Children* (2009)

Murphy, Patrick, *Tiger Smith* (1981)

——, *The Centurions* (2009)

Nicholson, Juliet, *The Perfect Summer* (2006)

——, *The Great Silence 1918–1920* (2009)

Nickalls, G.O., *With the Skin of their Teeth* (1951)

Noble, M.A., *Gilligan's Men* (1925)

——, *Those Ashes 1926* (1926)

——, *The Fight for the Ashes 1928–29* (1929)

Oldfield, W.A., *Behind the Stumps* (1938)

——, *The Rattle of the Stumps* (1954)

Overy, Richard, *The Morbid Age: Britain Between the Wars* (2009)

Palgrave, Louis, *The Story of the Oval* (1949)

Parker, Eric, *The Game of Cricket* (1930)

Parkin, Cecil, *Cricket Triumph and Troubles* (1936)

Pawle, Gerald, *R.E.S. Wyatt: Fighting Cricketer* (1985)

Paynter, Eddie, *Cricket All the Way* (1962)

Peebles, Ian, *Woolley: The Pride of Kent* (1969)

——, *Patsy Hendren: The Cricketer and His Times* (1969)

——, *Spinner's Yarn* (1977)

Perkins, Anne, *A Very British Strike* (2006)

Perry, Roland, *The Don* (1996)

Pollock, William, *Talking about Cricket* (1941)

Porter, Clive, *The Test Match Career of Sir Jack Hobbs* (1988)

Porter, Roy, *London: A Social History* (1994)

Pugh, Martin, *We Danced All Night* (2009)

Reeve, F.A., *Victorian and Edwardian Cambridge* (1971)

Rendell, Brian, *Gubby Allen: Bad Boy of Bodyline?* (2008)

Rennles, Keith, *The War Diary of the Daylight Squadrons of the Independent Air Force* (2002)

Robertson-Glasgow, Raymond, *46 Not Out* (1948)

——, *More Cricket Prints* (1948)

——, *Crusoe on Cricket* (1966)

Rogerson, Sidney, *Wilfred Rhodes* (1960)

Root, Fred, *A Cricket Pro's Lot* (1937)

Ross, Gordon, *The Surrey Story* (1958)

——, *A History of Surrey County Cricket* (1971)

——, *The History of Surrey County Cricket* (1989)

Sewell, E.H.D., *A Searchlight on English Cricket* (1926)

Sheen, Steve and Kit Bartlett, *Tom Hayward* (1997)

Sissons, Ric, *The Players: A Social History of the Professional Cricketer* (1988)

—— and Brian Stoddart, *Cricket and Empire* (1984)

Smart, John Blythe, *The Real Colin Blythe* (2009)

Smith, Peter Jefferson and Alison Wilson, *Clapham in the Twentieth Century* (2002)

Smith, Rick, *Cricket Brawl: The 1912 Dispute* (1995)

Strudwick, Herbert, *25 Years behind the Stumps* (1925)

Streeton, Richard, *P.G.H. Fender: A Biography* (1981)

Sugg, Willie, *A Tradition Unshared: A History of Cambridge Town and County Cricket* (2002)

Sutcliffe, Herbert, *For England and Yorkshire* (1948)

Swanton, E.W., *Sort of a Cricket Person* (1972)

——, *Gubby Allen: Man of Cricket*, (1985)

Synge, Allen, *Sins of Omission* (1990)

Tate, Maurice, *My Cricketing Reminiscences* (1932)

Tebbutt, Geoffey, *With the 1930 Australians* (1930)

Tennyson, Lionel Lord, *Sticky Wickets* (1950)

Thomson, A.A., *Cricket My Pleasure* (1953)

——, *Hirst and Rhodes* (1959)

——, *Cricket: The Golden Ages* (1961)

Tinkler, Basil Ashton, *A Somerset Hero who Beat the Aussies* (2000)

Tranter, Neil, *Sport, Economy and Society in Britain 1750–1914* (1998)

Travers, Ben, *94 Declared: Cricket Reminiscences* (1981)

Trevor, Philip, *With the MCC in Australia 1907–08* (1908)

——, *Cricket and Cricketers* (1921)

Vamplew, Wray, *Play Up and Play the Game* (1988)

Van Emden, Richard and Steve Humphries, *All Quiet on the Home Front* (2004)

Warner, P.F., *England v Australia: The Record of a Memorable Tour* (1912)

—— *England v Australia* (1913)

——, *Cricket Reminiscences* (1920)

——, *The Fight for the Ashes in 1926* (1926)

——, *The Fight for the Ashes in 1930* (1930)

——, *Cricket Between Two Wars* (1942)

——, *Long Innings* (1951)

Williams, Jack, *Cricket in England* (2003)

Wilton, Iain, *C.B. Fry: An English Hero* (1999)

Woodhouse, Anthony, *The History of Yorkshire County Cricket Club* (1989)

Woods, Mike and Tricia Platts, *Bradford in the Great War* (2007)

Woods, S.M.J., *My Reminiscences* (1925)

Woolley, Frank, *The King of Games* (1936)

——, *Early Memoirs* (1976)

Wyatt, R.E.S., *Three Straight Sticks* (1951)

Wykes, A.P.A., *Golden Ages at the Fenner's Margin* (2005)

Young, Kenneth, *Harry, Lord Rosebery* (1974)

Acknowledgements and Sources

Whearched a biography of Geoff Boycott twelve years ago, much of the book was made up with first-hand testimony from interviews with a wide range of his friends, acquaintances, lovers and former colleagues. Even his tailor gave me a lively account, complete with verbal explosions, of a typical Boycott visit for a fitting. Sadly, it has not been possible to gather anything like the same amount of audio material about Sir Jack Hobbs, since none of his contemporaries are still alive. Indeed, given that he retired from first-class cricket almost eighty years ago, there are probably only a few people still around who even saw him play. However, I was able to track down several of his descendants who were able to provide me with some insights into Sir Jack's character and family. I would therefore like to record here my gratitude to Harry Hobbs, John and Margaret Witt, Martyn Hobbs and Mark Hobbs, who all spoke to me with thoughtfulness and candour. Johnnie Sandham, the daughter of Sir Jack's famous Surrey opening partner, also generously granted me an interview about her father, while David Pimblett, the manager of Hobbs Sports in Cambridge, gave me a host of insights about Sir Jack's early years in Cambridge, much of the information gleaned from his own superb collection of local newspaper cuttings on cricket. Frances Willmoth, the archivist at Jesus College, Cambridge, found for me useful documents about Sir Jack's father and Honor Rideout of the Cambridgeshire Association for Local History filled in some of the nineteenth century background. Further material on Sir Jack's Cambridge came from Willie Sugg, Stephen Harper-Scott, Fonz Chamberlain and Adrian Wykes, author of the fascinating *Golden Ages at the Fenner's Margin*. John Woodcock, the renowned cricket writer, kindly provided his memories of working alongside Sir Jack in the pressbox of the 1950s, as well as giving me some warm-hearted anecdotes about Sir Jack's playing days. The Conservative MP Bill Cash, a true cricket enthusiast, recounted to me his experience of buying a bat from Sir Jack's shop in the early 1960s.

There were many others who assisted me with their time and advice. The book could not have been written without the invaluable help of David Frith, one of cricket's greatest historians, who not only allowed me full access to his rich archive of documents and photographs, but was also a wonderful guide to the context of Hobbs's career. When I was first fired with a passion for cricket growing up in Belfast at the height of the Troubles, David Frith's majestic works like *The Golden Age of Cricket* had a profound influence on me and it was a privilege, more than three decades later, to be able to sit for hours with him chatting about the great game. Among the other cricket experts who advised me were Rob Brooke, David Jeater, Hugh Nathan, David Ryvern Allen, Tony Barker, Martin Howe and Roger Packham. I am also grateful to Philip Bailey for producing a fine statistical appendix with typical expertise and insight. Jo Miller, the archivist at Surrey County Cricket Club, could not have been more supportive about the project and the same is true of Neil Robinson at the MCC Library. I am also sincerely grateful to the professional researcher Ian Waller for his diligence in illuminating Sir Jack's family background, first jobs in Cambridge, and his war record. Guy Fletcher, the director of sport at Bedford School, arranged for me to have a happy day there going through records and seeing the grounds where Sir Jack first earned his living as a professional. Useful details on the Suffragette movement came from Joyce Kay of Stirling University and Beverley Cook of the Museum of London, while information on the General Strike of 1926 was provided by Helen Ford of Warwick University and Darren Treadwell of the People's History Museum in Manchester.

I am obliged to the staff of all the other reference libraries that helped me with my research, including the local history collection at Bedford, the Surrey History Centre at Woking, the Cambridgeshire archives in Cambridge Central Library, the British Newspaper Library at Colindale, the British Library at St Pancras, the RAF Museum at Hendon, the National Archive at Kew and the BBC archives at Caterham.

On the production side, I am indebted to Rowan Yapp of the Yellow Jersey Press both for commissioning the book and for overseeing the project so expertly. Her team have also been highly efficient throughout so my thanks to Justine Taylor, Kate Bland and Ruth Warburton.

I am also grateful, as always, to my excellent agent Bill Hamilton.

Finally, I must express my heartfelt gratitude to my long-suffering wife Elizabeth, who has been unstinting in her support throughout the long months of research and writing about Sir Jack. I would never have been able to do the book without her.

Leo McKinstry
Westgate-on-Sea
February 2011

Illustrations

1) Jack Hobbs in 1925 (Getty Images); 2) No.4 Rivar Place, Cambridge (Author's collection); 3) The backstreets of late Victorian Cambridge (Author's collection); 4) Hobbs on first-class debut, 1905 (David Frith collection); 5) Hobbs after his first Ashes tour, 1907/8 (Getty); 6) Hobbs batting in Cape Town 1909/10 (DF collection); 7) Hobbs in the Triangular Tournament 1912 (DF collection); 8) Hobbs with Tom Hayward (DF collection); 9) Wilfred Rhodes batting (Getty); 10) Hobbs leaping down the wicket (Press Association); 11) Lord Hawke (Getty); 12) The Surrey captain Percy Fender (Getty); 13) Hobbs in the indoor nets (Getty); 14) Hobbs in contemplation (DF collection); 15) Hobbs in Italy, with Rhodes, Woolley and Strudwick (DF collection); 16) Hobbs an ill man, Headingley 1921 (DF collection); 17) Hobbs batting against South Africa , 1924 (DF collection); 18) Hobbs equalling W.G.Grace's record of centuries, Taunton 1925 (Getty); 19) Hobbs toasts the cheers of the Taunton crowd (Getty); 20) Hobbs with Andy Sandham (Getty); 21) Hobbs with Herbert Sutcliffe (Getty); 22) Hobbs batting at Lord's 1926 (author's collection); 23) Hobbs leads out England, Old Trafford 1926 (author's collection); 24) Hobbs on his way to a century at the Oval, 1926 (author's collection); 25) Hobbs is congratulated by Herbie Collins on his innings (DF collection); 26) Hobbs's wife Ada on the beach at Margate (Getty); 27) Jack with his beloved Ada, 1929 (Getty); 28)

Jack and Ada teaching two of their children cricket (DF collection); 29) A crowd outside Hobbs's Fleet Street shop (Getty); 30) Hobbs choosing the willow for a new bat (Getty); 31) Hobbs signs his autograph for a schoolboy fan (Getty); 32) Hobbs scoring his last Test century (author's collection); 33) Hobbs hits out against Derbyshire, 1924 (Mirrorpix); 34) Hobbs bowled by Notts, 1929 (Kate Bland collection); 35) Hobbs driving into Lord's, 1930 (Getty); 36) Hobbs controversially caught by Ted a'Beckett, 1930 (author's collection); 37) The start of his last Test innings, Oval 1930 (Press Association); 38) In his retirement, coaching young schoolboys (Getty); 39) Opening of the Hobbs gates at the Oval, 1934 (DF collection); 40) Sir Jack at Buckingham Palace, 1953 (Press Association); 41) On his 70th birthday in his Fleet Street shop (author's collection).

Statistical Appendix

Test record series by series

Season		Matches	Inns	Not Out	Runs	HS	Average	100	50
1907/08	v Aus	4	8	1	302	83	43.14	0	3
1909	v Aus	3	6	1	132	62*	26.40	0	1
1909/10	v SAf	5	9	1	539	187	67.37	1	4
1911/12	v Aus	5	9	1	662	187	82.75	3	1
1912	v SAf	3	5	1	163	68	40.75	0	2
1912	v Aus	3	4	0	224	107	56.00	1	1
1913/14	v SAf	5	8	1	443	97	63.28	0	4
1920/21	v Aus	5	10	0	505	123	50.50	2	1
1921	v Aus	1	0						
1924	v SAf	4	5	0	355	211	71.00	1	1
1924/25	v Aus	5	9	0	573	154	63.66	3	2
1926	v Aus	5	7	1	486	119	81.00	2	2
1928	v WI	2	2	0	212	159	106.00	1	1
1928/29	v Aus	5	9	0	451	142	50.11	1	2
1929	v SAf	1	2	0	62	52	31.00	0	1
1930	v Aus	5	9	0	301	78	33.44	0	2
Total		61	102	7	5410	211	56.94	15	28

Test Career Bowling and Fielding

Balls	Mdns	Runs	Wkts	BB	Average	5wI	Catches
376	15	165	1	1-19	165.00	0	17

Methods of dismissal in Tests

Caught	54
Bowled	24
lbw	11
Stumped	3
Run out	2
Hit wicket	1

Opening partnerships with certain players

	Partnerships	Unbroken	Runs	Average	Highest
W. Rhodes	36	1	2146	61.31	323
H. Sutcliffe	38	1	3249	87.81	283

Notes: Hobbs and Sutcliffe had one further partnership of 90 for the 5th wicket when a changed batting order was used in 1924/25
Hobbs and Rhodes had four further partnerships totalling 148 runs for other wickets
Hobbs and Hayward had two opening partnerships of 23 and 16
Hobbs and Sandham played three Tests together but had only one partnership, 28 for the second wicket

Test hundreds

211	England	South Africa	Lord's	1924
187	England	South Africa	Cape Town	1909/10
187	England	Australia	Adelaide	1911/12
178	England	Australia	Melbourne	1911/12
159	England	West Indies	The Oval	1928
154	England	Australia	Melbourne	1924/25
142	England	Australia	Melbourne	1928/29
126*	England	Australia	Melbourne	1911/12
123	England	Australia	Adelaide	1920/21
122	England	Australia	Melbourne	1920/21
119	England	Australia	Adelaide	1924/25
119	England	Australia	Lord's	1926
115	England	Australia	Sydney	1924/25
107	England	Australia	Lord's	1912
100	England	Australia	The Oval	1926

Bowlers who dismissed Hobbs most times in Test cricket

C. V. Grimmett	9
A. A. Mailey	9
J. M. Gregory	7
J. V. Saunders	4
C. G. Macartney	4
J. M. Blanckenberg	4
G. A. Faulkner	4
A. Cotter	4
H. V. Hordern	4
A. W. Nourse	3
W. J. Whitty	3
A. E. E. Vogler	3

First-class record season by season

Season		Matches	Inns	Not Out	Runs	HS	Average	100	50
1905	England	30	54	3	1317	155	25.82	2	4
1906	England	31	53	6	1913	162*	40.70	4	10
1907	England	37	63	6	2135	166*	37.45	4	15
1907/08	Australia	13	22	1	876	115	41.71	2	6
1908	England	36	53	2	1904	161	37.33	6	7
1909	England	31	54	2	2114	205	40.65	6	7
1909/10	South Africa	12	20	1	1194	187	62.84	3	7
1910	England	38	63	3	1982	133	33.03	3	14
1911	England	36	60	3	2376	154*	41.68	4	13
1911/12	Australia	11	18	1	943	187	55.47	3	2
1912	England	38	60	6	2042	111	37.81	3	14
1913	England	32	57	5	2605	184	50.09	9	12
1913/14	South Africa	16	22	2	1489	170	74.45	5	8
1914	England	29	48	2	2697	226	58.63	11	6
1919	England	30	49	6	2594	205*	60.32	8	14
1920	England	31	50	2	2827	215	58.89	11	13
1920/21	Australia	12	19	1	924	131	51.33	4	1
1921	England	5	6	2	312	172*	78.00	1	1
1922	England	29	46	5	2552	168	62.24	10	9
1923	England	34	59	4	2087	136	37.95	5	8
1924	England	30	43	7	2094	211	58.16	6	10
1924/25	Australia	10	17	1	865	154	54.06	3	5

1925	England	30	48	5	3024	266*	70.32	16	5
1926	England	30	41	3	2949	316*	77.60	10	12
1927	England	23	32	1	1641	150	52.93	7	5
1928	England	28	38	7	2542	200*	82.00	12	10
1928/29	Australia	11	18	1	962	142	56.58	2	7
1929	England	24	39	5	2263	204	66.55	10	8
1930	England	30	43	2	2103	146*	51.29	5	14
1931	England	31	49	6	2418	153	56.23	10	7
1932	England	24	35	4	1764	161*	56.90	5	9
1933	England	12	18	0	1105	221	61.38	6	3
1934	England	12	18	1	624	116	36.70	1	4
Total		826	1315	106	61237	316*	50.65	197	270

First-Class Career Bowling and Fielding

Balls	Mdns	Runs	Wkts	BB	Average	5wI	Catches
5205	171	2676	107	7-56	25.00	3	337

Methods of dismissal

Caught	692
Bowled	287
lbw	126
Stumped	67
Run out	31
Hit wicket	6

Opening partnerships with certain players

	Partnerships	Unbroken	Runs	Average	Highest
W. Rhodes	92	2	4467	49.63	323
T. W. Hayward	394	9	16218	42.12	352
A. Sandham	405	9	21671	54.72	428
H. Sutcliffe	99	2	7492	77.23	283

Notes: the figures above are for first wicket partnerships only

First-class double hundreds

316*	Surrey	Middlesex	Lord's	1926
266*	Players	Gentlemen	Scarborough	1925
261	Surrey	Oxford University	The Oval	1926

226	Surrey	Nottinghamshire	The Oval	1914
221	Surrey	West Indians	The Oval	1933
215*	Surrey	Essex	Leyton	1914
215	The Rest	Middlesex	The Oval	1920
215	Surrey	Warwickshire	Birmingham	1925
211	England	South Africa	Lord's	1924
205*	Surrey	Australian Imperial Forces	The Oval	1919
205	Surrey	Hampshire	The Oval	1909
204	Surrey	Somerset	The Oval	1929
203*	Surrey	Nottinghamshire	Nottingham	1924
202	Surrey	Yorkshire	Lord's	1914
200*	Surrey	Warwickshire	Birmingham	1928
200	Surrey	Hampshire	Southampton	1926

Bowlers who dismissed Hobbs most times in first-class cricket

J. W. H. T. Douglas	25
C. Blythe	17
G. G. Macaulay	15
T. G. Wass	15
W. Rhodes	15
E. G. Dennett	15
J. A. Newman	14
J. C. White	13
F. E. Woolley	13
C. V. Grimmett	12
F. Barratt	12
A. S. Kennedy	12
C. W. L. Parker	12
N. E. Haig	12
A. A. Mailey	11
G. H. Hirst	11
A. E. Relf	11
J. H. King	10
A. P. Freeman	10
H. Dean	10
F. A. Tarrant	10
J. W. Hearne	10

Records still held by Hobbs

Most runs and most hundreds in first-class cricket by any one player
Most hundreds for England against one team (12 v Australia)
Highest opening partnership for England v Australia
Most runs for England v Australia in Tests (3636)

Note: the above figures for first-class matches include the match The Reef v MCC in 1909/10 later ruled not first-class by the South African Cricket Association and exclude the matches played by the Maharajah of Vizanagram's XI in India and Ceylon which are considered to be first-class by the Association of Cricket Statisticians. The ACS figures for these seasons and their total are as follows:

Season		Matches	Inns	Not Out	Runs	HS	Average	100	50
1909/10	South Africa	11	18	1	1124	187	66.11	3	7
1930/31	India	6	9	0	282	81	31.33	0	2
1930/31	Ceylon	3	3	1	311	144*	155.50	2	1
		834	1325	107	61760	316*	50.70	199	273

His career bowling based on the ACS match list:

Balls	Mdns	Runs	Wkts	BB	Average	5wI	Catches
5217	169	2704	108	7-56	25.03	3	342

Index